VOCATIONAL INTERESTS IN THE WORKPLACE

Vocational Interests in the Workplace is an essential new work, tying together past literature with contemporary research to present the most comprehensive coverage on vocational interests to date. With increasing recognition of the importance of vocational interests and their relevance to the workplace, this book emphasizes the strong links between vocational interests and work behavior. It proposes new models and approaches that facilitate thorough exploration of the implications of this relationship between interests and practice.

The authors, drawing on knowledge and experience from a range of professional backgrounds, cover essential topics, including: interest measurement; personnel selection; motivation and performance; expertise; meaningful work; effects of a global business environment; diversity; and the ongoing development of interests through adulthood to retirement.

Endorsed by the Society for Industrial and Organizational Psychology board, this book is a valuable resource for researchers, professionals, and educators in the fields of human resources, organizational behaviour, and industrial or organizational psychology.

Christopher D. Nye is Assistant Professor of Organizational Psychology at Michigan State University, USA. He has received awards from the University of Illinois, the Society for Industrial and Organizational Psychology, and the International Personnel Assessment Council for his work. More recently, Dr. Nye was awarded the Early Career Award from the Academy of Management Research Methods Division. He has also been a Consortium Research Fellow for the Defense Manpower Data Center and a Senior Consortium Research Fellow for the U.S. Army Research Institute.

James Rounds is Professor of Educational Psychology and Psychology and College of Education Distinguished Scholar at the University of Illinois at Urbana-Champaign, USA. His publications have appeared in numerous journals. He has received the American Psychological Association John L. Holland Award for outstanding achievement in career and personality research, American Educational Research Association Outstanding Research Award in Counseling and has been designated a Fellow of the Association of Psychological Science.

SIOP Organizational Frontiers Series

Series Editor

Richard Klimoski

George Mason University

The Organizational Frontiers Series is sponsored by the Society for Industrial and Organizational Psychology (SIOP). Launched in 1983 to make scientific contributions accessible to the field, the series publishes books addressing emerging theoretical developments, fundamental and translational research, and theory-driven practice in the field of Industrial-Organizational Psychology and related organizational science disciplines including organizational behavior, human resource management, and labor and industrial relations.

Books in this series aim to inform readers of significant advances in research; challenge the research and practice community to develop and adapt new ideas; and promote the use of scientific knowledge in the solution of public policy issues and increased organizational effectiveness.

The Series originated in the hope that it would facilitate continuous learning and spur research curiosity about organizational phenomena on the part of both scientists and practitioners.

The Society for Industrial and Organizational Psychology is an international professional association with an annual membership of more than 8,000 industrial-organizational (I-O) psychologists who study and apply scientific principles to the workplace. I-O psychologists serve as trusted partners to business, offering strategically focused and scientifically rigorous solutions for a number of workplace issues. SIOP's mission is to enhance human well-being and performance in organizational and work settings by promoting the science, practice, and teaching of I-O psychology. For more information about SIOP, please visit www.siop.org.

Tonidandel/King/Cortina: *(2014) Big Data at Work: The Data Science Revolution and Organizational Psychology*
Ashkanasy/Bennett/Martinko: *(2016) Understanding the High Performance Workplace: The Line Between Motivation and Abuse*
Ellingson/Noe: *(2017) Autonomous Learning in the Workplace*
Ferris/Johnson/Sedikides: *(2018) The Self at Work: Fundamental Theory and Research*
Nye/Rounds: *(2019) Vocational Interests in the Workplace: Rethinking Behavior at Work*

For more information about this series, please visit: https://www.routledge.com/SIOP-Organizational-Frontiers-Series/book-series/SIOP

VOCATIONAL INTERESTS IN THE WORKPLACE

Rethinking Behavior at Work

Edited by Christopher D. Nye and James Rounds

Routledge
Taylor & Francis Group
NEW YORK AND LONDON

First edition published 2019
by Routledge
52 Vanderbilt Avenue, New York, NY 10017

and by Routledge
2 Park Square, Milton Park, Abingdon, Oxon, OX14 4RN

Routledge is an imprint of the Taylor & Francis Group, an informa business

Library of Congress Cataloging-in-Publication Data
Names: Nye, Christopher D., editor. | Rounds, James, editor.
Title: Vocational interests in the workplace : rethinking behavior at work / edited by Christopher D. Nye and James Rounds.
Description: 1 Edition. | New York : Routledge, 2019. |
Series: SIOP organizational frontiers series | Includes bibliographical references and index.
Identifiers: LCCN 2018060311| ISBN 9781138932890 (hardback) | ISBN 9781138932883 (pbk.) | ISBN 9781315678924 (ebk)
Subjects: LCSH: Vocational guidance. | Interest (Psychology)
Classification: LCC HF5381 .V566 2019 | DDC 658.3/85—dc23
LC record available at https://lccn.loc.gov/2018060311

ISBN: 978-1-138-93289-0 (hbk)
ISBN: 978-1-138-93288-3 (pbk)
ISBN: 978-1-315-67892-4 (ebk)

Typeset in Bembo
by codeMantra

CONTENTS

FIGURES

TABLES

CONTRIBUTORS

Sarena Bhatia is a talent consultant in the Leadership Service Line at Aon. She consults with companies in diverse industries in the areas of leadership assessment and development, training design, competency modeling, performance management, and career pathing. She received her Ph.D. in Organizational Psychology from Michigan State University.

Alexander P. Burgoyne received his M.A. from Michigan State University, where he is currently pursuing a Ph.D. in cognition and cognitive neuroscience. His research focuses on individual differences in skill acquisition and expertise.

M. Teresa Cardador received her Ph.D. from the University of Illinois, Gies College of Business, and is currently Associate Professor of Labor and Employment Relations at the University of Illinois Urbana-Champaign. Her research focuses on identity, meaningfulness, and gender at work; she is particularly interested in these issues as they relate to the work and career experiences of women in male-dominated occupations.

Oleksandr S. Chernyshenko received his Ph.D. from the University of Illinois at Urbana-Champaign and is currently Associate Professor at the Nanyang Business School in Singapore. He researches various applied measurement topics and teaches talent acquisition and management courses to undergraduates, postgraduates, and executives. He was an Academic Director of Nanyang Fellows MBA and Nanyang EMBA programs, and now serves as the Associate Dean of Executive Education.

Filip De Fruyt received his Ph.D. from Ghent University and is currently appointed as Senior Full Professor in Differential Psychology and Personality Assessment at Ghent University in Belgium. He is holding the Institute Ayrton Senna (IAS) Endowed University Chair at Ghent University, studying the assessment and development of living and employability skills in youth. His research spans a broad domain including adaptive and maladaptive traits, interests, cross-cultural manifestations of personality, and applied personality psychology.

David Z. (Zach) Hambrick received his Ph.D. in experimental psychology from the Georgia Institute of Technology in 2000, and is currently Professor in the Department of Psychology at Michigan State University. His research focuses on the origins of human expertise, and especially the interplay between basic abilities and training in complex skill.

Suzanne E. Hidi is Adjunct Professor at the Ontario Institute for Studies in Education of the University of Toronto. Her early work focused on academic writing, followed by investigations of motivation in general and interest development in specific. Although her work has primarily focused on educational practice, she also addresses the applications of these findings in the work place. Her current work addresses the integration of neuroscientific and psychological research in the area of human motivation, performance and information search.

Robert Hogan, president of Hogan Assessment Systems, is an international authority on personality assessment, leadership, and organizational effectiveness. He was McFarlin Professor and Chair of the Department of Psychology at the University of Tulsa for 14 years. Prior to that, he was Professor of Psychology and Social Relations at The Johns Hopkins University. Dr. Hogan received his Ph.D. from the University of California, Berkeley, specializing in personality assessment.

Leaetta M. Hough is president and founder of the Dunnette Group, and a past president of the Society for Industrial and Organizational Psychology (SIOP) and of FABBS (Federation of Associations in Behavioral and Brain Sciences). She is best known for her independent thinking and work challenging "received wisdom" about what is and is not useful for predicting important outcomes in organizational settings. Dr. Hough received a doctorate in psychology from the University of Minnesota in 1981.

Jason L. Huang received his Ph.D. in Organizational Psychology from Michigan State University and is currently Associate Professor in the School of Human Resources and Labor Relations at Michigan State University. His research primarily addresses personality and adaptability at work, training and transfer, and organizational research methods.

Danielle D. King received her B.A. in Psychology from Spelman College and her Ph.D. in Organizational Psychology from Michigan State University. She is currently Assistant Professor of Industrial and Organizational Psychology at Rice University. Her research centers on the topics of employee resilience, workplace identity intersectionality and authenticity, and organizational citizenship behavior. Her work has been funded by the National Science Foundation and published as both book chapters and journal articles.

Mengqiao (MQ) Liu received her Ph.D. in Industrial/Organizational Psychology from Wayne State University. She is currently a consultant on the Product Development Team at DDI (Development Dimensions International). Her work revolves around selection, people analytics, and machine learning and natural language processing for I/O and HR.

Hanyi Min received her Ph.D. from Bowling Green State University and is currently Assistant Professor of Industrial/Organizational Psychology at University of Central Florida. Her primary research areas are psychometrics and measurement, such as, applying psychometric tools to develop, improve, and compare psychological measurements.

Frederick L. Oswald is currently Professor and Herbert S. Autrey Chair in the Department of Psychological Sciences at Rice University. His research addresses personnel selection, psychological measurement, big data, and statistical issues faced within organizational, military, and educational settings. He received his Ph.D. in industrial-organizational psychology from the University of Minnesota (1999). Learn more at workforce.rice.edu.

Joshua J. Prasad is a doctoral candidate in the Organizational Psychology program at Michigan State University. His research primarily focuses on the use of assessments across diverse groups, vocational interests, and determinants of performance over time.

Shan Ran received her Ph.D. in Industrial-Organizational Psychology from Wayne State University and is now Assistant Professor of Psychology at Mercer University. Her research interests focus on boosters (i.e., leadership capacity, training) and barriers (i.e., bias and discrimination) to individual success in the workplace, as well as how demographic (e.g., gender, age, etc.) and cultural characteristics influence these processes.

K. Ann Renninger is the Dorwin P. Cartwright Professor of Social Theory and Social Action at Swarthmore College. She teaches in the Department of Educational Studies. Her research focuses on the development of interest, where interest is conceptualized and measured as both a psychological state and a motivational variable. Her research addresses the conditions that support interest to develop. Although her work has primarily focused on educational practice, she also addresses the applications of these findings in the work place.

Ann Marie Ryan is Professor of organizational psychology at Michigan State University. Her major research interests involve improving the quality and fairness of employee selection methods, and topics related to diversity and justice in the workplace. In addition to publishing extensively in these areas, she regularly consults with organizations on improving assessment processes. She is a past president of the Society of Industrial and Organizational Psychology, past editor of the journal *Personnel Psychology,* and former associate editor of *American Psychologist.*

Ryne A. Sherman is currently the Chief Science Officer at Hogan Assessment Systems, a world leader in psychological assessment for employment purposes. He received his Ph.D. in personality psychology from the University of California, Riverside and was previously Professor at Florida Atlantic University and Texas Tech University. His research concerns psychological assessment, personality, leadership, and organizational effectiveness.

Stephen Stark received his Ph.D. from the University of Illinois in Urbana-Champaign in 2002 and is currently Professor and Director of the Industrial-Organizational Psychology program at the University of South Florida. His research focuses on the development and application of item response theory models for noncognitive testing, methods for detecting measurement bias and aberrant responding, individual difference constructs, and the validity of methods for predicting outcomes in educational and organizational contexts.

Gundula Stoll received her Ph.D. from Saarland University in Saarbrücken, Germany. Currently she is a senior researcher at the Hector Research Institute of Education Sciences and Psychology at the University of Tübingen, Germany. In her research, she studies the impact and development of vocational interests, as well as their interplay with other aspects of individual differences and life experiences.

Rong Su received her Ph.D. from the University of Illinois at Urbana-Champaign and is currently Assistant Professor of Management and Organizations at the Henry B. Tippie College of Business, University of Iowa. Her research centers on the role of personality, interests, and person-environment fit in explaining and predicting workplace outcomes, including job attitudes, performance, career success, as well as gender and diversity in organizations.

Laura Venz is a postdoctoral researcher in Work and Organizational Psychology at the University of Mannheim, Germany, where she also received her Ph.D. Her research interests include social relationships at work, occupational health and well-being, and the ageing workforce.

Mo Wang received his Ph.D. from Bowling Green State University and is currently the Lanzillotti-McKethan Eminent Scholar Chair at the University of Florida. He specializes in the research areas of retirement and older worker employment, occupational health psychology, expatriate and newcomer adjustment, leadership and team processes, and advanced quantitative methodologies.

Bart Wille currently works as Assistant Professor of Industrial-Organizational Psychology at Ghent University, from which he also received his Ph.D. He studies individual differences such as personality traits and vocational interests and their role in work and career contexts. Specific research topics include career development and management, interest development, leadership, multi-rater assessments and dark side personality.

Michael J. Zickar received his Ph.D. from the University of Illinois in Urbana-Champaign and is currently Professor and Chair of Psychology at Bowling Green State University. His research involves psychometrics and pre-employment testing as well as the history of applied psychology.

Chen Zuo is currently a doctoral graduate student in industrial-organizational psychology at Rice University. Her ongoing research focuses on selection and psychological measurement, with special interest in underrepresented groups such as first-generation college students, women, and minorities in educational and organizational settings.

FOREWORD

Why do people get into certain professions? Why do they seek out certain jobs or new work assignments? What causes individuals to expend time, resources, and effort in order to develop their professional skills? And importantly, how or why do people persist in working to a goal, even in the face of setbacks? There are many ways to frame how to best model such human behavior as it relates to the world of work. As described in this volume, a very traditional approach—that of using vocational interests—is clearly a leading contender. Toward this end, Christopher D. Nye and James Rounds provide a compelling case. They first reach back in time to set the stage of how, when, and where vocational interests emerged as a viable way to help us understand and predict the pursuit of educational opportunities and employment options. With this as the foundation, the chapters that follow go on to reveal how current thinking about vocational interests can be put to use in order to help us understand such phenomena as the development of task expertise, achieving high levels of job performance, managing career trajectories, or even making retirement decisions. Thus, each chapter adds to our understanding of the potential value of vocational interests as these relate to a wide range of work relevant behaviors. The authors contributing to this volume are all well-regarded thought leaders who provide a very readable compilation of what we know (and do not yet know) about vocational interests, based on the most up-to-date research. As such, this volume will be valuable to those who want to know about the state of the research literature on vocational interests, as well as those who may want to make use of research findings to address applied problems. But it will also appeal to those who wish to prepare the next generation of scholars to do work in this arena.

Richard Klimoski
Series Editor, SIOP Organizational Frontiers Series
11/26/2018

INTRODUCTION

Christopher D. Nye

MICHIGAN STATE UNIVERSITY

James Rounds

UNIVERSITY OF ILLINOIS

Interest in a particular topic can serve as a motivational force that drives individuals to focus attention, exert effort, and persist on related activities. The link between interest and behavior is intuitive. It makes sense that people are more likely to engage in tasks that they are interested in. This applies to all aspects of life—people watch tv shows, pay closer attention to school lectures, and pick hobbies that they believe will interest them. Interests can also guide career choices as people tend to choose academic majors, occupations, and jobs that they are interested in (Holland, 1997; Strong, 1943). As such, understanding interest in work, or vocational interest, can help to explain and predict how individuals will behave in the workplace.

There is a long history of research on vocational interests in the applied psychological literature. For example, some of the earlier writings on interests (at least as we think of them today) were published in the early 1900s (Savickas, 1999). Since that time, a substantial amount of research has been conducted and prominent theories of vocational interests (e.g., Holland, 1959, 1997) have been developed. In addition, these theories have had a substantial impact on organizational research, particularly in the area of person-environment (P-E) fit (cf. Schneider, 1987).

Despite these contributions and early excitement about the potential utility of vocational interests for predicting workplace behavior (Strong, 1943), research on this topic in organizational psychology declined drastically after the 1970s. In a recent review of the *Journal of Applied Psychology* (JAP), Sackett, Lievens, Van Iddekinge, and Kuncel (2017) noted that approximately 90% of the vocational interest articles in JAP were published between 1930 and 1979. In contrast, only seven interest articles were published in this journal between 1980 and 2008. Although this review only summarized a single journal, these results are representative of a broader trend in the organizational literature in which vocational interests have been ignored in recent research. As another example, interests have been almost completely left out of recent reviews of the employee selection literature (e.g., Cortina & Luchman, 2013; Ployhart, 2006; Sackett & Lievens, 2008; Schmitt, Cortina, Ingerick, & Weichmann, 2003) or have been mentioned only briefly in others (Ployhart, Schmitt, & Tippins, 2017), despite their potential to contribute to the selection process. As a consequence of the paucity of interest research in the recent organizational literature, both organizational theories and vocational interest theories describe workplace behavior and predict many of the same outcomes but have developed largely independently of each other.

More recently, the number of organizational studies examining vocational interests has begun to increase. For example, several recent studies have examined the importance of interests for predicting workplace behavior (Nye, Su, Rounds, & Drasgow, 2012, 2017; Van Iddekinge, Roth, Putka, & Lanivich, 2011). As a result of the increasing number of vocational interest studies, Sackett et al. (2017, p. 264) suggested that the period from 2009-present marked the "return of interest research."

In addition to the increased empirical attention, there has also been a corresponding increase in the awareness of vocational interests in practice. Consequently, some organizations are now starting to consider using vocational interests for personnel selection (Rounds, 2013). For example, although the U.S. Military has a history of assessing vocational interests dating back to the 1950s (Ingerick & Rumsey, 2014), several branches of the U.S. military have recently initiated new efforts to develop and/or evaluate vocational interest measures for military personnel. For example, the U.S. Navy is exploring a measure known as the Job Opportunities in the Navy (JOIN) as a way to help individuals identify jobs in the Navy that they will be satisfied with. In addition, research is being conducted by the U.S. Army and Air Force to develop and validate new interest assessments, the Adaptive Vocational Interest Diagnostic (AVID) and the Air Force Work Interest Navigator (AFWIN), respectively.

Given the growing "interest" in vocational interest research, more empirical research is needed to integrate the various streams of interest research in the educational and vocational psychology literatures with existing theories of workplace behavior from the organizational literature. The purpose of the present book is to do just that and to describe the ways in which vocational interests can contribute to organizational research and vice versa. Interests are defined as an individual's "trait-like preferences for activities, contexts in which activities occur, or outcomes associated with preferred activities that motivate goal-oriented behaviors and orient individuals toward certain environments" (Rounds & Su, 2014, p. 98). This definition suggests that vocational interests can play an important role in predicting a number of workplace phenomena such as job performance, training performance, motivation, job satisfaction, job choice, occupational/organizational diversity, work meaningfulness, and even retirement, among other topics. This book examines these issues and the potential contributions of vocational interests to workplace behavior research and practice.

Holland's Model

Holland's (1959, 1997) model of vocational interests provides an underlying theme in many of the chapters in this book. Holland's widely researched model of vocational interests is the dominant theoretical framework for understanding the structure and predictive validity of vocational interests. A major contribution of Holland's work was suggesting that interests could be classified into six primary interest types: Realistic interests reflect preferences for working with things and in the outdoors; Investigative interests involve activities in the sciences (e.g., physical, social, medical); Artistic interests include preferences for activities that allow creative expression; Social interests reflect preferences for social interactions that involve teaching or helping people; Enterprising interests include preferences for persuasive roles such as management and sales positions; and Conventional interests are associated with activities in well-structured environments such as business settings. Collectively, these six interest types are known by their acronym as the RIASEC model.

Holland organized these six RIASEC types into a hexagonal structure as shown in Figure I.1. An advantage of this model is that it also illustrates the relationships between the six interests. Adjacent interest types should be the most highly correlated with each other, alternate types should be slightly less correlated, and opposite interests on the hexagon should be the least highly correlated. Although some have criticized the circumplex structure (Gati, 1991), Holland's model has substantial empirical support. For example, Tracey and Rounds (1993) conducted a meta-analytic structural analysis of 104 RIASEC correlation matrices and found that both the quasi-circumplex and the circulent model adequately represented the data. Similarly, Day and Rounds (1998)

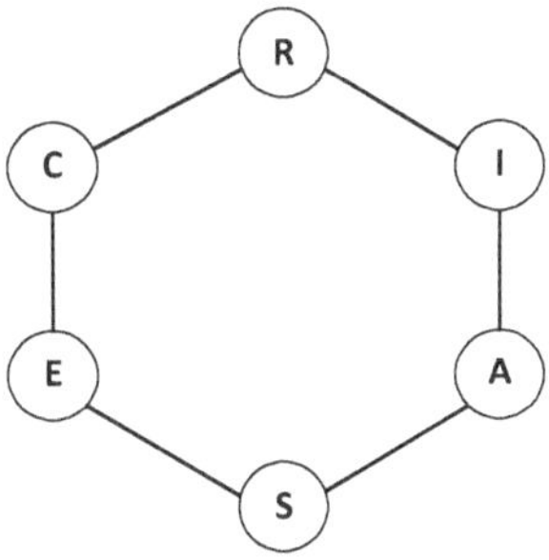

FIGURE I.1 Holland's Hexagonal RIASEC Structure.

and Day, Rounds, and Swaney (1998) demonstrated that the quasi-circumplex structure also fit well across diverse racial-ethnic groups.

Another major contribution of Holland's (1959, 1997) work was that he suggested that environments can also be categorized using the six RIASEC dimensions. In other words, profiles of the six RIASEC types can be developed for both individuals and environments. A number of different approaches have been used to operationalize the interest profile of the environment. One approach is to use the interest profiles of job incumbents (Campbell & Holland, 1972; Donnay & Borgen, 1996; Holland, 1997). However, sampling becomes an issue when generalizing the RIASEC codes to occupations because incumbent samples are rarely representative of many ill-defined occupations. Another approach to operationalizing the environment interest profile is to use job analysis information about work activities and requirements (Holland, Viernstein, Kuo, Karweit, & Blum, 1972; McCormick, Jeanneret, & Mecham, 1972; cf. Rounds, Shubsachs, Dawis, & Lofquist, 1978). However, the most direct way of assessing the environment interest profile is to rate it directly. For example, researchers can use the Position Classification Inventory (PCI; Gottfredson & Holland, 1996) to assess the RIASEC profile of an occupation. With this measure, employees or supervisors rate the extent to which individuals in the job perform various work activities related to each RIASEC type. A related approach is to train subject matter experts to rate the RIASEC dimensions for each environment (Rounds, Smith, Hubert, Lewis, & Rivkin, 1999).

Because both individuals and environments can be categorized using the RIASEC dimensions, Holland (1997) suggested that the match (or congruence) between individuals and their environments would be closely related to their behavior. A growing body of research has provided empirical support for this prediction (e.g., Holland, 1997; Nauta, 2010; Nye et al., 2012, 2017) and this research is summarized in several of the chapters in this book. Given the substantial amount of empirical support for Holland's model and his congruency hypothesis, this model has had a substantial impact on the study of vocational interests. As such, his model appears repeatedly throughout this book and is influential for many of the ideas expounded here. This largely represents the state of the literature and the impact that his model has had on the field.

Organization of This Book

Given the goals of this book, the chapters are organized into three sections. The chapters in Section 1 discuss topics related to the theory and measurement of vocational interests. These chapters focus on what interests are and how they can be measured. After discussing these issues, Section 2 reviews existing research on the value of vocational interests for predicting various work outcomes. The goal of this section is to discuss the theoretical and empirical implications of vocational interests at work and to identify how vocational interests fit in existing nomological networks of organizational variables. Finally, the chapters in Section 3 of this book describe how the broader work context can influence our understanding of vocational interests and their effects on workplace outcomes. Combined, the goal of these three sections is to review existing research and theory on vocational interests and to explore new and emerging topics in vocational interest research that can help to facilitate future research in this area. Below we provide a brief description of each chapter in this book.

Section 1

As noted above, Section 1 provides a description of what interests are and how they can be measured. As such, Chapter 1 by Rong Su, Gundula Stoll, and James Rounds attempts to address the question "what is the nature of vocational interests?" In this chapter, they integrate two divided perspectives—interests as traits and interest as a psychological state—and propose a unifying theoretical framework of Trait-State Interest Dynamics. Using this framework, they discuss how vocational interests are organized and represented in the human mind, how they develop through the dynamic process of person-environment interaction, and how they influence individual behavior in many aspects of an individual's work and life. Importantly, they also discuss the relationships between vocational interests and various other psychological characteristics such as personality, cognitive ability, motivation, values, and goals. Understanding these relationships is particularly important for understanding the unique contribution of vocational interests to organizational theories.

Although the chapter by Su et al. conceptualizes interests as both a trait and a state, the discussion in their chapter stems from the research literature on the more trait-like vocational interests. In contrast, Chapter 2 by K. Ann Renninger and Suzanne E. Hidi focuses on interest as both a cognitive and affective motivational variable that develops over time. They define interest as a psychological state *as well as* the predisposition to reengage particular content over time. These authors discuss their Four-Phase Model of Interest Development, which starts with an initial activation of interest and can progress to a well-developed interest. They explain the distinction between their discussion of interest and the discussion of vocational interests, and describe how a developmental approach to workplace interest could be beneficial. They point out that vocational interests represent later stages of the interest development process and can be developed with proper support.

After understanding the nature of vocational interests, these individual differences can then be measured. In fact, the history of research on vocational interests has been closely linked with the assessment of these individual differences. In Chapter 3, Michael Zickar and Hanyi Min review this history and several key advances in the assessment of interests over time. In this context, these authors discuss some of the key figures, including E. K. Strong and the various iterations of the Strong Interest Inventory and John Holland and the Vocational Preference Inventory, which have had a substantial influence on vocational interest research and the field of vocational psychology more broadly. They also discuss additional milestones in the history of interest assessment and more recent advances in interest assessment that have contributed to the use of vocational interests in the workplace.

Building on the history of interest assessments discussed in Chapter 3, Chapter 4 addresses psychometric considerations for modern interest measurement. In this chapter, Oleksandr Chernyshenko, Stephen Stark, and Christopher Nye discuss important dimensions of interest assessment, stimuli and response formats that are relevant for these assessments, and psychometric models that can help to advance the measurement of vocational interests in the future. These authors discuss the growing importance of basic interests (narrow dimensions of interest) and their utility for differentiating occupations and predicting work outcomes. In addition, they also discuss recent efforts to move beyond the broader RIASEC framework to identify additional dimensions of interest for occupational assessment. In sum, this chapter highlights potential directions for the next generation of vocational interest assessments and their use in the workplace.

Section 2

The development of high-quality measures paved the way for research on the utility of vocational interests for predicting attitudes and behavior. As such, Section 2 discusses research on the validity of vocational interests for predicting workplace outcomes. In Chapter 5, Christopher Nye, Sarena Bhatia, and Joshua Prasad discuss the relationships between vocational interests and a number of workplace outcomes, including job choice, job performance, job satisfaction, turnover, and career success. Importantly, these relationships are discussed in the context of current models of employee behavior including Campbell's (1990) model of job performance. This chapter also emphasizes the importance of interest fit (or congruence) in the vocational interest literature. In contrast to other individual differences such as personality, there are not specific dimensions of interest that are relevant to all jobs. Instead, it is the match between an individual's interests and his or her job that will be most important for predicting work outcomes.

Given the validity evidence discussed in Chapter 5, vocational interests may be useful for employee selection decisions. Therefore, Chapter 6 by Fred Oswald, Leaetta Hough, and Chen Zuo extends this discussion to note the implications of these relationships and additional factors that need to be considered in employee selection and classification settings. This chapter discusses not only the validity of vocational interests but also their incremental validity over other predictors of performance such as personality and cognitive ability. Another important consideration in this context is the potential for adverse impact and this chapter discusses previous research quantifying race and sex differences in vocational interests. Finally, the chapter ends by discussing issues related to the specificity of interests, faking on interest assessments, and the implications of vocational interests for the burgeoning "gig economy."

The discussion of the empirical relationships between interests and work outcomes continues in Chapter 7 where Teresa Cardador describes the links between interest fit and work meaningfulness. This author discusses various pathways to meaningful work and how vocational interests can map onto each one of these pathways. To help facilitate this discussion, she proposes a framework for understanding the contexts in which fit should create meaningful work and how organizations can help employees to find meaning by leveraging their work environment and their experiences on the job.

Another key outcome of vocational interests is turnover. Holland (1997) predicted that interest congruence should lead employees to stay on the job longer. Although research has demonstrated the validity of vocational interests for predicting workplace withdrawal behaviors, more research is needed to understand other types of withdrawal such as retirement. In Chapter 8, Laura Venz and Mo Wang discuss how interests can contribute to retirement decisions. They suggest that although interests are positively related to job tenure, they may also be the driving force behind retirement decisions and make theoretical predictions about when and how interests might facilitate this process. These authors also discuss the relevance of leisure interests for retirement decisions and the activities that are performed during retirement.

In Chapter 9, Robert Hogan and Ryne Sherman suggest several new directions for vocational interest research in the workplace. Specifically, they note that the concepts of employability and career success have been relatively understudied but that interests can contribute to the prediction of each of these outcomes. In addition, they discuss the conceptual relationships and distinctions between values, needs, personality, and interests and the roles that these individual differences can play in understanding and predicting employee behavior.

Through their effects on individual outcomes, vocational interests can also influence organizational outcomes and the broader work context. In Chapter 10, Ann Marie Ryan and Danielle King discuss how interests can contribute to diversity within an organization. Past research has demonstrated that there are sex and (slightly smaller) race differences in vocational interests. Therefore, these authors discuss how these subgroup differences might impact an organization's efforts to recruit and retain a diverse workforce. In addition, they also note that a diversity of interests may be a good thing in a group and may contribute to overall group/team performance.

Section 3

Finally, the chapters in the third section of this book describe the role of interests in the broader work context. In Chapter 11, Jason Huang, Shan Ran, and Mengqiao Liu discuss vocational interests in the global work environment. These authors review past research on the generalizability of vocational interests and their relationships with other variables across cultures. They identify several areas in which research findings have varied and suggest future directions for examining vocational interests across cultures. Importantly, these authors recommend conducting more studies in non-U.S. countries as a way to further understanding of the role of culture in the measurement and use of vocational interests.

In Chapter 12, Bart Wille and Filip De Fruyt discuss stability and change in vocational interests during adulthood. This chapter reviews the evidence showing that the rank order of trait vocational interests are relatively stable yet the mean levels can change over time. These authors propose a model of adult interest development that suggests that both stability and change occur through an individual's interactions with his or her work environment and the progression of person-environment fit over time. In addition, they discuss the implications of these processes in the context of recent changes to the nature of work that involve greater job flexibility and career mobility, an aging workforce, and an increased need to maintain a competitive workforce in a global business environment.

In Chapter 13, the final chapter, David Hambrick, Alexander Burgoyne, and Fred Oswald discuss the relationship between interests and expertise. Specifically, they propose that interest plays a key role in the development of expertise. Expert performance requires both ability and deliberate practice and interests help to determine who will be sufficiently motivated to engage in and sustain long-term deliberate practice over time. These authors describe these effects in the context of the Multifactorial Gene-Environment Interaction model of expertise (Ullén, Hambrick, & Mosing, 2016) and suggest future longitudinal research to examine the role of interests in the context of other factors that can influence the development of expertise over time.

Concluding Thoughts

The first goal of this book is to integrate organizational psychology research with the vocational interest literature. Both of these literatures examine individual behavior on the job, but theories and models of vocational interests have been largely ignored in the areas of organizational research where they could contribute the most. As such, the second goal of this book is to help facilitate research on the topic of vocational interests in the organizational literature. Although other recent books have focused on the use of vocational interests in educational or social psychology (e.g., Renninger & Hidi, 2016; Silvia, 2006) and vocational psychology (e.g., Savickas & Spokane, 1999), these books have devoted little space to addressing how vocational interest research can be applied within organizations. The present work attempts to fill this need.

References

Campbell, J. P. (1990). Modeling the performance prediction problem in industrial organizational psychology. In M. D. Dunnette & L. M. Hough (Eds.), *Handbook of industrial and organizational psychology* (Vol. 1, 2nd ed., pp. 687–732). Palo Alto, CA: Consulting Psychologists Press.

Campbell, D. P., & Holland, J. L. (1972). A merger in vocational interest research: Applying Holland's theory to Strong's data. *Journal of Vocational Behavior, 2*, 353–376.

Cortina, J. M., & Luchman, J. N. (2013). Personnel selection and employee performance. In N. W. Schmitt, S. Highhouse, & I. B. Weiner (Eds.), *Handbook of Psychology: Industrial and organizational psychology* (Vol. 12, 2nd ed., pp. 143–183). Hoboken, NJ: Wiley.

Day, S. X., & Rounds, J. (1998). Universality of vocational interest structure among racial and ethnic minorities. *American Psychologist, 53*, 728–736.

Day, S. X, Rounds, J., & Swaney, K. (1998). The structure of vocational interests for diverse racial-ethnic groups. *Psychological Science, 9*, 40–44.

Donnay, D. A. C., & Borgen, F. H. (1996). Validity, structure, and content of the 1994 Strong interest inventory. *Journal of Counseling Psychology, 43*, 275–291.

Gati, I. (1991). The structure of vocational interests. *Psychological Bulletin, 109*, 309–324.

Gottfredson, G. D., & Holland, J. L. (1996). *Dictionary of Holland occupational codes*. Odessa, FL: Psychological Assessment Resources.

Holland, J. L. (1959). A theory of vocational choice. *Journal of Counseling Psychology, 6*, 35–45.

Holland, J. L. (1997). *Making vocational choices: A theory of vocational personalities and work environments* (3rd ed.). Odessa, FL: Psychological Assessment Resources.

Holland, J. L., Viernstein, M. C., Kuo, H., Karweit, N. L., & Blum, Z. D. (1972). A psychological classification of occupations. *Journal Supplement Abstract Service, 2*, 84.

Ingerick, M., & Rumsey, M. G. (2014). Taking the measure of work interests: Past, present, and future. *Military Psychology, 26*, 165–181.

McCormick, E. J., Jeanneret, P. R., & Mecham, R. C. (1972). A study of the job characteristics and job dimensions as based on the Position Analysis Questionnaire. *Journal of Applied Psychology Monograph, 56*, 347–368.

Nauta, M. M. (2010). The development, evolution, and status of Holland's theory of vocational personalities: Reflections and future directions for counseling psychology. *Journal of Counseling Psychology, 57*, 11–22.

Nye, C. D., Su, R., Rounds, J., & Drasgow, F. (2012). Vocational interests and performance: A quantitative summary of over 60 years of research. *Perspectives on Psychological Science, 7*, 384–403.

Nye, C. D., Su, R., Rounds, J., & Drasgow, F. (2017). Interest congruence and performance: Revisiting recent meta-analytic findings. *Journal of Vocational Behavior, 98*, 138–151.

Ployhart, R. E. (2006). Staffing in the 21st century: New challenges and strategic opportunities. *Journal of Management, 32*, 868–897.

Ployhart, R. E., Schmitt, N., & Tippins, N. T. (2017). Solving the Supreme Problem: 100 years of selection and recruitment at the *Journal of Applied Psychology*. *Journal of Applied Psychology, 102*, 291–304.

Renninger, K. A., & Hidi, S. E. (2016). *The power of interest for motivation and engagement*. New York: Routledge.

Rounds, J. (2013, April). Rethinking interests. In J. W. Stuster (Chair), *New directions in assessing performance potential of individual and groups*. Invited paper at the National Research Council, Washington, DC.

Rounds, J. B., Jr., Shubsachs, A. P. W., Dawis, R. V., & Lofquist, L. H. (1978). A test of Holland's environment formulations. *Journal of Applied Psychology, 63*, 609–616.

Rounds, J., Smith, T., Hubert, L., Lewis, P., & Rivkin, D. (1999). *Development of Occupational Interest Profiles (OIPs) for the O*NET*. Raleigh, NC: National Center for O*NET Development.

Rounds, J., & Su, R. (2014). The nature and power of interests. *Current Directions in Psychological Science, 23*, 98–103.

Sackett, P. R., & Lievens, F. (2008). Personnel selection. *Annual Review of Psychology, 59*, 1–32.

Sackett, P. R., Lievens, F., Van Iddekinge, C. H., & Kuncel, N. R. (2017). Individual differences and their measurement: A review of 100 years of research. *Journal of Applied Psychology, 102*, 254–273.

Savickas, M. L. (1999). The psychology of interests. In M. L. Savickas & A. R. Spokane (Eds.), *Vocational interests: Their meaning, measurement and use in counseling* (pp. 19–56). Palo Alto, CA: Davies-Black.

Savickas, M., & Spokane, A. (Eds.) (1999). *Vocational interests: Their meaning, measurement and use in counseling*. Palo Alto, CA: Davies-Black.

Schmitt, N., Cortina, J. M., Ingerick, M., & Weichmann, D. (2003). Personnel selection and employee performance. In R. J. Klimoski, W. C. Borman, & D. R. Ilgen (Eds.), *Handbook of psychology: Industrial and organizational psychology* (Vol. 12, pp. 77–105). Hoboken, NJ: Wiley.

Schneider, B. (1987). The people make the place. *Personnel Psychology, 40*, 437–453.

Silvia, P.J. (2006). *Exploring the psychology of interest*. New York: Oxford University Press.

Strong, E. K., Jr. (1943). *The vocational interests of men and women*. Stanford, CA: Stanford University Press.

Tracey, T. J., & Rounds, J. B. (1993). Evaluating Holland's and Gati's vocational-interest models: A structural meta-analysis. *Psychological Bulletin, 113*, 229–246.

Van Iddekinge, C. H., Roth, P. L., Putka, D. J., & Lanivich, S. E. (2011). Are you interested? A meta-analysis of relations between vocational interests and employee performance and turnover. *Journal of Applied Psychology, 96*, 1167–1194.

Ullén, F., Hambrick, D. Z., & Mosing, M. A. (2016). Rethinking expertise: A multifactorial gene–environment interaction model of expert performance. *Psychological Bulletin, 142*, 427–446.

1

THE NATURE OF INTERESTS

Toward a Unifying Theory of Trait-State Interest Dynamics

Rong Su

TIPPIE COLLEGE OF BUSINESS, UNIVERSITY OF IOWA

Gundula Stoll

UNIVERSITY OF TÜBINGEN

James Rounds

UNIVERSITY OF ILLINOIS AT URBANA-CHAMPAIGN

The field of research on vocational interests has made significant progress over the last century. Interest research stemmed from an empirical measurement tradition to address the need of career guidance at the beginning of the twentieth century and accelerated in the late 1930s thanks to E. K. Strong's (1943) pioneering work on the criterion-related validity of interest assessment. In recent years, there is a resurgence in the study of vocational interests in industrial-organizational (I-O) psychology in light of burgeoning meta-analytic evidence on the relationship between interests and job performance (Nye, Su, Rounds, & Drasgow, 2012, 2017; Van Iddekinge, Roth, Putka, & Lanivich, 2011) and evidence on the incremental validity of interests over cognitive ability and personality traits for predicting performance and career success (Rounds & Su, 2014; Stoll et al., 2017; Van Iddekinge, Putka, & Campbell, 2011). Following the empirical tradition in interest research, most interest theories to date have focused on the mechanisms and boundary conditions for the relationship between interests and educational or occupational outcomes (e.g., Holland, 1959, 1997; Lent, Brown, & Hackett, 1994). However, theories about the nature of interests have lagged behind. Many scholars in the field lament the "dustbowl empiricism" in interest research and the underdevelopment of conceptual understandings of interests (e.g., Dawis, 1980; Savickas, 1999; Silvia, 2001a). What are interests? What psychological processes are involved in the experience and expression of interests? How do interests develop and to what extent can they change? Where are interests situated within the nomological network of traits and motives (Ackerman & Heggestad, 1997; Armstrong, Day, McVay, & Rounds, 2008)? Lack of knowledge about these fundamental questions will not only impede further advancement of interest research but also hinder successful development and application of interest assessment in the workplace.

In this chapter, we begin to establish a theoretical framework of what interests are, how interests are represented and organized in the human mind, and where interests are positioned in the nomological network. We integrate research from educational psychology and vocational psychology, in which interests are conceptualized as states and traits, respectively. We incorporate insights from other fields—notably, behavioral genetics, cognitive psychology, and developmental psychology—to bridge the state and trait perspectives on interests and to develop theoretical propositions that establish an integrative framework. Some of the fundamental issues addressed in the current chapter will be further elaborated on in other chapters of this book. Below, we first present an overview of current conceptualizations of interests, followed by a discussion of our proposed theoretical framework and a series of specific propositions.

Current Conceptualizations of Interests

Vocational interests have been defined as "trait-like preferences to engage in activities, contexts in which activities occur, or outcomes associated with preferred activities that motivate goal-oriented behaviors and orient individuals toward certain environments" (Rounds & Su, 2014, p. 98). These preferences are not simply characterized by the experience of enjoyment, but are more strongly associated with prolonged attention to objects of interest, a sense of curiosity, and persistent engagement in tasks and activities, even when they are complex or perplexing (Silvia, 2008; Turner & Silvia, 2006). As such, interests serve as a source of intrinsic motivation that drives the direction, effort, and persistence of human behaviors, knowledge acquisition, and performance on tasks (Su & Nye, 2017).

At the core of this definition of interests, and what distinguishes interests from other individual differences, is the idea that interests describe not only people but also their relationships with external environments. In other words, interests are contextualized and capture individuals' reactions toward target objects (Rounds & Su, 2014). An object of interest may be a task (e.g., "repair a car engine") or a work setting in which an individual is involved (e.g., "serve on the board of a large organization"). When interests are measured, these objects are often used as stimuli (items) and individuals indicate how they feel about each of the stimuli (items) using a Likert-type scale or a forced-choice scale. Responses to interest items are then scored into scales that represent interest constructs at various levels of specificity.

Defining interests as preferences for (work) activities and contexts is useful for the purposes of interest assessment and career guidance. However, to unpack the nature and meaning of interests, we need to answer further-reaching questions: What are the bases for individuals' preferences for various objects? How does an individual decide how to respond to a specific item and whether he/she prefers one item over another? Where does the information come from and how is this information stored? Do those responses represent meaningful latent traits of the individual and, if they do, can they be modified over time and change across situations? As Silvia (2001a) eloquently articulated, answering these questions about interests is not just valuable in itself, but may also serve as a vehicle for exploring broader theoretical quests and help us understand the dynamic relationship between transient experiences, cognitions, emotions, and relatively enduring individual differences.

Thus far, the way interest researchers approach the above questions and conceptualize interests has been largely dependent on their disciplinary affiliations and research traditions (for a comprehensive review of extant theoretical perspectives, see Renninger & Hidi, 2011). Most of these perspectives can be categorized into two approaches: interest as a psychological state and interests as traits. As a psychological state, interest is referred to as *situational interest* and is used in the singular form. Situational interest is defined as momentary feelings of curiosity, fascination, and enjoyment triggered by an environment or a task (e.g., Ainley, 2007; Krapp, 2007; Silvia, 2008). In addition to the affective component, situational interest may also involve cognitive evaluations of the value or importance of the environment or task (Eccles et al., 1983; Schiefele, 1991). Alternatively, interests have been conceptualized as traits or predispositions to reengage in activities or environments that individuals prefer (e.g., Ackerman & Heggestad, 1997; Holland, 1959, 1997; Lubinski, 2000; Savickas & Spokane, 1999; Rounds & Su, 2014). As traits, interests are referred to as *dispositional interests* or *individual interests* and are used in the plural form. Despite being frequently debated, these two approaches are not incompatible with each other. We see the two approaches as capturing different aspects of the nature of interests: the trait perspective mainly focuses on the origin and function of interests, whereas the state perspective primarily focuses on the experience and development of interest. Both perspectives, however, emphasize the importance of the object of interest, describe interests not just as characteristics of individuals but individuals in relation to their environments, and highlight links between interest and motivation, learning, and achievement in academic and work contexts.

A Theory of Trait-State Interest Dynamics

Figure 1.1 depicts our proposed theoretical framework on the origin, function, experience, and development of interests, termed the Trait-State Interest Dynamics. The section of the framework above the dotted line is a representation of the trait perspective, and the section below the dotted line is a representation

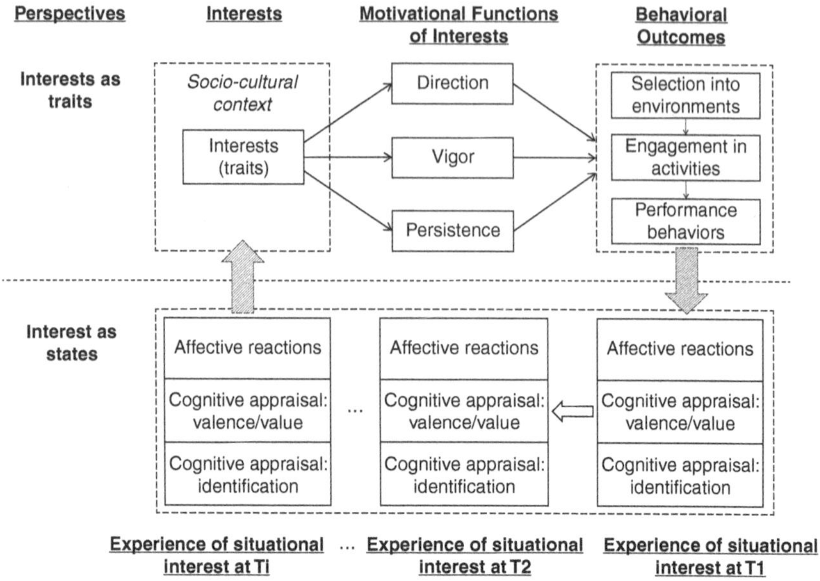

FIGURE 1.1 A Theoretical Framework of Trait-Situation Interest Dynamics.

of the state perspective. We propose that interests are traits embedded in socio-cultural contexts (Proposition 1); interests serve motivational functions by directing and sustaining individuals' effort and engagement in various activities and environments (Proposition 2); the experience of interest in specific situations as a collection of affective and cognitive responses further determines individuals' behaviors (Proposition 3) and helps shape existing mental representations of interests (Proposition 4); and through this dynamic process of person–environment interaction, either direct or vicarious, interests develop as an integral part of an individual's identity (Propositions 5 & 6). Below we elaborate on these theoretical propositions.

Proposition 1: Interests are traits embedded in socio-cultural contexts. Observed, relatively stable individual differences in interests are a result of both nature and nurture.

Two types of evidence are relevant for inferring the degree to which a psychological construct is a trait (Tellegen, 1991): (1) the extent to which observed (phenotypic) differences in the psychological construct among individuals are stable over time and across situations, and (2) the extent to which those phenotypic differences are attributable to genetic versus nongenetic sources. Between-individual differences in personality traits, for example, have been found to be fairly stable, with rank-order stability peaking in the .70s after age 50

(Roberts & DelVecchio, 2000). Heritability for personality traits has generally been found to be around .40-.50 (Bouchard, 1997), meaning that close to half of the between-person variances in personality is attributable to genetic influences while the other half is attributable to environmental factors.

Statistics on the stability and heritability of interests are very similar to what have been reported in personality research. Rank-order stability of interests was in fact found to be higher than that of personality traits for every age group before age 30 and to peak at .70 for the age group of 22–29 years old (Low, Yoon, Roberts, & Rounds, 2005). There have also been a series of behavioral genetics studies to date showing that genetic influences on interests are approximately as strong as those on personality traits (Betsworth et al., 1994; Harris, Vernon, Johnson, & Jang, 2006; Kandler, Bleidorn, Riemann, Angleitner, & Spinath, 2011; Lykken, Bouchard, McGue, & Tellegen, 1993; Moloney, Bouchard, & Segal, 1991; Schermer & Vernon, 2008). Importantly, these studies have found that interests share some common genetic influences with personality traits (Harris et al., 2006) and that only a modest amount of the genetic variance in interests can be explained by the interaction between personality genotypes and environmental influences. Taken together, these findings suggest that interests are dispositional in nature. Counter to previous views that interests are the byproducts or workplace instantiations of basic personality traits (e.g., Holland, 1997; McCrae & Costa, 1990), interests have a unique genetic basis and serve unique motivational functions in driving human behaviors (see Proposition 2).

As traits, interests do not exist in a vacuum. We view interests as an integral part of an individual's identity that is composed of a myriad of traits connected with each other (i.e., trait complexes, Ackerman, 2003; or trait constellations, Armstrong et al., 2008) as well as self-concepts and social roles to which individuals subscribe (e.g., Eagly & Karau, 2002; Eccles, Wigfield, Harold, & Blumenfeld, 1993; Gottfredson, 1981, 2005; Hogan & Blake, 1999; Marsh, Trautwein, Lüdtke, Köller, & Baumert, 2005; Super, 1963; Tyler, 1955). As we examine the dispositional nature of interests, it is important to clarify that relative stability and heritability of traits does not imply that traits are set in stone and do not change at all. This is a common misunderstanding characterizing many scholarly debates over whether a psychological construct is a trait or simply a state activated by specific situations (Kenrick & Funder, 1988). Personality traits and interests do change in meaningful ways over time at the within-person level (e.g., Hoff, Briley, Wee, & Rounds, 2018; Roberts, Luo, Briley, Chow, Su, & Hill, 2017; Roberts, Walton, & Viechtbauer, 2006). In the case of interest development, it is closely associated with the development of knowledge, cognitive ability, and personality (Ackerman & Heggestad, 1997). Individuals are also motivated to maintain and develop interests in ways that are consistent with their existing self-concepts and social roles (Eccles et al., 1993; Gottfredson, 1981, 2005; Super, 1963; Tyler, 1955).

Super (1963) viewed vocational development as the implementation of self-concept, which includes self-actualization needs and role expectations of important persons such as parents. Other theorists have emphasized the impact of socio-cultural contexts. Leona Tyler (1955), for example, found that children at an early age reported interests in activities that were consistent with their sex roles "as if at this stage boys and girls were certain about repudiating things characteristic of the opposite sex" (pp. 40–41). In the Theory of Circumscription and Compromise, Linda Gottfredson (1981, 2005) elaborated on this perspective and maintained that the expression of vocational interests is constrained by the broader social order that individuals try to adjust to and fit in. Variables such as gender and social class dictate one's place in the society ("social space") and the range of activities or occupations that one would consider as acceptable for oneself. In other words, individuals act on their interests and, in this process, shape their interests, according to the scripts and boundaries imposed by their socio-cultural contexts. We depict interest traits (box with solid lines) as embedded in the influence of broader socio-cultural contexts (box with dashed lines) in Figure 1.1.

Proposition 2: Interests serve motivational functions that drive individuals' self-selection into certain external environments, effort and engagement with activities in those environments, and performance outcomes.

Both state and trait perspectives have emphasized the volitional nature of interests. Arnold (1906a, 1906b), for example, described interest as a striving or a conative tendency toward an anticipated gratification. Similarly, Dewey (1913) commented that interest signifies an "organic union" among the person, the materials (that is, the objects of interest to the person), and the results of action (p. 17). This union means that interest marks "an identification in action, and hence in desire, effort, and thought, of self with objects; namely, with the objects in which the activity terminates (ends) and with the objects by which it is carried forward to its end (means)" (p. 90). Strong (1943, p. 17) famously analogized interests as the rudder of a motorboat, which determines the boat's direction, whereas abilities, like the motor of the boat, determines the boat's speed in the chosen direction. Fryer (1931, p. 352) maintained that "once initiated, interest provides its own quantitative energy or motivational drive in proportion to the strength of acceptance (of the target object)."

The above views highlighted three motivational properties of interests. First, interests steer the direction of behaviors. Direction of behavior is implied in individuals' choice of broad environments (e.g., Katherine strives to be an engineer instead of a musician) and in the engagement in specific experiences and tasks (e.g., as an engineer, Katherine is drawn to designing machines and structures more so than interacting with clients). Second, the strength of interests is reflected in the amount of energy or vigor in individuals' striving (e.g., the more Katherine is interested in designing machines and structures, the greater amount of time and effort she invests in collecting and reading books and articles on this topic). Third, interests are usually associated with end goals and will sustain effort until end goals are met. The association between interests and goals, much like a vector "pointing ahead and to the future" (Arnold, 1906b, p. 299), not only directs and energizes behaviors, but also defines the duration of behavioral effort till goal attainment. On a micro scale, when a task of interest is clearly specified (e.g., reading an article about the challenges of building a multiple-span cable-stayed bridge), interest will motivate a goal-oriented behavior until the task is completed. On a macro scale, having a dispositional interest in an area often means that it will repeatedly incite striving over time and across a series of similar situations that involve goal-oriented behaviors until a long-term goal is achieved (e.g., receive a PhD degree or attain a dream job).

These three motivational functions of interests (Rounds & Su, 2014; Su & Nye, 2017) have been supported by empirical studies on the relationship between interest(s) and individuals' *choice* of environment as well as individuals' *effort* in the environment both on a micro and on a macro scale. Accumulating evidence from the education literature has shown that interest is associated with heightened attention to objects, deepened engagement with and processing of reading materials, and increased time and effort devoted to tasks (Hidi, 1990; Schiefele, 1991; Silvia, 2008). Research from vocational psychology and I-O psychology has consistently linked interests with choice of academic majors and occupations (Strong, 1943; Campbell, 1971) and effort and performance in both academic and work environments (Nye et al., 2012, 2017; Van Iddkinge, Campbell, et al., 2011; Van Iddekinge, Roth, et al., 2011). Figure 1.1 depicts the motivational functions and outcomes of interests. We will discuss the overlap and differences between interests and other motivational constructs in the next section when we position interests in the nomological network.

Proposition 3: Interests are experienced as a collection of affective reactions and cognitive evaluations toward objects in external environments. These affective and cognitive experiences jointly determine individuals' behaviors.

The primary difference between the trait perspective on interests and the state perspective on interest is whether a researcher focuses on consistent conative tendencies across situations over time or a context-specific experience. Schiefele (1991) distinguished dispositional interests from situational interest by defining the former as "latent characteristics" that represent relatively long-term orientations of an individual toward certain types of objects or activities, and referring to the latter as "actualized individual interest" that represents the manifestations of individual interests in a specific context (pp. 302–304). In fact, when discussing situational interest, some researchers prefer the term *to be interested* over the noun to emphasize the experience of interest in the moment (Kitson, 1925).

So, what does the experience of interest entail? Even for scholars who take the state perspective on interest, the answers are different. Mainly, the experience of interest has been theorized either as feelings (e.g., Izard, 1977; Silvia, 2001a) or as cognitions (e.g., Eccles et al., 1983; Schiefele, 2001, 2009). Izard (1977) provided a description that nicely summarized the experience of interest at the affect level: "At the experiential level interest... is the feeling of being engaged, caught-up, fascinated, curious. There is a feeling of wanting to investigate, become involved, or extend or expand the self by incorporating new information and having new experiences with the person or object that has stimulated the interest. In intense interest or excitement, the person feels animated and enlivened. It is this enlivenment that guarantees the association between interest and cognitive or motor activity. Even when relatively immobile the interested or excited person has the feeling that he is 'alive and active'" (p. 216). There are several key points in this description of interest. First, interest has a positive valence. It entails a positive feeling toward the object or task of interest, such that the person wants to know more about it and be involved with it. When engaged in the task of interest or being in a context that arouses interest, this positive feeling reinforces that experience so that the person desires to reengage in similar experiences. Second, interest is different from other positive feelings such as pleasure or satisfaction in that it is the feeling of engagement and curiosity (Silvia, 2001a, 2008). It marks the start, rather than the end, of an individual's cognitive and behavioral pursuit of an object of interest. It is associated with a level of discontentment that motivates the individual to invest more time and effort in the object. As Magda Arnold (1960) has argued, to be interested is to want to know more, not to have or possess (and be happy and content about it). Third, interest, even when conceptualized as an affective state, is closely tied to cognition. It is well established in the education literature that interest narrows the perceptual field, focuses attention, and deepens cognitive processing (e.g., Hidi, 1990; Schiefele, 1991). Interest is key to knowledge acquisition and cognitive development (Denissen, Zarrett, & Eccles, 2007; Su & Nye, 2017). Therefore, although interests are frequently labeled and studied as "non-cognitive attributes" in the I-O literature to distinguish the role of interests from that of cognitive abilities, understanding the link between interest and cognition in the work setting is critical for unpacking the relationship between interests and performance.

Aside from feelings of engagement and curiosity, the experience of interest also involves cognitive appraisals of the object of interest as well as the object *in relation to* oneself. The first layer in the cognitive component of interest captures subjective beliefs about the positive value of an object. Schiefele (2009), for example, described interest as "a set of value beliefs" that requires continuous cognitive processing and, when activated in a context, directly impacts individuals' intrinsic motivation. Similarly, Eccles et al. (1983) used the term "intrinsic value" to describe individuals' interest in a task and proposed that perceived intrinsic value—along with attainment value (perceived importance) and utility value (perceived instrumentality)—of the task drives individuals' motivation and achievement behaviors. The cognitive appraisal of an object's positive value is at the consciousness level but is closely associated with spontaneous affective responses. The second layer in the cognitive component of interest, which is discussed less frequently in the literature, captures a sense of meaning or worth provided by an object and the closeness of the object to one's self-concept (Dewey, 1913; Super, 1963). In other words, in the first cognitive appraisal, individuals ask the question "Is this object intriguing?" whereas in the second cognitive appraisal, individuals process questions like "Is this object meaningful *to me*?" "Is my interest in this object compatible with my existing self-concept and social roles?" "Do I identify with this object?" It is at this stage of cognitive evaluation that objects perceived as compatible with an existing self-concept are incorporated and those perceived as incompatible are rejected, even if they possess positive valence emotionally and cognitively. For example, a girl may highly enjoy computer programming but rejects it because of its perceived incompatibility with her gender role (Eccles et al., 1983; Gottfredson, 2005).

We maintain that affective and cognitive processes are both essential to the interest experience and jointly affect individual behaviors in external environments. Positive emotions and cognitive appraisals not only promote individuals' engagement and persistence in an activity in the moment, but also reinforce individuals' interest in the activity and motivate individuals to pursue similar activities in the future. In Figure 1.1, these affective and cognitive processes are represented as "the experience of situational interest at T_1 (T_2, ..., T_i)." Next, we describe how these affective reactions and cognitive evaluations of objects are stored in the human mind, how these mental representations are organized, and how existing mental units are expanded or adjusted with new experiences and information about new objects.

Proposition 4: Individual interests are organized as abstract mental representations of external objects and activities. New experiences with similar objects and activities can strengthen or refine these mental representations.

The experience of interest is idiosyncratic to each individual. The same object or situation may elicit vastly different reactions from different people. Even the most intriguing piece of art may encounter an indifferent viewer, and even the most boring lecture may find an avid listener. The fact that interests are trait-like and are affected by genetic influences means that individuals are predisposed to like or dislike certain types of objects, activities, or environments. In other words, dispositional interests set the baseline for individuals' affective and cognitive reactions in a given situation, such that some people have a general tendency to enjoy art while others lack that tendency. On the other hand, two people with the exact same genotype may have different expressions of interests. Imagine Katherine and her identical twin sister Kristen, who share a strong dispositional interest in mechanical activities—tinkering with gadgets and tools, playing with various materials, building things by hand—and were reared apart by two families. Katherine's parents discovered her interest in this area and took her to the Museum of Science and Industry, signed her up for summer camps on robotics, and bought her LEGO kits and played with her. Meanwhile, Kristen, whose adoptive father owned an auto shop, let her play with tools in the shop, taught her how to fix broken machines, and built things with her using spare parts. Although Katherine and Kristen had very different experiences growing up and were exposed to different activities, they have both been able to strengthen their interests in mechanical activities and are both excited to fulfill their interests in this domain with additional experiences. What happened for Katherine and Kristen, we argue, was that over time they both formed a mental representation of mechanical activities, albeit through different examples in this abstract category.

We propose that individual interests are organized into and stored as abstract, schematic mental representations of homogenous groups of objects and activities in external environments, such as mechanical activities, mathematics, finance, and teaching. Each mental representation (schema) contains incidents of past experiences with similar objects and activities in that group. Stored in each incident is information about a particular object/activity as well as the individual's affective reactions to and cognitive appraisals of it. Incidents within a schema can vary for every person due to exposure to different activities or access to different opportunities, as was the case for Katherine and Kristen. Nonetheless, individuals are able to generalize specific incidents to construct general impressions about and reactions to a class of homogeneous objects/activities. When an individual encounters a new object or activity, the affective and cognitive experience is assimilated into an existing schema, either strengthening or refining this mental representation. For example, Kristen may watch a documentary on how engineers use clues from the natural world in ingenious ways to develop new buildings and machines, completely fascinated and absorbed. This documentary thus reinforces Kristen's interest in mechanical activities and, at the same time, broadens her mental representation of mechanical activities from her previous experiences related to automobiles to a more generalized category. In a sense, these generalized categories are akin to latent constructs, and individuals' experiences with specific activities are akin to indicators of latent constructs. Forming these abstract mental representations is important, because it allows individuals to categorize new and unfamiliar objects/activities and anticipate reactions to them. As such, these abstract mental representations serve as a mechanism for selecting environments by directing individuals to engage in activities and contexts similar to those that interested them in the past. This process of interest development is shown in Figure 1.1 with repeated experiences over multiple time points from T_1 to T_i.

Our proposition is consistent with evidence from cognitive psychology, particularly in the area of impression formation (e.g., Brewer, 1988; Fiske, 1993; Smith & Zárate, 1992). Smith and Zárate (1992), for example, have shown that humans refer to specific accounts of experiences ("exemplars") as well as abstract schematic knowledge to form perception and social judgment. Underneath the cognitive experience of interest is assimilation—the process of associating a new object or activity to a preexisting schema in mind (McDougall, 1960; Savickas, 1999). The role of affect in the process is to color the experience in a positive light and thus magnify its meaning to the individual. Silvan Tomkins (1987, 1991), in the script theory, proposed that individuals experience scenes, which are emotional "slices of life" as subjectively perceived, and connect one affect-laden scene with another to form scripts, which are groups of scenes based on shared features that provide "rules" (or meanings) to guide future behavior. Each script is subject to revision from the ongoing experience of emotional scenes that share a core theme (Silvia, 2001a). It is not difficult to draw the analogy between cognitive and affect theory: scenes are affect-coded exemplars in cognition, scripts are affect-coded schemata that organize scenes, and the assimilation of new objects and activities into existing schemata co-occurs with the magnification of positive emotions. Both cognitive and affect research support the idea that interests are organized hierarchically with abstract mental representations drawn from specific experiences. This research also suggests that, as abstract mental representations, interests can be shaped by specific incidents in an academic or work environment. An affective event experienced at work (Weiss & Cropanzano, 1996), for example, not only influences an individual's job attitudes and performance behaviors but also has implications for the individual's interest development. Below we elaborate on this point.

Proposition 5: Interest development is a dynamic process through person-environment interaction. Both direct and vicarious experiences can contribute to the maintenance and development of interests.

According to script theory, the meaning of a script and its implications about the objects involved and the broader world extend beyond the simple collection of scenes within the script. A script provides a stable, guiding idea that predicts the course of future behaviors (Silvia, 2001a). The relative stability of scripts (i.e., abstract mental representations of interests) is important because it enables us to understand individuals' choice, persistence, and performance in academic and work environments better than transient emotional and cognitive experiences and thus makes interest assessment useful tools for personnel selection, staffing, and other organizational functions. Meanwhile, scripts develop through repeated person–environment interaction: An existing script will influence individuals' selection of and engagement in environments and activities, for example, making Kristen more likely to be drawn to a documentary on engineering marvels than one on political movements; experience in an environment and engagement in activities, in turn, will further shape that script, for example, watching the documentary furthers and solidifies the meaning of her existing script (i.e., interest in mechanical activities). Conversely, a negative affective or cognitive incident experienced at work may cause an individual to reevaluate his/her interest in the work activity/environment. For example, if Kristen gets an internship at an engineering firm and overhears her male colleagues discussing her not being a great fit because of her gender, this incident may lead to the experience of negative emotions and the perception of incompatibility between engineering and her identity, which, in turn, dampens her interest in this area. In summary, interests provide a relatively stable baseline for individuals' attitudes and behaviors at work. Individuals' experience at work with various job characteristics, peers and supervisors, and other contextual factors, on the other hand, triggers the process of adjusting the affective reaction to and cognitive appraisal of an external environment or object, allowing interest to develop in a dynamic, cyclical manner over time.

The dynamic process of interest development is depicted in Figure 1.1 as the loop between trait and state perspectives of interests. This process has been highlighted by theories from the state perspective, such as Hidi and Renninger's (2006) four-phase model of interest development and Prenzel's (1992) selective persistence model of interest. It is also implied by person-environment (P-E) fit theories from the trait perspective (e.g., Holland, 1959, 1997), in that individuals seek out academic and work environments that are congruent with their existing interests and positive outcomes resulting from P-E fit further reinforce these interests. Intervention studies have also shown that interest in a school subject or an occupational field can be increased by emphasizing its personal relevance (e.g., Harackiewicz, Rozek, Hulleman, & Hyde, 2012; Hulleman, Godes, Hendricks, & Harackiewicz, 2010; Hulleman & Harackiewicz, 2009) or its compatibility with personal goals (e.g., Diekman, Clark, Johnston, Brown, & Steinberg, 2011).

Given the key role of person-environment interaction in interest development, nearly all interest theories emphasize the necessity of reengagement in similar experiences and repeated interactions with objects/activities that elicit interest. Silvia (2001a, p. 285), for example, claimed that if "interest is not experienced in the context of an activity and magnified over time, an interest will not develop, regardless of why the feelings of interest arose in the first place." Prenzel (1992) further suggested that an interest would dissipate without repeated engagement with an object/activity that provides a sense of novelty, complexity, and uncertainty. While we acknowledge the importance of repetition and magnification for interest development, we submit that both direct engagement with an object/activity and vicarious experiences may contribute to the maintenance and development of interests. Social learning theory (Bandura, 1977) suggests that new associations may be established without direct experience of a behavior and its consequences but through observing an activity and forming the meaning of the activity symbolically. Therefore, visiting a museum exhibition, viewing a documentary, or watching someone else do an activity of interest to oneself may all elicit the same positive emotions and cognitive appraisals as directly engaging in the activity, providing vicarious reinforcement for existing interests.

Further, we submit that it is not necessary for interests to be constantly activated to be maintained. As previously discussed, interests are trait-like. Genetic influence provides a set point for the level of interest in an area. Once an individual forms the abstract mental representation of interest in this area (a latent construct), it will maintain its strength until the individual has an opportunity to reengage in another activity (an indicator of the latent construct), either directly or vicariously, and revisit the existing interest schema. Without being experienced or stimulated, individual interest in an area may be dormant for years, but will not dissipate. Evidence for this proposition comes from studies of individuals with severe physical disabilities (e.g., Krause & Clark, 2014; Rohe & Krause, 1998). These studies have found that, for individuals who suffered from traumatic spinal cord injuries, their interests stayed relatively stable despite their inability to participate in any interest-related activities. Future longitudinal studies with repeated measures of interests are needed to further test this proposition in other populations, particularly individuals who have gaps in career transitions and return to work after a period of unemployment.

Proposition 6: Interests develop in tandem with other parts of self-concept and identity, including abilities, values, and roles.

Interests are an integral part of an individual's identity. Previously we proposed that the experience of interest includes cognitive appraisals of the value of an object and its compatibility with oneself. Over the life span, individuals are likely to form mental representations of interests that are consistent with other parts of their self-concept (self-schemata). Individuals tend to be interested in areas where they are knowledgeable, do well, and have high self-perceived abilities (Ackerman & Heggestad, 1997; Denissen et al., 2007). For example,

Denissen and colleagues (2007) examined the longitudinal development of approximately 1,000 students between grades 1 and 12 (ages 6–17) and found that interests were positively associated with students' self-concept of ability and academic achievement; more important, the within-person correlations among interests, self-concept of ability, and academic achievement increased over the course of 12 years. The increasing association between interests and abilities starts from an early age and continues throughout the life-span. Similarly, individuals tend to develop interests in areas that are perceived as compatible with their roles, scripts, and narratives determined by socio-cultural norms (e.g., gender role).

Our proposition is in line with studies on trait complexes and integrative theories of human development, such as Ackerman's (1996) Process, Personality, Interests, and Knowledge (PPIK) model (also see von Stumm, & Ackerman, 2013), Snow's aptitude complexes (Corno et al., 2002; Snow, Corno, & Jackson, 1996), and Holland's (1959, 1997) characterizations of the six RIASEC vocational personality types (which comprise not only associations among preferences for certain activities, but also associations between preferences and certain personality traits, abilities and skills, self-competence beliefs, specific styles of problem solving, as well as values and life goals; cf. Stoll & Trautwein, 2017). These theories examine individual difference variables jointly and organize them into clusters based on their shared variances (for reviews, see Ackerman & Heggestad, 1997; Armstrong et al., 2008; and Mount, Barrick, Scullen, & Rounds 2005). We believe that interests are indicators for such trait complexes rather than isolated individual difference variables.

Studies on trait complexes and integrative frameworks of individual differences (e.g., Ackerman, 1996, 2003; Armstrong et al., 2008; Anthoney & Armstrong, 2010; Armstrong & Anthoney, 2009) provide a new approach to understanding the nature of interests. By empirically examining the correlates and overlaps between interests and other psychological constructs such as personality traits and cognitive abilities, these integrative studies highlighted the importance of studying interest development across the life span and provided information on what individual difference variables to target in longitudinal research. Importantly, the trait complexes may be the best way to predict complex educational and career behaviors including performance and career success (Armstrong, Su, & Rounds, 2011).

Interests in the Nomological Network

Against the backdrop of the above propositions, we examine the nomological network in the second part of this chapter and discuss the similarities and differences between interests and related constructs. In the following, we address the relationships between interests and personality traits, cognitive abilities, motivation, values, goals, and intentions (expressed interests).

Interests and Personality Traits

Interests and personality traits are similar in that they both reflect important aspects of individual differences (Caspi, Roberts, & Shiner, 2005; Low et al., 2005; Lubinski, 2000). This similarity has been overlooked for a long time, as traditional models of personality (e.g., McCrae & Costa, 1990) regarded the Big Five personality dimensions as the core of traits, and regarded motivational constructs—that is, interests—as "downstream" instantiations of personality traits that are at a lower level of abstraction. This perspective is based on the assumption that motivational constructs are less stable and less heritable than the Big Five. However, as discussed previously, empirical findings do not support this assumption. Meta-analytic rank-order continuity coefficients were found to be higher for interests than for personality traits (Low et al., 2005) and heritability estimates of interests were found to be comparable (Betsworth et al., 1994; Lykken et al., 1993) or even higher (Kandler, Zimmermann, & McAdams, 2014) than those for personality traits. In line with these findings, newer theories like the neo-socioanalytic model of personality (Roberts & Wood, 2006; Roberts, Wood, & Caspi, 2008) conceptualize personality traits and motives (including interests) as parallel and separate domains of human functioning.

Meta-analytic results (Barrick, Mount, & Gupta, 2003) have demonstrated meaningful overlaps between vocational interest constructs in Holland's (1959, 1997) RIASEC model and Big Five personality traits, such as those between Extraversion and Enterprising and Social interests (ρ = .41 and .29, respectively) and those between Openness to Experience and Artistic and Investigative Interests (ρ = .39 and .25, respectively). This overlap may be partially due to the similarities in the conceptualization of these constructs. Other correlations between vocational interests and personality traits were found to be modest, mostly around or below .10. These findings suggest that personality traits and interests reflect somewhat different aspects of a person: Personality traits focus on the person as a social actor (see Kandler et al., 2014). They comprise enduring patterns of thoughts, feelings, and behaviors (Roberts & Wood, 2006) and describe how the person typically behaves and how the person is seen by others (or the self). Therefore, personality traits are essential for a person's reputation in social groups—reflecting the extent to which the person is considered as, for example, sociable, hard-working, or impulsive. However, personality traits do not fully capture the core preferences and aspirations of a person (Fleeson, 2012). In contrast, interests—and other motivational constructs—focus on the person as a motivated agent and represent what a person wants in life and what a person aims to achieve or avoid.

As discussed earlier (see Proposition 4), interests are organized as abstract mental representations that serve as a mechanism for selecting environments. By directing individuals to engage in activities and contexts similar to those that interested them in the past, interests predict human behaviors in particular environments. This might also explain why interests were found to be stronger predictors of certain life outcomes than personality traits—especially if these outcomes were related to volitional choices and decisions (Stoll et al., 2017; Su, 2012).

Interests and Cognitive Abilities

Cognitive abilities represent another important domain of individual differences (Lubinski, 2000; Sackett, Lievens, Van Iddekinge, & Kuncel, 2017; Schmidt, 2014). Abilities reflect what a person can do, whereas interests reflect what a person wants to do (i.e., direction of effort), how hard the person tries (i.e., vigor of effort), and how long the effort is sustained (i.e., persistence of effort; Rounds & Su, 2014; Su & Nye, 2017). It is proposed that interests, personality traits, and abilities develop along with each other (Ackerman & Heggestad, 1997). An individual's level of ability and personality traits influence the probability to succeed in a specific task, whereas interests determine the motivational forces put forth toward the task.

Although interests have been discussed as part of individuals' "non-cognitive" attributes, interests and cognitive abilities are mutually dependent (Su & Nye, 2017): On the one hand, a certain level of ability or knowledge is necessary for the development of interest in the first place; on the other hand, interest is an important precondition for skill- and knowledge development, as it facilitates more efficient seeking, acquisition, and organization of knowledge (Dewey, 1913; Hidi, 1990; Reeve, 1996; Schiefele, Krapp, & Winteler, 1992; Voss & Schauble, 1992). Interest leads to engagement in specific activities; whereas abilities enhance the probability of successful performance in these activities. Positive performance feedback will foster self-competence beliefs that, in turn, may reinforce the initial interest and foster its maintenance—leading to enduring interests (Hidi & Renninger, 2006). Enduring interests then, again, lead to increased engagement in specific activities, which, along with experiences associated with these activities, lead to the acquisition of new skills and the accumulation of abilities in these areas.

To better understand the dynamic and reciprocal causal relationship between interests and cognitive abilities, we draw from Cattell's (1963) investment theory that distinguishes between fluid intelligence (which is innate) and crystalized intelligence (which is acquired or learned). Investment theory postulates that individuals invest their fluid intelligence in the acquisition of crystalized intelligence. Empirical findings show that crystalized intelligence—manifested as skills and knowledge—is not solely caused by fluid intelligence, but also by a general interest in learning as well as specific interests—for example, RIASEC interests (see Schmidt, 2014, for a discussion). Specific interests are important for the development of crystalized intelligence in specific domains, as they lead people to engage in experiences in these domains. In doing so, interests determine the amount and type of knowledge and skills that people acquire. Again, the motivational functions of interests (as discussed in Proposition 2) differentiate them from cognitive abilities. Individuals need to invest their fluid intelligence in the development and acquisition of skills and knowledge (crystalized intelligence), but specific interests are the key factors that determine the areas in which people invest their fluid intelligence, how much effort they invest, and for how long. An example that demonstrates this mechanism is women's underrepresentation in science, technology, engineering, and mathematics (STEM) occupations despite little observed sex differences in general mental ability (GMA) and quantitative ability (Hyde & Linn, 2006). Schmidt (2011) demonstrated that the gender gap in STEM might be attributable to women's lower interest in technical or mechanical activities, which leads to fewer technical experiences (e.g., technical hobbies) and, in turn, less-developed technical knowledge and lower levels of technical aptitude. Because technical material is not emphasized in Grades K through 12, as are verbal or mathematical materials, lack of self-driven engagement in technical experiences outside of school means that gender gaps in technical interest and aptitude will likely persist. This evidence is consistent with our theoretical propositions 4–6.

Interests and Motivation

The term motivation can be used in two ways—in a narrow sense reflecting the state of being motivated to perform a specific behavior; or in a general sense reflecting the collection of motives that drive human decisions or choices. When it is used in the sense of being motivated to perform a specific task, we view motivation as a downstream construct and an outcome of interests. Interests determine the objects and activities into which people invest their energy and time. When a person has a strong interest in an activity, he or she will also be strongly motivated to engage in the activity. This assumption that interest influences motivation is in line with the educational psychology perspective on interest, which views interest as a source of intrinsic motivation (Renninger & Hidi, 2011; Schiefele, 1991, 2001).

When motivation is used in the general sense as a collection of motives that drive human decisions, interests are one of several motivational constructs that determine individuals' choices (Roberts & Wood, 2006; Walsh, 1999). Motivational constructs—values, goals, and interests—have in common that they involve appraisals of external objects and these appraisals are used as a basis for evaluating and prioritizing various behaviors and choices. As these constructs are closely connected (Rounds & Armstrong, 2014) and fulfill similar functions in motivating individuals' behaviors, a clear distinction between these constructs is sometimes difficult. Nonetheless, although all motivational constructs include an evaluative component, interests, values, and goals differ in the nature of their evaluations, their levels of granularity, and the specific ways in which they influence behaviors. We detail these differences in the following sections.

Interests and Values

Interests and values are similar in that they are both contextualized and involve external objects. In addition, interests and values both involve cognitive and affective appraisals of objects and activities, although the nature and level of these appraisals are different. The main difference between interests and values is that interests reflect evaluations of personal preference, whereas values reflect evaluations of importance (Dawis, 1991). By attaching importance to various objects in life, values describe the worth of more abstract entities (Kandler et al., 2014) and function as principles—standards or criteria—by which people behave (Dawis, 1991). Therefore, values are often considered to be broader and more general than interests (Allport & Vernon, 1931).

Another difference between interests and values is that interests are closely associated with the development of cognitive abilities, whereas values may develop independent of abilities (Sagiv, 2002). The accumulation of abilities, skills, and knowledge in a domain is key to individuals' evaluation of activities in the domain, as individuals tend to prefer activities that they can do well. In contrast, individuals may value something as important without being able to do it.

Finally, values often develop within certain social contexts and reflect both personally and socially approved life goals (Wach & Gosling, 2004). Therefore, values explain individuals' behaviors as well as social justification for the behaviors. Interests, in contrast, do not directly reflect social justification for behaviors. However, because interests involve cognitive appraisals of whether certain objects or activities are consistent with self-identity, social justification for behaviors can be internalized and integrated into personal preferences (see Proposition 3). For example, if an individual values social recognition or financial rewards, he/she may be drawn to tasks, contexts, or roles that have the potential to fulfill these values because they are seen as compatible with his/her self-identity. This may explain why a prestige component is often found in the factor structure of interests (e.g., Tracey & Rounds, 1996). Therefore, values—as socially approved evaluations of the importance of desirable end states—may direct individuals' choices and, over time, manifest in individuals' interests and preferences (Dawis, 1991). In addition, depending on what an individual values, it may strengthen or weaken the effects of interests on job attitudes and performance. For an individual who highly values work itself, interest fit (or misfit) is likely more strongly associated with job satisfaction and performance compared with someone who highly values pay and promotion and cares little about the interestingness of the job (Locke, 1976). Because personal values reflect socio-cultural norms, the importance of interests may vary by culture. Interests may be more important in cultures that value intrinsic rewards from work compared to those that more strongly value extrinsic rewards from work. More research is needed on the overlap, distinction, and mutual influence between interests and values.

Interests, Goals, and Goal-Setting

Similar to interests, goals affect behaviors and performance outcomes by directing attention, mobilizing effort, increasing persistence, and motivating strategy development (Locke, Shaw, Saari, & Latham, 1981). However, the mechanisms through which interests and goals affect behaviors are different. Interest in an activity is focused on the activity itself and the experiences associated with the activity. This means that interests direct behaviors, because people choose to engage in activities or objects for "their own sake" (Silvia, 2001a). By contrast, goals are related to specific end states that a person wants to achieve and commits to attain through action (Hennecke & Freund, 2017). Goals affect behaviors because people choose to engage in activities that will help them reach the desired end states. As such, goals combine ends with means, as they comprise cognitive representations of desired end states and cognitive representations of how to achieve them (Kruglanski et al., 2002). Therefore, goals could be viewed as more proximal to behavior and performance outcomes compared to interests—goals guide attention and action focused on possible opportunities for goal attainment (Kruglanski et al., 2002), whereas interests guide attention and action based on preferences for certain activities or environments.

The above discussion on different mechanisms through which interests and goals affect behaviors may lead to the assumption that goals have stronger associations with behavior and performance outcomes than interests. In fact, the strength of this association depends on the level of concreteness of a goal, as goals can range from very specific and concrete to very broad and abstract (see Roberts & Robins, 2000). When goals are contextualized and targeted at immediate actions for discrete events, they are closely associated with specific behaviors. When goals are conceptualized broadly (e.g., major life goals or global aspirations), they may be trans-situational and may not be as strongly tied to behaviors in specific situations (Rokeach, 1973; Wach & Gosling, 2004). The more specific and concrete a desired end state is, the clearer the behaviors or actions needed are for the achievement of this end state. For example, if a person aims to go to a concert of her favorite rock band, to reach this specific goal it is obvious that she has to buy tickets for the concert, organize the transportation to the concert venue, and maybe ask a friend to join. In contrast, if the person's goal is more abstract (e.g., she aspires to live a life that is helpful and supportive for others), then a great variety of possible actions could lead to the fulfillment of this goal, because the aspired end state itself could be manifested in various forms. Goals influence behaviors, but the associations between goals and behaviors will be much stronger if goals are tied to specific and concrete end states.

In contrast to goals, interests are not directly linked to end states. Nevertheless, interests are important for goal setting and goal achievement (Nye et al., 2012). Interests influence goal setting, as they direct activities toward specific domains (i.e., interest-based choices). Interests influence goal achievement, as they energize goal-striving effort, motivating people to work hard on a task. In addition, interests support goal persistence, sustaining goal-striving effort until a goal is achieved (Nye et al., 2012). As interests affect the direction, vigor, and persistence of goal-oriented behaviors, it is expected that interests will predict goal attainment (Rounds & Su, 2014; Su & Nye, 2017). Interests can predict achievement on a micro scale by attaining specific goals and, on a macro scale, by attaining a long-term overarching goal that requires the completion of many short-term specific goals.

Intriguingly, there have also been findings suggesting that specific ways of goal setting could foster the development of interest. Harackiewicz, Barron, Carter, Lehto, and Elliot (1997) demonstrated that setting performance goals improved college students' grades but did not affect their interest, whereas setting learning goals enhanced interest.

Interests and Intentions (Express Interests)

At the end of this chapter, we would like to clarify a confusion that many people—even researchers—have about interests and intentions. When lay people talk about "interest" as in "I am interested in applying to this engineer job," what they really mean is their intention or expressed interest in a specific action, not interest traits in the sense of individual differences as we have discussed in this chapter. Similarly, when young children talk about "interest" as in "I want to become a fire-fighter when I grow up" or "I want to be the President of the United States," they are expressing career aspirations, which, again, may to some extent reflect latent interest traits but are not interest traits per se. Although expressed interests—intentions and career aspirations—are sometimes used as indicators of interests, they are conceptually distinct from interest traits (Silvia, 2001b). In the Social Cognitive Career Theory, Lent and colleagues (1994) differentiated interests from *choice goals*, which are conceptualized as intentions to make certain academic or career choices and subsume the constructs of expressed interests and career aspirations. Interests and intentions are causally linked. Intentions are downstream constructs of interests and are more proximal to specific behavioral (choice) outcomes (e.g., occupational entry and membership), as interests may influence the intention to pursue a given occupation and direct behaviors through the formation of concrete intentions. This distinction between interests and intentions also explains why expressed interests are often better predictors for those specific behaviors than measured interests (Silvia, 2001b).

Summary and Conclusions

Is there a unique place for interests in organizational research? An intermediate answer

In the first part of this chapter we proposed that interests are traits that are embedded in socio-cultural contexts and serve motivational functions by directing and sustaining individuals' effort and engagement in various activities and environments. Additionally, we proposed that the experience of interest in an external environment as a collection of affective reactions and cognitive appraisals further determines individuals' behaviors and helps shape existing mental representations of interests. Through this dynamic process of person-environment interaction—either direct or vicarious—interests develop as an integral part of an individual's identity. In the second part of this chapter, we reviewed the similarities and differences between interests and other constructs of individual differences and demonstrated that interests are distinct from many relevant constructs, including personality traits, cognitive abilities, values, goals, and intentions.

We believe that there is a unique place for interests in work and organizational research. Occupations and organizations provide specific socio-cultural contexts, in which interests are embedded and serve various motivational functions. Interests direct individuals' occupational choices since individuals tend to select environments that correspond to their interests. In addition, interests direct and sustain the effort and engagement a person is willing to put into work-related tasks, which, in turn, influences the person's performance in the task and the success that is achieved—in the short term and over the course of one's career. Currently, the primary use of interest assessment is limited to guiding career choices. However, based on our discussion, interests can be useful for understanding emotions and attitudes at work and many other work outcomes, including effort on the job, job performance, and career success. Interest assessment has potential value-added beyond cognitive ability and personality assessments for many organizational functions including personnel selection and staffing.

With the integrative framework of Trait-State Interest Dynamics, we have attempted to reconcile the trait and state perspectives on interests and highlight the process of interest development through person-environment interactions. Understanding the experience of interest in organizations, aside from individual differences in interests, may provide unique insights into how individuals manage their careers, interpret their fit with work environments, and adapt to organizational life. Specifically, future research needs to examine how the subjective experience of interest—the collection of affective reactions and cognitive appraisals—may differ from interest traits and what contextual factors influence this experience. It may also prove to be fruitful for future research to investigate the actions that individuals take to cope with incongruence between their interests and jobs and the strategies that organizations may use to better socialize and manage employees who experience interest misfit. Understanding the consequences of and adaptive processes in response to the experience of interest misfit is equally important as studying the positive outcomes and predictive power of interests and interest fit. This also requires a shift from a static view of interests to a dynamic view of interests within the context of work environments.

As an integral part of individuals' identity, interests could be seen as the binding link between cognitive and non-cognitive traits, as well as motivational constructs like values, goals, and intentions. Instead of studying these domains of individual differences in isolation, future research should investigate how interests interact with these other constructs to form trait complexes or constellations and evolve within the organizational context and how they jointly influence individuals' work and career outcomes.

References

Ackerman, P. L. (1996). A theory of adult intellectual development: Process, personality, interests, and knowledge. *Intelligence, 22*, 227–257. doi:10.1016/S0160-2896(96)90016-1

Ackerman, P. L. (2003). Aptitude complexes and trait complexes. *Educational Psychologist, 38*(2), 85–93.

Ackerman, P. L., & Heggestad, E. D. (1997). Intelligence, personality, and interests: Evidence for overlapping traits. *Psychological Bulletin, 121,* 219–245.

Ainley, M. (2007). Being and feeling interested: Transient state, mood, and disposition. In P. Schutz (Ed.), *Emotion in education* (pp. 141–157). New York: Academic Press.

Allport, G. W., & Vernon, P. E (1931). A test for personal values. *Journal of Abnormal and Social Psychology, 26*, 231–248.

Anthoney, S. F., & Armstrong, P. I. (2010). Individual and environments: Linking ability and skill ratings with interests. *Journal of Counseling Psychology, 57,* 36–51.

Armstrong, P. I., & Anthoney, S. F. (2009). Personality facets and RIASEC interests: An integrated model. *Journal of Vocational Behavior, 75,* 346–359.

Armstrong, P. I., Day, S. X, McVay, J. P., & Rounds, J. (2008). Holland's RIASEC model as an integrative framework for individual differences. *Journal of Counseling Psychology, 55,* 1–18.

Armstrong, P. I., Su, R., & Rounds, J. (2011). Vocational interests: The road less traveled. In T. Chamorro-Premuzic, S. von Strumm, & A. Furnham, (Eds.), *Handbook of individual differences* (pp. 608–631). Oxford: Wiley-Blackwell.

Arnold, F. (1906a). The psychology of interest (I). *Psychological Review, 13*(4), 221–238.

Arnold, F. (1906b). The psychology of interest (II). *Psychological Review, 13*(5), 291–315.

Arnold, M. B. (1960). *Emotion and personality.* New York: Columbia University Press.

Bandura, A. (1977). *Social learning theory.* Englewood Cliffs, NJ: Prentice-Hall.

Barrick, M. R., Mount, M. K., & Gupta, R. (2003). Meta-Analysis of the relationship between the Five-Factor model of personality and Holland's occupational types. *Personnel Psychology, 56*(1), 45–74. doi:10.1111/j.1744-6570.2003.tb00143.x

Betsworth, D. G., Cooper, C. R., Grotevant, H. D., Hansen, J. I. C., Scarr, S., & Weinberg, R. A. (1994). Genetic and environmental influences on vocational interests assessed using adoptive and biological families and twins reared apart and together. *Journal of Vocational Behavior, 44*(3), 263–278.

Bouchard Jr, T. J. (1997). The genetics of personality. In K. Blum & E. P. Noble (Eds.), *Handbook of psychiatric genetics* (pp. 273–296). Boca Raton, FL: CRC Press.

Brewer, M. B. (1988). A dual process model of impression formation. In R. S. Wyer & T. K. Srull (Eds.), *Advances in social cognition* (Vol. 1, pp. 1–36). Hillsdale, NJ: Erlbaum.

Campbell, D. P. (1971). *Handbook for the strong vocational interest blank.* Palo Alto, CA: Stanford University Press.

Caspi, A., Roberts, B. W., & Shiner, R. L. (2005). Personality development: Stability and change. *Annual Review of Psychology, 56*(1), 453–484. doi:10.1146/annurev.psych.55.090902.141913

Cattell, R. B. (1963). Theory of fluid and crystallized intelligence: A critical experiment. *Journal of Educational Psychology, 54*(1), 1–22. doi:10.1037/h0046743

Corno, L., Cronbach, L. J., Kupermintz, H., Lohman, D. F., Mandinach, E. B., Porteus, A. W., & Talbert, J. E. (2002). *Remaking the concept of aptitude: Extending the legacy of Richard E. Snow.* Mahwah, NJ: Erlbaum.

Dawis, R. V. (1980). Measuring interests. In D. A. Payne (Ed.), *New directions for testing and measurement: Recent developments in affective measurement.* San Francisco, CA: Jossey-Bass.

Dawis, R. V. (1991). Vocational interests, values, and preferences. In M. D. Dunnette & L. M. Hough (Ed.), *Handbook of industrial and organizational psychology* (Vol. 2, 2nd ed., pp. 833–871). Palo Alto, CA: Consulting Psychologists Press.

Denissen, J. J., Zarrett, N. R., & Eccles, J. S. (2007). I like to do it, I'm able, and I know I am: Longitudinal couplings between domain-specific achievement, self-concept, and interest. *Child Development, 78*(2), 430–447.

Dewey, J. (1913). *Interest and effort in education.* Boston: Houghton Mifflin Company. doi:10.1037/14633-000

Diekman, A. B., Clark, E. K., Johnston, A. M., Brown, E. R., & Steinberg, M. (2011). Malleability in communal goals and beliefs influences attraction to stem careers: Evidence for a goal congruity perspective. *Journal of Personality and Social Psychology, 101*(5), 902–918.

Eagly, A. H., & Karau, S. J. (2002). Role congruity theory of prejudice toward female leaders. *Psychological Review, 109*(3), 573–598.

Eccles, J., Adler, T. F., Futterman, R., Goff, S. B., Kaczala, C. M., Meece, J., & Midgley, C. (1983). Expectancies, values and academic behaviors. In J. T. Spence (Ed.), *Achievement and achievement motives: Psychological and sociological approaches* (pp. 75–146). San Francisco: Freeman.

Eccles, J., Wigfield, A., Harold, R. D., & Blumenfeld, P. (1993). Age and gender differences in children's self-and task perceptions during elementary school. *Child Development, 64*(3), 830–847.

Fiske, S. T. (1993). Social cognition and social perception. *Annual Review of Psychology, 44*(1), 155–194.

Fleeson, W. (2012). Perspectives on the Person: Rapid growth and opportunities for Integration. In K. Deaux & M. Snyder (Eds.), *The Oxford handbook of personality and social psychology*. New York: Oxford University Press. Retrieved from http://www.oxfordhandbooks.com/view/10.1093/oxfordhb/9780195398991.001.0001/oxfordhb-9780195398991-e-003

Fryer, D. (1931). The measurement of interests in relation to human adjustment. Oxford, England: Holt.

Gottfredson, L. S. (1981). Circumscription and compromise: A developmental theory of occupational aspirations. *Journal of Counseling Psychology, 28*(6), 545–579. doi:10.1037/0022-0167.28.6.545

Gottfredson, L. S. (2005). Applying Gottfredson's theory of circumscription and compromise in career guidance and counseling. In S. D. Brown & R. W. Lent (Eds.), *Career development and counseling: Putting theory and research to work* (pp. 71–100). Hoboken, NJ: Wiley.

Harackiewicz, J. M., Barron, K. E., Carter, S. M., Lehto, A. T., & Elliot, A. J. (1997). Predictors and consequences of achievement goals in the college classroom: Maintaining interest and making the grade. *Journal of Personality and Social Psychology, 73*, 1284–1295.

Harackiewicz, J. M., Rozek, C. S., Hulleman, C. S., & Hyde, J. S. (2012). Helping parents to motivate adolescents in mathematics and science: An experimental test of a utility value intervention. *Psychological Science, 23*, 899–906.

Harris, J. A., Vernon, P. A., Johnson, A. M., & Jang, K. L. (2006). Phenotypic and genetic relationships between vocational interests and personality. *Personality and Individual Differences, 40*(8), 1531–1541.

Hennecke, M., & Freund, A. M. (2017). The development of goals and motivation. In J. Specht (Ed.), *Personality development across the lifespan* (pp. 257–274). London: Academic Press Elsevier.

Hidi, S. (1990). Interest and its contribution as a mental resource for learning. *Review of Educational Research, 60*, 549–571. doi:10.2307/1170506

Hidi, S., & Renninger, K. A. (2006). The four-phase model of interest development. *Educational Psychologist, 41*(2), 111–127. doi:10.1207/s15326985ep4102_4

Hoff, K. A., Briley, D. A., Wee, C. J. M., & Rounds, J. (2018). Normative changes in interests from adolescence to adulthood: A meta-analysis of longitudinal studies. *Psychological Bulletin, 144*, 426–451.

Hogan, R., & Blake, R. (1999). John Holland's vocational typology and personality theory. *Journal of Vocational Behavior, 55*(1), 41–56.

Holland, J. L. (1959). A theory of vocational choice. *Journal of Counseling Psychology, 6*(1), 35–45. doi:10.1037/h0040767

Holland, J. L. (1997). *Making vocational choices: A theory of vocational personalities and work environments* (3rd ed.). Odessa, FL: Psychological Assessment Resources.

Hulleman, C. S., Godes, O., Hendricks, B. L., & Harackiewicz, J. M. (2010). Enhancing interest and performance with a utility value intervention. *Journal of Educational Psychology, 102*(4), 880–895.

Hulleman, C. S., & Harackiewicz, J. M. (2009). Promoting interest and performance in high school science classes. *Science, 326*, 1410–1412.

Hyde, J. S., & Linn, M. C. (2006). Gender similarities in mathematics and science. *Science, 314*, 599–600.

Izard, C. (1977). *Human emotions*. New York: Plenum.

Kandler, C., Bleidorn, W., Riemann, R., Angleitner, A., & Spinath, F. M. (2011). The genetic links between the big five personality traits and general interest domains. *Personality and Social Psychology Bulletin, 37*(12), 1633–1643.

Kandler, C., Zimmermann, J., & McAdams, D. P. (2014). Core and surface characteristics for the description and theory of personality differences and development. *European Journal of Personality, 28*(3), 231–243. doi:10.1002/per.1952

Kenrick, D. T., & Funder, D. C. (1988). Profiting from controversy: Lessons from the person-situation debate. *American Psychologist, 43*, 23–34.

Kitson, H. D. (1925). *Psychology of vocational adjustment*. Philadelphia: Lippincott.

Krapp, A. (2007). An educational–psychological conceptualization of interest. *International Journal of Educational and Vocational Guidance, 7*, 5–21.

Kruglanski, A. W., Shah, J. Y., Fishbach, A., Friedman, R., Woo Young Chun, & Sleeth-Keppler, D. (2002). A theory of goal systems. *Advances in Experimental Social Psychology, 34*, 331–378. doi:10.1016/S0065-2601(02)80008-9

Krause, J. S., & Clark, J. M. R. (2014). Stability of vocational interests after recent spinal cord injury. *Rehabilitation Psychology, 59*, 321–328.

Lent, R. W., Brown, S. D., & Hackett, G. (1994). Toward a unifying social cognitive theory of career and academic interest, choice, and performance. *Journal of Vocational Behavior, 45*(1), 79–122. doi:10.1006/jvbe.1994.1027

Locke, E. A. (1976) The nature and causes of job satisfaction. In M. D. Dunnette (Ed.), *Handbook of industrial and organizational psychology* (Vol. 1, pp. 1297–1343). Chicago: Rand McNally.

Locke, E. A., Shaw, K. N., Saari, L. M., & Latham, G. P. (1981). Goal setting and task performance: 1969–1980. *Psychological Bulletin, 90*(1), 125–152. doi:10.1037/0033-2909.90.1.125

Low, K. S. D., Yoon, M., Roberts, B. W., & Rounds, J. (2005). The stability of vocational interests from early adolescence to middle adulthood: A quantitative review of longitudinal studies. *Psychological Bulletin, 131*(5), 713–737. doi:10.1037/0033-2909.131.5.713

Lubinski, D. (2000). Scientific and social significance of assessing individual differences: "Sinking shafts at a few critical points." *Annual Review of Psychology, 51*, 405–444. doi:10.1146/annurev.psych.51.1.405

Lykken, D. T., Bouchard, T. J. Jr., McGue, M., & Tellegen, A. (1993). Heritability of interests: A twin study. *Journal of Applied Psychology, 78*(4), 649–661.

Marsh, H. W., Trautwein, U., Lüdtke, O., Köller, O., & Baumert, J. (2005). Academic self-concept, interest, grades, and standardized test scores: Reciprocal effects models of causal ordering. *Child Development, 76*(2), 397–416.

McCrae, R. R., & Costa, P. T. (1990). *Personality in adulthood*. New York: Guilford Press.

McDougall, W. (1960). *An introduction to social psychology*. London: Methuen.

Moloney, D. P., Bouchard Jr, T. J., & Segal, N. L. (1991). A genetic and environmental analysis of the vocational interests of monozygotic and dizygotic twins reared apart. *Journal of Vocational Behavior, 39*(1), 76–109.

Mount, M. K., Barrick, M. R., Scullen, S. M., & Rounds, J. (2005). Higher-order dimensions of the big five personality traits and the big six vocational interest types. *Personnel Psychology, 58*(2), 447–478. doi:10.1111/j.1744-6570.2005.00468.x

Nye, C. D., Su, R., Rounds, J., & Drasgow, F. (2012). Vocational interests and performance: A quantitative summary of over 60 years of research. *Perspectives on Psychological Science, 7*(4), 384–403. doi:10.1177/1745691612449021

Nye, C. D., Su, R., Rounds, J., & Drasgow, F. (2017). Interest congruence and performance: Revisiting recent meta-analytic findings. *Journal of Vocational Behavior, 98*, 138–151.

Prenzel, M. (1992). The selective persistence of interest. In K. A. Renninger, S. Hidi, & A. Krapp (Eds.), *The role of interest in learning and development* (pp. 71–98). Hillsdale, NJ: Erlbaum.

Reeve, J. (1996). *Motivating others: Nurturing inner motivational resources.* Needham Heights, MA: Allyn & Bacon.

Renninger, K. A., & Hidi, S. (2011). Revisiting the conceptualization, measurement, and generation of interest. *Educational Psychologist, 46*(3), 168–184.

Roberts, B. W., & DelVecchio, W. F. (2000). The rank-order consistency of personality traits from childhood to old age: A quantitative review of longitudinal studies. *Psychological Bulletin, 126*(1), 3–25. doi:10.1037/0033-2909.126.1.3

Roberts, B. W., Luo, J., Briley, D. A., Chow, P. I., Su, R., & Hill, P. L. (2017). A systematic review of personality trait change through intervention. *Psychological Bulletin, 143*(2),117–141. doi:10.1037/bul0000088

Roberts, B. W., & Robins, R. W. (2000). Broad dispositions, broad aspirations: The intersection of personality traits and major life goals. *Personality and Social Psychology Bulletin, 26*(10), 1284–1296. doi:10.1177/0146167200262009

Roberts, B. W., Walton, K. E., & Viechtbauer, W. (2006). Patterns of mean-level change in personality traits across the life course: A meta-analysis of longitudinal studies. *Psychological Bulletin, 132*(1), 1–25.

Roberts, B. W., & Wood, D. (2006). Personality development in the context of the neo-socioanalytic model of personality. In D. K. Mroczek & T. D. Little (Eds.), *Handbook of personality development* (pp. 11–39). Mahwah, NJ: Erlbaum.

Roberts, B. W., Wood, D., & Caspi, A. (2008). Personality trait development in adulthood. In *Handbook of personality: Theory and research* (3rd ed., pp. 375–398). New York: Guilford Press.

Rohe, D. E., & Krause, J. S. (1998). Stability of interests after severe physical disability: An 11-year longitudinal study. *Journal of Vocational Behavior, 52*, 45–58. doi:10.1006/jvbe.1996.1560

Rokeach, M. (1973). *The nature of human values.* New York: Free Press. Retrieved from doi.apa.org/index.cfm?fa=search.exportFormat&uid=2011-15663-000&recType=psycinfo&singlerecord=1&searchresultpage=true

Rounds, J. & Armstrong, P. I. (2014). Integrating values and interests for career counseling. In M. Pope, L. Y. Flores, & P. J. Rottinghaus (Eds.), *The role of values in careers* (pp. 101–113). Greensboro, NC: Information Age Publishing.

Rounds, J., & Su, R. (2014). The nature and power of interests. *Current Directions in Psychological Science, 23*(2), 98–103. doi:10.1177/0963721414522812

Sackett, P. R., Lievens, F., Van Iddekinge, C. H., & Kuncel, N. R. (2017). Individual differences and their measurement: A review of 100 years of research. *Journal of Applied Psychology, 102*(3), 254–273. doi:10.1037/apl0000151

Sagiv, L. (2002). Vocational interests and basic values. *Journal of Career Assessment, 10*(2), 233–257. doi:10.1177/1069072702010002007

Savickas, M. L. (1999). The psychology of interests. In M. L. Savickas & A. R. Spokane (Eds.), *Vocational interests: Meaning, measurement, and counseling use* (pp. 19–56). Palo Alto, CA: Davies–Black.

Savickas, M. L., & Spokane, A. R. (Eds.) (1999). *Vocational interests.* Palo Alto, CA: Davies–Black.

Schermer, J. A., & Vernon, P. A. (2008). A behavior genetic analysis of vocational interests using a modified version of the Jackson Vocational Interest Survey. *Personality and Individual Differences, 45*(1), 103–109.

Schiefele, U. (1991). Interest, learning, and motivation. *Educational Psychologist, 26*, 299–323.

Schiefele, U. (2001). The role of interest in motivation and learning. In J. M. Collis & S. Messick (Eds.), *Intelligence and personality: Bridging the gap in theory and measurement* (pp. 163–194). Mahwah, NJ: Erlbaum.

Schiefele, U. (2009). Situational and individual interest. In K. R. Wenzel & A. Wigfield (Eds.), *Educational psychology handbook series. Handbook of motivation at school* (pp. 197–222). New York: Routledge/Taylor & Francis Group.

Schiefele, U., Krapp, A., & Winteler, A. (1992). Interest as a predictor of academic achievement: A meta-analysis of research. In K. A. Renninger, S. Hidi, A. Krapp, & K. A. Renninger (Eds.), *The role of interest in learning and development* (pp. 183–212). Hillsdale, NJ: Erlbaum.

Schmidt, F. L. (2011). A theory of sex differences in technical aptitude and some supporting evidence. *Perspectives on Psychological Science, 6*(6), 560–573. doi:10.1177/1745691611419670

Schmidt, F. L. (2014). A general theoretical integrative model of individual differences in interests, abilities, personality traits, and academic and occupational achievement: A commentary on four recent articles. *Perspectives on Psychological Science, 9*(2), 211–218. doi:10.1177/1745691613518074

Silvia, P. J. (2001a). Interest and interests: The psychology of constructive capriciousness. *Review of General Psychology, 5*(3), 270–290. doi:10.1037/1089-2680.5.3.270

Silvia, P. J. (2001b). Expressed and measured vocational interests: Distinctions and definitions. *Journal of Vocational Behavior, 59*(3), 382–393. doi:10.1006/jvbe.2001.1805

Silvia, P. J. (2008). Interest—The curious emotion. *Current Directions in Psychological Science, 17*(1), 57–60.

Smith, E. R., & Zárate, M. A. (1992). Exemplar-based model of social judgment. *Psychological Review, 99*(1), 3–21. doi:10.1037/0033-295X.99.1.3

Snow, R. E., Corno, L., & Jackson, D. (1996). Individual differences in affective and conative functions. In D. C. Berliner & R. C. Calfee (Eds.), *Handbook of educational psychology* (pp. 243–310). London: Prentice Hall International.

Stoll, G., Rieger, S., Lüdtke, O., Nagengast, B., Trautwein, U., & Roberts, B. W. (2017). Vocational interests assessed at the end of high school predict life outcomes assessed 10 years later over and above IQ and big five personality traits. *Journal of Personality and Social Psychology, 113*(1), 167–184. doi:10.1037/pspp0000117

Stoll, G., & Trautwein, U. (2017). Vocational interests as personality traits: Characteristics, development, and significance in educational and organizational environments. In J. Specht (Ed.), *Personality development across the lifespan* (pp. 401–417). London: Academic Press Elsevier.

Strong, E. K., Jr. (1943). *The vocational interests of men and women*. Stanford, CA: Stanford University Press.

Su, R. (2012). *The power of vocational interests and interest congruence in predicting career success* (Unpublished doctoral dissertation). University of Illinois at Urbana-Champaign. Retrieved from http://hdl.handle.net/2142/34329

Su, R., & Nye, C. D. (2017). Interests and person-environment fit: A new perspective on workforce readiness and success. In J. Burrus, K. D. Mattern, B. Naemi, & R. D. Roberts (Eds.), *Building better students: Preparation for the workforce*. New York: Oxford University Press.

Super, D. E. (1963). Self-concepts in vocational development. In D. E. Super, R. Starishevsky, N. Matlin, & J. P. Jordaan (Eds.), *Career development: Self-concept theory* (pp. 1–16). New York: College Entrance Examination Board.

Tellegen, A. (1991). Personality traits: Issues of definition, evidence, and assessment. In D. Cicchetti & W. Grove (Eds.), *Thinking clearly about psychology: Essays in honor of Paul Everett Meehl* (Vol. 2, pp. 10–35). Minneapolis: University of Minnesota Press.

Tomkins, S. S. (1987). Script theory. In J. Aronoff, A. I. Rabin, & R. A. Zucker (Eds.), *The emergence of personality* (pp. 147–216). New York: Springer.

Tomkins, S. S. (1991). *Affect, imagery, consciousness: Vol. 3. The negative affects: Anger and fear.* New York: Springer.

Tracey, T. J. G., & Rounds, J. (1996). The spherical representation of vocational interests. *Journal of Vocational Behavior, 48*, 3–41.

Turner, S. A., Jr., & Silvia, P. J. (2006). Must things be pleasant? A test of competing appraisal structures. *Emotion, 6,* 670–674.

Tyler, L. E. (1955). The development of "vocational interests": I. The organization of likes and dislikes in ten-year-old children. *Journal of Genetic Psychology, 86,* 33–44.

Van Iddekinge, C. H., Putka, D. J., & Campbell, J. P. (2011). Reconsidering vocational interests for personnel selection: The validity of an interest-based selection test in relation to job knowledge, job performance, and continuance intentions. *Journal of Applied Psychology, 96*(1), 13–33. doi:10.1037/a0021193

Van Iddekinge, C. H., Roth, P. L., Putka, D. J., & Lanivich, S. E. (2011). Are you interested? A meta-analysis of relations between vocational interests and employee performance and turnover. *Journal of Applied Psychology, 96*, 1167–1194. doi:10.1037/a0024343

von Stumm, S., & Ackerman, P. L. (2013). Investment and intellect: A review and meta-analysis. *Psychological Bulletin, 139*(4), 841–869.

Voss, J. F., & Schauble, L. (1992). Is interest educationally interesting? An interest-related model of learning. In K. A. Renninger, S. Hidi, & A. Krapp (Eds.), *The role of interest in learning and development* (pp. 101–120). Hillsdale, NJ: Erlbaum.

Wach, M., & Gosling, P. (2004). Values, interests and attitudes within vocational behaviour. *European Journal of Psychology of Education, 19*(3), 223–226. doi:10.1007/BF03173220

Walsh, W. B. (1999). What we know and need to know: A few comments. In M. L. Savickas & A. R. Spokane (Eds.), *Vocational Interests: Meaning, measurement and counseling use* (pp. 371–382). Palo Alto, CA: Davies-Black.

Weiss, H. M., & Cropanzano, R. (1996). Affective events theory. *Research in Organizational Behavior, 18*, 1–74.

2

INTEREST DEVELOPMENT AS A DYNAMIC PROCESS IN THE WORKPLACE

K. Ann Renninger

SWARTHMORE COLLEGE

Suzanne E. Hidi

UNIVERSITY OF TORONTO

In this chapter, we review literature suggesting the benefit of integrating current conceptions of workplace interest with research on the development of interest that has primarily been studied in educational contexts. Historically, vocational interest has been used to match individuals to the workplace. This practice in vocational psychology is based on the emphasis of the "trait-like" nature of interest (Rounds & Su, 2014; Su, 2018). Traits have been considered to be stable and thus have predictive utility for patterns of behavior, and vocational interest has been shown to be relatively stable from early adolescence to adulthood (e.g., Low & Rounds, 2006, 2007; Low, Yoon, Roberts & Rounds, 2005). Moreover, as Low and Rounds (2007) reported, vocational interest measures are even more stable than personality traits. Findings such as these have led to the use of vocational interest as an indicator of optimal academic and/or career choice.

Since the publication of Strong's (1943) volume on men's and women's vocational interests, there has been a plethora of studies supporting the use of a trait-based approach to study interest in the workplace. Recent studies demonstrate that vocational interest measures are highly correlated with student and employee performances (see Nye, Su, Rounds, & Drasgow, 2012, Rounds & Su, 2014, for reviews of this literature). Not surprisingly, those students and employees who have an interest in what they are doing have been shown to perform better and persist longer in a wider variety of situations and tasks than their uninterested peers. Thus, interest is predictive of job performance.

In the following, we discuss the implications of the Four Phase Model of Interest Development (Hidi & Renninger, 2006; Renninger & Hidi, 2016) for considering how vocational interest might be supported to develop and/or deepen (see also Renninger & Hidi, 2019a). Rather than describing vocational interest as a trait, we view it as mapping onto later (or more-developed) phases of interest development (see Table 2.1). As depicted in Table 2.1, earlier

TABLE 2.1 The Four Phases of Interest Development (Hidi & Renninger, 2006): Definitions and Learner Characteristics; adapted from Renninger & S. Su, 2012.

	Phases of Interest Development			
	Less-Developed (Earlier)		*More-Developed (Later)*	
	Phase I: Triggered Situational Interest	**Phase 2: Maintained Situational Interest**	**Phase 3: Emerging Individual Interest**	**Phase 4: Well-Developed Individual Interest**
Definition	• Psychological state resulting from short-term changes in cognitive and affective processing associated with a particular class of content	• Psychological state that involves focused attention to a particular class of content that reoccurs and/or persists over time	• Psychological state *and* the beginning of relatively enduring predisposition to seek reengagement with a particular class of content over time	• Psychological state *and* a relatively enduring predisposition to reengage a particular class of content over time
Learner Characteristics	• Attends to content, if only fleetingly • May or may not be reflectively aware of the experience • May need support to engage from others and through instructional design • May experience either positive or negative feelings	• Reengages content that previously triggered attention • Is developing knowledge of the content • Is developing a sense of the content's value • Is likely to be supported by others to find connections to content based on existing skills, knowledge, and/or prior experience • Is likely to have positive feelings	• Is likely to independently re-engage content • Has stored knowledge and stored value • Is reflective about the content • Is focused on their own curiosity questions • Has positive feelings	• Independently reengages content • Has stored knowledge and value • Is reflective about the content • Is likely to recognize others' contributions to the discipline • Self-regulates curiosity questions and seeks answers • Appreciates and may actively seek feedback • Can persevere through frustration and challenge in order to meet goals • Has positive feelings

(or less-developed) phases of interest development are less stable (and more malleable), whereas later phases have trait-like characteristics in that a person has a disposition to continue to reengage over time. In the four-phase model, interest has two related meanings. It refers to the psychological state of individuals engaging with some disciplinary content, object, or idea (henceforth, content) that is physiologically based and it also refers to their motivation to reengage with that content over time. The research literature has now confirmed that interest can be supported to develop (e.g., Harackiewicz, Durik, Barron, Linnenbrink, & Tauer, 2008; Nolen, 2007; Renninger & Riley, 2013). As interest is malleable, and can be promoted, it is not simply a trait. However, it does have a genetic component, which accounts for why interest is often associated with traits. People with genetic predispositions to figure out how things work or pursue music, for example, may have an easier time, but unless they have the opportunity and/or support to sustain these engagements, they may not develop an interest in these activities.

Whereas vocational interest focuses on already existing capacities that are used to identify interest, we study interest as a cognitive and affective motivational variable that develops by tracking the development of interest from the initial triggering of attention through to its development as an individual interest. From our perspective, individual interest, or the later phases of interest development, is the focus of research on vocational interest.

In the present chapter, we first describe the four-phase model, which was advanced on the basis of reviews of empirical studies. We then consider the relation of the four-phase model to vocational interest and describe issues raised in recent studies that may have implications for workplace interest. We conclude by pointing to the complementary nature of these approaches to the study of interest and highlight the utility of their integration for increasing understanding of interest and its role in the workplace.

The Four-Phase Model of Interest Development

The four-phase model describes interest as developing through phases regardless of age, or whether the context of its development is in the home, in or out of school, or in the workplace (see Renninger & Hidi, 2016). Research in neuroscience now provides evidence that the capacity to seek additional information about content is hardwired and the search for anticipated information that is also an aspect of interest is rewarding (Gottlieb, Oudeyer, & Baranes, 2013; Gruber, Gelman, & Ranganath, 2014; Panksepp, 1998). This also explains why developing an interest at any age is possible (Ainley & Hidi, 2014; Renninger & Hidi, 2016). Research in educational and social psychology further indicates that interest can be supported to develop through triggering.[1]

The triggering of interest directs attention to the content of interest, and is accompanied by an affective reaction, that is often, but not necessarily positive.

Triggering can refer to the response of an individual to the actions of other people (e.g. scaffolding, modeling), the design features of the environment (e.g., key words, highlighting; see related discussions in Järvela & Renninger, 2014; Renninger, Ren, & Kern, 2018), and serendipitous occurrence (e.g., the death of worms needed for an experiment, that leads to revised experimentation, see Renninger, Austin, Bachrach, Chau, Emmerson et al., 2014). Although it may seem that triggering only occurs in the first phase of interest development, other people (e.g., employers, educators, parents) can trigger the interest of individuals who already have enough interest to be involved in an activity or job, to help them focus on specific aspects of it. The triggering process is essential not only for initiation, but also for the continued deepening of interest. When interest is triggered, its continued development can be supported, leading to further engagements with content.

In any situation there are multiple potential triggers for interest (e.g., opportunities to work independently, opportunities to work in a group, novel information, challenge, personal relevance) (Renninger, Bachrach, & Hidi, 2019). Individuals may notice some of these, and others might be missed altogether. For example, an employer could provide information about educational training relevant to the workplace by posting it. One employee might recognize that he/she does not presently have the skill to be part of a select project in the office, and because of the posted information could decide to develop his or her skills. Another employee might not pick up on the notice, or think that he/she had any need to develop the skills it addressed. Follow-through to pursue additional training by an employee is likely to reflect the perception that the training could provide new ways to engage work and/or recognition of the relevance or utility of such training. Help to recognize that the training could be important may facilitate its pursuit.

Once triggered, two conditions determine whether interest is likely to continue to develop: (a) the types of connections that a person makes to the content, and (b) the forms of support (e.g., the type and extent of encouragement, modeling, collaboration) that are recognized and used. The development of interest always involves the interaction of a person and the environment. The environment (other people and/or the design of tasks, software, exhibits, etc.) may be adjusted in order to enable continued engagement. Thus, even though genetics contributes to the possibility that an interest will continue to develop, the environment has an essential role in whether this potential is realized. It is in relation to the environment that a person's interest can be triggered and supported to develop—and also that the development of new interests can be fostered. Effective triggers for interest stretch a person's understanding of the content, posing optimally discrepant problems related to the content of interest.

The triggers that are effective for persons in earlier and later phases of interest development are typically not the same (Renninger & Hidi, 2019b). For example, although novelty is a proven trigger for interest (e.g., Berlyne, 1960;

Durik & Harackiewicz, 2007), information that is novel for a person in an earlier phase of interest development is likely not to be novel for a person in a later phase (Bergin, 1999; Renninger & Bachrach, 2015). The same applies to triggers that provide a person with challenge, utility, relevance, and so forth (e.g., Dohn, 2013; Hulleman & Harackiewicz, 2009; Harackiewicz, Tibbetts, Canning, & Hyde 2014; Rotgans & Schmidt, 2014). If the content of a trigger is already familiar (e.g., individuals already know the information to be covered in the workshop), it may feel repetitive and is not likely to be an effective trigger for interest.

In addition, there is always a question about how direct or indirect support should be, as well as how extrinsic or intrinsic the triggers for interest are. Persons with little initial interest are most likely to need support that is tailored to focus their attention on relevant or key aspects of the tasks, and external triggers to enable sustained engagement. In later phases of interest individuals may also adapt their behaviors by identifying new questions to pursue and/or challenge themselves that may make what may appear to an outsider to be known, novel.

The difference between those with more and those with less developed interest is often obvious. People who have an interest in what they are doing like working on related problems (Barron, Mertl, & Martin, 2014; Lipstein & Renninger, 2007; Renninger & Riley, 2013), and if given time and opportunity, continue to develop their ability to solve these problems (Azevedo, 2006, 2013). They are likely to be creative, strategic, and successful (Barron et al., 2014). They are well able to set goals for themselves and follow through to accomplish them (Harackiewicz, et al., 2008). They ask curiosity questions and through these set new challenges for themselves (Renninger et al., 2014). They can also be expected to grow in their capacities, shouldering increasing amounts of responsibility, which can lead to creating opportunities or positions for themselves that did not exist previously (Renninger & Shumar, 2002).

In contrast, those who lack interest may not be willing to persevere to master challenge, invest additional time to make something work, or pick up on another's ideas and figure out ways in which these could be fit together with their own ideas (Lipstein & Renninger, 2007). In terms of the workplace, they also may be perceived as persons who do not fit. Supporting them to fit in, to understand and develop an interest in company goals, is possible, but also involves work on the part of the employer. Persons with little interest need to be supported for them to make connections to content, to want to persevere to master challenge, and to find engagement with content rewarding (Renninger & Hidi, 2019 a, 2019 b). The benefits of supporting a person to develop at least some interest makes the investment of time that it involves worthwhile.

Not surprisingly, interest and other motivational variables are more closely related in later phases of interest development than they are in earlier phases (Renninger & Hidi, 2016). Goal setting (the ability to set goals for oneself and then follow through to meet them), self-efficacy (the belief that one can accomplish a task, or do the work of a discipline), and self-regulation (the ability to organize oneself to continue to persevere to reach a goal, despite the time and frustration that it may involve) are each influenced by the phase of a person's interest. In earlier phases of interest a person is not likely to set related goals, feel self-efficacious about relevant content, and/or self-regulate to engage in related activities, unless there is assistance to do so. In later phases of interest, on the other hand, interest and these motivational variables are increasingly coordinated. With developing interest, a person is more likely to set goals, feel that he or she can achieve them, and self-regulate in order to do so.

The Four-Phase Model and Interest in the Workplace

We surmise that even though the psychological state and motivational disposition that characterize the process of engaging in different contexts such as the school, the home, or the workplace are similar (see related discussion in Vroom, 1964), the nature of these contexts has led to different questions about interest. Study of student learning and interest development can be traced back to early educators and psychologists who were interested in the way in which interest informs students' attention, memory, and recall, and what this suggests about instruction (e.g., Dewey, 1913; James, 1890; Herbart, 1806/1965; Pestalozzi, 1898/2004). When educators and parents seek to support the development of their students' or their children's interest in some content (such as mathematics, playing the piano), they may be encouraging the development of interests that are completely new, interests that are developing, and/or engagement with content that the students or children perceive to be too hard for them.

The four-phase model addresses the triggering and development of new interests, continuing support for the deepening of existing interests, and making connections to difficult content. Although how much a person "likes" particular content is often used to identify interest in the literature and in every day conversation, liking is only a proxy for interest in particular content. Liking does not distinguish between earlier and later phases in the development of interest. Instead, Renninger and Hidi (2016) suggest that measurement of interest as a variable that develops should be assessed using indicators targeting behavior: the frequency (e.g., Do you do engineering problems that are not assigned?) and depth of engagement (e.g., How easy is it for you to get absorbed in solving engineering problems?), as well as whether engagement is sometime voluntary (e.g., Do you talk about engineering outside of work you need to do for class?) and independent (e.g., Do you do engineering problems that are not assigned?). These indicators have been reliably found to form one factor (e.g., Renninger & Schofield, 2014; see also Renninger & Hidi, 2016), and can be assessed informally in the workplace, in addition to more formally using age, content, and context-appropriate methods such as observation, surveys, log files, and experience-sampling.

In contrast, the focus of studies of vocational interest has been the fit of the person to the environment, rather than how the environment might be adjusted to meet the needs of the person. Studies of vocational interest were first undertaken to match persons to different areas of engineering (Moore, 1921), which eventually led to studies of the match of persons to different jobs and the development of interest inventories (e.g., Holland, 1959; Paterson, Elliot, Anderson, Toops, & Heidbreder, 1930; Strong, 1943). Presumably because vocational interest is related to the workplace, and the associated expectation for efficient business practices that would not typically include assisting an employee to develop interest that does not already exist, it has not focused on the development of new interests. As such, even though findings from studies of interest indicate that new interests can be developed at any age and in any context, the research on vocational interest has not focused on how to support the development of new interest and/or existing interests.

We suggest not only that the phases of emerging and well-developed individual interest in the four-phase model map onto workplace interest, but also that research on the model's less-developed phases of triggered and maintained situational interest could inform workplace practices (Renninger & Hidi, 2019a). Renninger and Hidi (2016) use the four-phase model to describe the case of an engineer and his interest in problem solving that is associated with analysis and design of systems. They also describe the challenges he faces in his work at a relatively small firm. The engineer does not voluntarily engage in selling the firm's "products," despite the fact that selling is essential for engineering firms and brings in the business that provides the engineer with the types of problems he likes to solve. The engineer does not seem to recognize that selling really needs to be done, or that selling could be a kind of game/problem to be solved. However, selling is a related interest that the engineer may need to develop if he wants to continue to be employed by the firm.

Although a vocational interest inventory enables a person to identify a potential career such as engineering based on existing characteristics, or traits, it cannot ensure that the person who pursues engineering will be successful. Research that is the basis of the four-phase model suggests that the engineer's environment might be adjusted to enable him to understand the role of sales in whether the firm continues to win jobs on which he might work, and on the basis of this content knowledge lead him to appreciate the necessity of mastering sales (e.g., Harackiewicz, et al., 2014; Hulleman & Harackiewicz, 2009). Interactions with other people who support the engineer to understand how they think and go about selling could be important forms of support. The engineer needs content-specific support and encouragement to engage in selling. Chances are that the engineer knows that he is supposed to do selling and that he needs models and possibly some collaboration with others who are doing selling initially in order to figure out how he too can do selling. He also would benefit from recognition of whatever positive efforts he has invested in doing selling and an opportunity to reflect in a constructive way on the relative success of his efforts and what he might do differently another time (see related discussions and studies of similar situations with students in Azevedo, 2006; Nolan, 2007; Pressick-Kilborn, 2015; Renninger, 2010; Renninger et al., 2014).

It appears that the source of differences between research on the four-phase model and vocational interest stems from the contexts in which interest has been studied and the research questions that have been pursued. Renninger and Hidi (2011) identified five characteristics of interest on which researchers of interest tend to agree, regardless of the focus of their research questions. Interest:

- is always content specific
- exists in the interaction between a person and his or her environment
- has both an affective and a cognitive component
- may or may not be something of which a person is reflectively aware
- has a physiological/neurological basis.

Interest is considered to be content specific (e.g., interest in engineering) by both those studying interest in terms of the four-phase model and those studying vocational interest. However, the two groups of researchers differ in their conceptualizations of the second characteristic: that interest exists in the interaction between the person and his or her environment. Those studying the four-phase model are focusing on the dynamics of the interaction, which includes the adjustment that other people or the design of the environment can make to accommodate the level of a person's interest development. Although workplace interest research may be based in person-environment fit models that assume that the relation between interest and environment is dynamic (e.g., Su, Murdock, & Rounds, 2015), and the person and the environment components of the model can each be dynamic (Dawis & Lofquist, 1984), it has not focused on what to do if there is no fit between the person and the environment.

Both sets of researchers appear to agree on the third characteristic, that interest has both a cognitive and an affective component, but they also differ in their conceptualization of what the affective component references. Researchers focusing on the four-phase model identify cognition and affect as including knowledge and feelings (positive and negative), as well as value. They have pointed to the coordination of these components, as well as the likelihood that the relative importance of each changes as interest develops (see Hidi & Renninger, 2006). In earlier phases of interest development, they describe affect as assuming more prominence. In later phases, cognition and the development of knowledge become essential.

In contrast, in considering vocational interest to be a trait, vocational interest reflects or describes a person's preferences, or what they like (Strong, 1943).

However, developments in neuroscience now further distinguish among liking, wanting, and learning (e.g., Berridge, Robinson, & Aldridge, 2009). Liking may accompany interest as it develops, but does not distinguish among phases of interest (Ainley & Hidi, 2014); frequency and depth (in terms of knowledge) need to be assessed, as does whether activity is voluntary and/or independent when this is an option.

Although the fourth and fifth characteristics have not been a focus of research on vocational interest, they are relevant to the workplace. The fourth characteristic, that a person may or may not be aware of their interest, has implications for measurement of interest and for providing support for interest development. In earlier phases of interest especially, individuals may not realize that their interest has been triggered. They are not, as such, necessarily able to self-report about the triggering of their interest, nor are they making decisions to engage wilfully. Rather they engage because the conditions provided by other people or the environment support them to engage: their attention has been triggered, supported to continue to develop, and they want to learn something more. The predictive validity of vocational interest surveys suggests that in later phases of interest, a person can be expected to be more metacognitively aware and able to report on interest.

The fifth characteristic, that interest has a physiological/neurological basis, is important because it points to the association of interest with the reward circuitry in the brain. As noted earlier in this chapter, people are hardwired to develop interest, however, they need to be supported to find the connections to the content of interest worthwhile. In the earlier phases of interest development, support to trigger interest using novel information, promoting utility, and so forth, enables a person to make connections to content. Once interest is supported to develop, it becomes rewarding. Once interest has become rewarding, a person is in a position to self-trigger by identifying curiosity questions (problems that they want to solve) and seeking resources and opportunities to address them. Before interest has been triggered to develop, as well as in its early phases, those who are providing support for its development may need to employ related rewards in order to ensure that interest will develop.[2]

Interest Development in the Workplace

Interest in a career may be predicted on the basis of a person's existing characteristics or traits, and the triggering, development, and continued deepening of interest occurs through the interactions individuals have with the environment. The case of the engineer illustrates that employers and the workplace can support the development of interest, and also that they may contribute to the decline of interest. Research demonstrates that even individuals with more-developed interest need opportunities to continue to develop it

(Azevedo, 2013; Crowley, Barron, Knutson, & Martin, 2015; Renninger & Hidi, 2016); otherwise the activities that they were interested in may no longer be novel and challenging for them. The opportunity to continue to develop interest offsets the likelihood that employees will seek challenge and opportunity elsewhere.

Study of motivation in the workplace became an integral part of both vocational and industrial psychology in the mid-twentieth century (Vroom, 1964). Researchers asked questions about why people chose their jobs, why they stay in them, and how they perform. Concepts addressed included need, motive, goal, incentive, and attitudes. Vocational interest surveys were refined to identify the fit between individuals and their work. However, interest as a psychological state and the potential for interest to develop were not directly investigated, nor was the possibility that the fit between employees and their jobs could lessen.

In reviewing the quantitative literature, Nye et al. (2012) observed that despite its relation to workplace success, the employee selection literature has tended to overlook interest measures. Even in practice, the motivation provided by experiencing interest in the workplace has been considered only indirectly. For example, Kaye and Jordan-Evans (2002; Kaye, Jordan-Evans, & Career Systems International, 2014) identified the top 6 "stay factors" for people to continue in their jobs (see Figure 2.1). All of the factors, with the possible exception of fair pay, have interest as an underlying, and unidentified, component. They point either to the individual experience of interest or to the conditions that enable the experience of interest to be realized. The first and most influential factor (62% of 8,454 respondents), "exciting, challenging, or meaningful work," includes adjectives used to describe work that one is interested

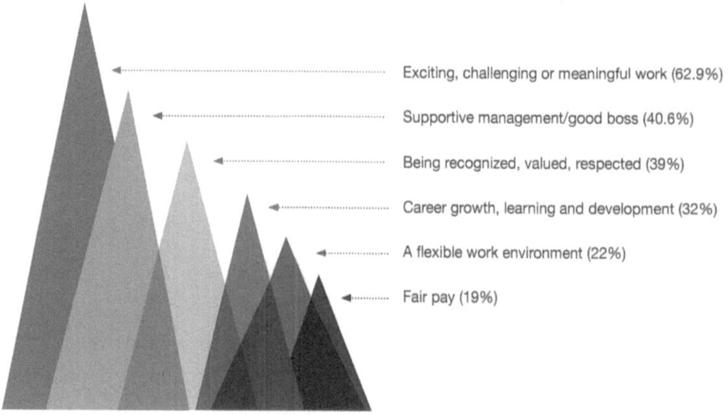

FIGURE 2.1 Top six "stay factors." Reprinted from, What Keeps You: A White Paper About Engaging and Retaining Talent (www.keepem.com/pdf/WKY_2014_pdf), with permission from Beverly Kaye, Sharon Jordan-Evans and Career Systems International.

to perform, and the experience that accompanies the psychological state of interest. This factor reflects interest that is maintained and is enabled to continue to develop.

The second factor, "supportive management/good boss," describes conditions that allow the development of interest to flourish, whereas the third factor, "being recognized, valued, respected," references the development of self-efficacy, which is coordinated with the development of interest. The fourth factor, "career growth, learning and development," points to developing content knowledge, which is critical to the continued development of interest and is useful for future goals. The fifth factor, "a flexible work environment," is another aspect of workplace conditions that provides support for a person to have their own ideas/needs and enables interest to continue to develop. Of note, the ranking of these factors was found to hold regardless of age, gender, position, industry, job function, geography, and company size (Kaye et. al., 2014).

It is possible, of course, for employees' initial interest in their jobs to fall off. This is a situation in which focusing on more than the latter phases of the four-phase model might be beneficial to understanding workplace interest. It seems very likely that when people lose their interest in the activity of their workplace, there are decreases in their job satisfaction and the quality and quantity of overall productivity. A decline in interest, or the onset of boredom, may well indicate that either they have the skills and capacity for the job, but find their activity boring and repetitive and do not experience interest in working with its content, or the conditions of their job have changed. As Renninger and Hidi (2016) concluded, if people's existing abilities to make connections to content are not aligned with available tasks and opportunities, this will very likely lead interest to fall off.

Examples of issues addressed in studies that focus on student interest, and inform the ways in which the four-phase model could contribute to the understanding of workplace interest, include the relations among conscientiousness, grit, and interest; social media and interest; and the role of other people in supporting the development of interest. We review this work briefly, pointing to its potential utility for understanding and enabling the development of interest in the workplace.

Conscientiousness, Grit, and Interest in the Workplace

Conscientiousness, grit, and interest have been associated with higher levels of individual effort and learning. Consider, for example, two lab technicians who are examining cells to detect those suspicious ones that may be signs of cancer. One finds a very unusual cell and marks it for the doctor to check it out. On finding the same atypical cell, the other technician goes to the medical library and, before handing over the findings to the doctor, tries to identify the cell. Is the difference between the acts of the two technicians due to differences in their conscientiousness or in their levels of interests, or both?

Both conscientiousness and interest could be influencing how a lab technician reacts when finding suspicious cells, just as these two variables are likely to influence individuals' reactions to a multitude of situations. Trautwein, Lüdtke, Nagy, Lenski, Niggli et al. (2015) examined how interest and conscientiousness are related to academic effort using self-reports. They found in four studies involving over 2,500 students that conscientiousness and interest uniquely predicted academic effort. More importantly, the researchers reported that there was a significant compensatory interaction between the two predictors. That is, conscientiousness was especially important for students who were not interested in their school subjects, and domain-specific interest seemed to play an important role in motivating students who were low in conscientiousness.

If we that assume the same patterns established for academic interest among the three variables hold true for vocational interest, these findings have important implications for employers to consider. As Trautwein et al. (2015) point out, conscientiousness has been characterized as a domain-general trait; one of the five personality traits in the Big Five Model of personality (e.g., Digman, 1990). As such, conscientiousness is considered to be both stable and domain general, and it is not usually expected to develop. However, as Nye and Roberts (2013) point out, there are exceptions. If the workplace provides adults with support, they are likely to become more extroverted, emotionally stable, and/or conscientious (see Roberts & Mroczek, 2008; Roberts, Walton, & Viechtbauer, 2006).

On the basis of Trautwein et al.'s data, it might be the case that as long as conscientiousness is present, an employee will be productive. However, if an employee is low on conscientiousness, the employer might focus on how an employee's interest can be supported to develop. Related to discussions of both conscientiousness and interest is the construct of grit, defined by Duckworth, Peterson, Matthews, & Kelly (2007) as the passion and perseverance to obtain long-term goals. If people are not interested, grit, similarly to conscientiousness, may be essential to assure performance. However, when people are engaged in activities that they are interested in, grit, or perseverance (also described as self-regulation, see Sansone, 2009) is a component of their engagement. As Sansone, Thoman, and Fraughton (2015) noted, when a person lacks interest, self-regulation is a problem. When people are supported to develop an interest in some content, they persevere independently, and are self-regulated and fully engaged because they want to be, not because they have to be. The development of even some interest can have a beneficial impact on attention, goal setting, and learning strategies (Renninger & Hidi, 2019b).[3]

Social Media and Interest in the Workplace

Recent studies have also examined how participating in social media is related to students' school activities and how interest influences this relation. Investigations repeatedly indicated that academic engagement and performance are adversely affected by participation in social media that is not an assigned part of the class. For example, Duncan, Hoekstra, and Wilcox (2012) reported that in-class use of cell-phones reduces learning; several others have reported that social media in general interferes with academic performance (e.g., Fries & Dietz, 2007; Junco, 2011).

Flanigan and Babchuk's (2015) review of the widespread use of social media in academia found that whereas many studies have demonstrated that university students' access to technological distractions diminishes their learning and achievements, only a few considered students' own perceptions of their social media use. To address this gap in the literature, they conducted a qualitative (phenomenological) study of semi-structured interviews that focused on students' perceptions of the impact of social media on their educational experience. Participants reported that in their view, using social media during academic activities diminishes achievement, increases the amount of time it takes to complete tasks, and reduces how much information they retain from study and lecture sessions. Additionally, the students also noted that their own lack of situational and topic interest increased the temptations of social media.

In the workplace, the personal use of electronically mediated activities is referred to as cyberloafing or cyberslacking (see Baturay & Toker, 2015, for a review of the literature). Findings from this literature suggest that similar associations are identified for cyberloafing and workplace productivity as those of social media use in academic settings. Although we could not find any direct reference to interest in studies that investigated cyberloafing, researchers indirectly refer to the lack of interest as one of the underlying reasons for social media use—the reasons for cyberloafing include de-motivating jobs and poor employee–job fit leading to low-engagements. For example, Jian (2013) analyzed data from the Pew Internet and American Life Project's sponsored Networked Workers Survey (Madden & Jones, 2008) and concluded that job variety improves employee engagement and reduces personal use of online communications such as gambling, shopping, emailing, and social media use.

Several studies have examined the use of social media in the workplace and its effect on productivity. Based on surveys of employees in workplaces with internet connectivity, Munene and Nyaribo (2013) observed that there are potentially both positive and negative outcomes of using social media in the workplace. For example, seeking relevant information (like the conscientious and interested lab technician described above who researched the cell identified) can be beneficial to productivity. However, Munene and Nyaribo also reported that there were more negative than positive influences. They found that employees spent most of the time on social media enhancing their personal networks, which, in turn, distracted them from work-related expectations.

To eliminate the negative effects of cyberloafing, employers can ban, control, or set limits on their employees ability to use social media. However, such restrictions may also have undesirable outcomes (Ugrin, Pearson, & Odom, 2007). As Garrett and Danziger (2008) observed: "Restricting personal Internet use may be an effective deterrent to cyberslacking.......it can [also] backfire by reducing job satisfaction and ...productivity" (p. 291). Flanigan and Babchuk's (2015) findings suggest that developing interest may be another way to reduce inappropriate use of social media. Importantly, their findings corroborate those of Trautwein and his colleagues (2015) who reported the potential utility of supporting interest to develop as a way to balance the impact of low conscientiousness and improve prospects for productivity.

The Role of Other People and Interest in the Workplace

Although there are instances in which environmental conditions result in the serendipitous triggering of interest (e.g., unintentional modeling of behavior by a person with whom the engineer has a connection; a person hears a new bird song and starts searching online resources on birds), other people's interactions with the person, as well as the conditions or design of the environment (e.g., work climate, software features) are primary sources of interest development (see Schneider, 1987). People are in a position to help adjust the way in which an individual engages with content, and are able to support changes in their engagement. Xu, Coats, and Davidson (2012), for example, reported that when teachers both have an interest in the discipline that they teach and have an interest in supporting their students to develop interest, the students do develop interest and also succeed. Employers need to understand that their employees' interest can be supported to develop (that interest is not simply a trait), and thus appreciate that they can provide support (e.g., encouragement, information) that could have a pivotal role in their employees' interest development. By doing so, such change may offset workplace difficulties such as employees who are lacking in conscientiousness or who are inclined to spend time on social media instead of on their work.

If we reexamine the reasons for individuals staying in their jobs (Figure 2.1), two of them (supportive management/good boss [40.6%] and being recognized, valued, respected, [39%]) demonstrate the importance of others to workplace satisfaction. In school settings, Bergin (2016) described social influences as one of the important sources of more-developed individual interests. In his review, Bergin identified parents, friends, and affinity groups among those who can contribute to social experiences leading to triggering and supporting students' interest. He noted how social influences affect students' interest, and maintained that students' need to belong leads them to seek social links that influence the development of their individual interest. Although Bergin did not discuss social influences on interest development in the workplace, his notion that social influences can nurture interest development should also be relevant to this setting. Both employers and coworkers are likely to be in the position to provide triggers and support for interest development.

Summary and Conclusions

In this chapter, we have described how vocational interest maps onto later phases of interest development and pointed to the utility of employers understanding that their employees' interest can be supported to develop. We have suggested that if interest can be supported to develop, grit and self-regulation become components of their activities, and this can compensate for lack of conscientiousness if it is present. We also note the beneficial impact of interest on attention to the workplace and the negative effects of social media and distraction. Finally, we point to the importance of other people in encouraging the development of interest.

There are also a number of unresolved questions. For example, we wonder if the successful prediction of fit by vocational interest measures would be strengthened if distinctions between the last two phases in the development of interest were considered? That is, does the predicted fit between person and environment based on vocational interest measures vary if a person has an emerging individual interest, rather than a well-developed individual interest (see Table 2.1). According to the four-phase model, the difference between these two phases is in the person's capacity to persevere in problem solving despite frustration, and his or her vision of what can be achieved. In contrast to consideration of vocational interest as trait-like, we describe the effectiveness of supports for interest to develop. For educational contexts, and we would argue for the workplace as well, the fact that interest is malleable—that it can be supported to develop—is critical. Its malleability suggests that investing effort in supporting interest to develop will yield results that make this investment worthwhile.

Research such as this is as central to researchers and practitioners working with the four-phase model as they are to those concerned with vocational interest. It is our sense that the integration of research on the four-phase model with that on vocational interest is overdue, and that it could be relatively easy to accomplish. The integration of these two lines of study has the potential to clarify understanding of interest and its utility in the workplace.

Notes

1 Our conceptualization of triggers for interest differs from Goldsmith and Reiter's (2015) in that they speak of triggers for behavior, whereas we refer to triggers for interest, resulting in an information search related to a specific mental activity.

2 Findings from neuroscience provide evidence that people are hardwired to develop interest and that once interest is developed it becomes its own reward (e.g., Gruber, et al., 2014; Panksepp, 1998). However, rewards are needed to support engagement

when an individual does not have interest, as Hidi (2016) points out. This is a point that is consistent with findings from self-determination theory, although it has not been emphasized in that literature (see Deci, 1971; Marsden, Ma, Deci, Ryan, & Chiu, 2014; Ryan & Deci, 2017).

3 As noted earlier in this chapter, developments in motivation research and in neuroscience have now made it clear that people (including employers, parents, teachers, etc.) need to recognize that we are all hardwired to develop interest (that activates the reward circuitry in the brain) and that all people, regardless of age or previous experience, may be supported to develop interest—and also that interest needs support to develop, especially in its earliest phases.

References

Ainley, M., & Hidi, S. (2014). Interest and enjoyment. In R. Pekrun & L. Linnenbrink-Garcia (Eds.), *The international handbook of emotions in education* (pp. 205–227). New York: Taylor and Francis. doi:10.4324/9780203148211.ch11

Azevedo, F. S. (2006). Personal excursions: Investigating the dynamics of student engagement. *International Journal of Computers for Mathematical Learning, 11,* 57–98. doi:10.1007/s10758-006-0007-6

Azevedo. F. S. (2013). The tailored practice of hobbies and its implication for the design of interest-based learning environments. *The Journal of the Learning Sciences, 22*(3), 462–510. doi:10.1080/10508406.2012.730082

Barron, B., Mertl, V., & Martin, C. K. (2014). Appropriating the process: Creative production within informal interactions and across settings. In B. Barron, K Gomez, N. Pinkard, & C. K. Martin (Eds.), *The digital youth network: Cultivating digital media citizenship in urban communities* (pp. 167–190). Cambridge, MA: MIT Press.

Baturay, M. H. & Toker, S. (2015). An investigation of the impact of demographics on cyberloafing from an educational setting angle. *Computers in Human Behavior, 50,* 358–366.

Berlyne, D. E. (1960). *Conflict, arousal, and curiosity.* New York: McGraw-Hill Book Company.

Bergin, D. A. (1999). Influences on classroom interest. *Educational Psychologist, 34*(2), 87–98. doi:10.1207/s15326985ep3402_2

Bergin, D. A. (2016). Social influences on interest. *Educational Psychologist.* doi: 10.1080/00461520.2015.1133306

Berridge, K. C., Robinson, T. E., & Aldridge, J. W. (2009). Dissecting components of reward: "liking," "wanting," and learning. *Current Opinion in Pharmacology, 9*(1), 65–73. doi:10.1016/j.coph.2008.12.014

Crowley, K., Barron, B.J., Knutson, K., & Martin, C. (2015). Interest and the development of pathways to science. In K. A. Renninger, M. Nieswandt, & S. Hidi (Eds.), *Interest in mathematics and science learning* (pp. 297–314). Washington, DC: American Educational Research Association.

Dawis, R. V., & Lofquist, L. H. (1984). *A psychological theory of work adjustment.* Minneapolis: University of Minnesota Press.

Deci, E. L. (1971). Effects of externally mediated rewards on intrinsic motivation. *Journal of Personality and Social Psychology, 18*(1), 105–115. doi:10.1037/h0030644

Dewey, J. (1913). *Interest and effort in education.* Boston, MA: Houghton Mifflin. doi:10.1037/14633-000

Digman, J. M. (1990). Personality structure: Emergence of the five-factor model. *Annual Review of Psychology, 41,* 417–440. doi:10.1146/annurev.ps.41.020190.002221

Dohn, N. B. (2013). Situational interest in engineering design activities. *International Journal of Science Education, 35*(12), 2057–2078. doi:10.1080/09500693.2012.757670

Duckworth, A. L., Peterson, C., Matthews, M. D., & Kelly, D. R. (2007). Grit: Perseverance and passion for long-term goals. *Journal of Personality and Social Psychology, 92*(6), 1087–1101.

Duncan, D. K., Hoekstra, A. R., & Wilcox, B. R. (2012). Digital devices, distraction, and student performance: Does in-class cell phone use reduce learning? *Astronomy Education Review, 11*(1) 10108. Retrieved from *https://www.learntechlib.org/p/88569/*

Durik, A. M., & Harackiewicz, J. M. (2007). Different strokes for different folks: How individual interest moderates the effects of situational factors on task interest. *Journal of Educational Psychology, 99*(3), 597–610. doi:10.1037/0022-0663.99.3.59

Flanigan, A. E., & Babchuk, W. A. (2015). Social media as academic quicksand: A phenomenological study of student experiences in and out of the classroom. *Learning and Individual Differences, 44,* 40–45. doi: 10.1016/j.lindif.2015.11.003

Fries, S., & Dietz. F (2007). Learning in the face of temptation: The case of motivational interference. *The Journal of Experimental Education, 76*(1). 93–112.

Garrett, R. K., & Danziger, J. N. (2008). On cyberslacking: Workplace status and personal Internet use at work. *Cyberpsychology & Behavior, 11,* 287–292. doi:10.1089/cpb.2007.0146

Goldsmith, M., & Reiter, M. (2015). *Triggers: Creating behavior that lasts—Becoming the person you want to be.* New York: Penguin Random House.

Gottlieb, J., Oudeyer, P-Y., Lopes, M., & Baranes, A. (2013). Information seeking, curiosity and attention: Computational and neural mechanisms. *Trends in Cognitive Sciences, 17*(11) 585–593. doi:10.1016/j.tics.2013.09.001

Gruber, M. J., Gelman, B. D., & Ranganath, C. (2014). States of curiosity modulate hippocampus-dependent learning via the dopaminergic circuit. *Neuron, 84*(2), 486–496. doi:10.1016/j.neuron.2014.08.060

Harackiewicz, J. M., Durik, A. M., Barron, K. E., Linnenbrink, L., & Tauer, J. M. (2008). The role of achievement goals in the development of interest: Reciprocal relations between achievement goals, interest, and performance. *Journal of Educational Psychology, 100*(1), 105–122. doi:10.1037/0022-0663.100.1.105

Harackiewicz, J. M., Tibbetts, Y., Canning, E., & Hyde, J. S. (2014). Harnessing values to promote motivation in education. In S. A. Karabenick, & T. C. Urdan (Eds.), *Advances in motivation and achievement. Vol. 18: Motivational Interventions.* (pp. 71–107). Bingley, UK: Emerald Group Publishing. doi:10.1108/s0749-742320140000018002

Herbart, J. F. (1806/1965). Allgemeine Pädagogik, aud dem Zweck der Erziehung abgeleitet. In J. F. Herbart (Ed), *Pädagogische schriften* (Vol. 2). Düsseldorf: Kupper.

Hidi, S. (2016). Revisiting the role of rewards in motivation and learning: Implications of neuroscientific research. *Educational Psychology Review, 28*(1), 61–93. doi:10.1007/s10648-015-9307-5

Hidi, S., & Renninger, K. A. (2006). The four-phase model of interest development. *Educational Psychologist, 41*(2), 111–127. doi: 10.1207/s15326985ep4102_4

Holland, J. L. (1959). A theory of vocational choice. *Journal of Counseling Psychology, 6,* 35–45.

Hulleman, C., & Harackiewicz, J. (2009). Promoting interest and performance in high school science classes. *Science, 326*(5698), 1410–1412. doi:10.1126/science.1177067

James, W. (1890). *The principles of psychology.* London: Macmillan. doi:10.1037/11059000

Järvelä, S., & Renninger, K. A. (2014). Designing for learning: Interest, motivation, and engagement. In D. Keith Sawyer (Ed.), *Cambridge handbook of the learning sciences* (2nd. ed., pp. 668–685). New York: Cambridge University Press.

Jian, G. (2013). Understanding the wired workplace: The effects of job characteristics on employees' personal online communication at work. *Communication Research Reports, 30* (1), 22–33. doi:10.1080/08824096.2012.746221

Junco, R. (2011). Too much face not enough books: The relationship between multiple indices of Facebook use and academic performance. *Computers in Human Behavior, 28*, 187–198. doi: 10.101G/j.chb2011.08.026

Kaye, B., Jordan-Evans, S., & Career Systems International. (2014). *What keeps you: A white paper about engaging and retaining talent.* Retrieved from www.keepem.com/pdf/WKY_2014_pdf

Kaye, B., & Jordan-Evans, S. (2002). *Getting good people to stay.* San Francisco: Berrett-Koehler.

Lipstein, R., & Renninger, K. A. (2007). "Putting things into words": 12–15-year-old students' interest for writing. In P. Boscolo & S. Hidi (Eds.), *Motivation and writing: Research and school practice* (pp. 113–140). New York: Kluwer Academic/Plenum Press. doi:10.1163/9781849508216_008

Low, K. S. D., & Rounds, J. (2006). Vocational interests: Bridging person and environment. In D. L. Segal & J. Thomas (Eds.), *Comprehensive handbook of personality and psychopathology, Vol. I: Personality and everyday functioning* (pp. 251–267). New York: Wiley

Low, K. S. D., & Rounds, J. (2007). Interest change and continuity from early adolescence to middle adulthood. *International Journal of Educational and Vocational Guidance, 7*, 23–36.

Low, K. D., Yoon, M., Roberts, B. W., & Rounds, J. (2005). The stability of vocational interests from early adolescence to middle adulthood: A quantitative review of longitudinal studies. *Psychological Bulletin, 131*, 713–737. doi:10.1037/0033-2909.131.5.713

Madden, M., & Jones, S. (2008). Networked workers: Most workers use the internet or email at their jobs, but they say these technologies are a mixed blessing for them. *Pew Internet and American Life Project.* Retrieved from http://www.pewinternet.org/files/old-media//Files/Reports/2008/PIP_Networked_Workers_FINAL.pdf.pdf

Marsden, K. E., Ma, W. J., Deci, E. L., Ryan, R. M., & Chiu, P. H. (2014). Diminished neural responses predict enhanced intrinsic motivation and sensitivity to external incentive. *Cognitive, Affective, Behavioral Neuroscience, 15*, 276–286. doi:10.3758/s13415-014-0324-5

Moore, H. T. (1921). The comparative influence of majority and expert opinion. *American Journal of Psychology, 32*, 16–20. doi:10.2307/1413472

Munene, A. G., & Nyaribo, Y. M. (2013). Effect of social media pertication in the workplace on employee productivity. *International Journal of Advances in Management and Economics, 2*(2), 141–150.

Nolen, S. B. (2007). The role of literate communities in the development of children's interest in writing. In G. Rijlaarsdam (Series Ed.) & S. Hidi & P. Boscolo (Vol. Eds.), *Studies in writing. Vol. 19: Writing and Motivation* (1st ed., pp. 241–255). Oxford, UK: Elsevier.

Nye, C. D., & Roberts, B. W. (2013). A developmental perspective on the importance of personality for understanding workplace behavior. In N. Christiansen & R. Tett (Eds.), *Handbook of personality at work* (pp. 796–818). New York: Routledge.

Nye, C. D., Su, R. Rounds, J., & Drasgow, F. (2012). Vocational interests and performance: A quantitative summary of over 60 years of research. *Perspectives on Psychological Science, 7*(4), 384–403. doi: 10.1177/1745691612449021

Panksepp, J. (1998). *Affective neuroscience: The foundations of human and animal emotion.* New York: Oxford.

Paterson, D. G., Elliot, R. M., Anderson, L. D., Toops, H. A., & Heidbreder, E. (1930). *Minnesota Mechanical Ability Tests.* Minneapolis, MN: Minneapolis University Press.

Pestalozzi, J. H. (1898/2004). *Letters on education.* Syracuse, NY: C.W. Bardeen.

Pressick-Kilborn, K. (2015). Canalization and connectedness in the development of science interest. In K. A. Renninger, M. Nieswandt, & S. Hidi (Eds.), *Interest in mathematics and science learning* (pp. 353–367). Washington, DC: American Educational Research Association.

Renninger, K. A. (2010). Working with and cultivating interest, self-efficacy, and self-regulation. In D. Preiss & R. Sternberg (Eds.), *Innovations in educational psychology: Perspectives on learning, teaching and human development* (pp. 107–138). New York: Springer.

Renninger, K. A., Austin, L., Bachrach, J. E., Chau, A., Emmerson, M. S., King, R.B., … Stevens, S. J. (2014). Going beyond Whoa! That's Cool! Achieving science interest and learning with the ICAN Intervention. In S. Karabenick & T. Urdan (Eds.), *Motivation based learning interventions, Advances in Motivation and Achievement series* (Vol. 18, pp. 107–140). Bingley, UK: Emerald. doi:10.1108/S0749-74232014 0000018003

Renninger, K. A., & Bachrach, J. E. (2015). Studying triggers for interest and engagement using observational methods. *Educational Psychologist, 50*(1), 58–69. doi: 10.1080/00461520.2014.999920

Renninger, K. A. Bachrach, J. E., & Hidi, S. E. (2019). Triggering and maintaining in early phases of interest development. In H. Hedges & M. Birbili (Guest Eds.), Special Issue: Conceptualising and researching interest/s as a learning phenomenon. *Learning, Culture and Social Interaction.* https://doi.org/10.1016/j.lcsi.2018.11.007

Renninger, K. A., & Hidi, S. E. (2019a). Supporting the development of interest in the workplace. In F. L. Oswald, T. S. Behrens, & L. L. Foster (Eds.), *Workforce readiness* (pp. 19–34). New York: Routledge.

Renninger, K. A., & Hidi, S. E. (2019b). Interest development and learning. In K. A. Renninger & S. E. Hidi (Eds.), *The Cambridge handbook of motivation and learning* (pp. 265–296). Cambridge, UK: Cambridge University Press.

Renninger, K. A., & Hidi, S. E. (2016). *The power of interest for motivation and engagement.* New York: Routledge.

Renninger, K. A., & Hidi, S. (2011). Revisiting the conceptualization, measurement, and generation of interest. *Educational Psychologist, 46*(3), 168–184. doi:10.1080/00461520.2011.587723

Renninger, K. A., Ren, Y., & Kern, H. M. (2018). Motivation, engagement, and interest: "In the end, it came down to you and how you think of the problem." In F. Fischer, C. E. Hmelo-Silver, S. R. Goldman, & P. Reimann (Eds.), *International handbook of the learning sciences* (pp. 116–126). New York: Routledge.

Renninger, K. A., & Riley, K. R. (2013). Interest, cognition and case of L-and science. In S. Kreitler (Ed.), *Cognition and motivation: Forging an interdisciplinary perspective* (pp. 352–382). New York: Cambridge University Press. doi:10.1017/cbo9781139021463.021

Renninger, K. A., & Schofield, L. S. (2014). *Assessing STEM interest as a developmental motivational variable.* Poster presented in K. A. Renninger & S. E. Hidi (Chairs),

Current Approaches to Interest Measurement, American Educational Research Association, Philadelphia, PA.

Renninger, K. A., & Shumar, W. (2002). Community building with and for teachers: The Math Forum as a resource for teacher professional development. In K. A. Renninger & W. Shumar (Eds.), *Building virtual communities: Learning and change in cyberspace* (pp. 60–95). New York: Cambridge University Press.

Renninger, K. A., & Su, S. (2012). Interest and its development. In R. Ryan (Ed.), *Oxford handbook of motivation* (pp. 167–187). New York: Oxford University Press.

Ryan, R., & Deci, E. L. (2017). *Self-determination theory: Basic psychological needs in motivation, development, and wellness.* New York: Guilford Press.

Roberts, B. W., & Mroczek, M. (2008). Personality trait change in adulthood. *Current Directions in Psychological Science, 17*(1), 31–35. doi:10.1111/j.1467-8721.2008.00543.x

Roberts, B. W., Walton, K., & Viechtbauer, W. (2006). Patterns of mean-level change in personality traits across the life course: A meta analysis of longitudinal studies. *Psychological Bulletin, 132,* 1–25.

Rotgans, J. I., & Schmidt, H. G. (2014). Situational interest and learning: Thirst for knowledge. *Learning and Instruction, 32,* 37–50. doi:10.106/j.learninstruc.2014.01.00

Rounds, J., & Su, R. (2014). The nature and power of interests. *Current Directions in Psychological Science, 23*(2), 98–103. doi: 10.1177/0963721414522812

Sansone, C. (2009). What's interest got to do with it?: Potential trade-offs in the self-regulation of motivation. In J. P. Forgas, R. Baumiester, & D. Tice (Eds.), *Psychology of self-regulation: Cognitive, affective, and motivational processes* (pp. 35–51). New York: Psychology Press.

Sansone, C., Thoman, D., & Fraughton, T. (2015). The relation between interest and self-regulation in mathematics and science. In K. A. Renninger, M. Nieswandt, & S. Hidi (Eds.), *Interest in mathematics and science learning* (pp. 111–131). Washington, DC: American Educational Research Association.

Schneider, B. (1987). The people make the place. *Personnel Psychology, 40*(3), 437–453.

Strong, E. K., Jr. (1943). *Vocational interests of men and women.* Palo Alto, CA: Stanford University Press.

Su, R., Murdock, C. D., & Rounds, J. (2015). Person-environment fit. In P. J. Hartung, M. L. Savickas, & W. B. Walsh (Eds.), *APA handbook of career interventions* (pp. 81–98). Washington, DC: American Psychological Association.

Trautwein, U., Lüdtke, O., Nagy, N., Lenski, A., Niggli, A., & Schnyder, I. (2015). Using individual interest and conscientiousness to predict academic effort: Additive, synergistic, or compensatory effects? *Journal of Personality and Social Psychology, 109,* 142–162. doi:10.1037/pspp0000034

Ugrin, J. C., Pearson, J. M., & Odom, M. D. (2007). Profiling cyber-slackers in the workplace: Demographic, cultural, and workplace factors. *Journal of Internet Commerce, 6* (3), 75–89.

Vroom, V. H. (1964). *Work and motivation.* New York: Wiley.

Xu, J., Coats, L. T., & Davidson, M. L. (2012). Promoting student interest in science: The perspectives of exemplary African American teachers. *American Educational Research Journal, 49*(1), 124–154. doi: 10.3102/0002831211 426200

3

A HISTORY OF VOCATIONAL INTEREST MEASUREMENT

Michael J. Zickar and Hanyi Min

BOWLING GREEN STATE UNIVERSITY

In this chapter, we trace the beginnings of vocational interest measurement and the subsequent refinements of measures focusing in depth on several seminal measures (i.e., the Strong Vocational Interest Blank). Throughout this chapter, we discuss general trends but also concentrate on several key figures (i.e., Edward Strong and John Holland). In addition, we highlight several forgotten and less successful efforts to remind readers that history is not a linear and straight path from early days to the current situation. Finally, throughout this history we also focus on relevant sociopolitical and scientific events and contexts that influenced the measurement of vocational interests (see Zickar, 2015, for background on many of our historical decisions).

Early Days: The Scientists and the Reformers

The beginning of the previous turn of the century was an exciting and tumultuous time in the business community, in governmental affairs, and in the fledging social sciences. Historians typically refer to the era in the United States from the 1890s to the 1920s as the Progressive Era as reformers in public and private industry tried to make the country better by improving and expanding access to education, addressing worker safety, advocating for the right of women to vote, tackling serious problems like alcoholism and drug use, and improving the country's health through better food safety and nutrition. One of the first people to be concerned with vocational interests was Frank Parsons, a civil engineer for a railroad who then worked as a public school teacher before becoming a lawyer and then eventually a professor at Boston University and Kansas State Agricultural College. Mr. Parsons wrote and lectured on a variety of topics popular in the Progressive Era including abuses in the railroad industry, the importance of public ownership of utilities, and the need to expand democracy throughout our government (see Davis, 1969; Zytowski, 2001). Relevant to this chapter, one of the last passions of Parsons's was the idea of matching people to appropriate careers and occupations. By finding the right jobs for people, he argued that both productivity and happiness would be maximized. The last book that Parsons published (actually it was published posthumously) was entitled *Choosing a Vocation* (Parsons, 1909). In that book, he advocated the importance of matching an individual's aptitudes, abilities, ambitions, and limitations with the knowledge and requirements of jobs. In 1905, Parsons created a Breadwinner's Institute, which offered courses for the working poor. In 1908, he created the Vocation Bureau of Boston, which was designed to educate the working poor to increase their job skills and to make better vocational decisions (see Brewer, 1942; Mann, 1950). Unfortunately Parsons died tragically early, soon after the founding of the Vocation Bureau. Inspired by the work of the Vocation Bureau of Boston, a National Vocational Guidance Association was created in 1913 and work was stimulated around the country to help people make better career decisions.

One problem was that there were few tools to help individuals make better occupational choices. Parsons searched the extant psychological literature at the turn of the century but did not find much help. One subsequent commentator stated that "when he went to the psychological laboratories for techniques he found that the cupboard was bare" (Paterson, 1938, p. 37). A few early efforts were made at assessing vocational interests. Jesse Davis, a principal in Grand Rapids public schools, created a Student Vocational Self-Analysis tool for use by 10th graders; this tool had a structured set of items (e.g., "What can you do better than others of your age?" and "Have you any weakness or temptation that would endanger your career in any particular vocation?"), though there was no proposed way to score these open-ended items (Davis, 1914). Soon after, psychologists developed the technology, tests, and techniques needed to provide guidance counselors with useful information about individuals.

Psychological testing began in earnest with the United States' entrance into World War I (WWI). Prior to that time, the U.S. military was quite small and unprepared for the scale of combat faced on the European continent. Upon the entrance of the United States into WWI in April of 1917, the military was faced with the need to screen large numbers of applicants and place them into positions that were suited to their skills, talents, and abilities. Several psychologists, led by Robert Yerkes, took lessons learned from the recently published Stanford-Binet Intelligence Test (Terman et al., 1915), and developed a series of tools that could be administered in large groups to assess cognitive aptitude, temperament, and trade skills. Some of these tests were developed in time to be used operationally, whereas others were developed too late to be of use (see Yoakum & Yerkes, 1920).

Soon after the War, however, businesses and organizations started seeing the value of psychological testing to help them make better decisions (Katzell & Austin, 1992). Private consulting companies such as the Scott Company and the Psychological Corporation included key psychologists who had worked on the war testing effort and marketed psychological tests to industry for hiring purposes. Tests proliferated to measure a variety of constructs. Kornhauser and Kingsbury (1924), in an early survey postwar of psychological tests for industrial use highlighted tests designed to measure general intelligence, general mechanical aptitude, physical and motor abilities, sensory capabilities, character, temperament, and emotional traits. Several of these tests have names that are still well-recognized (e.g., Stanford-Binet), though many of them have faded into obscurity (e.g., Chicago Group Intelligence Test, Downey Will Temperament Test, and the Voelker Tests of Habits of Moral Trustworthiness). Although many of the complex statistical techniques (e.g., factor analysis) used to analyze tests had not yet been developed, nor had classical test theory been formulated, researchers such as Kornhauser and Kingsbury (1924), Freyd (1925), and Link (1919), among others, were advocating a scientific approach to test construction and evaluation.

Given all of the previously mentioned excitement related to vocational guidance and the sudden availability of psychological tests, it was not surprising that tests designed for selection were soon promoted to be used for vocational guidance, as well as new tests being developed specifically for that purpose (see Harrington & Long, 2013). Kornhauser and Kingsbury (1924) noted "professional vocational counselors, whether connected or not with schools, have hitherto made much less use of psychological tests than it seems likely they will in the future" (p. 156). They noted that intelligence tests were used by counselors to help guide decision-making. In addition, researchers studied the relationship between intelligence test scores and occupational achievement; Fryer (1922) studied military data for 96 occupations and found the average intelligence level differed, ranging from the highest for engineer officer and lowest for laborer. Feingold (1923) examined high school students and investigated the match between their intelligence and the intelligence demanded of their occupational choice, finding that over 50% of students made bad vocational choices based on a mismatch. This focus on ability was important as it highlighted some of the occupations for which an individual might be successful, but these tests did little to identify which tests might be most satisfying, motivating, and interesting to individuals.

One individual, who received some of his key training during the Great War effort, would take the knowledge gained from test construction in ability tests and apply these techniques to develop the first prominent vocational interest inventory. In the following section, we present a brief history of Edward K. Strong and then detail his creation of the Strong Interest Inventory, as well as follow subsequent developments.

Edward K. Strong and the Strong Interest Inventory

A Brief History of Strong

Edward K. Strong, according to his daughter, loved his work and he wanted others to enjoy their work, which might be the reason why he devoted a lot of time to develop Strong's Vocational Interest Blank (SVIB; Hansen, 1987). Strong got his PhD degree from Columbia University in 1911. During WWI, Strong served as a member of the Classification of Personnel Committee in the Army. During this time, Strong began to "identify the need that individuals have for career guidance and vocational development, and he began to appreciate the efficiency of the army trade tests in determining a person's fitness for a job" (Hansen, 1987, p. 120). After the war, Strong joined the Carnegie Institute of Technology, where a pool of 1,000 items used to differentiate people in various occupations was developed during a seminar conducted by Clarence S. Yoakum. The first Strong Vocational Inventory borrowed items from this item pool, as well as from several other existing vocational inventories, for example, the Occupational Interest Inventory and the Interest Report Blank (Donnay, 1997). Yoakum's item pool inspired several other vocational inventories, the Occupational Interest Inventory (Freyd, 1922), the Interest Report Blank (Cowdery, 1926), and the Carnegie Interest Inventory (Carnegie Institute of Technology, 1920), though none of these inventories had the staying power of Strong's inventory. In the fall of 1923, Strong moved to Stanford University and remained there for the rest of his career. At Stanford University, the first edition of the Strong Interest Inventory was published in 1927.

Introduction of the original Strong Interest Inventory: Strong's Vocational Interest Blank

Strong's original inventory was named Strong's Vocational Interest Blank, and then changed to Strong-Campbell Interest Inventory. Now Strong's original scales and other complementary scales developed later are referred to as the Strong Interest Inventory.

The first edition of the SVIB contained 10 Occupational Scales. The development of the SVIB was based on assumptions that interests are located on a dimension of liking and disliking, and that people interested in and people working in a particular occupation share similar likes and dislikes (Donnay, 1997).

Scoring method

The use of SVIB Occupational Scales rested on the differences in responses of members of various criterion groups and men-in-general or women-in-general groups (Strong, 1943, 1963). Reference groups of Strong's Vocational Interest Blank were made up of 150–500 individuals from a specific occupation (Super & Crites, 1962). The reference group was selected based on several standards: (1) they needed to work in the occupation for at least three years, (2) they needed to be satisfied with their work, and (3) they needed to have minimum proficiencies for their work, such as certification (Campbell, 1971). Responses of reference groups and that of men-in-general, or women-in-general, were compared. Then based on how large differences were between these two groups, items were selected or assigned different weights on the scoring scale for that occupation (Campbell, 1971). Scores of the original occupation sample were standardized on a scale with mean of 50 and standard deviation of 10, and used as norm of scoring. Because standardized scores can be difficult to interpret, letter grades were assigned to respondents based the range of scores, including A, B+, B, B-, C+, or C (Strong, 1943).

Worth noting is that the scoring of the SVIB should not focus on specific occupations, but on the patterns of scores. Score patterns allow interpretation of types of occupations rather than specific occupation. Also it is easier to see whether higher scores in one occupation are supported by high scores in other relevant occupations by looking at score patterns (Super & Crites, 1962). For example, it is more important to know that a respondent's primary interest patterns are in the scientific and literary occupations with a secondary pattern in the social welfare field, than to know that he or she scored A's as psychologist, physician, chemist, and other specific occupations (Super & Crites, 1962).

Reliability and validity of the SVIB

Results of the SVIB were proven to be consistent and stable over time. The average odd-even reliability coefficient of 36 revised scales was .88 for 285 Stanford senior males, with only one scale falling below .80 (Strong, 1943). And the average test-retest coefficient for an interval of a week was .91 (Strong, 1943). Also, studies indicated that reliabilities might differ for different types of respondents. For example: for 10th graders (135), average test-retest coefficient after two years was .57 for 7 typical scales; for 11th graders (813) after three years it was .71 (Van Fridagh Taylor, 1942). These results suggest that interests stabilize more as students get older.

Strong provided the first evidence of predictive validity for Vocational Interest Blank with a longitudinal study. Strong (1935) collected longitudinal data over a five-year interval from senior males at Stanford and found:

> (1) Men continuing in an occupation obtain a higher interest score in it than in any other occupation; (2) Men continuing in an occupation obtain a higher interest score in it than men entering some other occupation; (3) Men continuing in an occupation obtain higher scores in it

> than men who change from that occupation to some other; and (4) Men changing from other occupations to occupation X score higher in X prior to the change than they did in other occupations. (Strong, 1935, p. 335)

Numerous researchers also examined concurrent and predictive validity of the SVIB following Strong's early effort. Donnay (1997) summarized results of various validity studies and transformed them into consistent formats: percentage of good hits. Donnay (1997) showed that 24 studies reported direct and indirect good hits at the rate of 32% to 69%, which provided support for the validity of SVIB.

Revisions of the Strong Interest Inventory

As one of the earliest scales still in use, Strong's Vocational Interest Blank has gone through many revisions to avoid obsolescence. These revisions updated items of the original SVIB and expanded the number of Occupational Scales (Strong 1962; Strong, 1963; Donnay, 1997). Below are three major revisions of the SVIB.

1968 revision: Basic Interest Scales

In the 1968 revision, the first group of homogeneous content scales, Basic Interest Scales, were added to the Strong Interest Inventory. A few limitations of the Occupational Scales were hindering scale operation and interpretation: (1) further psychological interpretation of the empirical scales is difficult. For example, what does it mean if a respondent has interests that are similar to lawyers? (2) There was a large number of empirical occupation scales; and (3) the empirical scales were difficult to work with in research (Campbell, Borgen, Eastes, Johansson, & Peterson, 1968). The 22 Basic Interest Scales were developed aiming to address these limitations of the empirical Occupational Scales and to provide specific occupational areas that would be good fits for respondents.

Basic Interest Scales were built by identifying important clusters of interests represented in the SVIB (Campbell et al, 1968). Campbell (1971) pointed out that Basic Interest Scales were a supplement of the original Occupational Scales, with relatively less items and could be generalized beyond one particular occupation. Intercorrelations between items were examined. Then highly correlated items were treated as a cluster to represent one of the 22 general interests (e.g. Culinary Arts, Teaching and Education, and Medical Science).

The test-retest reliability of Basic Interest Scales was roughly equivalent to the SVIB Occupational Scale. Campbell et al. (1968) reported the average test-retest reliability was .89 for an interval of thirty days and .65 for an interval of two years. Seven concurrent and predictive validity studies (Donnay, 1997) showed that direct and indirect good hits of Basic Interest Scales at the rate of 21% to 75%, which was comparable with the Occupational Scales. Campbell et al. (1968) also reported the scores of Basic Interest Scales were related to occupational choice.

1974 revision: General Occupational Themes.

In 1974, David P. Campbell first combined separate forms for male and female into a single-sex form, called the Strong-Campbell Interest Inventory (Campbell, Crichton, Hansen, & Webber, 1974). The 1974 revision increased the number of Occupational Scales to 124 and added scales that assessed Academic Comfort and the personality trait of Introversion-Extroversion. Most importantly, the 1974 revision developed the General Occupational Themes. The General Occupational Themes incorporated Holland's theory of six personality types for classifying individuals and occupations: Realistic, Investigative/Intellectual, Artistic, Social, Enterprising, and Conventional (RIASEC). Campbell and Holland (1972) used the General Occupational Themes to analyze the vast Strong archival data and reported that the mean scores conformed well. This indicates "the first use of theory framework to organize and interpret the earlier empirical efforts of Strong" (Donnay, 1997, p. 12). The General Occupational Themes showed predictive validity nearly as high as the Occupational Scales for males, with direct and indirect good hits at the rate of 31% to 69%. But it was less predictive for females with the rate of good hits ranging from 13% to 53% (Donnay, 1997).

1994 revision: Personal Style Scales and Skills Confidence Inventory.

Four Personal Style Scales were added to the Strong Interest Inventory in the 1994 revision, measuring respondent's broad living and working preferences. The four scales were Work Style, Learning Environment, Leadership, and Risk Taking/Adventure (Harmon, DeWitt, Campbell, & Hansen, 1994). Researchers had found that there was a relationship between vocational interest and personality (Costa, McCrae, & Holland, 1984). In addition, within the field of Industrial and Organizational (IO) psychology in general, the inclusion of the five-factor model as well as the development of several popular Big Five personality inventories had resulted in the usage of personality in all aspects of work-related psychology (see Hough & Oswald, 2008). The inclusion of Personal Style Scales reflected this trend of incorporating personality into vocational interest measurement and interpretation (Borgen & Harmon, 1996). The four Personal Style Scales were found to differentiate occupational and educational groups consistent with theoretical expectations (Harmon et al., 1994).

Another innovation of the 1994 revision was development of the Skills Confidence Inventory (SCI) as a companion to the traditional interest inventory booklet. The development of the SCI was a combination of measurement for interest and self-efficacy in a particular interest dimension (e.g., interest and self-efficacy in Realistic occupations), in order to better interpret vocational interests (Betz, Harmon, & Borgen, 1996). The result of the SCI was a reflection of respondent's confidence level in the six Holland themes. Betz et al. (1996) reported that score patterns of SCI were consistent with predicted group and occupational differences and within-occupation score profiles were consistent with the Holland interest codes of each occupation, which supported the validity of the SCI. Betz et al. (1996) suggest that the measurement of interest-based self-efficacy can be used by counselors in giving career advice.

Contribution of Strong

The Strong Interest Inventory has had the longest history of *any* currently used psychological test (Donnay, 1997). Kuder (1977, p. xii) wrote "the firm foundation of scholarly research provided by Strong for further advance in interest measurement is so extensive that it is almost impossible to do anything in the field that does not have some background in Strong's work."

Many studies Strong conducted on vocational interests as early as the 1930s or 1940s are still meaningful for researchers today. For example, Strong realized there were gender differences in vocational interests and published separated forms of interest inventory for male and female. Strong (1943) also found that interests had cross-cultural similarity. Moreover, Strong (1955) pointed out that career counseling should not be restricted to youth and should occur all through life at the time when a majority thought career counseling was only appropriate for high school and college students.

The methods Strong used to develop Strong's Vocational Interest Blank were also influential for later studies. Strong's contrasted-groups method of empirical scale construction was adopted to develop many well-known and widely used questionnaires, such as the Minnesota Multiphasic Personality Inventory (Donnay, 1997; Hathaway & McKinley, 1940). Strong's criterion-related measurement used in the SVIB along with Kuder's content-related measurement represent the foundation of vocational interest measurement (Donnay, 1997).

Additional Early Vocational Interest Inventories

Although we devote a large amount of space to Strong's work, other vocational interest inventories were developed and had various degrees of success. For example, in the Buros Mental Measurement Yearbook of 1940, seven tools were mentioned, including Strong's inventory, as well as Cleeton's Vocational Interest Inventory (1935), which used the original 1,000-item pool from Yoakum to create a 670-item inventory that provided scores for occupational groups. Other inventories included Brainard and Stewart's Specific Interest Inventory (1932), Thurstone's Vocational Interest Schedule (1935), and Le Suer's Occupational

Interest Blank (1937). In addition, the Diagnostic Interest Blank was a projective interest inventory with 80 incomplete sentences that were scored on a variety of dimensions (Forer, 1948). Excepting Strong's inventory, these tests generally fell out of favor in a short amount of time. The one other test from that time that had staying power was the Kuder Preference Inventory (Kuder, 1939) which was developed by Dr. Frederic Kuder.

To pursue a career in vocational guidance, Frederic Kuder received a master's degree in education at the University of Michigan. After graduation, he went to Procter & Gamble where he worked with Marion Richardson to develop a scale used to measure the effectiveness of sales personnel, work that resulted in the Kuder-Richardson index of reliability, one of the first statistical indexes of that important psychometric concept. During the Great Depression, P&G closed their research shop and he went to Ohio State University where he studied with Herbert Toops, receiving his dissertation in 1937. He began his academic career at the University of Chicago where he worked as a university examiner; while at Chicago he developed the Kuder Preference Record interest inventory, which he continued to refine after moving to Duke University (see Zytowski & Austin, 2001).

The Kuder Preference Record (KPR) was originally published by the University of Chicago Bookstore (later by Science Research Associates) and included 330 pairs of forced-choice items where respondents had to express their preference between pairs of activities such as "Visit the U.S. Senate" or "Visit an art museum." The inventory was scored on seven basic interests: Scientific, Computational, Musical, Artistic, Literary, Social Service, and Persuasive. One of the key selling points to the KPR was a self-scoring edition that included a stylus and a specialized answer key that could be used to generate gender-specific percentile scores (see Zytowksi, 2014). Before computerized editions of tests that would make collection and scoring of data extremely easy, such practical advantages of tests were often important in helping marketing. Subsequent editions of the KPR added scales for Mechanical and Clerical, and Outdoor. The KPR remained in print until 2002. Kuder-related products still remain in use, with Kuder, Inc. providing many other career-planning tools.

Borgen (1986) identified the Strong Vocational Interest Blank and the Kuder Preference Record as two of the "Big Three" interest inventories, scales that had the largest impact in the field. The third of the Big Three, John Holland's Self-Directed Search is the focus of the next section.

Holland's RIASEC Model

Brief introduction of Holland as a Person

John L. Holland was one of the most prominent theorists in the field of vocational interests and warrants a short biographical foray. Holland grew up in Omaha Nebraska and received bachelor's degrees in psychology, French, and mathematics. After graduating in 1942, he served in the Army for 3.5 years. Given his psychology major, he was given the responsibilities to interviewing hundreds of new recruits, as well as administering psychological tests. This experience led him to start thinking that people fall into a relatively small number of types (Hansen, 2011; Weinrach, 1980). Holland got his PhD degree in psychology in 1952 at the University of Minnesota, in a department well-versed in scale development and individual differences. Even though Holland is well known as a theorist for his six typologies in vocational interests, he was also "an effective empirical researcher and a psychologist who valued the importance of applied psychology" (Hansen, 2011; p. 1213). He started his career by working in applied settings such as the Counseling Center at the Western Reserve University and the American College Testing Program. In 1969, he moved to Johns Hopkins University where he stayed until retirement. This variety of applied and academic settings might have been responsible for his work, which was both theoretically important, rigorously conducted, and with significant applied implications.

Introduction of RIASEC Model and Measurement

Development of the Vocational Preference Inventory (VPI)

The limitations of existing vocational interest inventories, such as Strong's Vocational Interest Inventory (SVIB; Strong, 1927) and the Kuder Preference Record (KPR; Kuder, 1939), motivated Holland to develop the Vocational Preference Inventory (VPI). First, the existing inventories were difficult to interpret and extrapolate beyond what their occupation scales assessed directly (Nauta, 2010). Meanwhile, it took a long wait to score existing vocational interest inventories, a concern for someone like Holland who had experience using inventories in counseling settings (Nauta, 2010; Weinrach, 1980). Finally, the existing inventories did not allow easy linkage between the respondent's score and environments (Nauta, 2010). Thus, the VPI was constructed aiming to give a maximum amount of reliable and valid information with a minimum amount of testing and scoring time, skill, and expense (Holland, 1958).

The VPI was published in 1958. Holland obtained the formulations of VPI by reviewing 30-plus Occupational Scales of the SVIB and writing brief interpretations (Weinrach, 1980). Holland considered the VPI as a personality inventory using occupational title for content. Subjects respond to 300 items in the VPI by indicating either "interest" (appeal) or "dislike." Result of the VPI reflects respondents' feelings and attitudes about occupational titles (Holland, 1958).

Holland (1958) provided evidences of reliability and validity of the VPI. The internal consistency coefficients of the VPI ranged from .72 to .95 and .68 to .90 for male and female samples, respectively. Test-retest reliability coefficients ranged from .70 to .87. Also, the VPI significantly differentiated a number of defined criterion groups, which proved construct validity of the inventory. Moreover, the VPI scales were found to be consistent with the SVIB and KPR (Weinrach, 1980).

Development and brief introduction of RIASEC typology

The hexagonal RIASEC typology is the core of Holland's theory and also one of the most influential theories in vocational psychology. The typology is often referred to by individuals who have no training in psychology and might be the second most popular psychological typology after the Myers-Briggs personality types. The typology came out of elaboration of the VPI rationale; the rationale for the first 6 scales of the VPI formed a primitive account of the RIASEC typology. Then when Holland and Whitney were searching for a way to order the typology by recording the correlations between the different scales of the VPI, the hexagonal model was built (Weinrach, 1980).

The main idea of Holland's theory is that people resemble a combination of the six orientations: Realistic, Investigative, Artistic, Social, Enterprising, and Conventional (abbreviated to RIASEC).

> Each orientation represents a somewhat distinctive life style which is characterized by preferred methods of dealing with daily problems and includes such variables as values and interests, preferences for playing various roles and avoiding others, interpersonal skills and other personal factors. (Holland, 1959, p. 36)

Each person has his/her own hierarchy or quasi-serial order of orientations according to those orientations' relative strengths (Holland, 1959). When making vocational choices between different classes of occupations, people actively search for environments that satisfy their hierarchy of orientation based on their knowledge for themselves and their environments (Holland, 1959).

Holland (1959) also developed a corresponding typology for occupational environments in his theory. Holland based this part of his theory on Linton's (1945) notion that environment can be shaped by people in it. Holland pointed out that environments were dominated by one type of people and people would behave in a way that was consistent with their typology (Holland, 1997). People would find environments reinforcing and satisfying when environment patterns resembled their personality pattern (Holland, 1997). Also, the parallel typologies of person and environments provided theory framework for development of Self-Directed Search, which will be more specifically discussed below.

Moreover, Holland pointed out that people and environment would interact with each other to influence behavior. Person-environment congruence was found to predict a person's occupation choices (Holland, 1997) and occupation stability (Donohue, 2006). Employed adults in the process of changing their career move in a direction of greater congruence (Oleski & Subich, 1996). This idea would later be elaborated upon by Benjamin Schneider in his Attraction-Selection-Attrition (ASA) model (Schneider, 1987).

Development of Self-Directed Search (SDS)

The Self-Directed Search (SDS) is an extension of Holland's RIASEC model and "a practical, self-help device—a pair of booklets that helps a person summarize who he/she seems to be and explore some occupational alternatives" (Weinrach, 1980; p. 408). The result of the SDS is a three-letter summary code, which represents a preference style. The order of the three letters is hierarchical, with the first letter representing the strongest preference (Weinrach, 1996).

The development of SDS was a long process. After the VPI, Holland kept constructing interest inventories believing that interest inventories could be made more helpful to clients (Nauta, 2010). Holland constructed the Personal Survey and the ACT College Guidance Profile before SDS. The personal survey was developed to assess people's resemblance for different typologies; however, this scale did not seem to outperform VPI; the ACT College Guidance Profile was a combination of many different sections, which made the scale difficult to self-score or direct compare scores of different sections (Weinrach, 1980). He then constructed the SDS in 1971 by "looking at old item analyses; old monographs in which life goals, self-ratings, activities, personality scales had been organized around the VPI; selected SVIB scales; and field of study" (Weinrach, 1980, p. 409). Later revisions of the SDS simplified the scoring procedure (Nauta, 2010) and reduced sex differences (Weinrach, 1980).

Nauta (2010) reported that test-retest reliability of the SDS was from .73 to .88 for an interval of 12 weeks. Gottfredson and Holland (1975) examined the validity of the SDS by looking at the percentage of correctly predicted career choice categories for each predictor: hits for the SDS range from 25.5% to 52.1% for men and from 49.5% to 72.4% for women.

Other components of Holland's theory

The RIASEC typology, VPI, and SDS are the major part of Holland's theory and measurements, but Holland's theory and instruments were not limited to these. Holland's theory also incorporated self-evaluation and self-knowledge. Holland (1959) pointed out that people's choices within an occupation class were a function of self-evaluation and ability to perform adequately in their chosen environment.

In addition to measurements for person, such as SDS, Holland also constructed instruments for assessing environments with respect to the RIASEC types. For example, the Position Classification Inventory (Gottfredson & Holland, 1991) and the Environmental Assessment Technique (Astin & Holland, 1961) were developed to classify work and educational environments using the RIASEC types. With these measurements classifying environments into RIASEC, respondents could have a better idea about whether the environment typology is congruent with their personality typology, therefore facilitating their career decisions.

Contribution of Holland and RIASEC

Holland's theory had a great influence on research and practice in vocational psychology. One commentator stated: "Prior to the introduction of Holland's theory, the majority of the research on test development was atheoretical and empirical. Holland's theory brought order to the entire field and provided a much sharper and more clear-cut focus" (Hansen, 2011, p. 1215).

Holland's works not only represented a breakthrough in the field at his time, but also has had continuous influence in vocational psychology. Nauta (2010) calculated articles in various counseling-related and career-related journals between 1999 and 2009 and found that 47% of the articles published in the *Journal of Career Assessment*, 32% of those in the *Career Development Quarterly*, 18% of those in the *Journal of Vocational Behavior*, and 18% of those in the *Journal of Career Development* had cited Holland's work at least once.

Recent Advances

Although this chapter has focused on relatively distant history, we did want to summarize some recent history, especially drawing connections with this earlier history. Here we summarize a few key contributions to the vocational interest literature.

*Occupational Information Network (O*NET)*

The United States Department of Labor created the *Dictionary of Occupational Titles* (DOT) during the throes of the Great Depression to help better categorize the fundamental attributes of jobs so that unemployed workers could be matched with appropriate jobs (see U.S. Department of Labor, 1993). In 1990, the secretary of labor commissioned an advisory panel to evaluate the DOT and recommend improvements. That panel recommended the development of a new system that provided technical and scientific improvements as well as a computerized database system that would integrate various types of occupational information. This panel led to the creation of the Occupational Information Network, also known as O*NET. O*NET is an internet-based system that provides job analytic data on a large number of jobs and links characteristics of jobs to individual assessments in a way that facilitates use by both employers and job-seekers (see Peterson et al., 2001). Within the O*NET, occupations are assessed using the Interest Profiler (Lewis & Rivkin, 1999), which is based on Holland's RIASEC taxonomy. In addition, Rene V. Dawis's 6-dimension taxonomy of work values, which is assessed by the Work Importance Locator (McCloy et al., 1999), was used to describe common values for each occupation (Dawis, 1991). Occupations are described on other characteristics such as education required, physical skills needed, and many other aspects.

O*NET is a significant leap forward in the matching of individuals to relevant jobs because it combines individual assessments with occupational information. Converse, Oswald, Gillespie, Field, and Bizot (2004) demonstrated the utility of matching individuals as assessed through O*NET tests with occupations. Specifically, the integration of abilities and personality data along with correspondent interest data along with job requirement data allow for identification of occupations that are consistent with a person's abilities, personality, and interest. The development of the O*NET, its comprehensiveness, and its accessibility have significantly advanced the practice of person-job matching. The work of Holland continues through the internet age.

Latest Methodology of Vocational Interest Measurement

In the early days of vocational interests, statistical theory was just developing with statistical technology lagging behind. As statistical practice developed, vocational interest researchers took advantage of the new insights provided. For example, Strong used exploratory factor analysis to refine his individual scales. As a further extension of the role of statistics, Jackson (1977) used exploratory factor analysis to develop the scales and dimensions of the Jackson Vocational Interest Survey. In one step further, as factor analysis has developed to include confirmatory methods, Armstrong, Rounds, and Hubert (2007) applied confirmatory factor analysis on an old dataset (Guilford, Christensen, Bond, & Sutton, 1953). They found that the data did not fully support Holland's RIASEC model and investigations into alternative basic interest typologies were recommended.

There have been several other creative usages of modern psychometric and statistical techniques to develop important insights into the nature of vocational interests. Structural equation modeling (SEM) has been used to examine short-term consistency in vocational interest, given SEM can help disentangle the effect of measurement error and true consistency (Gaudron & Vautier, 2007). SEM was also used to investigate the relationship between vocational interests and other constructs, such as career choice (Tokar & Jome, 1998) and career indecision (Guay, Senécal, Gauthier, & Fernet, 2003). The ability to untangle measurement error and construct-relevant variance provides an important advance as does the rigorous approach to goodness-of-fit that allows researchers to determine whether hypothesized structures fit the data. In addition, more recent advances in applying SEM-based approaches to longitudinal data and multilevel data will likely provide more insights into the measurement of vocational interests.

Item response theory (IRT) is a psychometric framework that uses a statistical model to relate properties of items and latent traits to item response behavior (see Drasgow & Hulin, 1990). This approach, in contrast to classical test theory, allows researchers to choose between various models and provides rigorous tests of fit to see which particular model fits best (Zickar & Broadfoot, 2008). In addition, IRT allows researchers to use powerful psychometric tools such as computerized adaptive testing and differential item functioning (DIF), tools that could be useful in vocational interest measurement. Tracey (2010) used IRT to develop a short version of the Personal Globe Inventory and delete items with DIF across either gender or ethnicity. IRT is extremely useful in determining how best to shape a test to maximize psychometric information and minimize the number of items, and to identify items that function differently across groups. Tay, Drasgow, Rounds, and Williams (2009) applied a new IRT model—the generalized graded unfolding model (GGUM)—to three vocational interest inventories: the Occupational Preference Inventory, the Interest Profiler, and the Interest Finder, and they found that GGUM showed better fit across all three inventories. This research is important and should spur additional research. The unfolding model that Tay et al. (2009) used relies on a psychometric model radically different from traditional psychometric approaches. Under this model, the probability of affirming an item depends on the distance between a person's latent trait and an item's location parameter. People can reject an item because they are too low on a latent trait *or too high on the latent trait*, relative to the item. This is different from traditional models in which more is always better. This assumption seems appropriate with ability items in which having more of an ability should result in a higher likelihood of answering an item correctly. With vocational interests, however, it may be possible that a person who rejects an item may have too much of a particular type of interest or too little of it. Tay et al.'s (2009) interesting findings should be explored in future work.

Several researchers have applied more than one method to investigate the structural validity of vocation interest models. Nagy, Trautwein, and Lüdtke (2010) used the randomization test of hypothesized order relations (RTOR) and confirmatory factor analysis (CFA) to three vocational interest models with a German sample: Holland's circular model, Gati's (1979, 1982, & 1991) hierarchical model, and Rounds and Tracey's (1996) alternative hierarchical model. They found RTOR supported all three models, whereas CFA only supported Holland's model. Although these two techniques did not provide identical results, the ability of contemporary statistical techniques to compare the model fit of various models has the potential to clarify the underlying structure of vocational interests. Gupta, Tracey, and Gore (2008) examined Holland's RIASEC model across five ethnic groups, Caucasian/Euro-Americans, African Americans, Asian American, Latinos, and Native Americans, using four different methods, RTOR, multidimensional scaling (MDS), Circular Stochastic Process Model with a Fourier series correlation function (CSPMF), and circular unidimensional scaling (CUS). Their results indicated that nonparametric methods showed more support for Holland's RIASEC model whereas SEM-based ones showed less support. Because these studies indicated that different methods might lead to different results, application of multiple statistical methods and investigation into potential reasons for inconsistency were recommended. As methodology keeps developing, we expect that these new methods will continue to be applied to vocational interest measurement. The ability to evaluate goodness-of-fit is perhaps the most useful advance of these various new techniques.

Vocational Interests and Performance

Another area of focus in recent research is exploring the relation between occupational interests and job performance. Early researchers such as Holland and Strong did consider the relationship of interests with job performance, specifically that the congruence between job demands and persons interests could result in increased performance. Advances in meta-analysis, however, provided the stimulation of being better able to synthesize the results across a large number of primary studies. Hunter and Hunter (1984) meta-analyzed the relation between interests measured by the Strong Interest Inventory and job performance and found a corrected correlation of only $\rho = .13$, discouraging future research. Recent researchers, however, have focused on how occupational interests may correlate with a wider variety of criteria. Van Iddekinge, Putka, and Campbell (2011) found cross-validated Rs that varied from .25 to .46 across a variety of criteria, including job knowledge, job performance, and intent to stay at an organization. In addition, they found that vocational interests predicted criterion even after controlling for cognitive ability and Big Five personality traits. Nye, Su, Rounds, and Drasgow (2012), in a meta-analysis of 60 primary studies, found that interest inventory scores correlated with performance and persistence in both academic and work contexts. In addition, they found that congruence measures correlated even higher with these outcomes. These studies suggest that measurement of vocational interests is not only helpful for providing individuals with information that may improve their vocational decision-making, such information may be useful for helping organizations make better hiring decisions. Much more research needs to be done about using interest inventories in this manner, but this research is promising.

Summary and Conclusions

In this chapter, we traced the beginnings of vocational interest measurement to the Progressive Era's urge to improve living conditions, as well as the passion for psychological testing that grew out of the World War I efforts. The history of vocational interest inventories is one that combines a concern for psychometric theory and testing along with a notion for using these tests to help individuals make better life decisions. As can be seen in our brief review of some of the major test creators, they combined these two passions. We believe the history of vocational testing is an area that psychologists can point to with pride, an area where their scientific rigor was used to help improve the lives of countless individuals.

References

Armstrong, P. I., Rounds, J., & Hubert, L. (2007). Re-conceptualizing the past: Historical data in vocational interest research. *Journal of Vocational Behavior, 72*, 284–297.

Astin, A. W., & Holland, J. L. (1961). The Environmental Assessment Technique: A way to measure college environments. *Journal of Educational Psychology, 52*(6), 308–316.

Betz, N. E., Harmon, L. W., & Borgen, F. H. (1996). The relationships of self-efficacy for the Holland themes to gender, occupational group membership, and vocational interests. *Journal of Counseling Psychology, 43*(1), 90–98.

Borgen, F. H. (1986). New approaches to the assessment of interests. In W. B. Walsh & S. H. Osipow (Eds), *Advances in vocational psychology. Vol. 1: The Assessment of interests* (pp. 83–102). Hillsdale, NJ: Erlbaum.

Borgen, F. H., & Harmon, L. W. (1996). Linking interest assessment and personality theory: An example of convergence between practice and theory. In M. L. Savickas & W. B. Walsh (Eds), *Handbook of career counseling theory and practice* (pp. 251–266). Palo Alto, CA: Davies-Blank.

Brainard, P. P., & Stewart, F. G. (1932). *Specific interest inventory*. New York: The Psychological Corporation.

Brewer, J. M. (1942). *History of vocational guidance*. New York: Harper.

Campbell, D. P. (1971). *Handbook for the Strong Vocational Interest Blank*. Stanford, CA: Stanford University Press.

Campbell, D. P., Borgen, F. H., Eastes, S. H., Johansson, C. B., & Peterson, R. A. (1968). A set of basic interest scales for the Strong Vocational Interest Blank for men. *Journal of Applied Psychology, 52*(6, pt. 2), 1–54.

Campbell, D. P., Crichton, L., Hansen, J. I., & Webber, P. (1974). A new edition of the SVIB: The Strong-Campbell Interest Inventory. *Measurement & Evaluation in Guidance, 7*, 92–95.

Campbell, D. P., & Holland, J. L. (1972). A merger in vocational interest research: Applying Holland's theory to Strong's data. *Journal of Vocational Behavior, 2*(4), 353–376.

Carnegie Institute of Technology: Bureau of Personnel Research. (1920). *Carnegie Interest Inventory*. Pittsburgh, PA: Author.

Cleeton, G. U. (1935). *Vocational interest inventory*. Bloomington, IN: McKnight & McKnight.

Converse, P. D., Oswald, F. I., Gillespie, M. A., Field, K. A., & Bizot, E. B. (2004). Matching individuals to occupations using abilities and the O* NET: Issues and an application in career guidance. *Personnel Psychology, 2*, 57–451.

Costa, P. T., McCrae, R. R., & Holland, J. L. (1984). Personality and vocational interests in an adult sample. *Journal of Applied psychology, 69*(3), 390–400.

Cowdery, K. M. (1926). Measurement of professional attitudes: Differences between lawyers, physicians, and engineers. *Journal of Personnel Research, 5*, 131–141.

Davis, H. V. (1969). *Frank Parsons; Prophet, innovator, counselor.* Carbondale: Southern Illinois University Press.

Davis, J. B. (1914). *Vocational and moral guidance.* Boston: Ginn & Company.

Dawis, R. V. (1991). Vocational interests, values, and preferences. In M. D. Dunnette & L. M. Hough (Eds), *Handbook of industrial and organizational psychology* (Vol. 2, 2nd ed., pp. 833–871). Palo Alto, CA: Consulting Psychologists Press.

Donnay, D. A. (1997). EK Strong's legacy and beyond: 70 years of the Strong Interest Inventory. *The Career Development Quarterly, 46*(1), 2–22.

Donohue, R. (2006). Person-environment congruence in relation to career change and career persistence. *Journal of Vocational Behavior, 68*(3), 504–515.

Drasgow, F., & Hulin, C. L. (1990). Item response theory. *Handbook of industrial and organizational psychology* (2nd ed., 577–636). Palo Alto, CA: Consulting Psychologists Press.

Feingold, G. A. (1923). The relation between the intelligence and vocational choices of high school pupils. *Journal of Applied Psychology, 7*, 143–153.

Forer, B. R. (1948). A diagnostic interest blank. Rorschach Research Exchange and Journal of Projective Techniques, 12, 119–129.

Freyd, M. (1922). The measurement of interests in vocational selection. *Journal of Personnel Research, 1*, 319–328.

Freyd, M. (1925). The statistical viewpoint in vocational selection. *Journal of Applied Psychology, 9*, 349–354.

Fryer, D. (1922). Occupational-intelligence standards. *School & Society, 16*, 273–277.

Gati, I. (1979). A hierarchical model for the structure of vocational interests. *Journal of Vocational Behavior, 15*, 90–106.

Gati, I. (1982). Testing models for the structure of vocational interests. *Journal of Vocational Behavior, 21*, 164–182.

Gati, I. (1991). The structure of vocational interests. *Psychological Bulletin, 109*, 309–332.

Gaudron, J. P., & Vautier, S. (2007). Estimating true short-term consistency in vocational interests: A longitudinal SEM approach. *Journal of Vocational Behavior, 71*(2), 221–232.

Gottfredson, G. D., & Holland, J. L. (1975). Vocational choices of men and women: A comparison of predictors from the Self-Directed Search. *Journal of Counseling Psychology, 22*(1), 28–34.

Gottfredson, G. D., & Holland, J. L. (1991). *Position Classification Inventory (PCI): Professional manual.* Odessa, FL: Psychological Assessment Resources.

Guay, F., Senécal, C., Gauthier, L., & Fernet, C. (2003). Predicting career indecision: A self-determination theory perspective. *Journal of counseling psychology, 50*(2), 165–177.

Guilford, J. P., Christensen, P. R., Bond, N. A., & Sutton, M. A. (1953). A factor analysis study of human interests. *United States Air Force Human Resources Research Center Research Bulletin*, 11–53

Gupta, S., Tracey, T. J., & Gore, P. A. (2008). Structural examination of RIASEC scales in high school students: Variation across ethnicity and method. *Journal of Vocational Behavior, 72*(1), 1–13.
Hansen, J. I. C. (1987). Edward Kellog Strong, Jr.: First author of the strong interest inventory. *Journal of Counseling & Development, 66*(3), 119–125.
Hansen, J. I. C. (2011). Remembering John L. Holland, PhD. *The Counseling Psychologist, 39*(8), 1212–1217.
Harmon, L. W., DeWitt, D. W., Campbell, D. P., & Hansen, J. I. C. (1994). *Strong interest inventory: Applications and technical guide: Form T317 of the Strong vocational interest blanks*. Stanford, CA: Stanford University Press.
Harrington, T., & Long, J. (2013). The history of interest inventories and career assessments in career counseling. *The Career Development Quarterly, 61*, 83–92.
Hathaway, S. R., & McKinley, J. C. (1940). A multiphasic personality schedule (Minnesota): I. Construction of the schedule. *The Journal of Psychology, 10*(2), 249–254.
Holland, J. L. (1958). A personality inventory employing occupational titles. *Journal of Applied Psychology, 42*(5), 336–342.
Holland, J. L. (1959). A theory of vocational choice. *Journal of Counseling Psychology, 6*(1), 35–45.
Holland, J. L. (1997). *Making vocational choices: A theory of vocational personalities and work environments* (3rd ed.). Odessa, FL: Psychological Assessment Resources.
Hough, L. M., & Oswald, F. L. (2008). Personality testing and industrial–organizational psychology: Reflections, progress, and prospects. *Industrial and Organizational Psychology, 1*, 272–290.
Hunter, J. E., & Hunter, R. F. (1984). Validity and utility of alternative predictors of job performance. *Psychological bulletin, 96*, 72–98.
Jackson, D. N. (1977). *Manual for the Jackson Vocational Interest Survey*. Port Huron, MI: Research Psychologist Press.
Katzell, R. A., & Austin, J. T. (1992). From then to now: The development of industrial-organizational psychology in the United States. *Journal of Applied Psychology, 77*, 803–835.
Kornhauser, A. W., & Kingsbury, F. (1924). *Psychological tests in business*. Chicago: University of Chicago Press.
Kuder, G. F. (1939). *Manual for the preference record*. Chicago: Science Research Associates.
Kuder, G. F. (1977). *Activity interests and occupational choice*. Chicago: Science Research Associates.
Le Suer, B. V. (1937). *Occupational interest blank*. New York: The Psychological Corporation.
Lewis, P., & Rivkin, D. (1999). Development of the O* NET interest profiler. Raleigh, NC: National Center for O* NET Development.
Link, H. C. (1919). Employment psychology, labor and industry. In H. C. Link, *Employment psychology: The application of scientific methods to the selection, training, and rating of employees* (pp. 376–391). New York: MacMillan Co.
Linton, R. (1945). *The cultural background of personality*. New York: Century.
Mann, A. (1950). Frank Parsons: The professor as crusader. *Mississippi Valley Historical Society, 37*, 471–490.
McCloy, R., Waugh, G., Medsker, G., Wall, J., Rivkin, D., & Lewis, P. (1999). *Development of the O* NET computerized work importance profiler*. Raleigh, NC: National Center for O* NET Development.

Nagy, G., Trautwein, U., & Lüdtke, O. (2010). The structure of vocational interests in Germany: Different methodologies, different conclusions. *Journal of Vocational Behavior, 76*(2), 153–169.

Nauta, M. M. (2010). The development, evolution, and status of Holland's theory of vocational personalities: Reflections and future directions for counseling psychology. *Journal of Counseling Psychology, 57*(1), 11–22.

Nye, C. D., Su, R., Rounds, J., & Drasgow, F. (2012). Vocational interests and performance: A quantitative summary of over 60 years of research. *Perspectives on Psychological Science*, 7(4), 384–403.

Oleski, D., & Subich, L. M. (1996). Congruence and career change in employed adults. *Journal of Vocational Behavior, 49*(3), 221–229.

Parsons, F. (1909). *Choosing a vocation*. Boston, MA: Houghton Mifflin.

Paterson, D. G. (1938). The genesis of modern guidance. *Educational Record, 29*, 36–46.

Peterson, N. G., Mumford, M. D., Borman, W. C., Jeanneret, P. R., Fleishman, E. A., Levin, K. Y., . . . & Dye, D. M. (2001). Understanding work using the Occupational Information Network (O* NET): Implications for practice and research. *Personnel Psychology, 54*, 451–492.

Rounds, J., & Tracey, T. J. G. (1996). Cross-cultural structural equivalence of RIASEC models and measures. *Journal of Counseling Psychology, 43*, 310–329.

Schneider, B. (1987). The people make the place. *Personnel Psychology, 40*, 437–453.

Strong, E. K., Jr. (1927). Vocational Interests tests. *Educational Record, 8*, 107–121.

Strong, E. K. (1935). Predictive value of the vocational interest test. *Journal of Educational Psychology, 26*(5), 331–349.

Strong, E. K. (1943). *Vocational interests of men and women*. Stanford, CA: Stanford University Press.

Strong, E. K., Jr. (1955). *Vocational interests 18 years after college*. Minneapolis: University of Minnesota Press.

Strong, E. K. (1962). Good and poor interest items. *Journal of Applied Psychology, 46*(4), 269–275.

Strong, E. K. (1963). Reworded versus new interest items. *Journal of Applied Psychology, 47*(2), 111–116.

Super, D. E., & Crites, J. O. (1962). *Appraising vocational fitness* (Revised edition). New York: Harper and Row.

Tay, L., Drasgow, F., Rounds, J., & Williams, B. A. (2009). Fitting measurement models to vocational interest data: Are dominance models ideal? *Journal of Applied Psychology, 94*(5), 1287–1304.

Terman, L. M., Lyman, G., Ordahl, G., Ordahl, L., Galbreath, N., & Talbert, W. (1915). The Stanford revision of the Binet-Simon scale and some results from its application to 1,000 non-selected children. *Journal of Educational Psychology, 6*, 551–562.

Thurstone, L. L. (1935). Vocational interest schedule. *Psychological Bulletin, 32*, 719.

Tokar, D. M., & Jome, L. M. (1998). Masculinity, vocational interests, and career choice traditionality: Evidence for a fully mediated model. *Journal of Counseling Psychology, 45*(4), 424–435.

Tracey, T. J. (2010). Development of an abbreviated Personal Globe Inventory using item response theory: The PGI-Short. *Journal of Vocational Behavior, 76*(1), 1–15.

United States Department of Labor. (1993). *The new DOT: A database of occupational titles for the 21st century*. Washington, DC: Author.

van Fridagh Taylor, K. (1942). The reliability and permanence of vocational interests of adolescents. *The Journal of Experimental Education, 11*(1), 81–87.

Van Iddekinge, C. H., Putka, D. J., & Campbell, J. P. (2011). Reconsidering vocational interests for personnel selection: The validity of an interest-based selection test in relation to job knowledge, job performance, and continuance intentions. *Journal of Applied Psychology, 96*(1), 13–33.

Weinrach, S. G. (1980). Have hexagon will travel: An interview with John Holland. *The Personnel and Guidance Journal, 58*(6), 406–414.

Weinrach, S. G. (1996). The psychological and vocational interest patterns of Donald Super and John Holland. *Journal of Counseling & Development, 75*(1), 5–16.

Yoakum, C. S., & Yerkes, R. M. (Eds.). (1920). *Army mental tests.* New York: H. Holt.

Zickar, M. J. (2015). Digging through dust: Historiography for the organizational sciences. *Journal of Business and Psychology, 30*(1), 1–14.

Zickar, M. J., & Broadfoot, A. A. (2008). The partial revival of a dead horse? Comparing classical test theory and item response theory. In C. E. Lance & R. J. Vandenberg (Eds.), *Statistical and methodological myths and urban legends* (pp. 37–59). New York: Routledge.

Zytowski, D. G. (2001). Frank Parsons and the progressive movement. *The Career Development Quarterly, 50,* 57–65.

Zytowski, D. G. (2014). The origins and development of Frederic Kuder's Preference Record. *Journal of Career Assessment, 23,* 686–692.

Zytowski, D. G., & Austin, J. T. (2001). Obituary: Frederic Kuder (1903–2000). *American Psychologist, 56,* 1170.

4

INTEREST MEASUREMENT

Oleksandr S. Chernyshenko

NANYANG TECHNOLOGICAL UNIVERSITY, SINGAPORE

Stephen Stark

UNIVERSITY OF SOUTH FLORIDA, USA

Christopher D. Nye

MICHIGAN STATE UNIVERSITY, USA

Vocational interests are among the most important classes of individual differences in applied psychology (Chernyshenko, Stark, & Drasgow, 2010) and can be simply defined as "preferences for certain work activities" (Hansen,1984; Van Iddekinge, Putka, & Campbell, 2011). To measure interests, one typically asks examinees to rate, rank, or choose between work activities, school subjects, or occupations. Because numerous studies have linked interests to occupational preferences (Campbell, 1971; Clark, 1961; Holland, 1997; Kuder, 1977; Strong, 1943), interest measures are widely used by vocational and career counselors in guiding individuals' choices of study majors, occupations, and alternative career paths. Vocational interests are also gaining traction in personnel selection and classification research as valid predictors of job performance, satisfaction, and turnover (Bizot & Goldman, 1993; Nye, Su, Rounds, & Drasgow, 2012; Van Iddekinge, Roth, Putka, & Lanivich, 2011). Not surprisingly, in the past one hundred years, numerous vocational interest measures have been developed. Readers of this chapter are likely to be among the tens of millions of people who have taken at least one interest measure at some point in their lives, including either the Strong Interest Inventory (SII; Harmon, Hansen, Borgen, & Hammer, 1994), the Kuder Occupational Interest Survey (KOIS; Kuder & Zytowski, 1991), or the Self-Directed Search (SDS; Holland, Fritzsche, & Powell, 1994).

In this chapter, we do not intend to revisit the history of interest measurement nor do we intend to provide descriptions of specific measures as such reviews have already appeared elsewhere (e.g., Harrington & Long, 2013). Our goal is to focus primarily on psychometric considerations involved in the measurement of vocational interests. First, we will discuss dimensions measured by vocational interest inventories. We will review broad factor taxonomies (a.k.a., general occupational themes) and discuss why basic interests have been recently receiving more attention. Next we will focus on the kinds of stimuli and response formats that are used to collect vocational interest preference data. Third, we will mention some psychometric models that are used to scale and score various interest assessments and highlight some of the recent research involving ideal point item response theory (IRT) models. We will conclude the chapter with some suggestions for future directions.

Dimensions Assessed by Interest Inventories

Hansen (1984) and Day and Rounds (1997) noted that nearly all vocational interest taxonomies can be organized into three levels of specificity with general interest factors representing the broadest level, basic interests representing the middle level of specificity, and occupational scales representing the narrowest job-specific interests. Below we highlight some of the most influential interest taxonomies and applications.

The Search for a Broad Factor Taxonomy

The quest to understand the factorial structure of vocational interests has largely mirrored efforts in other individual difference domains (e.g., Carroll, 1993; McCrae & Costa, 1987). The earliest interest inventories, such as the Carnegie Interest Inventory (Carnegie Institute of Technology, 1920) and the Strong Vocational Interest Blank (SVIB; Strong, 1927), addressed primarily applied concerns, for example, documenting the occupational preferences of men and women or trying to differentiate the characteristics of various occupations (e.g., sales engineers vs. design engineers). Soon, however, researchers turned their attention to analyzing responses to interest questions. Thorndike (1935), for example, analyzed Carnegie Interest Inventory data and reported that ratings of sixteen activity preferences were stable over a two-year period. He also noted that, unlike the high correlations observed among measures of cognitive abilities, interests exhibited a more complex pattern of relations, with some interests correlating positively and others correlating negatively or not at all. Thurstone (1931) was among the first researchers to apply newly developed factor analysis methods to interest data. He found, for example, that correlations among interests in eighteen occupations measured using the SVIB could be accounted for by just four factors, which he labeled *interest in science, language, people, and business*. Strong (1943) later factor analyzed four additional correlation matrices, comprising increasingly larger numbers of occupations, and also found that four to five factors, similar to those found by Thurstone, were "sufficient to account mathematically for all or nearly all of the variations in interests among the occupational groups so far studied" (p. 147). Finally, Ferguson, Humphreys, and Strong (1941) factor analyzed a correlation matrix of several interests and values scales and identified three of the four factors described by Thurstone (i.e., interest in -language, -people, and -science). These and other early papers indicated that the interest domain is multidimensional and likely to have a replicable underlying factor structure.

The next wave of taxonometric studies employed a variety of analytic techniques (factor analysis, cluster analysis, multidimensional scaling) and resulted in several researchers proposing comprehensive general factor models of vocational interests. Guilford, Christensen, Bond, and Sutton (1954) conducted a landmark study where they analyzed preferences for one hundred work activities and found six broad interest factors, often called General Occupational Themes: Mechanical, Scientific, Aesthetic Expression, Social Welfare, Business, and Clerical. These factors were very similar to those proposed by Holland (1959, 1997) as part of his hexagonal RIASEC (Realistic, Investigative, Artistic, Social, Enterprising, and Conventional) model of vocational interests. At about the same time, Roe (1956) proposed a circular model of interests including eight factors (Technology, Science, Outdoor, Arts and Entertainment, Service, General Culture, Organization, and Business). Her model was very similar to the RIASEC model, but split the Realistic factor into Mechanical and Outdoor interests and the Social factor into Service and General Culture interests.

Both Holland and Roe essentially based their models on a two-dimensional multidimensional scaling solution and, as was noted by Meir and Ben-Yehuda (1976), were essentially the same models. Prediger (1976, 1982) and Prediger and Vansickle (1992) defined these two broad dimensions as *people-things* and *ideas-data*. Building on their work, Tracey and Rounds (1996) proposed a spherical model of vocational interests that incorporated Prediger's two bipolar dimensions and a third, orthogonal, *prestige* dimension.

Finally, Gati (1979, 1991), after conducting a series of factor analyses, proposed a hierarchical model of interests. He postulated that the highest level of interests had two general factors, Soft and Hard Sciences, which could be progressively subdivided to form any number of hexagonal or circular general factors; and the next level had smaller subsets that could be further subdivided. Individual difference researchers familiar with taxonometric research in intelligence (e.g., Carroll, 1993) or personality (DeYoung, Quilty, & Peterson, 2007) would probably find Gati's representation most appealing, but his model has not received nearly as much attention as Holland's. Perhaps this is due to the influential paper by Tracey and Rounds (1993), who found that Holland's representation was a more adequate fit for 104 correlation matrices than Gati's model.

In sum, it has been nearly one hundred years since the first interest inventories were developed, but the field of vocational interest research has yet to converge on a set of factors to adequately describe the vocational interest domain. Although Holland's RIASEC model is currently the most popular (its 3-digit system, for example, is used to classify and suggest occupations in the Department of Labor O*NET system) and widely supported (Tracey & Rounds, 1993), more studies and frameworks are continuously being proposed to address this important research issue. The lack of consensus may also indicate the fluid nature of vocational preferences. Many activities that historically fell into the mechanical interest domain, for example, are quickly disappearing due to robotization, while those relating to information technology have been rapidly evolving and expanding (see Day & Rounds [1997] for more discussion of the changing nature of work). Liao, Jin, Tay, Su, and Rounds (2015), for example, recently conducted exploratory structural equation modeling analyses using responses to a large set of contemporary work activities. They found a well-defined Information Systems broad factor that reflects interest in analyzing data and managing information including mathematics, programming, and computer tasks. Such a factor was not found fifty years ago and, perhaps, best illustrates why the structure of vocational interests may have to be continuously updated.

Emerging Importance of Basic Interests

The second type of dimensions measured and reported by interest inventories is typically referred to as *basic interests*. According to Hansen (1984) and Day and Rounds (1997), basic interests represent an intermediate level of aggregation of work activity preferences, lying between the specific occupations and general interest factors. Essentially, these can be seen as narrow interest factors, akin to personality facets or specific intelligence factors. As was noted by Day and Rounds (1997), most people actually describe their vocational interests using the language of basic interests such as "I was born to teach," or "I like to fix things."

At the basic interest level, work preference items are grouped into homogenous composites based on some shared property, such as occupational context, work setting, objects of interest, and work processes. There are several reasons why basic interests have emerged as an important component of many interest inventories. First, as was noted by Jackson (1977), early interest inventories reported scores for a very large number of occupations, which could be overwhelming for a typical career counseling client. Also, because many occupations were similar, much of the information provided was redundant. Basic interests organize occupations into clusters, so the volume of information presented to an individual and the level of redundancy is therefore reduced. One of the earliest examples of a basic interest structure, which was developed by Campbell Borgen, Eastes, Johansson, and Peterson (1968) for the SVIB (Campbell, 1971; Strong, 1943), was introduced specifically to provide interpretive information for the Strong Occupational Scale scores.

Second, in comparison to the general factor level, basic interests make finer distinctions between areas of vocational interests, thus allowing for a more precise theoretical interest structure (Rounds, 1995). As a consequence, basic interest models are more nimble than broad factor models in their ability to detect and accommodate changes in the labor market (e.g., emerging work activities and occupations).

Finally, from an applied perspective, basic interests offer incremental validity in predicting occupational group membership, because they "more effectively deal with the reality of a complex multivariate space" (Donnay & Borgen, 1996, p. 288). For example, Ralston, Borgen, Rottinghaus, and Donnay (2004) analyzed Strong Interest Inventory scores from 17,074 college students who majored in 24 different areas and found that the addition of basic interest scores to the general factor scores added significantly to prediction for 22 out of 24 study majors.

In addition to the Campbell et al.'s (1968) basic interest scales for the SVIB, a number of other basic interest models have been introduced; many have been based on factor or cluster analyses of occupational preferences. The most frequently cited primary studies are by Guilford et al. (1954) who identified 12 interest factors, Jackson (1977) who identified 28 primary work role factors, Kuder (1977) who identified 16 factors, Droege and Hawk (1977) who identified 11 factors, and Rounds and Dawis (1979) who identified 14 factors for men and 13 factors for women in the SVIB. Rounds and colleagues (Rounds, 1995; Day & Rounds, 1997; Liao, Armstrong, & Rounds, 2008) wrote a series of papers that attempted to integrate these various taxonomies. Ultimately, they settled on 31 basic interest dimensions and they identified 6–14 markers (activities) that could be used to measure each basic interest factor or dimension (see Liao et al. [2008] for more detail). In Table 4.1, we list those 31 basic interests, together with their brief descriptions and examples of typical measurement markers. Liao et al. (2008) grouped the 31 basic interests into 9 clusters (see the first column in the table), but any other general factor model can be used to aggregate these narrow dimensions. For example, the seven basic interest dimensions from the Physical Activity and Technical clusters would fall under the Realistic General Occupational Theme in the RIASEC taxonomy.

Occupational Interests

Occupational interests are located at the most specific end of the interest range and are often labeled using generic job names such as "nurse," "reporter," or "zookeeper." The number of job-focused, occupational interests measured by most inventories can be very large. For example, the 1977 version of the Strong-Campbell Interest Inventory (Strong & Campbell, 1981) listed 116 occupational interests, Kuder (1977) referenced 217, and the 1994 Strong Interest Inventory contained 211 (Harmon et al., 1994). It is important to note that these occupational interests were actually the main reason why interest inventories had been developed. After completing an inventory, each test taker

TABLE 4.1 Liao et al. (2007) Basic Interest Taxonomy

Interest cluster	*Basic Interests*	*Description*	*Representative Item (Activity)*
Physical activity	Athletic coaching	Involvement in teaching exercise, sports, and games	Participate in competitive sports
	Physical/risk taking	Taking risks and seeking novel situations	Do work that is dangerous and exciting
Technical	Outdoor-agriculture	Working in outdoor settings with animals and plants	Protect crops from diseases and pests
	Manual labor	Performing work that requires routine physical activity	Load and unload freight materials
	Skilled trades	Building, repairing, using tools and materials	Install the piping and fixtures of a drainage system
	Engineering	Developing and using technology to produce and maintain things	Modify an equipment design to reduce sound level
	Protective	Guarding, ensuring safety, and enforcing rules and laws	Search for explosives in an airport
Applied mathematics	Technical writing	Writing for business and record-keeping purposes	Write complex technical information in an understandable way
	Information technology	Using computers and electronic devices for communication	Design a technology system for distance learning
	Mathematics	Working with quantitative concepts and mathematical formulas	Solve an algebraic equation
Science	Medical service	Applying medical knowledge and skills to the diagnosis, prevention, & treatment of disease and injury	Research new drugs to cure cancer
	Life science	Research, development, and consulting activities relating to plants and animals	Learn about the life cycle of an animal species
	Physical science	Research, development, and consulting activities relating to inanimate materials	Study the laws of gravity

(*Continued*)

Interest cluster	*Basic Interests*	*Description*	*Representative Item (Activity)*
Arts	Creative arts	Activities involving the visual arts or music	Sketch a picture
	Performing arts	Performing for an audience	Study one of the performing arts
	Creative writing	Developing and creating stories	Study creative writing
Social service	Teaching	Instructing people	Develop a lecture
	Social service	Helping people cope with problems	Assist people with disabilities to find employment
	Social science	Research, development, and consulting activities relevant to human behavior and social organizations	Learn about human behavior
	Religious activities	Leading spiritual groups, altruistic teaching	Read a religious text
Personal service	Family activity	Performing domestic activities	Take care of children at home
	Personal service	Performing everyday tasks for others	Wait on tables in a neighborhood restaurant
Law–politics	Law	Researching, documenting, and debating legal matters	Research case law
	Politics	Influencing ideas of individuals and governing a group of people in a political realm	Persuade people to vote for your candidate
Business	Professional advising	Advising people in meeting professional goals	Advise people in meeting their professional goals
	Human relations	Arranging positive interpersonal settings within organizations	Meet with workers to mediate disagreements
	Office work	Performing clerical tasks	Perform office work
	Finance	Managing assets and debts	Understand economics principles
	Business	Dealing with structured wholesale and retail activities	Understand the qualities of an effective business
	Management	Planning, organizing, and coordinating the activities of others	Direct the business affairs of a university
	Sales	Selling marketing products	Describe features and benefits of a product or service you sell

would receive a list of most/least suitable occupations and their brief descriptions, and vocational guidance counselors would use occupational interest information to help their clients in the job search process.

To develop these job-focused, occupational interest scales, most test developers have relied on empirical keying of work activity items. This is done by determining the most preferred work activities of a criterion group (i.e., individuals working in a particular occupation or studying in a particular major). Subject matter expert opinions may also be used to identify the likely set of most preferred activities. One consequence of empirical keying is that the resulting sets of preferred work activities can be fairly heterogeneous and, thus, responses to the item sets do not exhibit high internal consistency reliability or adequate fit when single-factor models are applied. For this reason, referring to occupational interests as "dimensions" may be misleading. Many researchers instead prefer terms such as "occupational interest scales" or "job-specific scales" and use test-retest correlations as estimates of reliability.

Other Dimensions Measured by Interest Inventories

In addition to the three kinds of interest dimensions discussed above, interest inventories sometimes measure dimensions from other individual difference domains to aid educational or vocational guidance. For example, some inventories measure perceived efficacy in performing certain tasks. The Skills Confidence Inventory is a 60-item supplement to the SII that asks respondents to indicate their confidence in performing a particular task or school subject. The Self-Directed Search–Form R (Holland, 1985) contains two 6-item sets that ask respondents to estimate their proficiency level of a particular ability or skill.

Other inventories may include a handful of personality or values dimensions. The Jackson Vocational Interest Survey (JVIS; Jackson, 2000), for example, makes a distinction between work role scales, which are basic interest scales, and work style scales, which include personality dimensions (e.g., planfulness, interpersonal confidence, dominant leadership) and value dimensions (personal independence, job security, accountability). In addition, the SII includes items assessing various personal styles. In contrast to traditional vocational interest items, which assess more specific aspects of work activities, the Personal Style Scales assess broader preferences for styles of living and working. For example, the 2004 version of the SII includes a Team Orientation scale that differentiates individuals who prefer to work alone from those who enjoy working in teams. In addition, the 2004 SII also includes a Risk-Taking scale to explore preferences for taking chances versus living or working in a safe environment.

Perhaps the most eclectic interest inventory is the Motives, Values, Preference Inventory (MVPI; Hogan & Hogan, 2010). Its authors argue that motives, needs, values, interests, and personality are closely related concepts. The developers cited Super (1973), who saw values and interests as specific avenues to satisfy their needs, Dawis (1980), who suggested that interests, attitudes, needs, and values all represent "an affective orientation toward stimulus objects" (p. 77), and Holland (1997) who construed vocational interests as the expression of personality in work, school subjects, hobbies, recreational activities, and preferences. Consequently, the MVPI groups all these constructs under the term "motives." For example, the MVPI Power Motive scale reflects "a desire for success, accomplishment, status, competition, and control."

Summary

In summary, a substantial amount of work has been conducted on the hierarchy and structure of vocational interest dimensions. This research has shown that there are both broad dimensions of work activities (e.g., Prediger, 1982) and narrower dimensions (Liao et al., 2008). Although the exact composition of broad dimensions is still being debated (see, for example, a recent criticism of Prediger's bipolar dimensions by Tay, Su, and Rounds [2011]), Holland's (1997) six interest types, which lie somewhere between the broad two-dimensional structure proposed by Prediger and the 31 basic interest dimension structure proposed by Liao et al. (2008), are currently the most dominant and widely used dimensions in vocational interest assessment. The majority of existing interest measures assess Holland's six types to some degree (i.e., either with scales that assess these types directly or by aggregating scales to get scores for each type). Despite the ubiquity of Holland's structure in interest assessment, more research is needed to integrate Holland's interest types with existing research proposing both broader and narrower dimensions. This research may consist of examining hierarchical models consistent with the types of factor structures identified in the literatures on cognitive ability (Carroll, 1993) and personality (DeYoung et al., 2007).

In addition to questions about the number and ordering of interest dimensions, the assessment of interests has also explored both general occupational themes (e.g., RIASEC) and narrower occupational scales. Each of these types of scales has both advantages and disadvantages. For example, although the general occupational themes are closely linked to Holland's theory and have substantial empirical support for their validity, some have argued that these dimensions may be too broad to predict outcomes like job choice in the modern workplace where jobs and the nature of work are changing rapidly (Liao et al., 2008). On the other end of the spectrum, occupational scales may be too narrow, which raises questions about faking (i.e., it may be easier to identify a high-prestige occupation than the activities associated with it) and/or their generalizability across jobs (i.e., an engineer in one organization may perform different tasks than an engineer in another organization). We discuss these advantages and disadvantages in more detail below but, as a result of these issues, we agree with previous research (Liao et al., 2008) that basic interests may provide a more flexible approach to assessing vocational interests in the future.

General Approaches to Measuring Interests: Stimuli, Response Formats, and Psychometric Models for Scoring

To date, several dozen vocational interest inventories have been developed for use in educational and civilian work settings. Some notable examples include the Strong Interest Inventory (Harmon et al., 1994), the Kuder Occupational Interest Survey (KOIS; Kuder & Zytowski, 1991), the Self-Directed Search (SDS; Holland et al., 1994), the Campbell Interest and Skills Survey (CISS; Campbell, Hyne, & Nilsen, 1992), the O*NET Interest Profiler (Lewis & Rivkin, 1999), the Revised Unisex Edition of the American College Testing (ACT) Interest Inventory (UNIACT-R; ACT, 1995), the Oregon Vocational Interest Scales (ORVIS; Pozzebon, Visser, Ashton, Lee, & Goldberg, 2010), and the Jackson Vocational Interest Survey (Jackson, 1977, 2000). Below, we attempt to distill some of the general approaches to scaling vocational interest preferences.

All interest inventories contain large sets of work activity statements, similar to those shown in Column 4 of Table 4.1. Presenting activity statements is, undoubtedly, the most straightforward way to scale interests, as preferences for work activities lie in the heart of the interest construct definition (e.g., Hansen, 1984). Most inventories ask respondents to indicate the degree of their preference for each individual activity; some utilize dichotomous (like/dislike) or trichotomous (like, indifferent/?, dislike) response formats, while many others have settled on a popular five-option Likert response format. Regardless, the response options are typically assigned successive integers and classical test theory methods (a.k.a., total score methods) are used to score respondents. Because activity statements are phrased in a consistent direction, no reverse-scoring is needed prior to computing total scale scores.

A small number of interest inventories have used a forced-choice format (e.g., JVIS, KOIS). In this format, items are shown in blocks of two or three activity statements and respondents are asked to choose an activity they prefer the most/least; scoring is done by summing the observed ranks for statements belonging to the same interest dimension. The main advantage of forced-choice formats is that they appear to be less susceptible to response biases commonly associated with Likert-type formats (e.g., social desirability, halo, acquiescence). The disadvantage is that the resulting scores are often ipsative (see Hicks, 1970; Mead, 2004 for review), which creates difficulties for computing reliabilities, conducting factor analytic studies, and making inter-individual comparisons. Note, however, that many ipsativity issues historically associated with forced-choice measures can now be overcome using more recently developed IRT methods (see Stark, Chernyshenko, & Drasgow, 2005; Brown &

Maydeu-Olivares, 2011; Hontangas et al., 2015), but we have yet to see research papers on this topic involving vocational interests.

In addition to presenting activity statements, many interest inventories (e.g., SII) include supplementary items such as checklists of specific occupations, confidence ratings for various abilities, skills, and competencies, or items describing work styles and work environment preferences. Responses to these kinds of items may be added to activity preference responses to compute the final primary, basic, and occupational interest scale scores, or used on their own for vocational counseling and guidance purposes. Although appealing, adding more item types carries some inherent psychometric risks. Respondents are now asked to navigate more complex sets of instructions, counselors must deal with more and possibly conflicting information, and scoring may need to accommodate mixed-item formats (e.g., reconcile combining dichotomous and polytomous items into a single scale score).

In terms of measurement models, the currently used inventories rely exclusively on classical test theory. To that extent, test developers screen and select items based on item-total correlations, estimate internal consistency reliabilities, and report various scale-level statistics for occupational, gender, or age groups. Factor analysis, which involves an underlying item response model, has been used primarily to investigate the factor structure rather than to improve scale construction and scoring (e.g., Nagy, Trautwein, & Lüdtke, 2010).

However, studies involving IRT models are emerging. Some of them have focused on improving existing measures by conducting in-depth analyses to identify poorly discriminating or biased items (e.g., Poitras, Guay, & Ratelle, 2012; Wetzel & Hell, 2014). Other studies have questioned some commonly held assumptions about interest scales. For example, Athanasou (2001) fit a Rasch IRT model to four-option Likert-type interest data and found that the distances between any two of the rating categories varied considerably across items. Based on those results, he cautioned against summing response category values in favor of more accurate, IRT-based scoring. In another paper, Wetzel and Hell (2014) applied multidimensional IRT methods to a German vocational interest inventory designed to assess RIASEC primary dimensions and found about 20% of items were multidimensional (i.e., had high loadings on two or more RIASEC dimensions). Their results have implications for how dimension scores may need to be estimated, because ignoring multidimensionality in data could result in biased trait estimates. Finally, a study by Tay, Drasgow, Rounds, and Williams (2009) questioned whether classical test theory and common factor models even make sense for interest items. Underlying all traditionally used models is the dominance response process assumption, which posits that the probability of endorsing an item increases monotonically as an individual's standing on the latent trait increases. Tay et al. (2009) suggested that the dominance process is most appropriate for items dealing with maximal performance (e.g., cognitive ability), but, for items requiring introspection (making judgements about likes/dislikes), the ideal point response process assumption would provide a better description of the way individuals respond to interest items. The ideal point response process assumes that individuals are most likely to endorse items *near* their location on the trait continuum, and they will disagree with items that are too distal in either the positive or negative direction. Tay et al.'s (2009) empirical results supported this claim and indicated that an ideal point model provided better fit to data for three vocational interest measures.

What are the implications of the findings by Tay et al. and other recent psychometric papers? At the very least, they suggest that using more complex and better-fitting item response models will lead to improved scoring accuracy. Assuming equally spaced response options, unidimensional data, and a dominance response process can all result in biased trait estimates. Also, as was discussed in Chernyshenko, Stark, Drasgow, and Roberts (2007), the scale development processes may need to be reconsidered, because the rules for evaluating the quality of items are different when, for example, multidimensional or ideal point IRT models are used. In the personality domain, it has been shown that highly discriminating items in the middle of a trait continuum (a.k.a., neutral items) tend to have low item-total correlations; so they are usually discarded when classical test theory methods are used. However, such items may be particularly informative for respondents at high and low trait levels so there is value in retaining them in interest measures (see Chernyshenko et al., 2007). Finally, the use of more complex models could pave the way for computer adaptive tests (CAT) of vocational interests. CAT could reduce the number of items needed for adequate precision by half, which is particularly important when a large number of dimensions is assessed (e.g., basic interests).

Summary and Conclusions

Psychometricians unfamiliar with the vocational interest domain may likely see the assessment landscape as surprising. On the one hand, interest assessments have nearly a one-hundred-year history with dozens of instruments developed and administered to millions of respondents worldwide. The field has generated a tremendous number of papers on the structure of interests and the effect of vocational interest congruence on important work and life outcomes (e.g., Nye et al., 2012). Finally, there is a sizable infrastructure to support a variety of practitioners that help individuals interpret and use vocational interest scores to make educational and occupational choices.

On the other hand, there is still an apparent lack of consensus concerning the structure of vocational interests, especially at the level of basic interests. Also, despite the availability of large quantities of item response data, relatively little advanced psychometric work has been done to improve assessment processes in this domain. The field continues to rely almost exclusively on classical test theory methods, even though published, albeit limited, research has questioned the tenability of many existing assumptions. Finally, hardly any innovation can be seen in how interest measures are delivered. Most inventories are fixed length, nonadaptive, and use text-based stimuli such as activity descriptors or checklists of occupations.

For these reasons, we see a number of opportunities for advancing assessments in the vocational interest area. First, more item types should be explored. One example is the recent work of Wetzel, Hell, and Passler (2012) who used only verbs instead of more traditional activity descriptors to develop the Verb Interest Inventory. Another example is the JOIN inventory (Farmer, Watson, Alderton, Michael, & Hindelang, 2006), which used pictures to complement text activity descriptors (e.g., images of Navy personnel performing selected work activities). Phan and Rounds (2018) also suggested that capturing affective responses to work activities may lead to new types of congruence indices and better prediction of career outcomes.

A second possible way to advance interest assessment is to use modern psychometric models to develop more informative interest measures and leverage CAT technology to increase the precision of interest assessments or, alternatively, to reduce current testing times. Along these lines, it may be fruitful to consider multidimensional forced choice CAT methods (Stark et al., 2005) that may help to reduce response sets, which can inflate correlations among work activity preferences and distort relationships with criteria in educational and personnel testing contexts. It is no longer beyond our capabilities to combine these technologies to create efficient, video-based CATs that illustrate performance in occupational or educational settings and instruct respondents to "select all" or "choose between" scenarios they find most appealing. It is also worth considering whether game-based assessments can be a more effective and enjoyable method of gathering data, particularly among elementary and high schoolers. With informed consent, it may also be possible to use posts and likes on social media sites or news boards to match website users with information about college majors and careers given that this technology is already widely used for targeted advertising.

As a third opportunity for future interest assessment research, it would be worthwhile to explore what can be learned by using factor-mixture models that account for subpopulation heterogeneity and latent profile methods that may reveal unpredicted patterns of responses. Finally, and perhaps foremost, it is necessary to avidly explore the utility of vocational interest measures for predicting academic performance, work performance, and how interest congruence affects psychological well-being. Until recently, it was widely believed that vocational interests have only weak relationships with motivation and performance in employment settings, but as was demonstrated by Nye et al. (2012), focusing on interest congruence can dramatically increase the magnitude of relationships and may help to clarify and advance theory in this area. Also, as was shown by Ralston, Borgen, Rottinghaus, and Donnay (2004), focusing on narrow factors (i.e., basic interest dimensions) may also provide incremental validity over the currently dominant broad-factor measures. In sum, we see many new and exciting research opportunities in the vocational interest area and are eager to see how future methods of interest assessment can be used to improve outcomes for individuals and organizations alike.

References

American College Testing Program. (1995). Technical manual: Revised unisex edition of the ACT interest inventory (UNIACT). Iowa City, IA: ACT.

Athanasou, J. A. (2001).Analysis of responses to vocational interest items: A study of Australian high school students. *Journal of Career Assessment, 9*, 61–79.

Bizot, E. B., & Goldman, S. H. (1993). Prediction of satisfactoriness and satisfaction: An 8-year follow-up. *Journal of Vocational Behavior, 43*, 19–29.

Brown, A., & Maydeu-Olivares, A. (2011). Item response modeling of forced-choice questionnaires. *Educational and Psychological Measurement, 71*, 460–502.

Campbell, D. P. (1971). *Handbook for the Strong Vocational Interest Blank*. Stanford, CA: Stanford University Press.

Campbell, D. P., Borgen, F. H., Eastes, S. H., Johansson, C. B., & Peterson, R. A. (1968). A set of basic interest scales for the Strong Vocational Interest Blank for men. *Journal of Applied Psychology Monograph, 52*, 1–54.

Campbell, D. P., Hyne, S. A., & Nilsen, D. L. (1992). *Manual for the Campbell Interest and Skill Survey*. Minneapolis, MN: National Computer Systems.

Carnegie Institute of Technology: Bureau of Personnel Research. (1920). *Carnegie Interest Inventory*. Pittsburgh, PA: Author.

Carroll, J. B. (1993). *Human cognitive abilities: A survey of factor-analytic studies*. New York: Cambridge University Press.

Chernyshenko, O. S., Stark, S., & Drasgow, F. (2010). Individual differences, their measurement and validity. In S. Zedeck (Ed.), APA *Handbook of industrial and organizational psychology* (pp. 117–151). Washington, DC: American Psychological Association.

Chernyshenko, O.S., Stark, S., Drasgow, F., & Roberts, B.W. (2007). Constructing personality scales under the assumptions of an ideal point response process: Toward increasing the flexibility of personality measures. *Psychological Assessment, 19*, 88–106.

Clark, K. E. (1961). *Vocational interests of nonprofessional men*. Minneapolis: Univesity of Minnesota Press.

Dawis, R. V. (1980). Measuring interests. In D. A. Payne (Ed.), *New directions for testing and measurement: Recent developments in affective measurement* (pp. 77–92). San Francisco: Jossey-Bass.

Day, S. X., & Rounds, J. (1997). "A little more than kin, and less than kind": Basic interests in vocational research and career counseling. *The Career Development Quarterly, 45*, 207–220.

DeYoung, C. G., Quilty, L. C., & Peterson, J. B. (2007). Between facets and domains: 10 aspects of the Big Five. *Journal of Personality and Social Psychology, 93*, 880–896.

Donnay, D. A. C., & Borgen, F. H. (1996). Validity, structure, and content of the 1994 Strong Interest Inventory. *Journal of Counseling Psychology, 43*, 275–291.

Droege, R. C., & Hawk, J. (1977). Development of a U.S. Employment Services interest inventory. *Journal of Employment Counseling, 14*, 65–71.

Farmer, W. L., Watson, S. E., Alderton, D. L., Michael, P. G., & Hindelang, R. (2006). *Improving person-job congruence during the classification process: Item development and initial testing of a pictorial interest instrument* (Technical Note No. 06–8). Millington, TN: Navy Personnel Research, Studies, and Technology Division, Bureau of Naval Personnel.

Ferguson, L. W., Humphreys, L. G., & Strong, F. W. (1941). A factorial analysis of interests and values. *Journal of Educational Psychology, 32*, 197–204.

Gati, I. (1979). A hierarchical model for the structure of interests. *Journal of Vocational Behavior, 15*, 90–106.

Gati, I. (1991). The structure of vocational interests. *Psychological Bulletin, 109*, 309–324.

Guilford, J. P., Christensen, P. R., Bond, N. A., & Sutton, M. A. (1954). A factor analysis study of human interests. *Psychological Monographs, 68 (4), no. 375*, 1–38.

Hansen, J. C. (1984). The measurement of vocational interests: Issues and future directions. In S. D. Brown & R. W. Lent (Eds.), *Handbook of counseling psychology* (pp. 99–136). New York: Wiley.

Harmon, L. W., Hansen, J. C., Borgen, F. H., & Hammer, A. L. (1994). *Strong Interest Inventory: Applications and technical guide*. Stanford, CA: Stanford University Press.

Harrington T., & Long, J. (2013). The history of interest inventories and career assessments in career counseling. *The Career Development Quarterly, 61*, 83–92.

Hicks, L. E. (1970). Some properties of ipsative, normative, and forced-choice normative measures. *Psychological Bulletin, 74*, 167–184.

Hogan, R., & Hogan, J. (2010). *Motives, values, preference inventory manual*. Tulsa, OK: Hogan Assessment Systems.

Holland, J. L. (1959). A theory of vocational choice. *Journal of Counseling Psychology, 6*, 35– 45.

Holland, J. L. (1985). *The Self-Directed Search professional manual*. Odessa, FL: Psychological Assessment Resources.

Holland, J. L. (1997). *Making vocational choices* (3rd ed.). Odessa, FL: Psychological Assessment Resources.

Holland, J. L., Fritzsche, B. A., & Powell, A. B. (1994). *The Self-Directed Search (SDS): Technical manual*. Odessa, FL: Psychological Assessment Resources.

Hontangas, P. M, de la Torre, J., Ponsoda, V., Leenen, I., Morillo, D., & Abad, F. J. (2015). Comparing traditional and IRT scoring of forced-choice tests, *Applied Psychological Measurement, 39*, 598–612.

Jackson, D. N. (1977). *Manual for the Jackson Vocational Interest Survey*. Port Huron, MI: Research Psychologist Press.

Jackson, D. N. (2000). *Jackson vocational interest survey manual* (2nd ed.). Port Huron, MI: Research Psychologists Press.

Kuder, F. G. (1977). *Activity interests and occupational choice*. Chicago: Science Research Associates.

Kuder, F., & Zytowski, D. G. (1991). *Kuder Occupational Interest Survey Form DD: General manual* (3rd ed.). Monterey, CA: Macmillan/McGraw-Hill.

Liao, H.-Y., Armstrong, P. I., & Rounds, J. (2008). Development and initial validation of public domain Basic Interest Markers. *Journal of Vocational Behavior, 73*, 159–183.

Liao, H.-Y., Jin, J., Tay, L., Su, R., & Rounds, J. (2015, May). Finding the big factors in interests: A factor analytic model of basic interests. In R. Su (Chair), *New directions in interest assessment: Methodological issues, debates, and solutions*. Symposium presented at Association of Psychological Science Annual Convention, New York, NY.

Lewis, P., & Rivkin, D. (1999). *Development of the O*NET Interest Profiler.* Raleigh, NC: National Center for O*NET Development.
McCrae, R. R., & Costa, P. T., Jr. (1987). Validation of the five-factor model of personality across instruments and observers. *Journal of Personality & Social Psychology, 57*, 17–40.
Meade, A. W. (2004). Psychometric problems and issues involved with creating and using ipsative measures for selection. *Journal of Occupational and Organizational Psychology, 77*, 531–552.
Meir, E. L, & Ben-Yehuda, A. (1976). Inventories based on Roe and Holland yield similar results. *Journal of Vocational Behavior, 8*, 269–274.
Nagy, G., Trautwein, U., & Lüdtke, O. (2010). The structure of vocational interests in Germany: Different methodologies, different conclusions. *Journal of Vocational Behavior 76*, 153–169.
Nye, C. D., Su, R., Rounds, J., & Drasgow, F. (2012). Vocational interests and performance: A quantitative summary of over 60 years of research. *Perspectives on Psychological Science, 7*, 384–403.
Phan, W. M. J., & Rounds, J. (2018). Examining the duality of Holland's RIASEC types: Implications for measurement and congruence. *Journal of Vocational Behavior, 106*, 22–36.
Poitras, S., Guay, F., & Ratelle, C.F. (2012). Using the Self-Directed Search in research: Selecting a representative pool of items to measure vocational interests. *Journal of Career Development, 39*, 186–207.
Pozzebon, J. A., Visser, B. A., Ashton, M. C., Lee, K., & Goldberg, L. R. (2010). Psychometric characteristics of a public-domain self-report measure of vocational interests: The Oregon Vocational Interest Scales. *Journal of Personality Assessment, 92*, 168–174.
Prediger, D. J. (1976). A world of work map for career exploration. *Vocational Guidance Quarterly, 24*, 198–208.
Prediger, D. J. (1982). Dimensions underlying Holland's hexagon: Missing link between interests and occupations? *Journal of Vocational Behavior, 21*, 259–287.
Prediger, D. J., & Vansickle, T. R. (1992). Locating occupations on Holland's hexagon: Beyond RIASEC. *Journal of Vocational Behavior; 40*, 111–128.
Ralston, C. A., Borgen, F. H., Rottinghaus, P. J., & Donnay, D. A. C. (2004). Specificity in interest measurement: Basic Interest Scales and major field of study. *Journal of Vocational Behavior, 62*, 203–216.
Roe, A. (1956). *The psychology of occupations.* New York: Wiley.
Rounds, J. (1995). Vocational interests: Evaluating structural hypotheses. In D. J. Lubinski & R. V. Dawis (Eds.). *Assessing individual differences in human behavior: New concepts, methods, and findings* (pp. 177–232). Palo Alto, CA: Davies-Black.
Rounds, J. B., Jr., & Dawis, R. V. (1979). Factor analysis of strong vocational interest blank items. *Journal of Applied Psychology, 64*, 132–143.
Stark, S., Chernyshenko, O. S., & Drasgow, F. (2005). An IRT approach to constructing and scoring pairwise preference items involving stimuli on different dimensions: An application to the problem of faking in personality assessment. *Applied Psychological Measurement, 29*, 184–201.
Strong, E. K. (1927). *Vocational Interest Blank.* Palo Alto, CA: Stanford University Press.
Strong, E. K. (1943). *Vocational interests of men and women.* Palo Alto, CA: Stanford University Press.

Strong, E. K., Jr., & Campbell, D. P. (1981). *Strong-Campbell Interest Inventory*. Stanford, CA: Stanford University Press.

Super, D. E. (1973). The Work Value Inventory. In D. G. Zytowski (Ed.), *Contemporary approaches to interest measurement*. Minneapolis, MN: University of Minnesota Press.

Tay, L., Su, R., & Rounds, J. (2011). People—Things and data—Ideas: Bipolar dimensions? *Journal of Counseling Psychology, 58*, 424–440.

Tay, L., Drasgow, F., Rounds, J. & Williams, B. A. (2009). Fitting measurement models to vocational interest data: Are dominance models ideal? *Journal of Applied Psychology, 94*, 1287–1304.

Thorndike, E. L. (1935). *The psychology of wants, interests and attitudes*. Oxford, England: Appleton-Century.

Thurstone, L. L. (1931). A multiple factor study of vocational interests. *Personnel Journal, 3*, 198–205.

Tracey, T. J., & Rounds, J. (1993). Evaluating Holland's and Gati's vocational-interest models: A structural met-analysis. *Psychological Bulletin, 113*, 229–246.

Tracey, T. J. G., & Rounds, J. (1996). The spherical representation of vocational interests. *Journal of Vocational Behavior, 48*, 3–41.

Van Iddekinge, C. H., Putka, D. J., & Campbell, J. P. (2011). Reconsidering vocational interests for personnel selection: The validity of an interest-based selection test in relation to job knowledge, job performance, and continuance intentions. *Journal of Applied Psychology, 96*(1), 13–33.

Van Iddekinge, C. H., Roth, P. L., Putka, D. J., & Lanivich, S. E. (2011). Are you interested? A meta-analysis of relations between vocational interests and employee performance and turnover. *Journal of Applied Psychology, 96*, 1167–1194.Washington, DC: American Psychological Association.

Wetzel, E., & Hell, B. (2014). Multidimensional item response theory models in vocational interest measurement: An Illustration Using the AIST-R, *Journal of Psychoeducational Assessment, 32*, 342–355.

Wetzel, E., Hell, B., & Passler, K. (2012). Comparison of different test construction strategies in the development of a gender fair interest inventory using verbs. *Journal of Career Assessment, 20*, 86–102.

5

VOCATIONAL INTERESTS AND WORK OUTCOMES

Christopher D. Nye, Sarena Bhatia, and Joshua J. Prasad

MICHIGAN STATE UNIVERSITY

Theory in the vocational psychology literature suggests that vocational interests should be related to individual attitudes and behaviors at work. If individuals like the work that they are doing, they should be more engaged (both mentally and physically) in their work. For this reason, early researchers suggested that vocational interests would be "one of the great, if not the greatest, contributions to applied psychology" (Strong, 1943, p. vii). Despite this early enthusiasm and the theoretical relationships between interests, work attitudes, and behavior, the research on these topics has been mixed. For example, many studies fail to find strong relationships between vocational interests and job satisfaction (Tinsley, 2000). In addition, although past research suggested that the relationship between interests and work performance is negligible (Hunter & Hunter, 1984), recent work has found much stronger relations between these constructs (Nye, Su, Rounds, & Drasgow, 2012, 2017; Van Iddekinge, Roth, Putka, & Lanivich, 2011). However, the validity of interests for predicting job performance appears to only apply to some aspects of performance (e.g., task performance and organizational citizenship behavior [OCB]) while the findings related to other performance outcomes are still unclear (e.g., counterproductive work behavior [CWB]).

In this chapter, we discuss the theoretical and empirical links between interests and work outcomes as well as the potential mechanisms for these relationships. The goal is to combine the vocational psychology literature on interests with the substantial literatures on job satisfaction, job performance, and career success from industrial and organizational psychology research. Below, we first discuss the importance of congruence in vocational interest theories before discussing the relationships between interests and work outcomes.

The Importance of Congruence

One of the most influential and long-lasting theories on the relationships between interests and work outcomes is Holland's (1959, 1997) theory of vocational choice. Holland's theory makes a number of predictions about the relationships between interests, attitudes, and behaviors at work. However, a key element of these predictions is the extent of person-environment fit. In contrast to the personality literature, where a few traits have been shown to predict performance across a broad range of jobs (conscientiousness and neuroticism; Barrick & Mount, 1991; Hogan & Holland, 2003), there is not a specific interest type that is relevant to all jobs. Instead, the work activities performed on each job are associated with different interest factors and it is the match (Holland used the term "congruence") between an individual's interests and the activities performed on his or her job that should affect attitudes and behavior. This emphasis on congruence is consistent with the broader P-E fit literature in psychology and Holland's early work on congruence was the basis for organizational theories of person-environment fit like Schneider's (1987) Attraction-Selection-Attrition (ASA) model.

Holland's (1963) original conceptualization of congruence focused on matching the first-letter code of the person to the occupation. However, in his subsequent work, Holland (1997) also recognized that both persons and occupations are complex and rarely homogenous. In other words, an individual may have multiple interests that vary in strength but influence behavior simultaneously. In addition, most jobs require individuals to perform a wide range of tasks and activities that rarely fall under the same broad RIASEC type. As a result, although comparing the dominant interest type associated with both the person and occupation is informative, it creates a narrow and incomplete view of the individual and his or her behavioral tendencies. Therefore, subsequent work has focused on comparing profiles of interests and work activities to calculate congruence (see Brown & Gore, 1994 for a discussion).

Broadly speaking, congruence indices provide a way to quantify the similarity between a person and his or her environment (Camp & Chartrand, 1992). However, given the importance of congruence for the study of interests, a broad range of congruence indices have been proposed. Table 5.1 describes several of these indices, how they are calculated, the number of interest dimensions included in the profile, and their impact (i.e., citation count) in the literature. Based on Holland's theory of congruence, we would expect congruence indices to be most important for predicting employees' attitudes and behaviors at work. In addition, given the diversity of tasks performed on the job, we would also expect congruence indices to be better predictors of work outcomes than simply matching first-letter codes and recent research has provided support for this prediction (Nye et al., 2017).

Despite the widespread use of Holland's theory, recent research has questioned the utility of congruence for predicting behavior. In particular, Tinsley (2000) has been one of the most vocal opponents of congruence, suggesting that congruence indices for vocational interests "appear to be the exception to the generally positive performance of P-E fit models" (p. 154). This statement was largely based on the seemingly contradictory findings related to the validity of congruence in the vocational interest literature. For example, despite strong correlations between P-E fit indices and job satisfaction in other areas of psychology (e.g., Kristof-Brown, Zimmerman, & Johnson, 2005), research on the validity of interest congruence for predicting this outcome has been relatively disappointing (e.g., Assouline & Meir, 1987; Tranberg, Slane, & Ekeberg, 1993). Based on evidence like this, Holland (1996) also noted that "despite the usefulness of the congruency hypothesis, there are some empirical anomalies that require resolution. The most striking anomaly is the general inefficiency of the congruency hypothesis" (p. 401).

Tinsley (2000) and others (Cronbach, 1958; Edwards, 1993) have noted other conceptual and statistical limitations of congruence indices more generally. Although these limitations have a number of implications for the study of interest congruence, the most salient consequence in the context of the present chapter is that the mathematical conceptualization of congruence indices can place limits on their validity (Edwards, 1994) and influence conclusions about the relationships between interests and work outcomes. Recently, Nye, Prasad, Bradburn, and Elizondo (2018) demonstrated the potential effects of these limitations on vocational interest research. Building on previous research (Edwards, 1993), these authors proposed using polynomial regression to operationalize interest congruence and showed that using this approach resulted in validities that were three to four times higher than with congruence indices for predicting both academic performance and job satisfaction. These results suggest that the polynomial regression approach may be a useful alternative to traditional congruence indices.

Regardless of how congruence is operationalized, Holland's model suggests that individuals who are congruent with the occupation that they are in will be more satisfied and successful on the job. For example, interest fit should predict work outcomes like job choice, motivation, job knowledge, job performance, and job satisfaction. Next, we review the validity evidence for vocational interests predicting each of these criteria with a particular emphasis on findings related to congruence indices. We divide this review into the proximal and distal work outcomes of vocational interests. The purpose behind dividing outcomes in this way is to provide a clearer explanation of the theoretical relationships between vocational interests and work outcomes and the psychological mechanisms underlying these relationships. In doing so, we hope to integrate Holland's model of vocational preferences with the industrial and organizational psychology literature on each of these outcomes to identify areas where future research in the organizational literature is needed.

Proximal Work Outcomes

Occupational Choice

One of the most salient proximal outcomes of vocational interests is occupation or academic major choice. In fact, Holland's (1997) model of vocational interests is a model of vocational preferences. According to Holland, a person's dominant interests will determine "the primary direction of his or her vocational choice" (1997, p. 36). In other words, an individual's first-letter RIASEC code will determine the type of occupation he or she will choose. However, as described above, most occupations can require individuals to perform a wide range of tasks and these tasks rarely fall under the same broad RIASEC type. Therefore, a single occupation may involve activities that are associated with multiple interest types and individuals will choose occupations based on the full range of activities. For example, an individual may be interested in Realistic occupations (i.e., his or her first-letter code) but may have secondary or tertiary interests in Investigative or Conventional activities. Therefore, the first-letter code may provide information about the general occupational category a person is interested in but a broader profile of interests will provide more detailed information about the specific occupation that he or she may choose. Consequently, Holland emphasized using profiles of interests and congruence indices to predict occupational choice.

Based on Holland's theory, the link between vocational interests and occupational choice has been fundamental to the development and use of many interest measures (e.g., Donnay, Morris, Schaubhut, & Thompson, 2005; Kuder, 1977; Spokane & Decker, 1999). The assumption here is that the interests of individuals within an occupation will be somewhat homogeneous (e.g., all police officers have similar interests; Holland, 1997). This assumption is consistent with Schneider's (1987) ASA model and past studies evaluating this model have provided empirical support for the homogeneity assumption in the context of employee personality (King et al., 2016; Schneider, Smith, Taylor, & Fleenor, 2007). However, some people have questioned the belief that the interest profile within an occupation will be homogeneous (e.g., Zytowski & Hay, 1984). For example, Dolliver and Nelson (1975) noted that work tasks vary substantially even within occupations, which can result in the within-occupation variability of interests. More recently, Nye, Perlus, and Rounds (2018) examined the homogeneity of interests in two separate datasets and found that the extent of homogeneity varied substantially across occupations.

Despite evidence contradicting the homogeneity assumption, there is still substantial evidence that interests are related to occupational choice. For example, Holland, Fritzsche, and Powell (1994) found that between 48% and 76% of individuals in a particular academic major or occupation had similar interest profiles. In a qualitative review of the literature, Fouad (1999) concluded that between 50% and 70% of individuals within an occupation or major will share the same interest profile, though these numbers do appear to be moderated by age such that homogeneity is higher for older individuals (Holland et al., 1994). In the context of these findings, it is worth noting that the meta-analytic corrected correlation between person-job (P-J) fit (not including interests) and job choice is a very disappointing -.06 (Chapman, Uggerslev, Carroll, Piasentin, & Jones, 2005). With this in mind, past findings on the homogeneity of interests within an occupation seem promising in light of the much lower effect of P-J fit.

The past studies cited above indicate that, in many cases, a large proportion of individuals within a particular occupation will share the same interests. However, there are clearly moderators of this relationship given that, in some cases, fewer than 50% of an occupational sample share the same interest profile (Nye et al., 2018). There are a number of potential reasons for this variation. First, this variation could reflect the complexity of job choices. There are many reasons why an individual may or may not choose a particular occupation. For example, there are a number of other factors to consider that have nothing to do with interest but yet may still influence decisions including pay, availability, benefits, and proximity to family, among other considerations. Other factors like the quality of the labor market or the barriers to entering a particular field may also influence homogeneity within an occupation because they could limit an individual's options and result in him or her settling for a less desirable job (McKee-Ryan & Harvey, 2011). All of these factors could limit the homogeneity within a particular occupation. With these factors in mind, it is important to note that correlations between interest fit and acceptance intentions (i.e., whether the individual would accept the job if offered) are much higher than for actual job choices both for interest fit (r ranged from .36 to .40 for composites of interests; Tracey & Hopkins, 2001) and for P-J fit more broadly ($\rho = .45$; Chapman et al., 2005). In an earlier study on occupational intentions in both academia and at work, Lent, Brown, and Hackett (1994) found a meta-analytic correlation of .60 between interests and intentions. In other words, it appears that individuals are attracted to occupations that they are interested in but the actual decision to choose a particular occupation may be more complicated.

Another potential reason for the variation in homogeneity across occupations could be within-occupation variability in work tasks. As described above, Holland (1997) recognized the inherent variation within occupations and suggested using broader profiles of interests to reflect this variability. However, despite evidence linking interests to occupational choices, congruence is less successful at predicting narrower choices (Lowman & Carson, 2013). To address this issue, Meir (1989) suggested using "specialty congruence" (i.e., congruence with a specific specialty within an occupation) instead of the broader conceptualization of congruence with respect to an occupation and proposed that the validity of specialty congruence for predicting job choice would be higher than for occupational congruence. Other studies have not found support for this prediction. Borges, Savickas, and Jones (2004) examined whether different medical specialties could be differentiated based on their RIASEC codes. They found that different medical specialties had the same interest profiles and that most medical students could fit equally well in several different specialties. These results seem to call into question Meir's (1989) proposal to focus on specialty congruence. Given these differences, more research is needed to examine the utility of specialty congruence for predicting job choice.

Finally, time may also moderate the homogeneity assumption. Both Holland's (1997) theory and Schneider's (1987) ASA model suggest that, although individuals are attracted to jobs that they are interested in, fit perceptions will sometimes be inaccurate and the individual may realize that he or she does not fit a particular occupation only after working in that field for some time. The aforementioned theories predict that these individuals will leave the job to find a better fit. However, this is a process that plays out over time and we would predict that a particular sample from a single occupation would be more homogenous the longer employees are on the job. Although Nye, Perlus, & Rounds (2018) did not find support for this prediction, other research has found that homogeneity is moderated by age such that homogeneity is higher for older individuals (Holland et al., 1994). Unfortunately, there is not a lot of research examining congruence over time. A notable exception is recent work by Wille, Tracey, Feys, and De Fruyt (2014). These authors found that congruence was relatively stable over time, but did not control for the consistency of the environment over time as well.

Motivation

Another direct outcome of interest in one's work is motivation. Motivation is defined as the set of internal processes that directs, energizes, and sustains behavior over time (Kanfer, 1990). Although interest is often defined as a motivational variable (Renninger & Hidi, 2016), the bulk of the research investigating the link between interests and motivation have been conducted in the educational literature, particularly on the topic of student learning. A substantial amount of organizational research has examined the relationship between personality and motivation but interests have largely been excluded from this discussion (Kanfer, Chen, & Pritchard, 2008). This is evident in the fact that there is almost no mention of interests in several recent reviews of the work motivation literature (e.g., Latham & Pinder, 2005; Schmidt, Beck, & Gillespie,

2013), despite the fact that interests are conceptualized as antecedents of motivation (Renninger & Hidi, 2016).

Although the empirical links between vocational interests and work motivation have not been thoroughly examined, the two constructs are conceptually related. For example, the definition of motivation provided above makes clear that motivation has three potential processes that influence behavior: direction, effort, and persistence. Both theory and research suggest that vocational interests can affect all three of these motivational processes (Renninger & Hidi, 2016). First, interests motivate individuals to focus their attention and their behaviors on specific tasks and activities. In fact, interest and attention are so closely linked that many definitions of interest include aspects of attentional focus. Savickas (1999) suggested that "interest denotes awareness of and attention to some environmental person, object, or activity" (p. 24). In some of the earliest definitions of interest, Herbart (1891) noted that interest defines the object of our attention and Kitson (1925) defined interest as "being engaged, engrossed, or entirely taken up with some activity because of its recognized worth" (p. 25). As these definitions make clear, individuals who are interested in certain tasks and activities will direct their attention to those activities. The link between interest and occupational choice described above provides one example of the role of interests in directing attention. Individuals are attracted to occupations that match their interests and will focus their attention on tasks and activities associated with those occupations.

Another stream of research in the educational literature has tended to focus on the effects of interest on attention and learning (Ainley, Hidi, & Berndorff, 2002; Anderson, 1982; Schiefele, 1999). These studies have found that interesting tasks require fewer attentional resources (McDaniel, Waddill, Finstad, & Bourg, 2000) and can facilitate learning by focusing attention on task-relevant behaviors (e.g., Ainley et al., 2002). Although similar research has not yet been conducted in the organizational literature, the research in the educational literature suggests that employees who are interested in the work that they do will be more likely to focus attention on work tasks, which will decrease the amount of attentional resources allocated to off-task demands (McDaniel et al., 2000). This increased focus on task demands is likely to lead to improved performance (Beal, Weiss, Barros, & MacDermid, 2005; Kanfer & Ackerman, 1989).

Because interests focus attention on job-relevant task demands, interests may also increase effort (Kanfer & Ackerman, 1989). The effect of interest on effort was recognized early on in the interest literature (Dewey, 1913) and more recent works have continued to suggest a strong link between these variables (Renninger & Hidi, 2016; Silvia, 2006). Again, much of the research on this topic has been conducted in the educational literature (Ainley et al., 2002; Renninger & Hidi, 2016). For example, Krapp (1999) detailed a study that examined the effects of interest on the amount of effort students put into classes during a semester. Results indicated that interest was correlated .52 with the amount of time spent studying. In addition, research in the organizational literature has also provided some empirical support for this link. For example, Van Iddekinge et al. (2011) found a positive association between a composite of interests and peer and supervisor ratings of effort (multiple $R = .22$). However, more research is needed to explore these relationships.

Finally, interests are also related to persistence on a task. This includes persistence in both the short-term and the long-term. In the short term, individuals will be more likely to persist to solve a difficult problem or to learn difficult material when they are interested in the topic (Silvia, 2006). In the long-term, individuals are more likely to persist in jobs that are consistent with their interests (Nye et al., 2017; Van Iddekinge et al., 2011).

It is worth noting that the bulk of the educational research on learning and motivation has focused on situational interest, which is slightly different from the trait perspective on vocational interests that we focus on here. The trait perspective views interests as relatively stable individual preferences. In contrast, the situational perspective views interest as a psychological state that reflects an individual's momentary reaction to people, objects, or tasks in his or her environment (Renninger & Hidi, 2016). Readers are referred to the chapter by Renninger and Hidi (this volume), which provides a more detailed discussion of these issues. However, studies focusing on situational interests generally do not examine the concept of congruence in the context of the RIASEC model and do not calculate the congruence indices that are typically used in the trait literature. As such, although the findings in the situational interest literature do imply a relationship between trait interests and motivation (Silvia, 2006), more research is needed examine these relationships, particularly in the context of congruence.

Job Knowledge

Given the influence of interests on occupational choice, and their ability to direct attention and focus effort on relevant job-related tasks, vocational interests should also be related to both declarative and procedural job knowledge. Cattell's (1971) investment hypothesis suggests a mechanism for these relationships. Cattell suggested that individuals are born with a certain level of fluid intelligence, which reflects their capacity for learning and maximal performance. An individual will develop knowledge and skills in a particular area (i.e., Cattell's crystalized intelligence) by investing his or her time and fluid intelligence in tasks and activities that are associated with that domain. In the context of work, individuals would develop job knowledge by investing their time and intellectual resources in job-relevant tasks (or in activities related to those tasks). For example, a mechanic would develop mechanical knowledge and skills by spending time actually working on cars, either on the job or in their free-time. Fluid intelligence will set the upper bound on how much knowledge an individual can obtain and how quickly it is learned. On the other hand, Cattell (1971, 1987) suggested that one's interests would define which activities and tasks he or she invests in. As described above, there is empirical support for the idea that interests direct attention and effort toward certain occupational activities (Fouad, 1999). Therefore, the amount of declarative (knowledge of facts, details, and content) and procedural (knowledge and skills that facilitate actually doing the work) job knowledge that can be gained by a mechanic, for example, will be determined by his or her fluid intelligence. However, the choice to pursue a job as a mechanic and/or spend time on the weekends fixing cars will be determined by his or her interests.

Based on Cattell's (1971, 1987) theory, we would expect to find a relationship between interests and job knowledge. Although Cattell suggested a compelling mechanism for this relationship, he was certainly not the first to suggest a relationship between interest and knowledge acquisition. For example, Dewey (1913) suggested that "if we can secure interest in a given set of facts or ideas, we may be perfectly sure that the pupil will direct his (*sic*) energies toward mastering them" (p. 1). Although this relationship was suggested over a century ago, empirical research on this relationship is relatively scarce. For example, in their review and meta-analysis of the relationship between interests, personality, and job knowledge, Ackerman and Heggestad (1997) were limited to providing a qualitative review of the literature on the relationships between interests and job knowledge because an insufficient number of studies were available for a meta-analysis. Nevertheless, a few studies have examined this relationship. Alexander, Murphy, Woods, Duhon, and Parker (1997) examined the relationship between interests and domain-specific knowledge (i.e., knowledge about a particular major) in a sample of 329 undergraduate students. They found that pre-entry interests were significantly correlated with pre-entry domain knowledge. However, the effect was small and interests and domain knowledge assessed again after one semester in the major were not significantly correlated. In contrast, Reeve and Hakel (2000) showed that there were substantial relationships between vocational interests and domain-specific knowledge, with correlations ranging from .27 to .42 for Realistic, Investigative, and Artistic interests. However, correlations between Conventional interests and relevant domain-specific knowledge were nonsignificant and in the opposite direction of what was expected ($r = -.04$). Note that both of these studies only examined the correlations between a single RIASEC interest type and job knowledge. However, as described above, jobs may be more complex and, therefore, a single interest type may not predict all forms of domain-specific knowledge particularly well. More recently, Van Iddekinge, Putka, and Campbell (2011) used regression analyses to create a composite of all six interest types for predicting technical and interpersonal job knowledge. The adjusted multiple *R*'s for these models were .31 and .25, respectively.

In summary, occupational choice, motivation, and job knowledge will be direct outcomes of vocational interests. Individuals will be attracted to occupations that match their interests, will be more motivated to engage in work activities that are consistent with their interests, and will also increase their knowledge related to the tasks and activities associated with those interests. Although much of this research has been conducted in the educational literature and focused on educational outcomes (e.g., learning), these proximal outcomes of interest have direct implications for understanding workplace behaviors and attitudes. In the next section, we discuss the more distal outcomes of vocational interests. In many cases, the relationships between interests and these distal outcomes will be mediated through the proximal outcomes described above.

Distal Work Outcomes

Job Performance

As noted above, Holland (1997) predicted that interests would be related to performance both at work and in school. This prediction is also consistent with theories of work performance. The most widely cited model of performance in the organizational literature was proposed by Campbell (1990). Despite being several decades old, this model is still widely used. Campbell's model suggests that declarative knowledge, procedural knowledge, and motivation are direct antecedents of performance. Consistent with Holland's prediction, Campbell suggested that cognitive ability, personality, and interests were all distal predictors of performance, mediated through the more proximal predictors of knowledge and motivation. As described above, theory and research in the vocational interest literature suggests that interests are related to declarative knowledge, procedural knowledge, and motivation. Therefore, one would expect interests to be related to performance as well.

Despite this theoretical relationship, interests have largely been ignored as predictors of performance in the industrial and organizational psychology literature over the past several decades. One reason could be that early results relating interests to performance were relatively disappointing. For example, in an early meta-analysis, Hunter and Hunter (1984) suggested that vocational interests were only weak predictors of performance on the job, with a meta-analytic corrected correlation of only .10. This finding was cited by subsequent studies as an indication that interests did not contribute to the prediction of performance, particularly after controlling for cognitive ability (Schmidt & Hunter, 1998).

Although Hunter and Hunter's (1984) meta-analysis has been widely cited in the employee selection literature, their findings on the relationship between interests and performance had several limitations (Nye et al., 2012). A full discussion of these limitations is beyond the scope of this chapter, but one of the most striking limitations is that their results were based on only three studies. To address these limitations, two recent studies reexamined the relationship between interests and performance. First, Van Iddekinge, Roth et al. (2011) examined correlations between interests and a number of performance criteria. These authors focused on correlations from interest scales that matched the job tasks and found that interests were moderate predictors of performance criteria. They also examined the multiple *R*'s from composites of interest scores and found that those composites were better predictors of performance (corrected composite-level validity estimate was .37) than the matching interest scales. However, the validity of the regression composites was significantly reduced when the shrunken *R*s were calculated (corrected composite level validity was .18).

Nye et al. (2012) conducted a separate meta-analysis that also showed that interests were moderate predictors of job performance. In contrast to Van Iddekinge, Roth et al. (2011), these authors also examined many of the congruence indices shown in Table 5.1 and the prediction of academic performance. Using a regression-based approach to meta-analysis, they found that interests were important predictors of both work ($\hat{\rho}$ = .20)[1] and academic performance ($\hat{\rho}$ = .23). In addition, they found that congruence indices were much better predictors of performance ($\hat{\rho}$ = .36) than interest scores alone. This finding was significant due to the importance of congruence in Holland's model and in his prediction that interests should be related to performance. However, this finding also contradicted the study by Van Iddekinge, Roth et al. (2011), which found that congruence indices were only modestly related to job performance (ρ = .15). To address these contradictory findings, Nye et al. (2017) conducted an updated and more comprehensive meta-analysis and found that congruence indices were significantly better predictors of job performance than interest scores alone. Again, using a regression-based approach to meta-analysis, Nye et al. found that the baseline correlations for predicting performance (before considering moderators) were .32 for congruence indices and .16 for interest scores alone. In other words, it appears that including more information about an individual's profile of interests provided better prediction of performance.

These findings are consistent with Holland's (1997) predictions about the outcomes of interest congruence and indicate that interests are relevant predictors of job performance. However, the findings from these two meta-analyses indicated that interests were not equally related to all types of performance. Another contribution of Campbell's (1990) model is the idea that job performance is multidimensional. In the previous meta-analyses described above, the

TABLE 5.1 Frequently Used Congruence Indices

Congruence Index	*Scoring*	*Number of Interests Considered*	*Number of Citations*
Dichotomous first letter agreement (Holland, 1963)	A score of 1 is assigned to individuals where their primary interest matches their environment, otherwise 0	1	188
First letter agreement based on hexagon (Holland, 1973)	Scores of 1–4 are assigned based on the distance between the primary interest of the individual and the environment on hexagon	1	4,373[1]
Two-letter code agreement (Healy & Mourton, 1983)	Scores of 1–3 are assigned based on the similarity of the two highest interests for the individual and the environment. A score of 3 is assigned if the highest two interests are the same (e.g. both are IA, or IA and AI). If the person has one of the two highest interests in the environment a score of 2 is assigned. All other configurations receive a 1.	2	29
Z-S Index (Zener & Schnuelle, 1976)	Scores of 0–6 are assigned based on inverse probability of three letter code match. A series of questions is used to assign scores and can be found in Kwak and Pulvino (1982).	3	137
CI (Wiggins & Moody, 1981)	Scores of 0–8 are assigned based on the probability of matching the first three letters for the individual and the environment, with weighting to place more emphasis on the primacy of interest. Scoring rules can be found in Wiggins, Lederer, Salkwoe, and Rys (1983).	3	26
K-P Index (Kwak & Pulvino, 1982)	Scores ranging from 0 to 1 assigned based on a weighted composite of the first through third interest matches. Value of match based on correlations between dimensions from Holland (1973) and combined with the following formula: $X = 7^{-1}(4AD + 2BE + 1CF)$ where A-C correspond to the individual's top three interests and D-F correspond to the environment.	3	69
M Index (Iachan, 1984)	Scores range from 0 to 28 and are based on the sum of weights for matches of first three interests ranging from 0–22. Direct matches between primary, secondary, and tertiary interests are assigned scores of 22, 5, and 1, respectively. When the primary interest of one entity matches the secondary interest of the other, a score of 10 is assigned. A score of 4 is assigned when the primary interest of one entity matches the tertiary interest of the other. Finally, a score of 2 is assigned when the secondary interest of one entity matches the tertiary interest of the other.	3	132

Note. The number of citations is based on the citation count of the original article based on a Google Scholar search.

1 The number of citations reported here is a bit misleading because this index was first proposed in the second edition of Holland's (1973) book on vocational interests. Therefore, most of these citations are unlikely to be related to his conceptualization of congruence.

authors examined the prediction of performance more broadly by including task performance, training performance, OCB, CWB, and turnover. In the most comprehensive and recent meta-analysis (Nye et al., 2017), results indicated that the validity of interest congruence was about equal for task performance ($\hat{\rho}$ = .27), training performance ($\hat{\rho}$ = .26), and turnover ($\hat{\rho}$ = .26). However, interests were much better predictors of OCB ($\hat{\rho}$ = .36). In other words, it appears that interests not only influence how an individual performs their specific job tasks, but also the additional peripheral tasks that may not be directly related to technical performance.

The finding that interests are most strongly related to OCB is important given the proposed mechanisms for the link between interests and performance described in Campbell's model. Although this finding is consistent with past work suggesting that noncognitive characteristics should be better predictors of OCB than cognitive ability (Borman, Penner, Allen, & Motowidlo, 2001), past research on the antecedents of OCB have generally focused on personality traits and the role of prosocial behavior in predicting these behaviors (e.g., De Dreu & Nauta, 2009; Joireman, Kamdar, Daniels, & Duell, 2006). Other research has focused on OCB as a social exchange whereby employees may use OCB as a resource to reciprocate the actions of others (Cortina & Luchman, 2013). In other words, the motivation to engage in OCB is different from the types of motivation that play a central role in task performance. It appears that individuals may be more motivated by the social aspects of OCB than by the technical aspects of the job. If this is the case, then why do interests predict OCB so well? We propose that one possible mediating mechanism could be the enjoyment and intrinsic motivation that comes from performing a task that one enjoys. Interest includes elements of enjoyment (Savickas, 1999). In other words, interest in a particular task leads to a certain level of enjoyment when performing that task. As a result, interest (specifically the enjoyment of the task) in work tasks may provide a form of intrinsic motivation to engage in those tasks. Therefore, individuals who are interested in the work that they do may be more willing to put forth extra effort on a task or to volunteer for activities that benefit the organization, which are both aspects of OCB (Cortina & Luchman, 2013). Of course, the mediating mechanisms between interests and OCB have not been examined so this link is purely speculation.

In contrast to OCB, Nye et al. (2017) found that the relationship between interest congruence and CWB was the lowest of any of the performance dimensions ($\hat{\rho}$ = –.19). In other words, individuals interested in their work were less likely to engage in CWB, but the effect was not substantial. As with OCB, the mediating mechanisms between interest congruence and CWB may be different from those for task performance. Although a lack of motivation is associated with increases in CWB (Thau & Mitchell, 2010), neither declarative knowledge nor procedural knowledge are conceptually related to this outcome. Recently, Iliescu, Ispas, Sulea, and Ilie (2015) proposed a model of the relationship between interests and CWB. They suggested that this relationship would be mediated by self-regulation processes such that a lack of fit would lead to frustration over having to perform tasks that are considered uninteresting. If this frustration is not resolved, individuals would engage in CWB as a way of adapting to their situation and reducing the discrepancy between the individual's desired and actual states. Iliescu et al. tested a mediation model and found support for this hypothesis.

In sum, interests appear to be related to behaviors on the job. Recent evidence suggests that interest congruence can lead to higher task and training performance, more OCBs, and less turnover. However, the relationship with CWB is less clear with some research finding only modest correlations with interests and other mediation studies finding stronger relationships. Therefore, more research is needed to understand the effects of interest (or disinterest) on CWB.

Job Satisfaction

In contrast to models of job performance, job satisfaction is not directly predicted by any of the direct outcomes of vocational interests. Nevertheless, Holland (1997) suggested that a key outcome of vocational interests would be job satisfaction. Individuals working in jobs that they are interested in should be more satisfied with their work. Holland and Gottfredson (1976) elaborated on the mechanism for this relationship and suggested that the mediating effect between interest and job satisfaction is the positive reinforcement that an individual receives in a congruent job. Individuals in jobs that match their interests will be rewarded both formally (through the effects of interest on competence and job performance) and informally (through the enjoyment and positive feelings that come from doing interesting work) on the job. Therefore, congruent individuals are also likely to be more satisfied with their job and a substantial amount of research has focused on the relationship between interests, particularly interest congruence, and job satisfaction. In fact, there have been at least four meta-analyses examining this relationship. Despite the theory supporting this association, the research linking these variables has been quite a bit more modest.

The first meta-analysis examining the relationship between interest congruence and satisfaction was conducted by Assouline and Meir (1987). Their study was conducted to provide a more quantitative approach compared to the qualitative review conducted by Spokane (1985). Although they found that the meta-analytic correlation was .21 (based on 53 correlations), the 95% confidence interval ranged from -.09 to .51. However, this value was only corrected for sampling error and not for range restriction or unreliability. The wide confidence interval for this correlation indicates substantial variability in the relationship. Consequently, the authors also examined potential moderators, the most important of which was the specificity of the interest congruence measure. When studies examined congruence within a specific occupational specialty (i.e., using an appropriate within-occupation measure) the mean corrected (for sampling error) correlation was .42 with a 95% confidence interval that ranged from .20 to .65. However, this correlation was based on only eight studies and a total sample size of 978, which may help to explain the relatively large confidence interval.

Tranberg et al. (1993) conducted an updated meta-analysis of this relationship. Interestingly, they included a little less than half (22) of the total number of correlations analyzed by Assouline and Meir (1987), despite adding six studies published since the first meta-analysis. This was partially explained by their decision to exclude unpublished studies, which could have influenced the results due to publication bias. Nevertheless, they found a slightly lower correlation (r = .17) with a confidence interval that also included zero (ranged from -.07 to .42). Tsabari, Tziner, and Meir (2005) revisited this relationship again but only included studies that were not included in the first two meta-analyses. They found a mean corrected (for several artifacts) correlation of .17 (across 53 correlations) with a 95% confidence interval ranging from -.09 to .42. In other words, they replicated the small effect size found in previous studies with more recent results. However, it is worth noting that these findings were based on only a subset of the results reported in the literature. Instead of including all of the correlations from each primary study included in their meta-analysis, Tsabari et al. (2005) picked a representative correlation from each study that reported multiple correlations for inclusion in their meta-analysis. As the authors pointed out, this approach reduced the total amount of information that was used in their analyses and limits the conclusions that can be drawn from them.

Each of these previous studies indicated that the relationship between interests and job satisfaction was lower than previously thought. However, each of these studies also had several methodological limitations that could have influenced results. For example, none of these three meta-analyses provided a comprehensive review of the literature. Assouline and Meir (1987) examined only studies of Holland's congruence hypothesis but excluded studies that did not fit within this framework. In addition, subsequent meta-analyses limited their analyses to only published studies (Tranberg et al., 1993) or to only some of the studies/effect sizes available at that time (Tsabari et al., 2005). In addition, the overall meta-analytic effects reported by these studies may be misleading because they included both job satisfaction and satisfaction with an academic major. When Assouline and Meir (1987) did examine correlations separately for occupations and majors, they found that the relationships between interest congruence and satisfaction was stronger for occupational samples (r = .32; i.e., the average correlation for occupations and occupational specialty) than in academia (r = .10). However, the latter was based on only 6 studies compared to 24 studies for the occupational correlation. Similar results were found by Tranberg et al. (1993).

An unpublished doctoral dissertation conducted by Morris (2003) attempted to address these limitations by examining satisfaction only in samples of employed adults and including a more comprehensive review of the literature. Using this approach, Morris found a corrected correlation of .24 across 76 studies. Although the overall effect was larger than in previous meta-analyses, the 95% confidence interval suggested that the effect still varied substantially across studies (ranged from .02 to .45). However, further analyses indicated that when a single large-sample study that accounted for over half of the total sample size was removed, the confidence interval got wider and included zero (ranged from -.05 to .52). In addition, this study also included only representative correlations from each study that reported multiple correlations (rather than all of the correlations within a study), limiting the amount of information used for the analyses.

More recently, Song, Wee, Earl, and Rounds (2016) conducted an updated meta-analysis that attempted to address the methodological limitations of the previous studies. They tested a number of moderators and found an overall corrected correlation between interest congruence and satisfaction of .20 with a 95% confidence interval ranging from .17 to .22. This estimate was based on 108 studies, 94 years of research, and a total sample size of 38,870. As such, this meta-analysis is the most comprehensive to date. Given the meta-analytic relationship identified in this study, the authors concluded that interest fit is moderately related to satisfaction but that this relationship may have been overemphasized in the literature relative to the relationship between interest fit and job performance.

Given the emphasis that Holland's theory placed on job satisfaction, the relatively low correlation between interest congruence and job satisfaction is surprising. In fact, these findings have been used by some as evidence that congruence indices, and Holland's hexagonal structure, are problematic (Tinsley, 2000). Although there are certainly limitations to congruence indices (e.g., Edwards, 1993), this claim contradicts recent findings on the relationship between interest congruence and job performance (Nye et al., 2017). Therefore, another possibility may be that interests are simply not strongly related to job satisfaction.

One reason for the lack of a relationship may stem from the fact that interests do not completely fulfill an individual's requirements for being satisfied. Many models of job satisfaction tend to focus on discrepancies between the characteristics that a person wants in a job and what the job actually provides. This focus on what a person wants is more closely linked to values than to interests. This distinction was made by Katz (1993) who suggested that values were more closely related to "feelings and judgments about the satisfactions and rewards that may be expected as outcomes" (p. 106) while interests are primarily concerned with the process rather than the outcome. In other words, Katz viewed values as essential to determining satisfaction while interests determine the means by which these values are achieved. For example, some individuals may value making lots of money in their job but their interests will guide them to occupations that will help them to achieve that goal. In this case, these individuals will be satisfied with their jobs if they make lots of money but a job that they are interested in may be one of many ways of accomplishing this goal. In other words, it may be the case that value congruence is a necessity for job satisfaction but interest congruence is not. This places values as a more proximal determinant of job satisfaction while interests are only one of many ways of finding value in work. This view is consistent with the popular value-percept model of job satisfaction (Locke, 1976), which suggests that satisfaction is a function of discrepancies between what an individual wants in his or her job and what the job actually provides multiplied by their importance. Here, the importance of a particular job characteristic is determined by the value the individual places on it.

Indirect evidence for the importance of values relative to interests was provided by Edwards (1996), who compared two different types of person-environment fit. First, he examined the similarities between the values of the individual and the characteristics of the environment that met those values. Edwards also examined the fit between the abilities of the individual and the demands of the job. These two types of fit have been labeled supplies-values (SV) fit and demands-abilities (DA) fit, respectively (French, Caplan, & Harrison, 1982). Edwards (1996) found that SV fit was a much better predictor of job dissatisfaction than DA fit. In other words, an individual's job satisfaction was more closely linked to whether or not the job had characteristics that matched his or her values than whether the individual had the knowledge, skills, and abilities to perform the job.

Note that interest congruence is most closely associated with the DA conceptualization of P-E fit. As described above, interests are directly related to declarative knowledge, procedural knowledge, and motivation. In this way, interests provide individuals with the knowledge, skills, and abilities (KSAs) to meet the demands of jobs that are congruent with those interests. Again, this provides indirect evidence that the more proximal outcomes associated with interests may fit well with models of job performance (Nye et al., 2017) but not with models of job satisfaction.

These findings suggest an interesting interpretation of the relationship between interest congruence and job satisfaction. Interest may not necessarily affect job satisfaction unless it is valued by the employee. In fact, individuals may vary in the extent to which they value interesting work. Holland's (1997) theory implicitly assumes that everybody values interesting work. This may be true to a certain extent but the rank of interesting work among the characteristics that are valued by an individual may vary from person-to-person

(Judge & Bretz, 1992). So, even though a person may say that he or she wants to do interesting work, he or she may prioritize other job characteristics above interest when evaluating job satisfaction. However, some have questioned the role of importance in determining satisfaction (Dalal, 2013), suggesting that more research is needed to determine the role that the perceived importance of interesting work plays in the interest–satisfaction correlation.

Career Success

Career success is defined as the psychological and job-related rewards one receives as a result of work experiences (Judge, Cable, Boudreau, & Bretz, 1995; Seibert & Kraimer, 2001). Historically, researchers have been interested in extrinsic measures of career success, such as whether a person earns a promotion or a raise in salary. These measures are generally viewed as indicators of upward mobility (Rasdi, Ismail, Uli, & Noah, 2009). In the late 1970s, an additional conceptualization of career success emerged: intrinsic career success (Van Maanen & Schein, 1979). Intrinsic career success is defined as "an individual's perception of their own success (e.g. work role, interpersonal success) evaluated against their own personal standards, age, aspirations, and views of significant others" (Nabi, 2003, p. 654). Career or job satisfaction is frequently used as a measure of intrinsic career success because it denotes how happy one is with his or her position and work, separately from external evaluations (Ng, Eby, Sorenson, & Feldman, 2005; Su & Nye, 2017). Extrinsic and intrinsic measures of career success are correlated, possibly because it is hard to fully separate one's internal evaluation from society's expectations, and because job satisfaction and job performance are linked (Baruch, 2004; Judge et al., 1995; Ng et al., 2005). However, as described above, past research has indicated that interests are generally not strongly related to intrinsic forms of career success (i.e., job satisfaction; Song et al., 2016). Therefore, in this section, we focus on the research examining the association between interests and forms of extrinsic career success like salary, occupational status, and promotions.

Extrinsic indicators of career success are obviously closely related to job performance. An individual is more likely to earn a higher salary or to be promoted if he or she is performing well in his or her job. However, career success can be conceptualized as occurring over a longer period of time because extrinsic indicators of success often include outcomes that are accumulated over many years (Su & Nye, 2017). For example, an individual's salary will be based on an accumulation of factors over his or her career including level of performance, amount of time in the job, availability of alternative job offers, and a number of other factors that may reflect effectiveness on the job. Therefore, although job performance is an indicator of short-term effectiveness in employees' current jobs, extrinsic career success may be more indicative of sustained effectiveness over a longer period of time. In terms of evaluating the relevance of vocational interests for understanding workplace behavior, both short- and long-term effectiveness will be important.

There are two mechanisms through which interests can influence extrinsic career success. The first mechanism is occupational choice. As described above, there is convincing evidence that interests are related to occupational membership (Savickas & Spokane, 1999); individuals are attracted to and likely to stay in jobs that they are interested in (Holland, 1959, 1997; Schneider, 1987). Given that occupations tend to vary on a number of factors such as income, authority, and prestige, job choice may be one possible mediator of the relationship between interests and career success. Strong (1943) recognized this link and developed the Occupational Level interest scale to reflect this variation across occupations. Across five studies, he found a median correlation of .61 between occupational level and income (correlations ranged from .12 to .77).

Other research has also suggested that a broad range of occupations can be represented well by including a higher-order prestige dimension of interests (Tracey & Rounds, 1996). As occupations increase in prestige, they will also provide more extrinsic indicators of career success, such as financial compensation, higher levels of responsibility, and greater authority. Again, this indicates that vocational interests may be related to extrinsic indicators of career success through their impact on occupational membership.

Interests may also influence career success through their influence on motivation. As described above, interests are related to motivation, which is a proximal predictor of job performance (Nye et al., 2012). As such, interests may influence career success through their indirect effects on performance. Over time, long-term sustained high performance can result in higher income, more authority, and faster promotions. However, the effects of interests on motivation may also have a direct influence on career success through the motivational components of self-efficacy and goal setting. Lent et al. (1994) proposed the Social Cognitive Career Theory (SCCT) that relates interests to career goals, which then influence actions and performance. Specifically, SCCT suggests that interests will focus an individual's attention on a particular career path by influencing the goals that he or she sets. These goals will help to motivate individuals by guiding and sustaining their energy toward a particular outcome. The well-documented literature linking goals to performance then comes into play to explain how these career success objectives are accomplished (Erez & Kanfer, 1983; Locke & Latham, 1990; Locke & Latham, 2002; Mento, Steel, & Karren, 1987). Interests, through their influence on motivation and career goals, thus influence career success.

Despite the theoretical link between interests and career outcomes, very little research has been conducted on this topic compared to the research on job performance. While very few studies have investigated this link, the studies that have been done mostly support the idea that interest congruence can lead to success. In one of the few studies to look at the relationship between interests and extrinsic career success, Huang and Pearce (2013) utilized data from the U.S. Bureau of Labor Statistics and O*NET to examine the relationship between the RIASEC types and income. Examining more than 650 occupations, these authors found that interests accounted for over half of the variance in income, with Investigative and Enterprising interests both positively related to this outcome. Realistic and Conventional interests were negatively related to income while the results for Social and Artistic interests were mixed. This study also found that the stronger an individual's interest in a particular type of work relative to other types (a concept Holland called differentiation), the stronger the relationship with income.

Another study examined the relationship between congruence and income in a sample of over 93,000 college alumni (Neumann, Olitsky, & Robbins, 2009). Here, interest congruence was calculated using Euclidean distances where lower scores indicated higher congruence. In this study, a one standard deviation decrease in the Euclidean distance resulted in a 5.0% increase in income. Interest congruence also offered incremental validity above standardized test scores and years of education, providing compelling evidence for the value of interests in predicting extrinsic career success even beyond other important measures.

Finally, in an unpublished doctoral dissertation, Su (2012) examined the relationship between interests and career success in a sample of nearly 400,000 high school students. She found that interests in high school predicted career success eleven years later, with a multiple correlation of .49 with income when all of the interest types were included in a regression model. In addition, results also indicated that interests predicted career success above and beyond cognitive ability, personality, and other human capital predictors.

Although existing evidence is limited, the studies that do exist indicate that vocational interests are valid predictors of extrinsic career success. Again, these findings differ from the results for intrinsic indicators (i.e., job satisfaction) of career success described above. The key seems to be the psychological mechanisms that mediate these relationships. However, to fully understand the differences between extrinsic and intrinsic indicators of career success, more research is needed to examine the mechanisms proposed here.

Conclusions and Future Directions

Holland's model of vocational interests suggests that congruence should be related to important work outcomes. As described above, the empirical evidence seems to support this claim for some criteria (e.g., performance, turnover, career success) but not necessarily for others (e.g., job satisfaction). In general, however, these findings support the conclusion that vocational interests can be useful for predicting workplace behavior. This finding is important, not only because of the potential implications for organizational models and theories, but also because vocational interests have been largely ignored over the past several decades in organizational research.

Although a number of organizational studies focusing on vocational interests were published in the 1940s and 1950s, recent decades have seen few interest studies published in organizational journals. The bulk of the research on vocational interests has been published in the educational or counseling literatures. Although a substantial amount of progress has been made in these literatures, this means that the role of interests in many organizational theories has yet to be thoroughly examined. Therefore, below we discuss several potential directions for future research on vocational interests in the organizational literature.

Psychological Mechanisms Underlying the Validity of Interests

One direction for future research is to examine the psychological mechanisms underlying the relationships between interest congruence and important work outcomes. As described above, a good amount of research has examined the relationships between interest and their distal outcomes. For many of these variables, theories help to explain why interests should predict attitudes and behavior. However, very little research has actually tested these psychological mechanisms and their roles as mediators in models of organizational behavior.

The research on vocational interests and job performance provides a compelling example. Although a number of studies have examined this relationship, very few have actually tested the full model with declarative knowledge, procedural knowledge, and motivation as mediators. Therefore, it is unclear whether these intervening variables can fully explain the link between interests and performance (full mediation) or whether additional psychological mechanisms may also account for variance in this model. Without this information, the mediating mechanisms of this relationship, and others, can only be speculated.

Examining the full predictive model of interests is important for testing theory and for explaining empirical findings. This is particularly important given that much of the research on the relationships between interests, knowledge acquisition, and motivation has been examined in the context of situational interest and short-term recall of information (Silvia, 2006). As described above, situational interests focus more on momentary interest in a particular topic and are frequently examined in the educational literature as a way of describing variation in interest across learning materials. In contrast, the review presented here focuses primarily on vocational interests, which are more enduring trait-like characteristics that guide preferences. Note that the distinction between situational and vocational interests is not trivial and a number of differences exist between the theoretical and empirical work on these perspectives. In fact, some theories suggest that situational interest is a precursor to the development of vocational interests (e.g., Renninger & Hidi, this volume). Due to the differences between these perspectives, it is unclear whether the relationships identified within a situation will generalize across situations or translate into general preferences. Therefore, more research is needed to evaluate the psychological mechanisms mediating the relationships between interests and attitudes and behavior at work.

Basic Interests

In addition to examining the psychological mechanisms underlying the relationships between vocational interests and workplace behavior, additional research is also needed on the measurement of interests. The origins of modern interest assessments date back to at least 1919 in a seminar conducted by C. S. Yoakum at the Carnegie Institute of Technology. Since that time, a number of interest inventories have been developed and are widely used in the literature. Across these measures, interests have been assessed at three different levels of specificity. At the broadest level, and probably the most common type of interest assessment, are measures that are sometimes referred to as *general occupational themes* (GOT), which assess the broader RIASEC types. The RIASEC types were developed to describe broad occupational preferences and each interest type is generally associated with a number of occupations. However, narrower dimensions of interest can also be assessed and are referred to as *basic interests*. Basic interests are more homogeneous dimensions of interest that group together work activities that may be relevant to a number of occupations. These narrow interest dimensions are analogous to trait facets in personality research and a number of basic interest dimensions will underlie each RIASEC type. The narrowest types of interest assessments are *occupational scales*, which ask individuals about the types of occupations that they would be most interested in. In contrast to GOT and basic interest measures, occupational scales are specific to a single occupation and are unlikely to generalize much beyond that vocation. Some interest inventories, like the Strong Interest Inventory (Donnay et al., 2005), include all three types of scales.

Although GOTs are commonly assessed in the interest literature, some have suggested that these assessments may be too broad and heterogeneous and may not reflect the changing nature of work (e.g., Day & Rounds, 1997). Although this framework was useful for describing interests and job classification at a time when employees stayed in a job or at a company for their entire career, these broad interest types are less useful for understanding the current workforce, which is characterized by frequent job/occupation changes and increased overall mobility. As a result, some have suggested assessing basic interests as an alternative to the broader occupational themes represented by the RIASEC (Jackson, 1977; Liao, Armstrong, & Rounds, 2008). Assessing the narrower basic interests can provide both the content specificity and the flexibility required to more accurately select and classify individuals into a broad range of occupations. In this way, basic interest scales may also have an advantage over occupational scales, in that they can be more representative of a broader range of occupations than the occupational scales, which are unique to one and only one occupation.

As with other constructs, a key consideration here is matching the breadth of the predictor and the criterion (Donnay & Borgen, 1996; Fishbein & Ajzen, 1974; Ralston, Borgen, Rottinghaus, & Donnay, 2004). From this perspective, narrower basic interests should be most appropriate for predicting narrower outcomes and occupational scales may predict even narrower outcomes still. However, past research has also indicated that the narrower facets of personality can add incremental validity to the broader Big Five traits when predicting broad criteria like job performance (Dudley, Orvis, Lebiecki, & Cortina, 2006). This finding may be due to the heterogeneity of the Big Five traits. It is possible that the Big Five are simply too broad and heterogeneous for prediction while the narrower facets provide purer estimates of personality constructs that may be related to theoretically relevant outcomes (Paunonen, Rothstein, & Jackson, 1999; Paunonen & Ashton, 2001). The narrow basic interest dimensions or occupational scales may be able to provide incremental validity over the broader RIASEC types for this same reason. In fact, past research has provided support for this prediction and shown that narrow basic interests can outperform the broader RIASEC types for predicting membership in specific occupations and academic majors (Donnay & Borgen, 1996; Ralston et al., 2004).

In addition, in the context of vocational interests, single interest scales are not the focus of prediction studies—interest profiles and their match to the job are more important. As such, matching the breadth of the interest scale to the criterion may be less useful for understanding prediction. Recent research has indicated that a profile of interests and combining multiple interest dimensions will be most useful for predicting work outcomes (Nye et al., 2017; Nye, Prasad et al., 2018). With this in mind, combining basic interests may provide a clearer description of a job and more flexibility for combining different interests to predict important work outcomes.

Interest Congruence

Finally, as noted throughout this chapter, the concept of congruence plays a central role in vocational interest theories. In particular, the most dominant theory of interests (Holland, 1997) emphasizes the importance of congruence for predicting workplace outcomes. Support for the benefits of congruence has been provided by recent meta-analyses indicating that interest congruence is a better predictor of behavior than interest scores alone (Nye et al., 2017). Given the importance of congruence for interest theories and research, more research is needed to improve our understanding of the fit between an individual's interests and his or her job. This research is particularly important given that recent reviews of the person-environment fit literature have excluded interest congruence from the conversation (Kristof-Brown et al., 2005).

In the context of congruence, a number of topics may be useful to study in future research. First, the vast majority of studies on interest fit have focused on a broad range of congruence indices developed to fit with Holland's model of interests (e.g., see Table 5.1; Brown & Gore, 1994). Although these indices have proven useful (Nye et al., 2017), some have questioned their utility for vocational interest research (Tinsley, 2000). In addition, the limitations of congruence indices have been widely recognized for a number of years (Cronbach, 1958; Edwards, 1993). Therefore, despite their potential for validity, other approaches to examining interest fit may be more useful.

One particularly relevant limitation of congruence indices is that they often impose unjustified constraints on the relationships between the various components of congruence (i.e., parts of the individual or environment profiles) and the outcomes being studied. Edwards (1993) demonstrated that these constraints could limit the validity of congruence indices and suggested that other methods of operationalizing congruence could provide higher validity than has been observed for traditional indices. For example, using regression to empirically estimate the relationships between an outcomes and each element of the individual and environment profiles can help to address this issue. Van Iddekinge, Roth et al. (2011) examined the use of regression composites that matched the importance of each interest type to the sample being studied. They found that these regression composites provided higher validity for predicting job performance (multiple R = .36) and turnover (R = -.33), among other criteria, than interest scores alone (corrected correlations were .14 and -.15, respectively). However, in some cases, the validity of these regression composites decreased substantially after accounting for shrinkage in the model (shrunken R's were .18 and -.29 for job performance and turnover, respectively).

Another way to operationalize congruence could be to use polynomial regression. A number of papers have been written advocating the use of polynomial regression as an alternative to congruence indices (Edwards, 1993, 1994). This methodology has a number of advantages over traditional congruence indices. For example, polynomial regression can be used to relax the constraints imposed by congruence indices and increase the validity of congruence as a result (Edwards, 1993). Despite the advantages of this approach, very few studies have used polynomial regression to examine interest fit. As noted above, Nye, Prasad et al. (2018) used polynomial regression to examine the relationships between interests, academic performance, and job satisfaction. They found that polynomial regression resulted in much higher validity than more traditional congruence indices used in the interest literature. In addition, Su (2012) examined polynomial regression in the prediction of career success and again found that polynomial regression improved the prediction of income and occupational prestige. Based on these findings, it appears that polynomial regression may be useful for examining the validity of interests.

In addition to examining the way that congruence is calculated, future research would also benefit from examining the level of congruence. As described above, the concept of interest congruence can be conceptualized at multiple levels. An individual's interests can match a particular task, a job, or an occupation and the question is which of these conceptualizations is most appropriate. Meir (1989) examined these issues in the context of the interest congruence–job satisfaction relationship and found that interests were more highly correlated with satisfaction when the focus was on congruence with the narrower occupational specialty rather than the broader occupation as a whole. Kristof-Brown et al. (2005) found something similar in the broader P-E fit literature. These authors found that person-job fit generally had higher correlations with outcomes than either person-organization fit or person-group fit. However, few studies have examined this issue in the interest literature and, therefore, more research is needed to examine these possibilities in models of vocational interests.

Summary and Conclusions

In conclusion, vocational interests appear useful for predicting attitudes and behavior at work. Despite these empirical relationships, the influence of interests is often ignored in many organizational theories. Therefore, integrating the broad literature on interests in vocational and educational psychology with theories and research on workplace behavior may provide a fruitful direction for future research. There are still many unanswered questions about the role of interests at work and the goal of the present chapter was to highlight a few of these areas in relation to the predictive validity of interest congruence.

Note

1 In the regression-based approach to meta-analysis, meta-analytic correlations are calculated as the predicted scores from a regression model developed using the coded data set. Therefore, we represent these correlations as $\hat{\rho}$. These values should be comparable to corrected correlations calculated using the Hunter and Schmidt (2004) approach.

References

Ackerman, P. L., & Heggestad, E. D. (1997). Intelligence, personality, and interests: Evidence for overlapping traits. *Psychological Bulletin, 121*(2), 219–245.

Ainley, M., Hidi, S., & Berndorff, D. (2002). Interest, learning, and the psychological processes that mediate their relationship. *Journal of Educational Psychology, 94*(3), 545–561.

Alexander, P. A., Murphy, P. K., Woods, B. S., Duhon, K. E., & Parker, D. (1997). College instruction and concomitant changes in students' knowledge, interest, and strategy use: A study of domain learning. *Contemporary Educational Psychology, 22*, 125–146.

Anderson, R. C. (1982). Allocation of attention during reading. In A. Flammer & W. Kintsch (Eds.), *Discourse processing* (pp. 292–305). Amsterdam: North Holland.

Assouline, M., & Meir, E. I. (1987). Meta-analysis of the relationship between congruence and well-being measures. *Journal of Vocational Behavior, 31*(3), 319–332.

Barrick, M. R., & Mount, M. K. (1991). The Big Five personality dimensions and job performance: A meta-analysis. *Personnel Psychology, 44*(1), 1–26.

Baruch, Y. (2004). *Managing careers: Theory and practice.* Glasgow, Ireland: Pearson Education Limited.

Beal, D. J., Weiss, H. M., Barros, E., & MacDermid, S. M. (2005). An episodic process model of affective influences on performance. *Journal of Applied Psychology, 90*(6), 1054–1068.

Borges, N. J., Savickas, M. L., & Jones, B. J. (2004). Holland's theory applied to medical specialty choice. *Journal of Career Assessment, 12*(2), 188–206.

Borman, W. C., Penner, L. A., Allen, T. D., & Motowidlo, S. J. (2001). Personality predictors of citizenship performance. *International Journal of Selection and Assessment, 9*(1-2), 52–69.

Brown, S. D., & Gore, J. P. A. (1994). An evaluation of interest congruence indices: Distribution characteristics and measurement properties. *Journal of Vocational Behavior, 45*, 310–327.

Camp, C. C., & Chartrand, J. M. (1992). A comparison and evaluation of interest congruence indices. *Journal of Vocational Behavior, 41*(2), 162–182.

Campbell, J. P. (1990). Modeling the performance prediction problem in industrial and organizational psychology. In M. D. Dunnette & L. M. Hough (Eds.), *Handbook of industrial and organizational psychology* (2nd ed., Vol. 1, pp. 687–732). Palo Alto, CA: Consulting Psychologists Press.

Cattell, R. B. (1971). *Abilities: Their structure, growth and action.* Boston: Houghton Mifflin.

Cattell, R. B. (1987). *Intelligence: Its structure, growth and action.* Amsterdam: North-Holland.

Chapman, D. S., Uggerslev, K. L., Carroll, S. A., Piasentin, K. A., & Jones, D. A. (2005). Applicant attraction to organizations and job choice: A meta-analytic review of the correlates of recruiting outcomes. *Journal of Applied Psychology, 90*(5), 928–944.

Cortina, J. M., & Luchman, J. N. (2013). Personnel selection and employee performance. In N. W. Schmitt, S. Highhouse, & I. B. Weiner (Eds.), *Handbook of psychology: Vol. 12. Industrial and organizational psychology* (2nd ed., pp. 143–183). Hoboken, NJ: Wiley.

Cronbach, L. J. (1958). Proposals leading to analytic treatment of social perception scores. In R. Tagiuri & L. Petrullo (Eds.), *Person perception and interpersonal behavior* (pp. 353–379). Stanford, CA: Stanford University Press.

Dalal, R. S. (2013). Job attitudes: Cognition and affect. In N. Schmitt & S. Highhouse (Eds.), *Handbook of psychology: Industrial and organizational psychology* (Vol. 12; pp. 341–366). Hoboken, NJ: Wiley.

Day, S. X., & Rounds, J. (1997). "A little more than kin, and less than kind": Basic interests in vocational research and career counseling. *The Career Development Quarterly, 45*(3), 207–220.

De Dreu, C. K., & Nauta, A. (2009). Self-interest and other-orientation in organizational behavior: Implications for job performance, prosocial behavior, and personal initiative. *Journal of Applied Psychology, 94*(4), 913–926.

Dewey, J. (1913). *Interest and effort in education*. Carbondale: Southern Illinois University Press.

Dolliver, R. H., & Nelson, R. E. (1975). Assumptions regarding vocational counseling. *Vocational Guidance Quarterly, 24*(1), 12–19.

Donnay, D. A., & Borgen, F. H. (1996). Validity, structure, and content of the 1994 Strong Interest Inventory. *Journal of Counseling Psychology, 43*, 275–291.

Donnay, D., Morris, M., Schaubhut, N., & Thompson, R. (2005). *Strong Interest Inventory Manual: Research, development and strategies for interpretation*. Mountain View, CA: Consulting Psychologists Press.

Dudley, N. M., Orvis, K. A., Lebiecki, J. E., & Cortina, J. M. (2006). A meta-analytic investigation of conscientiousness in the prediction of job performance: Examining the intercorrelations and the incremental validity of narrow traits. *Journal of Applied Psychology, 91*(1), 40–57.

Edwards, J. R. (1993). Problems with the use of profile similarity indices in the study of congruence in organizational research. *Personnel Psychology, 46*(3), 641–665.

Edwards, J. R. (1994). Regression analysis as an alternative to difference scores. *Journal of Management, 20*(3), 683–689.

Edwards, J. R. (1996). An examination of competing versions of the person-environment fit approach to stress. *Academy of Management Journal, 39*(2), 292–339.

Erez, M., & Kanfer, F. H. (1983). The role of goal acceptance in goal setting and task performance. *The Academy of Management Review, 8*(3), 454–463.

Fishbein, M., & Ajzen, I. (1974). Attitudes towards objects as predictors of single and multiple behavioral criteria. *Psychological Review, 81*(1), 59–74.

Fouad, N. A. (1999). Validity evidence for interest inventories. In M. L. Savickas & A. R. Spokane (Eds.), *Vocational interests: Meaning, measurement, and counseling use* (pp. 193–209). Palo Alto, CA: Davies-Black.

French, J. R., Caplan, R. D., & Harrison, R. V. (1982). *The mechanisms of job stress and strain*. Chichester, England: Wiley.

Healy, C C., & Mourton. D. L. (1983). Derivatives of the self-directed search: Potential clinical and evaluative uses. *Journal of Vocational Behavior, 23*(3), 318–328.

Herbart, J. F. (1891). *A text-book in psychology: An attempt to found the science of psychology on experience, metaphysics, and mathematics*. New York: D. Appleton.

Hogan, J., & Holland, B. (2003). Using theory to evaluate personality and job-performance relations: A socioanalytic perspective. *Journal of Applied Psychology, 88*(1), 100–112.

Holland, J. L. (1959). A theory of vocational choice. *Journal of Counseling Psychology, 6*(1), 35–45.

Holland. J. L. (1963). Explorations of a theory of vocational choice and achievement: II. A four-year prediction study. *Psychological Reports, 12*, 547–594.

Holland, J. L. (1973). *Making vocational choices: A theory of careers*. Englewood Cliffs, NJ: Prentice-Hall.

Holland, J. L. (1996). Exploring careers with a typology: What we have learned and some new directions. *American Psychologist, 51*(4), 397–406.

Holland, J. L. (1997). *Making vocational choices: A theory of vocational personalities and work environments*. Odessa, FL: Psychological Assessment Resources.

Holland, J. L. & Gottfredson, G. D. (1976). Using a typology of persons and environments to explain careers: Some extensions and clarifications. *The Counseling Psychologist, 6*, 20–29.

Holland, J. L., Fritzsche, B. A., & Powell, A. B. (1994). *The self-directed search (SDS): Technical manual*. Odessa, FL: Psychological Assessment Resources.

Huang, J. L., & Pearce, M. (2013). The other side of the coin: Vocational interests, interest differentiation and annual income at the occupation level of analysis. *Journal of Vocational Behavior, 83*(3), 315–326.

Hunter, J. E., & Hunter, R. F. (1984). Validity and utility of alternative predictors of job performance. *Psychological Bulletin, 96*(1), 72–98.

Hunter, J. E., & Schmidt, F. L. (2004). *Methods of meta-analysis: Correcting error and bias in research findings*. Newbury Park, CA: Sage.

Iachan, R. (1984). A measure of agreement for use with the Holland classification system. *Journal of Vocational Behavior, 24*(2), 133–141.

Iliescu, D., Ispas, D., Sulea, C., & Ilies, A. (2015). Vocational fit and counterproductive work behaviors: A self-regulation perspective. *Journal of Applied Psychology, 100*(1), 21–39.

Jackson, D. N. (1977). *Manual for the Jackson Vocational Interest Survey*. Port Huron, MI: Research Psychologist Press.

Joireman, J., Kamdar, D., Daniels, D., & Duell, B. (2006). Good citizens to the end? It depends: Empathy and concern with future consequences moderate the impact of a short-term time horizon on organizational citizenship behaviors. *Journal of Applied Psychology, 91*(6), 1307–1320.

Judge, T. A., & Bretz, R. D. (1992). Effects of work values on job choice decisions. *Journal of Applied Psychology*, 77(3), 261–271.

Judge, T. A., Cable, D. M., Boudreau, J. W., & Bretz, R. D. (1995). An empirical investigation of the predictors of executive career success. *Personnel Psychology, 48*(3), 485–519.

Kanfer, R. (1990). Motivation theory and industrial and organizational psychology. In M. D. Dunnette & L. Hough (Eds.), *Handbook of industrial and organizational psychology*, (Vol. 1, pp. 75–130) Palo Alto, CA: Consulting Psychologists Press.

Kanfer, R., & Ackerman, P. L. (1989). Motivation and cognitive abilities: An integrative/aptitude-treatment interaction approach to skill acquisition. *Journal of Applied Psychology, 74*(4), 657–690.

Kanfer, R., Chen, G., & Pritchard, R. D. (2008). Work motivation: Forging new perspectives and directions in the post-millennium. In R. Kanfer, G. Chen, & R.D. Pritchard (Eds.), *Work motivation: Past, present, and future* (pp. 601–632). New York: Routledge.

Katz, M. R. (1993). *Computer-assisted career decision making*. Hillsdale, NJ: Erlbaum.
King, D. D., Ott-Holland, C. J., Ryan, A. M., Huang, J. L., Wadlington, P. L., & Elizondo, F. (2016). Personality homogeneity in organizations and occupations: Considering similarity sources. *Journal of Business and Psychology*, 1–13.
Kitson, H. D. (1925). *The psychology of vocational adjustment*. Oxford, England: Lippincott.
Krapp, A. (1999). Interest, motivation and learning: An educational-psychological perspective. *European Journal of Psychology of Education, 1*, 23–40.
Kristof-Brown, A. L., Zimmerman, R. D., & Johnson, E. C. (2005). Consequences of individual's fit at work: A meta-analysis of person-job, person-organization, person-group, and person-supervisor fit. *Personnel Psychology, 58*(2), 281–342.
Kuder, F. (1977). *Activity interests and occupational choice*. Chicago: Science Research Associates.
Kwak. J. C, & Pulvino, C. J. (1982). A mathematical model for comparing Holland's personality and environmental codes. *Journal of Vocational Behavior, 21*(2), 231–241.
Latham, G. P., & Pinder, C. C. (2005). Work motivation theory and research at the dawn of the twenty-first century. *Annual Review of Psychology, 56*, 485–516.
Lent, R. W., Brown, S. D., & Hackett, G. (1994). Toward a unifying social cognitive theory of career and academic interest, choice, and performance. *Journal of Vocational Behavior, 45*(1), 79–122.
Liao, H. Y., Armstrong, P. I., & Rounds, J. (2008). Development and initial validation of public domain Basic Interest Markers. *Journal of Vocational Behavior, 73*(1), 159–183.
Locke, E. A. (1976). The nature and causes of job satisfaction. In M. D. Dunnette (Ed.), *Handbook of industrial and organizational psychology* (pp. 1297–1347). Chicago: Rand McNally.
Locke, E. A., & Latham, G. P. (1990). *A theory of goal setting & task performance*. Englewood Cliffs, NJ: Prentice-Hall.
Locke, E. A., & Latham, G. P. (2002). Building a practically useful theory of goal setting and task motivation: A 35-year odyssey. *American Psychologist, 57*(9), 705–717.
Lowman, R. L. & Carson, A.D. (2013). Conceptualization and assessment of interests. In J. Graham & J. Naglieri (Eds.), *Handbook of psychology, Assessment psychology* (2nd ed., pp. 534–557), New York: Wiley.
McDaniel, M. A., Waddill, P. J., Finstad, K., & Bourg, T. (2000). The effects of text-based interest on attention and recall. *Journal of Educational Psychology, 92*(3), 492–502.
McKee-Ryan, F. M., & Harvey, J. (2011). "I have a job, but...": A review of underemployment. *Journal of Management, 37*(4), 962–996.
Meir, E. I. (1989). Integrative elaboration of the congruence theory. *Journal of Vocational Behavior, 35*(2), 219–230.
Mento, A. J., Steel, R. P., & Karren, R. J. (1987). A meta-analytic study of the effects of goal setting on task performance: 1966–1984. *Organizational Behavior and Human Decision Processes, 39*(1), 52–83.
Morris, M. A. (2003). *A meta-analytic investigation of vocational interest-based job fit, and its relationship to job satisfaction, performance, and turnover* (Doctoral dissertation). Retrieved from ProQuest Information & Learning. (UMI No. 3089788)
Nabi, G. R. (2003). Situational characteristics and subjective career success: The mediating role of career-enhancing strategies. *International Journal of Manpower, 24*(6), 653–672.

Neumann, G., Olitsky, N., & Robbins, S. (2009). Job congruence, academic achievement, and earnings. *Labour Economics, 16*(5), 503–509.

Ng, T. W., Eby, L. T., Sorensen, K. L., & Feldman, D. C. (2005). Predictors of objective and subjective career success: A meta-analysis. *Personnel Psychology, 58*(2), 367–408.

Nye, C. D., Perlus, J. G., & Rounds, J. (2018). Do ornithologists flock together? Examining the homogeneity of interests in occupations. *Journal of Vocational Behavior, 107*, 195–208.

Nye, C. D., Prasad, J. J., Bradburn, J., Elizondo, F., (2018). Improving the operationalization of interest congruence using polynomial regression. *Journal of Vocational Behavior, 104*, 154–169.

Nye, C. D., Su, R., Rounds, J., & Drasgow, F. (2012). Vocational interests and performance: A quantitative summary of over 60 years of research. *Perspectives on Psychological Science*, 7(4), 384–403.

Nye, C. D., Su, R., Rounds, J., & Drasgow, F. (2017). Interest congruence and performance: Revisiting recent meta-analytic findings. *Journal of Vocational Behavior, 98*, 138–151.

Paunonen, S. V., & Ashton, M. C. (2001). Big Five factors and facets and the prediction of behavior. *Journal of Personality and Social Psychology, 81*(3), 524–539.

Paunonen, S. V., Rothstein, M. G., & Jackson, D. N. (1999). Narrow reasoning about the use of broad personality measures for personnel selection. *Journal of Organizational Behavior, 20*(3), 389–405.

Ralston, C. A., Borgen, F. H., Rottinghaus, P. J., & Donnay, D. A. (2004). Specificity in interest measurement: Basic Interest Scales and major field of study. *Journal of Vocational Behavior, 65*, 203–216.

Rasdi, R. M., Ismail, M., Uli, J., & Noah, S. M. (2009). Towards developing a theoretical framework for measuring public sector managers' career success. *Journal of European Industrial Training, 33*(3), 232–254.

Reeve, C. L., & Hakel, M. D. (2000). Toward an understanding of adult intellectual development: Investigating within-individual convergence of interest and knowledge profiles. *Journal of Applied Psychology, 85*(6), 897–908.

Renninger, K. A., & Hidi, S. E. (2016). *The power of interest for motivation and engagement.* New York: Routledge.

Savickas, M. L. (1999). The psychology of interests. In M. L. Savickas & A. R. Spokane (Eds.), *Vocational interests: Meaning, measurement, and counseling use* (pp. 19–56). Palo Alto, CA: Davies–Black.

Savickas, M. L., & Spokane, A. R. (1999). *Vocational interests: Meaning, measurement, and counseling use.* Davies-Black.

Schiefele, U. (1999). Interest and learning from text. *Scientific Studies of Reading, 3*(3), 257–279.

Schmidt, A. M., Beck, J. W., & Gillespie, J. Z. (2013). Motivation. In N. W. Schmitt, S. Highhouse, & I. Weiner (Eds.), *Handbook of psychology. Vol. 12: Industrial and organizational psychology* (2nd ed., pp. 311–340). Hoboken, NJ: Wiley.

Schmidt, F. L., & Hunter, J. E. (1998). The validity and utility of selection methods in personnel psychology: Practical and theoretical implications of 85 years of research findings. *Psychological Bulletin, 124*(2), 262–274.

Schneider, B. (1987). The people make the place. *Personnel Psychology, 40*(3), 437–453.

Schneider, B., Smith, D. B., Taylor, S., & Fleenor, J. (1998). Personality and organizations: A test of the homogeneity of personality hypothesis. *Journal of Applied Psychology, 83*(3), 462–470.

Seibert, S. E., & Kraimer, M. L. (2001). The five-factor model of personality and career success. *Journal of Vocational Behavior, 58*(1), 1–21.
Silvia, P. J. (2006). *Exploring the psychology of interest.* New York: Oxford University Press.
Song, C., Wee, C., Earl, K., & Rounds, J. (April, 2016). In C. D. Nye (Chair), *Advancing the validity of vocational interests in the workplace.* Symposium presented at the 31st annual conference of the Society for Industrial and Organizational Psychology, Anaheim, CA.
Spokane, A. R. (1985). A review of research on person-environment congruence in Holland's theory of careers. *Journal of Vocational Behavior, 26*(3), 306–343.
Spokane, A. R., & Decker, A. R. (1999). Expressed and measured interests. In M. L. Savickas & A. R Spokane (Eds.), *Vocational interests: Meaning, measurement, and counseling use* (pp. 211–233). Palo Alto, CA: Davies–Black.
Strong, E. K. (1943). *Vocational interests of men and women.* Stanford, CA: Stanford University Press.
Su, R. (2012). *The power of vocational interests and interest congruence in predicting career success* (Unpublished doctoral dissertation). University of Illinois at Urbana-Champaign. Retrieved from http://hdl.handle.net/2142/34329
Su, R., & Nye, C. D. (2017). Interests and person-environment fit: A new perspective on workforce readiness and success. In J. Burrus, K. D. Mattern, B. Naemi, & R. D. Roberts (Eds.), *Building better students: Preparation for the workforce* (pp. 177–206). New York: Oxford University.
Thau, S., & Mitchell, M. S. (2010). Self-gain or self-regulation impairment? Tests of competing explanations of the supervisor abuse and employee deviance relationship through perceptions of distributive justice. *Journal of Applied Psychology, 95*(6), 1009–1031.
Tinsley, H. E. A. (2000). The congruence myth revisited. *Journal of Vocational Behavior, 56*(3), 405–423.
Tracey, T. J., & Hopkins, N. (2001). Correspondence of interests and abilities with occupational choice. *Journal of Counseling Psychology, 48*(2), 178–189.
Tracey, T. J., & Rounds, J. (1996). The spherical representation of vocational interests. *Journal of Vocational Behavior, 48*(1), 3–41.
Tranberg, M., Slane, S., & Ekeberg, S. E. (1993). The relation between interest congruence and satisfaction: A meta-analysis. *Journal of Vocational Behavior, 42*(3), 253–264.
Tsabari, O., Tziner, A., & Meir, E. I. (2005). Updated meta-analysis on the relationship between congruence and satisfaction. *Journal of Career Assessment, 13*(2), 216–232.
Van Iddekinge, C. H., Putka, D. J., & Campbell, J. P. (2011). Reconsidering vocational interests for personnel selection: The validity of an interest-based selection test in relation to job knowledge, job performance, and continuance intentions. *Journal of Applied Psychology, 96*(1), 13–33.
Van Iddekinge, C. H., Roth, P. L., Putka, D. J., & Lanivich, S. E. (2011). Are you interested? A meta-analysis of relations between vocational interests and employee performance and turnover. *Journal of Applied Psychology, 96*(6), 1167–1194.
Van Maanen, J., & Schein, E.H. (1979). Toward a theory of organizational socialization. In B. M. Staw (Ed.), *Research in organizational behavior* (Vol. 1, pp. 209–264). Greenwich, CT: JAI Press.
Wiggins, J. D., Lederer, D. A., Salkowe, A., & Rys. G. S. (1983). Job satisfaction related to tester congruence and differentiation. *Journal of Vocational Behavior, 23*(1), 112–121.

Wiggins, J. D., & Moody, A. (1981). *Compatibility index description*. Dover, DE: Training and Associates.

Wille, B., Tracey, T. J., Feys, M., & De Fruyt, F. (2014). A longitudinal and multi-method examination of interest–occupation congruence within and across time. *Journal of Vocational Behavior, 84*(1), 59–73.

Zener, T. B., & Schnuelle, L. (1976). Effects of the self-directed search on high school students. *Journal of Counseling Psychology, 23(4),* 353–359.

Zytowski, D. G., & Hay, R. (1984). Do birds of a feather flock together? A test of the similarities within and the differences between five occupations. *Journal of Vocational Behavior, 24*(2), 242–248.

6

PERSONNEL SELECTION AND VOCATIONAL INTERESTS

Recent Research and Future Directions

Frederick L. Oswald

RICE UNIVERSITY

Leaetta M. Hough

THE DUNNETTE GROUP

Chen Zuo

RICE UNIVERSITY

Many of us (present authors included) reached our current jobs by variously walking, skipping, and staggering through our occupational development. A high school biology teacher might turn you away from an interest in medicine—forever. You might watch a TV show about dangerous jobs, where some of those actually seem interesting and realistic to pursue. On the job, you might meet after work with your colleagues to work on electronics projects that grow your knowledge and stimulate further interests. To some extent, all of these scenarios reflect a range of *vocational interests* (e.g., Realistic, Investigative, Artistic, Social, Enterprising and Conventional [RIASEC] interests) that come to light as a function of the person selecting and interacting with the situation at hand.

For decades, research and application involving vocational interests have fallen within the purview of career counselors and counseling researchers, who ultimately seek to inform students of their occupational potential and occupational choices. Interests pervade the cycle of education and work, long before someone becomes a job applicant (Figure 6.1). As early as kindergarten, vocational information is deliberately conveyed to children in the classroom. One of the reasons to do so (among others) is to develop an early and broad classroom interest in the STEM fields (i.e., science, technology, engineering, and math), that ideally will strengthen, leading to greater STEM-related confidence and competencies as one enters college (Le, Robbins, & Westrick, 2014), with the long-term hopes of increasing economic competitiveness and prosperity at a national level. We know with great certainty that students' vocational interests, even more than a decade later, can reliably predict occupational choice (Austin & Hansich, 1990), employment status, and income (Stoll et al., 2017). Although much is known about the predictive value of an individual's vocational interests, we need a better understanding of the developmental process of interests (in STEM and otherwise) that shape a student's educational and career pursuits long before personnel selection enters into this process. Theories of vocational interest describe how general factors such as occupational exposure (e.g., in the classroom, at home, with peers, and in the media), and a strong sense of a career as a calling (Kaminsky & Behrend, 2015), translate into individuals' later decisions and commitments over time that lead to gaining deeper occupational knowledge and skill (Hidi & Renninger, 2006). A little occupational or vocational knowledge early on can go a long way to shape interests—in tandem with information from guidance counselors, parents, and peers—to enhance a variety of behaviors and strategies when students are readying themselves for success in school and the workplace (e.g., course taking, extracurricular activities technical training, choice of college major, job search).

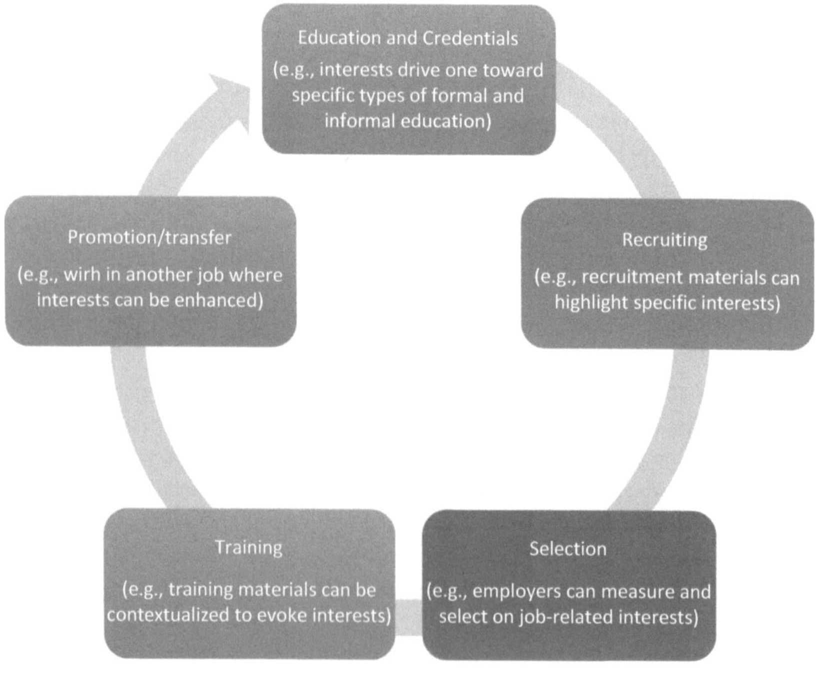

FIGURE 6.1 Interests Permeate the Education and Employment Cycle.

In this context, measures of vocational interests usually report information about how a respondent's interest profile matches the profiles of a wide range of occupations. Whereas the individual (or job candidate) profile of interests is almost always determined through taking a vocational interest inventory, the interest profiles for occupations can be determined using several approaches.

The first way one might determine interest profiles for occupations is through a *job analysis*. The Department of Labor's O*NET occupational data base serves as a prime example, where job analysts have provided data on RIASEC characteristics across all available occupations (see https://www.onetonline.org/find/descriptor/browse/Interests/). The database of interest profiles is constantly being updated as new occupations are added to the O*NET taxonomy (Rounds, Su, Lewis, & Rivkin, 2013).

A second reasonable way to determine interest profiles for occupations is by calculating the *average interest profile* of employees within each occupation. The assumption here is that when particular interests are higher for a particular occupation (vs. others), then those interests are job relevant for that occupation (see, for example, the Strong Interest Inventory; Harmon, Hansen, Borgen, & Hammer, 1994). This assumption may not be true, of course, and in low-stakes developmental settings, this may not matter; however, if interests are to be used for personnel selection purposes, then the job relevance of vocational interests and interest profiles becomes more important to the organization for ensuring validity and minimizing adverse impact.

A third approach is more indirect than the previous two, as it involves examining *complementary profiles*. With this approach, job applicants' profiles of vocational interests (e.g., RIASEC scores) are matched with occupational profiles of characteristics that are relevant to those interests. For example, organizations often seek knowledge, skills, abilities, and other characteristics (KSAOs) that are interest-related and address their business needs, such as the need for technical knowledge and teamwork. These KSAOs might represent the organizational profile. As another example, an organization's policies or management will vary in terms of their ability to reward applicants' interest-related outcomes (e.g., greater autonomy, security, variety). The ability to reward these different outcomes could indeed be represented as an organizational profile. Because these organizational profiles are complementary, they relate to applicants' vocational interest profiles indirectly (not one-to-one). They are thus more conceptually challenging to develop, and more empirically difficult to match to the applicant profile. Nonetheless, organizational profiles are important: They are motivated by the things that applicants and organizations both have to offer one another—and the things that both of them ultimately want—where *none* of these things may be the same for either party. This sort of complementarity is featured prominently in the Theory of Work Adjustment (e.g., Dawis, 2005).

Note that many vocational interest and work adjustment theories incorporate all three of these profile-based approaches (e.g., Dawis & Lofquist,

1984; Holland, 1997). Also, as the discerning reader might appreciate by now, there is a remarkable alignment between these vocational approaches and those theories found in the organizational literature regarding employees' fit to jobs, occupations, and organizational environments (e.g., Edwards, Cable, Williamson, Lambert, Shipp, 2006; Ehrhart & Makransky, 2007; Judge, 1994; Kristof-Brown, Zimmerman, & Johnson, 2005).

Vocational Interests in Personnel Selection Research

Industrial-organizational psychologists have extended the phenomenon of interest-job fit to personnel selection using measures that are more traditionally and directly aligned with those found in the vocational counseling literature than in the industrial-organizational literature. For example, in a large military sample of incumbents (N = 408–418), a web-based RIASEC measure of vocational interests was found to yield cross-validated R^2 values of .02 to .09 for predicting technical and interpersonal knowledge, task proficiency, effort, and continuance intentions in separate linear regression models (Van Iddekinge, Putka, & Campbell, 2011). Some of the zero-order correlations with other self-report measures, although exploratory, are also noteworthy: realistic interests correlated -.26 with concern for others; artistic interests correlated .31 with innovation; and enterprising interests correlated .23 with leadership orientation. Although these findings involved an incumbent sample as opposed to a higher-stakes applicant sample, the authors do correct for range restriction effects (as there was direct selection on the Armed Services Vocational Aptitude Battery (ASVAB), which correlates with interests). These large-sample findings at least show some initial promise for the use of vocational interests measures in an employment setting.

That said, for vocational interest measures to be useful operationally, they need to show incremental validity above more typical cognitive and personality tests used in employment settings. When that analysis was applied by the authors (see Van Iddekinge, Putka, & Campbell, 2011, Table 3), the incremental R^2 values were only .01 at most over cognitive ability and personality for predicting these outcomes. By contrast, when the outcome is the type of employment that one attains after college, RIASEC vocational interests predict well and predict incrementally above the Big Five personality measures (De Fruyt & Mervielde, 1999), reinforcing the profile-matching approach when determining broader person-occupation fit.

Organizations and personnel selection psychologists alike are keenly concerned about mean score differences between ethnic/racial and gender groups, because in upholding Title VII of the Civil Rights Act of 1964, they seek to guard against the use of selection procedures that result in adverse impact and employment discrimination. In the Van Iddekinge, Putka, and Campbell (2011) study, gender differences favoring males were large for Realistic interests (males, d = .83), whereas moderate differences favoring females were found for

Social and Conventional interests (*d* = -.45 and -.34, respectively). Black/White race differences were moderate-to-large for Realistic interests, favoring Whites (*d* = .62) and small-to-moderate for Artistic, Social, Enterprising, and Conventional, all favoring Blacks (*d* values of -.38, -.50, -.39 and -.47, respectively). In a much larger military study (Hough, Barge, & Kamp, 2001; Hough & Barge, 2001), similar mean score differences were found between men and women (male sample size ~7,500, female sample size ~850) and between Whites and Blacks (White sample ~5,500, Black sample ~2,200). Likewise, these patterns of findings are rather similar to those found in larger meta-analyses of gender (Su, Rounds, & Armstrong, 2009) and both gender and race (Jones, 2013). More continuous variables might help explain some of these group differences. For example, gender differences may be at least partially explained by continuous measures of masculinity (instrumentality) and femininity (expressiveness; Ludwikowski, Armstrong, & Lannin, 2018). But regardless, the magnitudes of many of these reported race and gender differences are important in that they may or may not tend to result in adverse impact against a protected class.

Two meta-analyses of vocational interests in the workplace complement the findings above. In the first one, the authors (Van Iddekinge, Roth, Putka, & Lanivich, 2011) compared the validity of interests (RIASEC and otherwise) for predicting several organizational outcomes (i.e., job performance, training performance, turnover intentions, and turnover). Several types of validities for vocational interests were provided: the single-interest scale most relevant to the job (e.g., Realistic interests for a hand-on military job), a regression-weighted composite of interest scales, and congruence indices (i.e., any of several indices that relate the interest profiles of applicants with those from jobs or organizations). Operational validities (i.e., validities corrected for measurement error variance in the criterion) were the highest for regression-weighted interest composites. These validities were shrinkage-corrected to avoid capitalizing on chance and were $r \approx .14$ for performance, $r \approx .15$ for training, $r \approx -.24$ for turnover intentions, $r \approx -.13$ for actual turnover. Importantly, validities across organizational outcomes were consistently higher when the interest measure was focused on specific job-relevant interests (magnitudes for validity are about .20).

The second is a pair of meta-analyses by the same authors (Nye, Su, Rounds, & Drasgow, 2012, updated and expanded in 2017) that focused on a comparison of the validity of individual interest scales with interest congruence indices. Here, after correcting for both incidental range restriction and measurement error variance in the criterion, the magnitudes of correlations based on interest profiles were uniformly higher than correlations based on individual scales across all organizational criteria: task performance, organizational citizenship behaviors, persistence, and counterproductive work behaviors (for CWBs, also see Iliescu, Ispas, Sulea, & Ilie, 2015). The authors suggested that profiles had higher validity because each profile reflects *relative* levels of interests aligned with the job or organization, and thus reflects the motivational characteristics of applicants and employees more so than scale scores, which reflect *absolute* levels of particular interests. Another possibility is that like regression analysis, profiles simply allow more variables to be involved in prediction; these profiles can be "driven" either by multiple variables (i.e., an interaction effect reflecting unique profile characteristics) or by single variables (i.e., a particularly high or low point within a given profile.).

In short, the revival of vocational interests in the domain of personnel selection is promising and very much welcome. Recent research findings are compelling enough to stimulate a wealth of selection-related research and practice that is likely to benefit both employees and organizations alike.

Future Research Directions

Taken together, the studies and meta-analyses described above offer several suggestions for researching vocational interests in personnel selection. First, research can explore how adding interest measures will affect protected classes (e.g., women and Black subgroups) in terms of reductions in adverse impact, also considering those reductions in light of criterion-related validity. Second, research can explore how interests relate to the modern circumstances of a "gig economy," which has implications for how interests might be measured and used to predict outcomes relevant to employers and job applicants in such an economy. Third, vocational interests that are specific to jobs can be examined further, given the meta-analytic evidence for higher criterion-related validity of specific (vs. general) interests for predicting performance ratings; historically, there was promise for specific interests reducing turnover as well (Bolanovich, 1948). Fourth, if interest measures are to be used in high-stakes personnel selection settings, then continued research on faking such measures is of concern, as it has been for decades with personality testing (see Garry, 1953, who showed how two samples of college students could elevate their vocational interest scores under instructed faking conditions).

Subgroup Differences and Adverse Impact

Because vocational interest measures are rarely used in the employment setting, group mean differences in interests are rarely examined; for instance, they were not mentioned in a wide-ranging research review of group differences found across constructs often used in personnel selection (Hough, Oswald, & Ployhart, 2011). However, we have long known that vocational interest measures are reliable, and they are remarkably stable over time like traits (even over twenty years; see the longitudinal meta-analysis of interests by Low, Yoon, Roberts, & Rounds, 2005). Vocational interests also show at least some evidence for validity and incremental validity, as noted above; and all of this is to justify the final point, that along with the evidence for reliability, stability, and validity, vocational interests also demonstrate durable patterns of mean differences by gender and race/ethnicity.

Personnel selection researchers are well aware of the "validity-adverse impact tradeoff," namely, that in many selection settings, cognitive ability measures tend to show the highest validity for predicting job performance, yet they also tend to show the largest mean differences by racial/ethnic subgroups, such as a .6 to 1.0 standard deviation difference between the means of African Americans and Whites in the selection context (see Roth, Bevier, Bobko, Switzer, & Tyler, 2001, and the review by Ones, Dilchert, Viswesvaran, & Salgado, 2017). If a cognitive ability test is included in a selection battery, research has demonstrated mathematically that this mean difference is very difficult to remove. For instance, if a cognitive ability measure has a group mean difference of $d = 1.0$, and an uncorrelated measure of conscientiousness is added to the selection battery $d = .00$ (no group mean difference), then the mean difference of the composite is not $d = .50$ as one might expect through averaging, but rather it is $d = .71$ (the square root of .50; see Sackett & Ellingson, 1997).

A more effective way to counter the adverse impact for cognitive ability would be to locate measures of constructs that are job-relevant yet show an *opposite* mean difference that favors the minority group. Such a tentative possibility is found with vocational interest measures: Given the d values that are in the .40s but favor African Americans (vs. Whites) for Artistic, Social, Enterprising, and Conventional interests (see Van Iddekinge, Putka, & Campbell, 2011, above), and given that these interests correlate low—and sometimes even negatively—with cognitive ability (Ackerman & Heggestad, 1997), then introducing these interest scales into a selection composite that included cognitive ability could greatly reduce the d-value of the overall selection composite. But this is a tentative suggestion that would need to be implemented with professional care.

Taking a conservative approach (yielding a higher estimate of d), let us assume that a d value between African Americans and Whites involving cognitive ability was as high as $d = 1.0$, and Enterprising and Social d values were -.39 and -.47 favoring African Americans as reported above; let us also assume the correlations between these three constructs were low, say zero even. Then using the formula for composites (Sackett & Ellingson, 1997), the composite d value would be $d = .08$. Note that this point in no way solves the "diversity-adverse impact tradeoff" because the incremental validity for vocational interests over cognitive ability is often quite low, although it depends upon the outcome to be predicted. Additional selection research involving interests is needed that pursues the real-world nature of the diversity-validity tradeoff in organizations (see a series of useful recommendations by Ployhart & Holtz, 2008).

Interests in the "Gig Economy"

Typical vocational interest measures center on one's interest in the skills, activities, and fit of traditional full-time occupations. But consider the gig economy, where organizations call upon people and teams to take on specific jobs or tasks on a temporary (if not fleeting) basis; where the work may be increasingly remote (e.g., work from home online); and the employment relationship might reflect less organizational loyalty and greater economic risks or burdens on the part of the employee (Friedman, 2014). New interest measures should not only involve different modes of administration (e.g., video-based, adaptive, online) but also be tailored to reflect the diverse, yet more specific, work found in the gig economy. This approach has also been recently advocated in the military, in order for recruits to understand that a wide range of possibilities for work and careers is possible, extending well beyond combat-related military occupational specialties (Ingerick & Rumsey, 2014).

Specific Interest Areas

Future research could determine whether these aforementioned types of tailored or specific interest measures might yield higher than the typical near-zero incremental validity for predicting overall job performance when added to personality and cognitive ability test batteries. We suspect that such tailored, specific interest inventories are likely to produce incremental validity, especially when outcomes such as turnover are considered.

The Big Five factor model of personality has been examined in terms of more refined facets, such as a measure of two facets within each of the Big Five (e.g., Industriousness and Orderliness within Conscientiousness; DeYoung, Quilty, & Peterson, 2007). Likewise, RIASEC interest factors have been examined at a facet level, such as the 23 Basic Interest Scales [BIS] measured in the Strong Interest Inventory, where Adventure, Agriculture, Nature, Military, and Mechanical Activities reside within Realistic interests (Hansen & Campbell, 1985); or the 31 Basic Interest Markers that are publicly available (Liao, Armstrong, & Rounds, 2008). Therefore, going beyond an analysis at the broad factor level, where for instance the Extraversion personality factor is related to the Social interest factor (Mount, Barrick, Scullen, & Rounds, 2005), an analysis at a more refined level of measurement interest level may reveal specific vocational interests that distinguish themselves from specific aspects of personality and thus have greater potential for incremental validity (for inspiration, see Larson & Borgen, 2002).

We noted earlier that Van Iddekinge, Roth et al. (2011) found higher validities for vocational interests predicting performance when interest measures were focused on specific jobs. Likewise, Gutentag and Gati (2016) enumerated 31 specific *aspect-based* career preferences that include vocational interests, but other aspects as well (e.g., amount of travel, management, indoors-outdoors, income). With four samples of college students (reflecting two cultures) who were administered the Career Preferences Questionnaire (CPQ; Gati & Asher, 2001), the authors found that these 31 aspects varied greatly in their stability; but clustering them suggested job-related interest areas beyond RIASEC, of concern to young and educated employees (e.g., interest in the work "package" that includes income, work hours, and prestige; interest in advancement and going into management; interest in organizational skills and teamwork). These clusters and other, more refined interest clusters could be developed (e.g., interest in combat vs. combat support in the military; Hough, Barge, & Kamp, 2001). Clusters could then, for instance, be aligned with the O*NET occupational database to enhance career development and selection tools beyond RIASEC interests. Refined interest clusters also could encourage criterion development and even a program of selection research at a commensurate level of refinement, when appropriate (e.g., how does a refined interest profile help an applicant select from among multiple job offers?).

Mean differences by race and/or gender in specific interest areas (as opposed to general RIASEC scores) may also help understand why such differences occur, with implications for how one might intervene (e.g., via recruitment, selection, and training) to mitigate those differences. In the U.S. Air Force context (Johnson, Trent, & Barron, 2017), a large basic training sample ($N = 1{,}008$) responded to interest-related items. Large item-level gender differences were found in participants' interest in job contexts (women tend to prefer jobs that are indoors, in the office, nonhazardous, and predictable; $d \approx .25\text{-}.50$) and work environments (women tend to prefer work involving analyzing, maintaining, and creating documents; and interacting, training, and serving people and customers; $d \approx .25\text{-}.65$). Regarding race and job context: African Americans generally preferred jobs that are indoors, in the office, nonhazardous, and predictable, with $d \approx .50\text{-}.65$ compared to Whites. In terms of work characteristics, African Americans relative to Whites also generally preferred analyzing, maintaining, and creating documents; and interacting, training, and serving people and customers, with $d \approx .25\text{-}.60$. Interestingly, the authors found these gender and race effects to be independent; that is, race and gender do not appear to be confounded, despite roughly similar patterns of mean differences.

Faking and the Measurement of Interests

Given the infrequency that vocational interests have been used in high-stakes settings, such as personnel selection, intentional distortion (e.g., lying) with regard to one's measured interests is an area ripe for research. Earlier military research indicates this need, where Hough, Barge, and Kamp (2001) administered a specially constructed interest inventory in a Military Entrance Processing Station, an applicant-like setting where enlistees completed the interest inventory and were told their responses would be used to make decisions about their careers in the military. In addition to this field setting, this interest inventory was also administered to military participants in three experimental conditions: fake a combat applicant, fake a noncombat applicant, and respond-honestly. Perhaps unsurprisingly, results indicated that when instructed to do so, soldiers could distort their responses in the experimental faking conditions. However, comparisons of data from the applicant-like setting and the honest experimental condition did not suggest any particular pattern to the mean score differences, although much more needs to be learned in future research about the impact of high-stakes settings on applicant responses to interest measures.

Summary and Conclusions

In the long term, it remains to be seen how frequently and effectively vocational interest measures might be implemented in personnel selection settings. As with any new constructs and new measures that are introduced, both organizations and applicants alike may have reservations—or at least they would like to obtain a better understanding of the benefits and drawbacks from empirical, rational, and practical standpoints, in comparison with the current state of affairs. More specifically, organizations and HR experts likely have limited knowledge about the nature of vocational interests, its benefits in personnel selection in terms of potential incremental validity and reductions in adverse impact, and its potential legal liabilities. Given the organizational research just reviewed, academics, practitioners, and organizations themselves likely agree that "more research is needed" to understand how, in what contexts, with what measures, at what level of refinement, and for what criteria vocational interests will be most effective for selecting employees in organizations.

Note: The authors wish to thank Amy Shaw, graduate student at Rice University, for contributing an initial search of existing vocational interest measures.

References

Ackerman, P. L., & Heggestad, E. D. (1997). Intelligence, personality, and interests: Evidence for overlapping traits. *Psychological Bulletin, 121,* 219–245.

Austin, J. T., & Hansich, K. A. (1990). Occupational attainment as a function of abilities and interests: A longitudinal analysis using Project TALENT data. *Journal of Applied Psychology, 75,* 77–86.

Bolanovich, D. J. (1948). Reduce factory turnover. *Personnel Psychology, 1,* 81–92.

Dawis, R. V. (2005). The Minnesota theory of work adjustment. In S. D. Brown & R. W. Lent (Eds.), *Career development and counseling: Putting theory and research to work* (pp. 3–23). Hoboken, NJ: Wiley.

Dawis, R. V. & Lofquist, L. H. (1984). *A psychological theory of work adjustment.* Minneapolis: University of Minnesota Press.

De Fruyt, F., & Mervielde, I. (1999). RIASEC types and Big Five traits as predictors of employment status and nature of employment. *Personnel Psychology, 52,* 701–727.

DeYoung, C. G., Quilty, L. C., & Peterson, J. B. (2007). Between facets and domains: 10 aspects of the Big Five. *Journal of Personality and Social Psychology, 93,* 880–896.

Edwards, J. R., Cable, D. M., Williamson, I. O., Lambert, L. S., & Shipp, A. J. (2006). The phenomenology of fit: Linking the person and environment to the subjective experience of person-environment fit. *Journal of Applied Psychology, 91,* 802–827.

Ehrhart, K. H., & Makransky, G. (2007). Testing vocational interests and personality as predictors of person-vocation and person-job fit. *Journal of Career Assessment, 15,* 206–226.

Friedman, G. (2014). Workers without employers: Shadow corporations and the rise of the gig economy. *Review of Keynesian Economics, 2,* 171–188.

Garry, R. (1953). Individual differences in ability to fake vocational interest tests. *Journal of Applied Psychology, 37,* 33–37.

Gati, I., & Asher, I. (2001). The PIC model for career decision making: Prescreening, in-depth exploration, and choice. In F. T. Leong & A. Barak (Eds.), *Contemporary models in vocational psychology* (pp. 7–54). Mahwah, NJ: Erlbaum.

Gutentag, T., & Gati, I., (2016). The consistency and structure of aspect-based career preferences. *Journal of Vocational Behavior, 93,* 33–46.

Hansen, J. C., & Campbell, D. P. (1985). *Manual for the Strong Interest Inventory* (4th ed.). Stanford, CA: Stanford University Press.

Harmon, L. W., Hansen, J. C, Borgen, F. H., & Hammer, A. L. (1994). *Strong Interest Inventory applications and technical guide.* Palo Alto, CA: Consulting Psychologists Press.

Hidi, S., & Renninger, K. A. (2006). A four-phase model of interest development. *Educational Psychologist, 41,* 111–127.

Holland, J. L. (1997). *Making vocational choices: A theory of vocational personalities and work environments* (3rd Ed.). Odessa, FL: Psychological Assessment Resources.

Hough, L. M., & Barge, B. (2001). *Development of vocational interests and needs inventories: AVOICE and JOB* (Institute Report #260). Minneapolis, MN: Personnel Decisions Research Institutes.

Hough, L. M., Barge, B., & Kamp, J. (2001). Assessment of personality, temperament, vocational interests, and work outcome preferences. In J. P. Campbell & D. J. Knapp (Eds.), *Exploring the limits of personnel selection and classification* (pp. 111–154). Mahwah, NJ: Erlbaum.

Hough, L. M., Oswald, F. L., & Ployhart, R. E. (2001). Determinants, detection and amelioration of adverse impact in personnel selection procedures: Issues, evidence and lessons learned. *International Journal of Selection and Assessment, 9*(1–2), 152–194.

Iliescu, D., Ispas, D., Sulea, C., & Ilie, A. (2015). Vocational fit and counterproductive work behaviors: A self-regulation perspective. *Journal of Applied Psychology, 100,* 21–39.

Ingerick, M., & Rumsey, M. (2014). Taking the measure of work interests: Past, present, and future. *Military Psychology, 26,* 165–181.

Johnson, J. F., Trent, J. D., & Barron, L. G. (2017). Gender, racial, and ethnic differences in job context and work-activity preferences. *Military Psychology, 29,* 542–559.

Jones, K. S. (2013). *Considering vocational interests in adverse impact: A meta-analysis of race, cognitive ability, and vocational interests* (Doctoral dissertation). University of Illinois at Urbana-Champaign.

Judge, T. A. (1994). Person–organization fit and the theory of work adjustment: Implications for satisfaction, tenure, and career success. *Journal of Vocational Behavior, 44,* 32–54.

Kaminsky, S. E., & Behrend, T. S. (2015). Career choice and calling: Integrating calling and social cognitive career theory. *Journal of Career Assessment, 23,* 383–398.

Kristof-Brown, A. L., Zimmerman, R. D., & Johnson, E. C. (2005). Consequences of individuals' fit at work: A meta-analysis of person-job, person-organization, person-group, and person-supervisor fit. *Personnel Psychology, 58,* 281–342.

Larson, L. M., & Borgen, F. H. (2002). Convergence of vocational interests and personality: Examples in an adolescent gifted sample. *Journal of Vocational Behavior, 60,* 91–112.

Le, H., Robbins, S. B., & Westrick, P. (2014). Predicting student enrollment and persistence in college STEM fields using an expanded PE fit framework: A large-scale multilevel study. *Journal of Applied Psychology, 99,* 915–947.

Liao, H. -Y., Armstrong, P. I., & Rounds, J. (2008). Development and initial validation of public domain Basic Interest Markers. *Journal of Vocational Behavior, 73,* 159–183.

Low, K. S., Yoon, M., Roberts, B. W., & Rounds, J. (2005). The stability of vocational interests from early adolescence to middle adulthood: A quantitative review of longitudinal studies. *Psychological Bulletin, 131,* 713–737.

Ludwikowski, W. M., Armstrong, P. I., & Lannin, D. G. (2018). Explaining gender differences in interests: The roles of instrumentality and expressiveness. *Journal of Career Assessment, 26,* 240–257.

Mount, M. K., Barrick, M. R., Scullen, S. M., & Rounds, J. (2005). Higher-order dimensions of the big five personality traits and the big six vocational interest types. *Personnel Psychology, 58,* 447–478.

Nye, C. D., Su, R., Rounds, J., & Drasgow, F. (2012). Vocational interests and performance: A quantitative summary of over 60 years of research. *Perspectives on Psychological Science, 7,* 384–403.

Nye, C. D., Su, R., Rounds, J., & Drasgow, F. (2017). Interest congruence and performance: Revisiting recent meta-analytic findings. *Journal of Vocational Behavior, 98,* 138–151.

Ones, D. S., Dilchert, S., Viswesvaran, C., & Salgado, J. F. (2017). Cognitive ability: Measurement and validity for employee selection. In J. Farr & N. Tippins (Eds.), *Handbook of employee selection* (2nd ed., pp. 251–276). New York: Routledge.

Ployhart, R. E., & Holtz, B. C. (2008). The diversity-validity dilemma: Strategies for reducing racioethnic and sex subgroup differences and adverse impact in selection. *Personnel Psychology, 61,* 153–172.

Roth, P. L., Bevier, C. A., Bobko, P., Switzer III, F. S., & Tyler, P. (2001). Ethnic group differences in cognitive ability in employment and educational settings: A meta-analysis. *Personnel Psychology, 54,* 297–330.

Rounds, J., Su, R., Lewis, P., & Rivkin, D. (June, 2013). *Occupational Interest Profiles for new and emerging occupations in the O* NET system: Summary.* Raleigh, NC: National Center for O*NET Development.

Sackett, P. R., & Ellingson, J. E. (1997). The effects of forming multi-group predictor composites on group differences and adverse impact. *Personnel Psychology, 50,* 707–721.

Stoll, G., Rieger, S., Lüdtke, O., Nagengast, B., Trautwein, U., & Roberts, B. W. (2017). Vocational interests assessed at the end of high school predict life outcomes assessed 10 years later over and above IQ and Big Five personality traits. *Journal of Personality and Social Psychology, 113,* 167–184.

Su, R., Rounds, J., & Armstrong, I. (2009). Men and things, women and people: A meta-analysis of sex differences in interests. *Psychological Bulletin, 135,* 859–884.

Van Iddekinge, C. H., Putka, D. J., & Campbell, J. P. (2011). Reconsidering vocational interest for personnel selection: The validity of an internet-based selection test in relation to job knowledge, job performance, and continuance intentions. *Journal of Applied Psychology, 96,* 13–33.

Van Iddekinge, C. H., Roth, P. L., Putka, D. J., & Lanivich, S. E. (2011). Are you interested? A meta-analysis of relations between vocational interests and employee performance and turnover. *Journal of Applied Psychology, 96,* 1167–1194.

7

VOCATIONAL INTERESTS AND MEANINGFUL WORK

M. Teresa Cardador

UNIVERSITY OF ILLINOIS

Vocational interests—trait-like preferences for vocational activities that energize goal striving (Rounds, 1995; Strong, 1943)—have long been considered critical in the areas of vocational counseling, and educational and occupational choice (Barrick & Mount, 1991; Low & Rounds, 2006; Rounds & Su, 2014; Walsh & Osipow, 1986). Moreover, the degree to which individual interests fit their work environment has been linked to important work outcomes such as job performance and persistence behaviors, as well as career success (e.g., Nye, Su, Rounds, & Drasgow, 2012). Because interests reflect preferences for situations, contexts, and behaviors (Rounds, 1995), it seems plausible that interests should not only reflect one's career preferences and work outcomes, but also how individuals make sense of the purpose and significance of the work in which they are engaged. That is, how people experience their work as meaningful. The aim of this chapter is to build theory at the intersection of the vocational interest and meaningful work literatures. In particular, I draw on theories of meaningful work to explain why and how people with different vocational interests may experience meaningful work through unique pathways. I then describe the relationship between the structure of interest profiles and individuals' experiences of work meaningfulness, and conclude with implications for how organizations might attempt to foster meaningfulness for individuals with different vocational interests.

Meaningful Work

Meaningful work refers to the amount and type of purpose and significance work holds for an individual (Pratt & Ashforth, 2003; Rosso, Dekas, & Wrzesneiwski, 2010). Research on meaningful work examines questions such as: How and where do workers find meaningfulness in their work? How do people derive different types of meaningfulness from similar jobs? And how do work meanings differ across cultures? Recent research has linked meaningful work to some of the most important outcomes in organizational science, such as performance (Wrzesniewski, 2003), absenteeism (Wrzesniewski, McCauley, Rozin, & Schwartz, 1997), organizational attachment (Cardador, Dane, & Pratt, 2011), engagement (May, Gilson, & Harter, 2004), and employee stress (Elangovan, Pinder, & McLean, 2010).

Scholars have identified several sources of meaningfulness in work. The term "source" is used to refer to ways in which meaningfulness is experienced and derived through work. In their comprehensive review, Rosso and colleagues identified others, the work context, and the self as three primary sources of work meaningfulness (Rosso et al., 2010). Research on the role of others in shaping perceptions of work meaningfulness has offered theoretical and empirical insight into how individuals experience meaningfulness in connection with interpersonal relationships with coworkers (Kahn, 2006; Wrzesniewski, Dutton, & Debebe, 2003), group and community memberships associated with work (Pratt & Ashforth, 2003), and leader behaviors that help employees grasp the purpose and significance of their work (Podolny, Khurana, & Hill-Popper, 2004). Research on the role of work contexts in shaping work meaningfulness has highlighted the critical influence of factors such as job design (Fried & Ferris, 1987; Grant, 2007; Hackman & Oldham, 1976), sense of community at work (Blatt & Camden, 2007), and organizational mission (Pratt, 2000; Thompson & Bunderson, 2003). Finally, research on the self and meaningful work has focused on how individual work values, motives, and orientations influence perceptions of the meaningfulness of work (Nord, Brief, Atieh, & Doherty 1990; Rokeach, 1960; Super & Šverko, 1995; Wresniewski et al., 1997).

While this literature has presented important insights, it is limited in a least two ways relevant to theory presented in this chapter. First, it has largely ignored the role of individual traits in people's experiences of meaningful work. Second, there is a paucity of research examining how and why different types of occupations may provide individuals with differential access to sources of meaningful work. Because interests are traits predictive of occupational preferences (Rounds, 1995; Walsh & Osipow, 1986), understanding the link between meaningful work and vocational interests begins to address both these gaps. Moreover, given that vocational interests are considered to be relatively stable and enduring (Low, Yoon, Roberts, & Rounds, 2005), understanding how interests link to individual sources of work meaningfulness may not only provide theoretical advances in understanding how and why workers experience the meaningfulness of their work, but may also have practical implications for helping workers to realize greater meaningfulness in their work.

The Relationship Between Pathways to Meaningful Work and Vocational Interests

Rosso and colleagues (2010) proposed a theoretical framework that highlights four main pathways to meaningful work. The four pathways rest at the intersection of two dimensions reflecting types of individual motives: (1) desire for agency versus communion and (2) action directed toward the self versus others. Desire for agency refers to the drive to master, assert, expand, and create, while desire for communion refers to the desire to connect, attach, contact, and unite (Bakan, 1966; Schneider, Ryan, Tracey, & Rounds, 1996). Action directed toward the self versus others refers to the degree to which work experiences are perceived as internal or external to the self. Internal experiences include authenticity and identity affirmation, while external experiences may include social impact or interpersonal connectedness (see also Dutton & Heaphy, 2003; Gecas 1982; Grant, 2008; Shamir, 1991). Rosso and colleagues (2010) identify four pathways to meaningful work associated with different combinations of these dimensions: (1) Individuation, (2) Contribution, (3) Self-Connection, and (4) Unification.

Individuation (agency-self dimensions) refers to work meaningfulness stemming from actions or outcomes that primarily define and distinguish the self as competent, valuable, and worthy. For example, individuals may experience meaningfulness in conjunction with personal achievement, or the opportunity to work on freely chosen tasks or projects. *Contribution* (agency-other dimensions) refers to work meaningfulness sourced from actions or outcomes in the service of making a difference to identifiable others (e.g., coworkers, clients, customers, one's work unit or organization). For example, individuals may experience contribution-based meaningfulness when they see that their work has a positive impact on clients or that they are part of a collective (e.g., team, organization) that values what they contribute. *Self-Connection* (communion-self dimensions) refers to work meaningfulness stemming from actions or outcomes that provide individuals with a sense of authenticity. That is, they allow for personal expressiveness or bring individuals into concordance with how they see themselves. Examples include having the chance to express one's "true self" among colleagues or "being heard" at work. Finally, *Unification* (communion-other dimensions) refers to actions or outcomes that help individuals experience a harmony with broader values, ideals, or principles (e.g., belongingness, altruism, morality, beauty). For example, one may experience unification when they feel their work improves society and/or when they experience their work environment as characterized by mutual closeness and support.

Before linking these meaningful work pathways to vocational interests, a brief overview of the RIASEC types is in order. Holland's theory (1973, 1997) states that vocational interests are multilevel dispositional traits, represent preferences for distinct work relevant characteristics, and can be used to meaningfully categorize people and work environments into six types—Realistic (R), Investigative (I), Artistic (A), Social (S), Enterprising (E), and Conventional (C). The Realistic person prefers activities involving the systematic manipulation of machinery, tools, or animals. The Investigative person tends to be analytical, curious, methodological, and precise. Artistic individuals are expressive, nonconforming, original, and introspective. Those with Social interests enjoy working with and helping others, as well as developing relationships, but avoid ordered activities involving tools and machinery. Enterprising individuals prefer activities that entail managing and persuading others to attain organizational goals or economic gain, but they tend to lack scientific ability. Finally, Conventional individuals enjoy the systematic manipulation of data, filing records, or reproducing materials.

How and why do vocational interests map on to the four different pathways to work meaningfulness? In particular, I theorize that individuals with E, R, I, and A interests should be more likely to experience work meaningfulness via Individuation; individuals with S, E, and C interests should be more likely to experience work meaningfulness via Contribution; individuals with A and E interests should be more likely to experience work meaningfulness via Self-Connection; and individuals with I and S interests should be more likely to experience work meaningfulness via Unification. See Table 7.1 for a summary of how the six RIASEC types relate to the four meaningful work pathways.

Before theorizing about the specific interest-pathway linkages, a note about interest fit is instructive. Previous research has shown that individuals find jobs and work environments reinforcing and satisfying to the extent that they fit with their interests (Low & Rounds, 2006; Nye et al., 2012). In line with this previous research, I suggest that accessing specific sources of work meaningfulness should be dependent on "interest-meaningfulness source" congruence—that is, being able to access the source of work meaningfulness that fits with your interests. However, departing a bit from the previous interest fit literature, I also suggest that perceptions of interest-meaningfulness source fit are not necessarily dependent on the job or environment fitting with one's interests, but

TABLE 7.1 Summary of Relationships Between RIASEC Types and Pathways to Meaningful Work

Interest	*Primary Pathway(s)*
R	Individuation
I	Individuation and Unification
A	Individuation and Self-Connection
S	Contribution and Unification
E	Individuation, Contribution, and Self-Connection
C	Contribution

rather on whether the context affords access to the source(s) of meaningfulness preferred. For example, a person high on SEC interests may or may not find him/herself in a job that matches this interest profile (e.g., Early Education Administration), but regardless of the job they hold, Contribution should be an important source of work meaningfulness. Consistent with the meaningful work literature, this means that all jobs have the potential for meaningfulness (Wrzesniewski, 2003), but preferred sources will vary according to interests.

Individuation and E, R, I, and A Interests

Individuals who are high on Enterprising (E), Realistic (R), Investigative (I) and Artistic (A) interests should be most likely to experience work as meaningful when they are able to define and distinguish themselves as worthy and valuable. Individuation places emphasis on experiencing a sense of mastery, control, and autonomy through work (Rosso et al., 2010). While these four interests differ in significant ways, all three share in common valuing the opportunity to experience differentiation and competence through work. E individuals prefer opportunity to manage and influence others, and be involved in administration, R type individuals prefer opportunities that allow them to develop technical and mechanical skills, I individuals seek intellectual challenge and growth, and A types show a preference for being recognized for their personal uniqueness (Holland, 1997; Su, Rounds, & Armstrong, 2009). All four interests show a preference for developing and demonstrating skill in a particular domain, and for experiencing differentiation and control in the forms of management (E), technical mastery (R), intellectual challenge (I), and artistic expression (A). Accordingly, those with combinations of E, R, I, and A interests should experience work meaningfulness when they experience high degrees of autonomy and control over their work, and when they have opportunities to experience progressive development and a sense of mastery through work (Baumeister & Vohs, 2002; Deci & Ryan, 2000; Masten & Reed, 2002).

Illustrating occupations, high on combinations of E, R, I, and A types are lawyers and designers (O*Net, 2016). Though very different occupations, both are individualist professions in the sense that they emphasize competitiveness (law [Shneidman, 1984]) and one's personal artistic expression (design [Hauge & Hracs, 2010]). Table 7.2 lists additional occupations in which individuals should value meaningfulness through Individuation. Individuals in these professionals seek out and are rewarded for mastery and distinguishing themselves from others in the chosen field.

The following prediction follows:

Proposition 1: Individuals who are high on E, R, I and A interests should be more likely than those high on S and C interests to experience meaningful work via Individuation.

TABLE 7.2 Jobs Linked to Pathways to Meaningful Work via RIASEC Types

Pathway (Associated RIASEC Types)	*Jobs*
Individuation (RIAE)	Commercial Pilot (RIE) Materials Engineer (IRE) Reporter (AEI) Urban Planner (IEA) Landscape Architect (AIR) Biochemist (IAR)
Contribution (SEC)	Human Resources Manager (ESC) Librarian (CSE) Clinical Nurse Specialist (ESC) Education Administrator – Early Education (SEC) Medical and Health Services Managers (ECS) Equal Opportunity Officer (SEC)
Self-Connection (AE)	Actor (AE) Musician (AE) Art Director (AE) Advertising Agent (EA) Public Relations Specialist (EA)
Unification (IS)	Registered Nurse (SI) Community Health Worker (SI) Special Education Teacher (SI) Judge (IS) Clinical Psychologist (IS) Physician (IS)

Contribution and S, E, and C Interests

Individuals who are highest on Social (S), Enterprising (E), and Conventional (C) interests should be most likely to experience meaningfulness when their work makes a difference to identifiable others or they see that their effort benefits their organization or work unit. Contribution as a source of meaningfulness places emphasis on perceived impact on others through work (Rosso et al., 2010; see also Grant, 2007, and Lips-Wiersma, 2002). Because it emphasizes a combination of personal agency and a focus on others, it differs from Individuation because the attention is on meaningfulness stemming from work that extends beyond the self to benefit and impact others (Grant, 2007; Lips-Wiersma & Morris, 2009).

Those with S, E, and C interests should experience meaningfulness through Contribution, but via different mechanisms. Individuals with S interests like to use their abilities to help others and/or solve social problems. Individuals with strong E interests show a preference for managing others and administration. And, individuals with C types engage tasks in a dutiful way. Based on these differences, for S types meaningfulness through contribution should be linked to experiences of being helpful and altruistic (Holland, 1997; Armstrong & Anthoney, 2009); for E types Contribution might be linked to having the ability to have a positive impact on others or one's organization through one's leadership; for C types, Contribution should be linked to their strong sense of duty, and tendency to show strong self-discipline and self-sacrifice (Armstrong & Anthoney, 2009). The C person's propensity for self-sacrifice should be associated with subordinating oneself to something larger than the self (e.g., one's family, an organization's mission, etc.). For S, E, and C types, meaningful work should be experienced to the extent that one's work provides them with opportunities to feel that they are having a positive impact on important others—that is, family, coworkers, customers, followers, the organization.

Occupations high on combinations of S, E, and C are clinical nurse specialists and social workers (O*Net, 2016). Both are social mission occupations that emphasize social contribution to individuals in need (Aldridge, 1994). Individuals in these occupations typically seek out and prefer opportunities to have a positive impact on patients and clients. See Table 7.2 for additional occupations in which individuals are likely experience meaningfulness through Contribution.

Thus, I predict the following:

Proposition 2: Individuals who are high on S, E, and C interests should be more likely than those high on R, I, and A interests to experience meaningful work via Contribution.

Self-Connection and A and E Interests

Self-Connection refers to integrity with how one sees oneself and the experience of authenticity or personal identity-affirmation (Rosso et al., 2010: see also Kahn, 2006; Waterman, 1993). Thus, Self-Connection is associated with experiencing one's "true" self at work (Gecas, 1982; Guevara & Ord, 1996; Waterman, 1990; Wrzesniewski et al., 2003), and individuals who experience meaningfulness through Self-Connection value opportunities to fully express themselves at work. Because Self-Connection is about being seen as you see yourself, those with certain types of interests may have a stronger need for Self-Connection to experience work meaningfulness. Specifically, those with A and E interests should be most likely to experience meaningfulness through Self-Connection, but, again, for different reasons. Those with A interests are adventurous, imaginative, creative, expressive, and original (Armstrong & Anthoney, 2009; Armstrong, Day, McVay, & Rounds, 2008; Holland, 1997). Because of these strong personal expressiveness traits, individuals with A interests should be likely to need to experience opportunities for personal expressiveness in order to experience work as meaningful (Waterman, 1993). Individuals with E interests generally seek positive affirmation from others, and benefit from verification that others are influenced by their actions (Holland, 1997; Su et al., 2006), thus they also should be likely to need self-affirmation and self-verification to experience work meaningfulness. For A and E types, meaningfulness should be associated with work experiences that suggest that others see them as they see themselves.

Occupations high on A and E interests include musicians and public relations specialists (O*Net, 2016). Both are creative occupations, and require individuals to have strong personal communication with stakeholders, such as clients or the public (Christopherson, 2004; Kent & Taylor, 2002). High degrees of personal expressiveness are required for such encounters, and to the extent that stakeholders validate such personal expression, individuals in these occupations should experience greater meaningfulness. Table 7.2 lists additional occupations in which individuals should experience meaningfulness through Self-Connection.

Thus, the following prediction:

Proposition 3: Individuals who are high on A and E interests should be more likely than those high on R, I, S, and C interests to experience work meaningfulness via Self-Connection.

Unification and I and S Interests

Individuals with strong Investigative (I) and Social (S) interests should be most likely to experience work meaningfulness through Unification (i.e., a harmony with others or valued ideals). Unification emphasizes finding meaningfulness through a strong value system (e.g., social, moral, religious), and sense of belongingness in a like-minded community (Rosso et al., 2010; see also Baumeister, 1991 and Baumeister & Leary, 1995). Value systems provide a compass for right and wrong, and acting in accordance with value systems gives individuals purpose associated with work (Schwartz, 1992; Weiner, 1988). For individuals who experience work meaningfulness through Unification, guiding ideals are fundamental to their work experience, and/or they feel a strong connection or shared identity with work-related social groups (such as their coworkers, units, or organizations [Rosso et al., 2010; see also Pratt & Ashforth, 2003]).

Individuals with I interests should find meaningfulness from being part of social groups that allow them to further value ideals, such as rigorous scientific inquiry or intellectual pursuit (Glenna, Welsh, Erwin, Lacy, & Biscotti, 2001; Holland, 1997). Those with strong S interests value helping and cooperating with others (Armstrong & Anthoney, 2009, Holland, 1997). These individuals should experience meaningfulness when they further altruistic or social ideals, and/or when they experience a sense of belongingness at work (Rosso et al., 2010; Dutton & Heaphy, 2003).

Occupations high on I and S interests include physicians and physical therapists (O*Net, 2016). In their work, individuals in these occupations are likely to be committed to furthering values such as scholarly pursuit, cooperation, and service (Hartung, Taber, & Richard, 2005; Stenmar & Nordholm, 1994), and should desire opportunities to experience meaningfulness in association with furthering these values through their work. See Table 7.2 for additional occupations in which individuals should value meaningfulness through Unification.

Accordingly, I predict the following:

Proposition 4: Individuals who are high on I and S interests should be more likely than those high R, A, E, and C interests to experience meaningful work via Unification.

Thus far, I have suggested that different interests should be associated with unique pathways to meaningful work. In particular, E, R, I, and A types should be most likely to experience meaningful work through Individuation, S, E, and C types through Contribution, A and E types through Self-Connection, and I and S types through Unification. This means that each interest type is linked to between one and three pathways to work meaningfulness: R types through the Individuation pathway; I types through the Individuation and Unification pathways; A types through the Individuation and Self-Connection pathways; S types through the Contribution and Unification Pathways; E types through the Individuation, Contribution, and Self-Connection pathways; and C types through the Contribution pathway. See Figure 7.1 for a visual representation of the integration of RIASEC interests with the pathways to meaningful work.

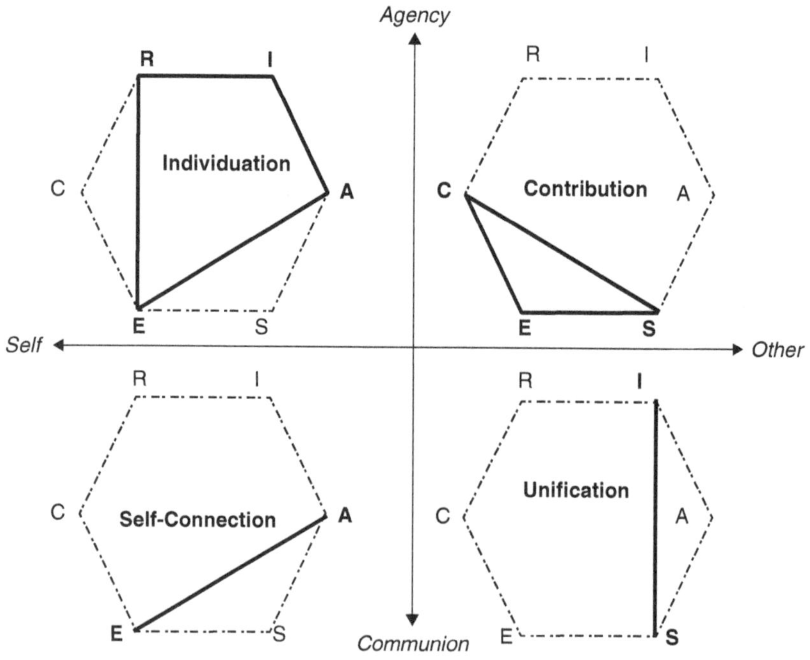

FIGURE 7.1 Integrating the RIASEC Interests with Pathways to Meaningful Work.

An interesting pattern that emerges from the preceding predictions is that, starting with C and R interests and moving to the right around the RIASEC hexagon, the number of relevant pathways to meaningful work increases. One possible explanation for this pattern may be provided by the two bipolar task dimensions underlying Holland's hexagon—working with "people" versus "things" and working with "ideas" versus "data" (Prediger, 1982; Su et al., 2009). When the RIASEC types are overlaid onto these dimensions, the following categorizations are evident: R anchors the "things" dimension; I is associated with "ideas" and "things"; A is associated with "people" and "ideas"; S anchors the "people" dimension; E is associated with "people" and "data"; and C is associated with "data" (Su et al., 2009). Using these dimensions as a foundation, the pattern suggests that one reason that R and C interests link with fewer sources of work meaningfulness may be that working with "people" and "ideas" increases the likelihood that one will experience work meaningfulness (Thompson & Bunderson, 2003; Wrzesniewski et al., 2003). Thus:

Proposition 5: Individuals will experience higher levels of work meaningfulness when they work in occupational environments characterized by "people" and "ideas."

In the next section, I present evidence that meaningful work pathways should be linked, not only to certain interests across individuals, but also to the pattern of a particular individual's interest profile.

Patterns of Interest Profiles and Meaningful Work

Holland (1973) proposed, and researchers have found evidence to support, additional constructs derived from interest scores. Two frequently examined constructs are differentiation and elevation. Differentiation captures the degree to which an individual shows a strong preference for one interest type over others (Holland, 1997; Im, 2011; Lowe, 1981; Nauta & Kahn, 2007). When profiles are high on differentiation, individuals demonstrate significantly higher levels of one or two interests; when profiles are low on differentiation, individuals display a "flat profile," representing almost equal interests across the six RIASEC types. Elevation refers to the strength of interest scores (Swanson & Hansen, 1986; Holland, 1997). High elevation interest profiles show strong interest scores across all types; low elevation interest profiles are those in which interest scores are depressed across RIASEC types. Low elevation profiles are indicative of people who don't like any of the activities associated with the RIASEC types; high elevation people like them all.

Based on these profile distinctions, certain profiles of interests should be differently linked to the pathways to meaningful work. In particular, I suggest that different interest profiles will lead to differences in potentiality for experiencing work meaningfulness connected with interests, and criticality of certain pathways for experiencing meaningful work. Those individuals who are low on differentiation and high on elevation should have the greatest potential to experience meaningful work. These individuals should be more likely to experience work meaningfulness since they are likely to have more options for pathways through which work meaningfulness can be realized. Individuals with high levels of multiple interests should be more likely to experience meaningfulness because if one pathway is blocked (e.g., few high-quality connections are available in the work environment, and thus the Unification pathway is blocked), then the individual can look to other pathways to experience work as meaningful (e.g., having opportunities for a high level of social impact, and thus experiencing meaningful work through the Contribution pathway). This type of flexibility should allow workers more opportunity to experience meaningfulness in work (Cardador & Caza, 2012). Thus:

Proposition 6: Individuals with high elevation and low differentiation of RIASEC types should have the greatest potential to experience work meaningfulness.

In contrast, those who are high on differentiation and high on elevation should consider a more limited number of pathways to be most critical to their experience of meaningful work for two reasons. First, a narrowness of interests limits the individual's ability to adapt to the conditions of his/her work environment with respect to opportunities for work meaningfulness (Cardador & Caza, 2012). For example, if someone's profile is characterized by high elevation on the R type, and high differentiation of the R type from others interests, he/she should experience work meaningfulness primarily through opportunities for Individuation, and is less likely to experience work meaningfulness through the other three pathways—Contribution, Self-Connection, and Unification. This means that avenues for experiencing Individuation will be critical to this individual's experience of meaningful work. For this individual, if opportunities to experience Individuation are not available, the ability to experience work meaningfulness will be significantly undermined.

Second, the criticality of certain meaningful work pathways for those with high differentiation and high elevation can also be explained using a certainty-authenticity argument (Gecas 1982). Individuals with strong interests in few areas are likely to be highly certain about their work preferences and to seek opportunities that allow these preferences to be more readily realized. Thus, they may look to critical pathways not because others are unavailable, but because their strong preferences dictate a clear and specific path to work meaningfulness though a smaller number of potential pathways.

Based on these arguments, I predict the following:

Proposition 7: Individuals with high elevation and high differentiation of RIASEC types should require fewer, and thus more critical, pathways to experience work as meaningful.

In contrast to individuals with high elevation in interest profiles just described, individuals with low elevation of RIASEC types should be less likely to experience work as meaningful. Meaningful work scholars point out that meaningful work refers to not only the *type* of meaning that one experiences at work, but also the *amount* of meaningfulness (Pratt & Ashforth, 2003; Wrzesniewski, 2003). Individuals with low elevation in their interest profiles should experience low levels of work meaningfulness regardless of their level of interest differentiation because they are less likely to show a preference for any of the four pathways to meaningful work. For these individuals, non-work avenues for meaningfulness—for example, marriage, hobbies and leisure pursuits, religion—may provide stronger pathways to meaningfulness than work avenues. Thus:

Proposition 8: Regardless of their level of differentiation of RIASEC types, individuals with low elevation of RIASEC types should be most likely to experience meaningfulness outside of the work domain.

To summarize this section, individuals with more and stronger interests should have access to more and varied sources of work meaningfulness, while those with fewer and weaker interests should have less access to fewer sources of meaningful work. While RIASEC types and interest profiles are important, given that a major assumption of Holland's (1973, 1997) theory is that the degree of congruence between a person's interest type and the environment is predictive of beneficial outcomes for individuals (e.g., Nye et al., 2012), considering the role of the organizational context should also be important. In the next section, I describe how organizations might foster meaningful work in connection with interests.

The Role of Organizations in Fostering Meaningfulness via Interest Profiles

Research has shown that people find environments reinforcing and satisfying when they fit with their interests (Low & Rounds, 2006). Additionally, because the experience of meaningful work is based on the fit between individual traits and what the work context provides (Rosso et al., 2010), organizations are seen as instrumental to individuals' experiences of meaningful work (Cardador, Dane, & Pratt, 2011; Podolny et al., 2004). This begs the question of how organizations might foster work meaningfulness for individuals with different interests, and suggests that workers may find work more meaningful when organizations are able to create conditions that allow individuals with different interests to access preferential sources of meaningfulness through work. I present organizational practices that foster meaningfulness via the four pathways—Individuation, Contribution, Self-Connection, and Unification. Figure 7.2 presents a summary of how the organizational practices summarized below apply to each of the six RIASEC types.

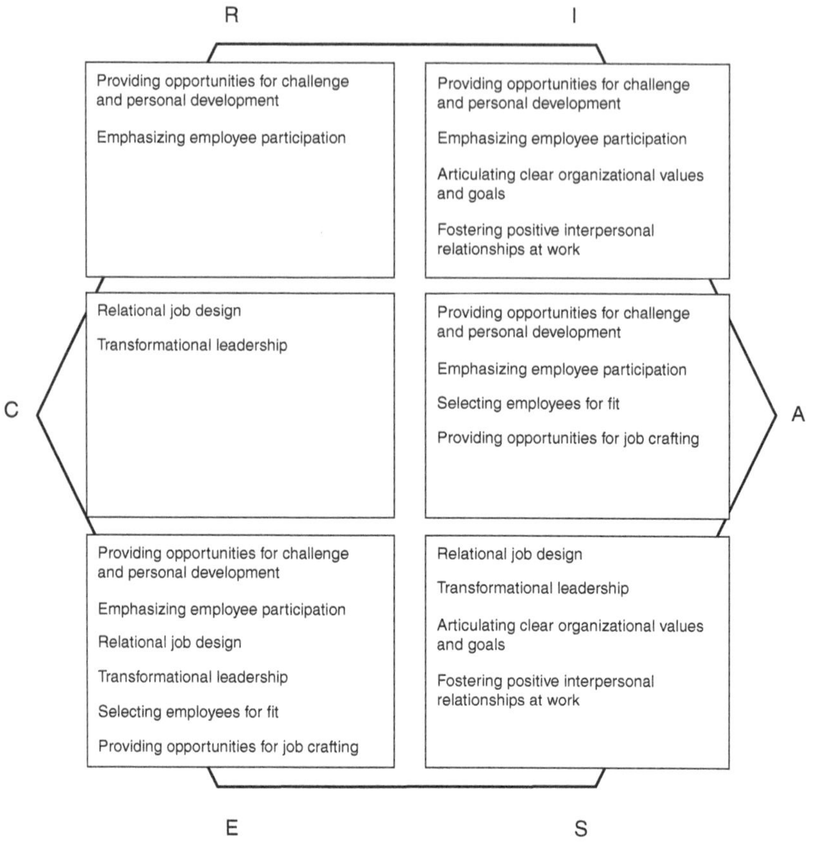

FIGURE 7.2 Role of Organizations in Fostering Work Meaningfulness via Interest Profiles.

Organizational Role in Fostering Meaningfulness Through Individuation

Because meaningful work via Individuation is about employees experiencing meaningfulness through a sense of personal competence, control, and autonomy in the workplace, (Rosso et al., 2010), organizational strategies to promote these conditions should increase employee access to meaningfulness. Based on the theorizing above, these strategies should be most useful for those with E, R, I, and A interests.

To address competency, control, and autonomy needs, organizations can engage in several practices. First, provide employees with opportunities for challenge, learning, and growth. Learning and growth provides individuals with a sense of progression in their work and improves feelings of personal mastery (Amabile & Kramer, 2011; Deci & Ryan, 2000; Gagne & Deci, 2005; Humphrey,

Nahrgang, & Morgeson, 2007; Masten & Reed, 2002). Experiencing challenge, learning, and growth increases workers' sense of efficacy and self-determination, thus providing greater access to opportunities to experience meaningful work through Individuation. A second organizational practice is managing employees in ways that foster greater participation and personal initiative (Deci, Connell, & Ryan, 1989). For example, managers can provide employees with voice in decision making, and flexibility to decide how their work tasks will be carried out (Baumeister & Vohs, 2002; Wrzesniewski & Dutton, 2001). Personal involvement and choice of work and task engagement can enhance employee feelings of autonomy and control and should thus promote greater meaningfulness via Individuation. Together, these practices—providing opportunities for challenge and development, and managerial styles that emphasize employee participation and initiative should be most effective for E, R, I, and A interests because of their preference for meaningful work via Individuation. Thus:

Proposition 9: Organizational practices that foster Individuation, such as opportunities for challenge and development, and managerial styles that emphasize employee participation and initiative, should be most effective at increasing work meaningfulness for those with E, R, I, and A interests.

Organizational Role in Fostering Meaningfulness Through Contribution

Because meaningful work via Contribution is about having a positive impact on others (Rosso et al., 2010), organizational strategies to promote perceptions of impact should increase employee access to meaningfulness. Based on the theorizing above, these strategies should be most useful for those with S, E, and C interests. Two specific practices for improving meaningful work via Contribution are relational job design and transformational leadership. First, research on relational job design—connecting employees with the impact that their work has on others (Grant, 2007)—shows that when employees have contact with, or receive information about, the beneficiaries of their work they experience greater perceptions of social impact (Grant, 2008; Grant et al., 2007). This idea is supported by research establishing that people are more likely to perceive the positive impact of their actions on others when they have clear and objective opportunities to benefit others through their work (Batson, 1998; Latane & Darley, 1970; Grant, 2007). Work designed to promote a positive sense of impact on others contributes to greater task significance, which is associated with more meaningful work (Grant, 2007, 2008). Organizations can play a role in helping employees see how their work is contributing to others through such strategies as providing employees with customer testimonials and customer profiles (Grant, 2011), or by encouraging employees to reflect—perhaps during performance reviews or other feedback sessions—about how their work has a positive impact on others (Cardador, 2014).

A second practice associated with employees' increased sense of meaningfulness via Contribution is transformational leadership. Transformational leaders articulate a vision that makes employees more aware of, and attentive to, how their work benefits others (Colby, Sippola, & Phelps, 2001; Grant, 2012; Podolny et al., 2004). Motivating employees to transcend self-interest by highlighting how and why employees' work has important consequences for others can help improve meaningfulness via Contribution.

Based on this evidence:

Proposition 10: Organizational practices that foster Contribution, such as relational job design and transformational leadership, should be most effective at increasing work meaningfulness for those with S, E, and C interests.

Organizational Role in Fostering Meaningfulness Through Self-Connection

Because meaningful work via Self-Connection relates to integrity with how one sees themselves, the experience of authenticity and personal identity-affirmation (Rosso et al., 2010; see also Kahn, 2006; Waterman, 1993), organizational practices that allow individuals to retain consistency of self, and to fully express themselves at work should increase employee access to this pathway to meaningfulness. Two practices that should promote greater meaningfulness through Self-Connection—and thus be most effective for employees with A and E interests—are selecting employees for organizational culture fit and providing opportunities for job crafting. First, when employees are selected for fit with an organization's culture, they should feel that they can express their true selves in the organization and should therefore feel more able to be personally expressive at work (Kristof-Brown, Zimmerman, & Johnson, 2005).

It is important to note that ensuring job-interest fit may be a strategy for fostering Self-Connection for employees with any of the RIASEC types. Though job-interest fit may not be necessary for employees to experience work meaningfulness, being hired into jobs and work environments that fit with one's interests may make it more likely for all employees to access their most impactful sources of work meaningfulness.

A second organizational practice for fostering personal authenticity and identity-affirmation is for organizations to provide workers with opportunities to engage in job crafting—that is, the opportunity to proactivity design (or redesign) the relational and task boundaries of their jobs to align them with employees' needs for personal expression (Wrzesniewski & Dutton, 2001). Providing opportunities for crafting can include small acts, such as allowing employees to personalize their workspaces and work environment (Elsbach, 2003), or can include more significant changes, such as providing employees options to create new task assignments that allow them to develop skills in preferred areas, or simply to feel that they are behaving in line with personal interests, goals, and values (Wrzesniewski & Dutton, 2001). For example, an individual who is highly artistic may feel more authentic when allowed to craft his work to allow for greater creativity and artistic expression.

Proposition 11: Organizational practices that foster Self-Connection, such as selecting employees for culture fit and allowing opportunities for job crafting, should be most effective at increasing work meaningfulness for those with A and E interests.

Organizational Role in Fostering Meaningfulness Through Unification

Because meaningful work via Unification is associated with individuals experiencing harmony with broader values, ideals, or principles (Rosso et al., 2010), organizational practices that increase this harmony should increase employee access to this pathway to meaningfulness, and should thus be most beneficial for those with I and S interests. Two organizational practices to improve work meaningfulness via Unification should be articulating clear organizational values and goals and fostering positive interpersonal relationships at work. First, organizational values and ideals can be expressed through a general belief system and/or through a set of organizational practices that guide and control organizational action and employee behavior (Bowen & Schneider, 1988). When organizations articulate clear goals and values—and communicate to employees how their work furthers them (Grant, 2012) —it makes it easier for employees to grasp how their work contributes to broader ideals beyond profit (Baumeister & Wilson, 1996: Podolny et al., 2004).

Another organizational strategy for fostering Unification is creating a social environment that encourages positive interpersonal interactions between individuals. Positive interpersonal interactions at work provide opportunities for workers to experience a sense of relatedness and closeness with others (Dutton & Heaphy, 2003), and to experience a sense of belongingness (Baumeister & Leary, 1995). Additionally, interpersonal relationships with coworkers influence workers' interpretation of the meaning of their work. Wrzesniewski and colleagues (2003) draw on information-processing theory to describe how interactions with others at work serve as sources of information regarding the value or significance of one's work. Through interpersonal cues provided by proximal coworkers, employees come understand the significance of their work. Based on this evidence:

Proposition 12: Organizational practices that foster Unification, such articulating values and ideals, and fostering positive interpersonal relationships, should be most effective at increasing work meaningfulness for those with I and S interests.

To summarize this section, because different types of organizational practices should be most effective in fostering meaningfulness via unique pathways, different types of practices should be more or less effective depending on one's vocational interest profile. However, if organizations engage in an array of meaningfulness-fostering practices, they should increase their changes of fostering work meaningfulness among a greater number of employees.

Summary and Conclusions

The principal aim of this chapter was to integrate the vocational interests and meaningful work literatures to build theory on why and how vocational interests and profiles may be associated with different sources of work meaningfulness. The theory explains why those with particular interests should be expected to experience work meaningfulness through unique pathways. In particular, those with E, R, I, and A interests should be most likely to experience meaningful work through Individuation, those with S, E, and C interests through Contribution, those with A and E interests through Self-Connection, and those with I and S interests through Unification. Moreover, the theory presented here suggested that those with high interest elevation and low differentiation should have the greatest potential to experience work meaningfulness, while those with high interest elevation and high differentiation will experience some pathways as more critical to their experience of meaningfulness. Finally, I suggested ways that organizations might foster work meaningfulness for those with different types of interests.

This chapter contributes to both the vocational interests and meaningful work literatures. With respect to the vocational interests literature, previous research has demonstrated that interests play a critical role in educational and occupational choice (e.g., Rounds & Su, 2014; Walsh & Osipow, 1986), and—to the degree that individuals experience congruence between their interests and their work environment—interests predict beneficial work outcomes such as job performance and career success (e.g., Nye et al., 2012). Building on this prior research, this chapter shows that individual differences in interests may also be critical for how workers experience the meaningfulness of their work. Further, when there is congruence between the ways in which the worker is most likely to experience work meaningfulness and what the organization and job provide, the amount and degree of purpose and significance attached to work should be heightened. This chapter has highlighted how and why people with different interests may look to different sources for work meaningfulness, and that organizations can foster meaningful work by creating the conditions through which people with unique interests can access critical sources of meaningfulness.

While not specifically focused on occupations, the theory developed in this chapter may also have implications for fostering meaningful work among members of different occupational groups. Because interests are linked to occupations (i.e., teachers tend to be high on S, A, and C interests, and civil engineers high on R, I, and C interests [O*Net, 2016]), knowing the most likely sources of meaningful work for individuals with these types can help organizations to develop specific, actionable, and tailored strategies to increase meaningful work for individuals in certain occupations. Understanding the relationship between interests and pathways to meaningfulness may help researchers and practitioners to better understand why certain occupations experience certain types of meaningfulness, as well as how meaningfulness gets thwarted in certain occupations because employees may lack access to critical meaningful work pathways.

This research also makes contributions to the meaningful work literature by showing the relationship between traits and pathways to meaningful work. While previous research has considered the role of individual differences in factors such as values, intrinsic motivation, job involvement, and work orientation (see Rosso et al., 2010, for a review), researchers have paid scant attention to the role of individual differences in enduring traits, such as vocational interests. Paying attention to this linkage is important given calls to examine the effect of meaningful work on more multidimensional conceptualizations of self. For example, Rosso and colleagues (2010) have noted that one limitation of current research is that it "tends to use singular elements of the self-concept to conceptualize the self" (e.g., values, motivations, beliefs [p. 99]). These scholars have suggested that this focus on singular elements presents an incomplete picture of how individual differences affect experiences of meaningful work. Because interests encompass goals, motives, preferences, and beliefs (Holland, 1997; Rounds, 1995), linking interests to meaningful work may represent an important initial step in explaining how a more multi-dimensional individual-difference construct is linked to pathways to meaningful work. Because these multiple dimensions of the self combine to influence single interests or profiles of interests, a focus on interests may provide a more parsimonious and perhaps more actionable theoretical lens through which to understand when and how different types of individuals are most likely to experience their work as purposeful and significant.

Moreover, this chapter highlights the role of organizations in shaping employees' work meaningfulness by fostering greater "interest-meaningfulness" congruence. Though previous research has highlighted a role for organizations in fostering meaningful work through strategies such as job design (Fried & Ferris, 1987; Grant, 2007; Hackman & Oldham, 1976), transformational leadership (Grant, 2012), organizational values (Poldony et al., 2005), and work environments characterized by positive interpersonal relationships (Dutton & Heaphy, 2003), this chapter offers a number of propositions suggesting that these different strategies should be more or less appealing and useful to individuals depending on their specific interest profile.

To conclude, while the vocational interest and meaningful work literatures have each provided unique and valuable insights into how workers make decisions about and experience their work environments, this research bridges these two literatures to provide new insights to each and to suggest interest-tailored avenues for organizations (and occupations) to improve the experience of meaningfulness for workers.

References

Aldridge, M. (1994). Unlimited liability? Emotional labour in nursing and social work. *Journal of Advanced Nursing, 20*(4), 722–728.

Amabile, T. M., & Kramer, S. J. (2011). The power of small wins. *Harvard Business Review, 89*, 70–80.

Armstrong, P. I., & Anthoney, S. F. (2009). Personality facets and RIASEC interests: An integrated model. *Journal of Vocational Behavior, 75*(3), 346–359.

Armstrong, P. I., Day, S. X., McVay, J. P., & Rounds, J. (2008). Holland's RIASEC model as an integrative framework for individual differences. *Journal of Counseling Psychology, 55*(1), 1–18.

Bakan, D. (1966). *The duality of human existence: Isolation and Communion in Western man.* Boston: Beacon.

Barrick, M. R., & Mount, M. K. (1991). The Big Five personality dimensions and job performance: A meta-analysis. In C. L. Cooper & L. A. Pervin (Eds.), *Personality: Critical concepts in psychology* (Vol. 2, pp. 231–254). New York: Routledge.

Batson, C. D. (1998). Altruism and prosocial behavior. In D. T. Gilbert, S. T. Fiske, & G. Lindzey (Eds.), *The handbook of social psychology* (Vol. 2, pp. 282–316). New York: McGraw-Hill.

Baumeister, R. F. (1991). *Meanings of life.* New York: Guilford Press.

Baumeister, R. F., & Leary, M. R. (1995). The need to belong: Desire for interpersonal attachments as fundamental human motivation. *Psychological Bulletin, 117*(3), 497–530.

Baumeister, R. F., & Vohs, K. D. (2002). The pursuit of meaningfulness in life. In C. R. Snyder, and S. J. Lopez (Eds.), *The handbook of positive psychology* (pp. 608–618). New York: Oxford University Press.

Baumeister, R. F., & Wilson, B. (1996). Life stories and the four needs for meaning. *Psychological Inquiry,* 7(4), 322–377.

Blatt, R., & Camden, C. T. (2007). Positive relationships and cultivating community. In J. E. Dutton & B. R. Ragins (Eds.), *Exploring positive relationships at work: Building a theoretical and research foundation.* Mahwah, NJ: Erlbaum.

Bowen, D. E., & Schneider, B. (1988). Services marketing and management: Implications for organizational behavior. In B. M. Staw & L.L. Cummings (Eds.), *Research in organizational behavior* (Vol. 10, pp. 43–80). Greenwich, CT: JAI.

Cardador, M. T. (2014). The effects of positive versus negative impact reflection on change in job performance and work-life conflict. *Frontiers in Psychology, 5,* 1370–1377.

Cardador, M. T., & Caza, B. B. (2012) Relational and identity perspectives on healthy versus unhealthy pursuit of callings. *Journal of Career Assessment, 20,* 338–353.

Cardador, M. T., Dane, E. I., & Pratt, M. G. (2011). Linking calling orientations to organizational attachment via organizational instrumentality. *Journal of Vocational Behavior, 79,* 367–378.

Christopherson, S. (2004). The divergent worlds of new media: How policy shapes work in the creative economy. *Review of Policy Research, 21*(4), 543–558.

Colby, A., Sippola, L., & Phelps, E. (2001). Social responsibility and paid work in contemporary American life. In A. Rossi (Ed.), *Caring and doing for others: Social responsibility in the domains of family, work, and community* (pp. 349–399). Chicago: University of Chicago Press.

Dawis, R. V. (Eds), *Assessing individual differences in human behavior: New concepts, methods, and findings* (pp. 177–232). Palo Alto, CA: Davies-Black.

Deci, E. L., Connell, J. P., & Ryan, R. M. (1989). Self-determination in a work organization. *Journal of Applied Psychology, 74*(4), 580.

Deci, E. L., & Ryan, R. M. (2000). The "what" and "why" of goal pursuits: Human needs and the self-determination of behavior. *Psychological Inquiry, 11*(4), 227–268.

Dutton, J. E., & Heaphy, E. D. (2003). The power of high quality connections. In K. S. Cameron, J. E. Dutton, & R. E. Quinn (eds.), *Positive organizational scholarship* (pp. 263–278). San Francisco: Berrett-Koehler Publishers.

Elangovan, A. R., Pinder, C. C., & McLean, M. (2010). Callings and organizational behavior. *Journal of Vocational Behavior,* 76, 428–440.

Elsbach, K. D. (2003). Relating physical environment to self-categorizations: Identity threat and affirmation in a non-territorial office space. *Administrative Science Quarterly, 48*(4), 622–654.

Fried, Y., & Ferris, G. R. (1987). The validity of the job characteristics model: A review and meta-analysis. *Personnel Psychology, 40*(2), 287–322.

Gagné, M., & Deci, E. L. (2005). Self-determination theory and work motivation. *Journal of Organizational Behavior, 26*(4), 331–362.

Gecas, V. (1982). The self-concept. *Annual Review of Sociology, 8,* 1–33.

Glenna, L. L., Welsh, R., Ervin, D., Lacy, W. B., & Biscotti, D. (2011). Commercial science, scientists' values, and university biotechnology research agendas. *Research Policy, 40*(7), 957–968.

Grant, A. M. (2007). Relational job design and the motivation to make a prosocial difference. *Academy of Management Review,* 32(2), 393–417.

Grant, A. M. (2008). The significance of task significance: Job performance effects, relational mechanisms, and boundary conditions. *Journal of Applied Psychology, 93*(1), 108–124.

Grant, A. M. (2011). How customers can rally your troops. *Harvard Business Review, 89*(6), 96–103.

Grant, A. M. (2012). Leading with meaning: Beneficiary contact, prosocial impact, and the performance effects of transformational leadership. *Academy of Management Journal, 55*(2), 458–476.

Grant, A. M., Campbell, E. M., Chen, G., Cottone, K., Lapedis, D., & Lee, K. (2007). Impact and the art of motivation maintenance: The effects of contact with beneficiaries on persistence behavior. *Organizational Behavior and Human Decision Processes,* 103(1), 53–67.

Guevara, K. & Ord, J. (1996). The search for meaning in a changing work context. *Futures, 28,* 709–722.

Hackman, J. R., & Oldham, G. R. (1976). Motivation through the design of work: Test of a theory. *Organizational Behavior and Human Performance, 16,* 250–279.

Hartung, P. J., Taber, B. J., & Richard, G. V. (2005). The physician values in practice scale: Construction and initial validation. *Journal of Vocational Behavior, 67*(2), 309–320.

Hauge, A., & Hracs, B. J. (2010). See the sound, hear the style: Collaborative linkages between indie musicians and fashion designers in local scenes. *Industry and Innovation, 17*(1), 113–129.

Holland, J. L. (1973). *Making vocational choice: A theory of careers*. Englewood Cliffs, NJ: Prentice-Hall.

Holland, J. L. (1997). *Making vocational choices: A theory of vocational personalities and work environments* (3rd ed.). Odessa, FL: Psychological Assessment Resources.

Humphrey, S. E., Nahrgang, J. D., & Morgeson, F. P. (2007). Integrating motivational, social, and contextual work design features: A meta-analytic summary and theoretical extension of the work design literature. *Journal of Applied Psychology, 92*(5), 1332.

Im, S. (2011). The effect of profile elevation on the relationships between interest differentiation and vocational identity. *British Journal of Guidance and Counseling, 39*(2), 149–160.

Kahn, W. A. (2006). Meaningful connections: Positive relationships and attachments at work. In J. E. Dutton & B. R. Ragins (Eds.), *Exploring positive relationships at work: Building a theoretical and research foundation* (pp. 189–206). Mahwah, NJ: Erlbaum.

Kent, M. L., & Taylor, M. (2002). Toward a dialogic theory of public relations. *Public Relations Review, 28*(1), 21–37.

Kristof-Brown, A. L., Zimmerman, R. D., & Johnson, E. C. (2005). Consequences of individual's fit at work: A meta-analysis of person-job, person-organization, person-group, and person-supervisor fit. *Personnel Psychology, 58*(2), 281–342.

Latane, B., & Darley, J. (1970). *The unresponsive bystander: Why doesn't he help?* New York: Appleton-Century-Crofts.

Lips-Wiersma, M. (2002). The influence of spiritual "meaning making" on career behavior. *Journal of Managerial Development*, 7, 497–550.

Lips-Wiersma, M., & Morris, L. (2009). Discriminating between "meaningful work" and the "management of meaning." *Journal of Business Ethics, 88*(3), 491–511.

Low, K. S. D., & Rounds, J. (2006). Vocational interests: Bridging person and environment. In D. L. Segal & J. Thomas (Eds.), *Comprehensive handbook of personality and psychopathology, Volume 1: Personality and everyday functioning* (pp. 251–267). New York: Wiley.

Low, K. D., Yoon, M., Roberts, B. W., & Rounds, J. (2005). The stability of vocational interests from early adolescence to middle adulthood: A quantitative review of longitudinal studies. *Psychological bulletin, 131*(5), 713–737.

Lowe, B. (1981). The relationship between vocational interest differentiation and career undecidedness. *Journal of Vocational Behavior, 19*, 346–349.

Masten, A. S., & Reed, M. J. (2002). Resilience in development. In C. R. Snyder & S. J. López (Eds.), *Handbook of positive psychology* (pp. 74–88). New York: Oxford University Press.

May, D. R., Gilson, R. L., & Harter, L. M. (2004). The psychological conditions of meaningfulness, safety and availability and the engagement of the human spirit at work. *Journal of Occupational and Organizational Psychology*, 77(1), 11–37.

Nauta, M. M., & Kahn, J. H. (2007). Identity status, consistency and differentiation of interests, and career decision self-efficacy. *Journal of Career Assessment, 15*(1), 55–65.

Nord, W., Brief, A., Atieh, J., & Doherty, E. (1990). Studying meanings of work: The case of work values. In A. Brief & W. Nord (Eds.), *Meanings of occupational work* (pp. 21–64). Lexington, MA: Lexington Books.

Nye, C. D., Su, R., Rounds, J., & Drasgow, F. (2012). Vocational interests and performance: A quantitative summary of over 60 years of research. *Perspectives on Psychological Science, 7,* 384–403.

O★Net Online. (2016). https://www.onetonline.org/find/

Podolny, J. M., Khurana, R., & Hill-Popper, M. (2004). Revisiting the meaning of leadership. *Research in Organizational Behavior, 26,* 1–36.

Pratt, M. G. (2000). The good, the bad, and the ambivalent: Managing identification among Amway distributors. *Administrative Science Quarterly, 45*(3), 456–493.

Pratt, M. G., & Ashforth, B. E. (2003). Fostering meaningfulness in working and at work. In K. S. Cameron, J. E. Dutton, & R. E. Quinn (Eds.), *Positive organizational scholarship.* San Francisco: Berrett-Koehler Publishers.

Prediger, D. J. (1982). Dimensions underlying Holland's hexagon: Missing link between interests and occupations? *Journal of Vocational Behavior, 21*(3), 259–287.

Rokeach, M. (1960). *The open and closed mind.* New York: Basic Books.

Rosso, B. D., Dekas, K. H., & Wrzesniewski, A. (2010). On the meaning of work: A theoretical integration and review. *Research in Organizational Behavior, 30,* 91–127.

Rounds, J. (1995). Vocational interests: Evaluating structural hypotheses. In D. J. Lubinski & R. V. Dawis, (Eds), *Assessing individual differences in human behavior: New concepts, methods, and findings* (pp. 177–232). Palo Alto, CA: Davies-Black.

Rounds, J., & Su, R. (2014). The nature and power of interests. *Current Directions in Psychological Science, 23*(2), 98–103.

Schneider, P. L., Ryan, J. M., Tracey, T. J. G., & Rounds, J. (1996). Examining the relation between Holland's RIASEC model and the interpersonal circle. *Measurement and Evaluation in Counseling and Development, 29,* 123–133.

Schwartz, S. H. (1992). Universals in the content and structure of values: Theory and empirical tests in 20 countries. In M. P. Zanna (Ed.), *Advances in experimental social psychology* (Vol. 25, pp. 1–65). New York: Academic Press.

Shamir, B. (1991). Meaning, self and motivation in organizations. *Organization Studies, 12,* 405–424.

Shneidman, E. S. (1984). Personality and "success" among a selected group of lawyers. *Journal of Personality Assessment, 48*(6), 609–616.

Stenmar, L., & Nordholm, L. A. (1994). Swedish physical therapists' beliefs on what makes therapy work. *Physical Therapy, 74*(11), 1034–1039.

Strong, E. K., Jr. (1943). *Vocational interests of men and women.* Stanford, CA: Stanford University Press.

Su, R., Rounds, J., & Armstrong, P. I. (2009). Men and things, women and people: A meta-analysis of sex differences in interests. *Psychological Bulletin, 135*(6), 859.

Super, D. E., & Šverko, B. (Eds.). (1995). *Life roles, values, and careers: International findings of the Work Importance Study.* San Francisco: Jossey-Bass.

Swanson, J. L., & Hansen, J. I. C. (1986). A clarification of Holland's construct of differentiation: The importance of score elevation. *Journal of Vocational Behavior, 28*(2), 163–173.

Thompson, J. A., & Bunderson, J. S. (2003). Violations of principle: Ideological currency in the psychological contract. *Academy of Management Review, 28*(4), 571–586.

Walsh, W. B., & Osipow, S. H. (Eds.). (1986). *Advances in vocational psychology. Vol. 1: The assessment of interests.* Hillsdale, NJ: Erlbaum.

Waterman, A. S. (1990). Personal expressiveness: Philosophical and psychological foundations. *Journal of Mind and Behavior, 11,* 47–74.

Waterman, A. S. (1993). Two conceptions of happiness: Contrasts of personal expressiveness (eudaimonia) and hedonic enjoyment. *Journal of Personality and Social Psychology, 64*, 678–691.

Wiener, Y. (1988). Forms of value systems: A focus on organizational effectiveness and cultural change and maintenance. *Academy of Management Review, 13*(4.), 534–545.

Wrzesniewski, A. (2003). Finding positive meaning in work. In K. S. Cameron, J. E. Dutton, J. E. & R. E. Quinn (Eds.), *Positive organizational scholarship: Foundations of a new* discipline (pp. 296–308). San Francisco: Berrett-Koehler.

Wrzesniewski, A., & Dutton, J. E. (2001). Crafting a job: Reenvisioning employees as active crafters of their work. *Academy of Management Review, 26*, 179–201.

Wrzesniewski, A., Dutton, J. E., & Debebe, G. (2003). Interpersonal sensemaking and the meaning of work. In R. M. Kramer & B. M. Staw (Eds.), *Research in organizational behavior* (Vol. 25, pp. 93–136). Amsterdam: Elsevier.

Wrzesniewski, A., McCauley, C., Rozin, P., & Schwartz, B. (1997). Jobs, careers, and callings: People's relations to their work. *Journal of Research in Personality, 31,* 21–33.

8

THE IMPORTANCE OF INTERESTS FOR UNDERSTANDING RETIREMENT

Laura Venz

UNIVERSITY OF MANNHEIM, GERMANY

Mo Wang

UNIVERSITY OF FLORIDA

As a consequence of low birth rates and increased longevity, the populations in most industrialized countries are rapidly aging and the share of older people will grow in the next decades. These changes in population compositions will also impact the workforce, ultimately leading to a higher proportion of older workers and people of retirement age (Topa, Moriano, Depolo, Alcover, & Morales, 2009). As a consequence, many developed economies face a shortage of skilled workers, causing a higher need of labor market participation of older and even already retired workers in order to maintain critical talent (Dohm, 2000; Fasbender, Wang, Voltmer, & Deller, 2015). These developments raised the need for organizations and scholars alike to thoroughly understand the career decisions of older workers and retirees. Surprisingly, despite the fact that decades of research have identified interests as important determinants of career decisions in younger people (see Rounds & Su, 2014), the potential role of interests in retirement has, to date, been neglected in empirical research. The main aim of this chapter is to present a theoretical model on the importance of interests to understand retirement.

General Conceptualization of Interests

Interests are commonly defined as individual preferences for certain activities, situations in which activities occur, or outcomes of the preferred activities (Rounds, 1995). Interests possess trait-like qualities (i.e., they are relatively stable over time) that influence goal-oriented behaviors through motivational processes and, thus, play an important role in long-term planning and decision making (Low, Yoon, Roberts, & Rounds, 2005; Rounds & Su, 2014). For instance, interests are a major determinant of occupational choice (e.g., Holland,

1997; Tracey & Hopkins, 2001) as well as of the selection of leisure activities (Varca & Shaffer, 1982).

The focus in the field of vocational psychology is typically on individuals' vocational interests, which have been defined as individual preferences for certain work-related activities or environments. Vocational interests facilitate the fit between people and their work environments and are reflective of a person's identity or self-concept (Low et al., 2005; Rounds & Su, 2014). Empirical research on vocational interests largely relied on Holland's (1959, 1997) theory of vocational choice, according to which vocational interests can be summarized into Realistic, Investigative, Artistic, Social, Enterprising, and Conventional (RIASEC) interests (see Nye & Rounds, this volume, for a description of the model).

In addition to describing individuals' vocational preferences, the RIASEC system also characterizes work environments that parallel the six general interest types. When making vocational choices, individuals seek out work environments in which their interests are met. For example, a person with high Realistic interests seeks Realistic environments and is, thus, likely to pursue a career that involves hands-on work activities, whereas someone with high Social interests is more likely to seek an occupation where he or she works with people (Holland, 1997; see also Low & Rounds, 2006).

While scholarly attention has mainly been focused on vocational interests and their role for career choices, some effort has been made to also examine leisure (sometimes referred to as avocational) interests (e.g., Kerby & Ragan, 2002; Leuty, Hansen, & Speaks, 2015). Leisure is defined as a freely chosen, intrinsically motivating engagement in activities for personal enjoyment (Tinsley & Tinsley, 2015). Given that interests are commonly defined as stable person characteristics, Holland (1997) argued that interests affect a person's preferences in both work and leisure contexts and that vocational and leisure interests should, thus, be highly related (for empirical evidence see Gaudron & Vautier, 2007; Hansen & Scullard, 2002). Accordingly, using the RIASEC system, Kerby and Ragan (2002) showed that vocational interests are relevant to understanding leisure activities of older adults. Specifically, Kerby and Ragan identified six types of leisure activities, which coincide with Holland's RIASEC system: The Realistic type shows high interests in manual (e.g., carpentry) and sporting activities. The Investigative type likes science and historical activities. The Artistic type prefers artistic (e.g., writing, painting) and household (e.g., baking, knitting) activities. The Social type is mostly interested in social outings (e.g., going to concerts, dining out). The Enterprising type pursues activities related to personal development such as tutoring and volunteer work. Finally, the Conventional type shows preferences for more conventional activities such as playing traditional games.

Although leisure and vocational interests seem to show a certain amount of overlap (Armstrong & Rounds, 2008), empirical research that assessed both leisure and vocational interests concurrently revealed inconclusive results on their relationship (for an overview see Leuty et al., 2015). Consequently, researchers advocated that leisure and vocational interests might be considered independently; particularly as leisure interests have been identified as a valuable additional instrument in career counseling and life planning for college students, working-age adults, and retirees alike (see Hansen, Dik, & Zhou, 2008). In this chapter, we follow this approach and discuss the roles of both vocational and leisure interests for understanding retirement.

Conceptualization of Retirement as a Temporal Process

Retirement, as the point of officially leaving the workforce, is a historically rather new phenomenon. Along with the industrial revolution and the implementation of social security systems, only starting at the beginning of the twentieth century were workers encouraged to retire at a particular age (Shultz & Wang, 2011). Nowadays, as a consequence of demographic and economic changes, many highly developed countries shifted from a policy of promoting early retirement toward encouraging the labor market participation of older people (OECD, 2006) and more and more countries increase the statutory retirement age. For example, the United States and Germany, as two of the world's leading economies, recently increased the full retirement age from 65 to 67.

From a psychological viewpoint, however, retirement is not just the single event of exiting the workforce but rather is a complex process that unfolds over a period of several years (Shultz & Wang, 2011; Wang, Olson, & Shultz, 2013). In that view, retirement is a longitudinal adjustment process that incorporates several sequential phases, namely, retirement planning, retirement decision making, actual transition from employment to retirement, and a post-retirement trajectory—including adjustment processes and even continued employment (Beehr, 1986; Wang & Shi, 2014).

In more detail, the psychological retirement process typically starts when workers begin to think about retiring (e.g., asking themselves what they will do after retirement; Adams & Rau, 2011) and start discussing their retirement plans with others (Wang & Shi, 2014). This phase of retirement planning is accompanied by the retirement decision-making process, during which workers make a choice on whether, when, how, and where they want to retire, that is, to behaviorally withdraw from their main employment (Feldman, 1994). When workers, finally, put their plans into action and retire, they undergo a change in life roles as they withdraw from the work role and take the retirement role (Adams, Prescher, Beehr, & Lepisto, 2002; Super, 1980; Wang, 2007). However, this role change is not necessarily an abrupt one. Rather, during an adjustment process that comprises the actual retirement transition and a post-retirement trajectory (Wang, 2007), the work as well as the retirement role might increase and decrease in importance (Super, 1980), making adjustment a dynamic, fluctuating process (see Wang, Henkens, & van Solinge, 2011). These life role changes and fluctuating adjustment levels are also reflected in changes in individuals' daily activities in post-retirement life, not only including leisure activities, but also volunteer work, and post-retirement paid work (Adams & Rau, 2011).

The psychological perspective on retirement as a temporal process emphasizes putting the research focus on individual differences as antecedents of retirement (Shultz & Wang, 2011). While corresponding research identified a wide number of individual attributes (e.g., gender, age, health, and personality; see Wang & Shi, 2014) that impact different phases of the retirement process, scholars so far missed the opportunity to study individual interests in this regard. However, research that identified older workers' personal needs and values as important determinants of the retirement process provides an indication of the possible role of individual interests for retirement. For instance, retirees who value leisure activities are more likely to retire voluntarily (Shultz, Morton, & Weckerle, 1998), whereas retirees with high generative motives (Dendinger, Adams, & Jacobsen, 2005) and higher entrepreneurial orientations (Davis, 2003) are more likely to engage in post-retirement paid work (so-called bridge employment). Besides individual factors, job and organizational factors, family factors, and socioeconomic factors are important determinants of each individual's retirement process (for a review see Wang & Shi, 2014).

A Theoretical Model on the Role of Interests in Retirement

Concatenating the largely unconnected literatures on interests and retirement, the present chapter provides a theoretical model on the importance of interests for understanding retirement (see Figure 8.1). Given that retirement is an important life-course transition from work to leisure (Nicolaisen, Thorsen, & Eriksen, 2012), we include both vocational interests (i.e., preferences for activities in the work life domain) and leisure interests (i.e., preferences for activities in the non-work-life domain) when discussing the role of interests in retirement. This is in line with extant research that examined both work and non-work-related factors when studying individual retirement (e.g., Schmidt & Lee, 2008; Wang & Shi, 2014) as well as in line with calls to consider vocational and leisure interests independently of each other (Leuty et al., 2015).

Following a temporal view on retirement (Shultz & Wang, 2011), in the following sections, we derive a number of propositions on the role of interests for retirement, which are summarized in Table 8.1. Specifically, we first conceptualize vocational and leisure interests as antecedents of the retirement process. Holland's (1959) theory of interests provides a framework for the explanation of stability and change in people's careers (Holland, 1996). Accordingly, (vocational) interests have been identified as an important determinant of young adults'

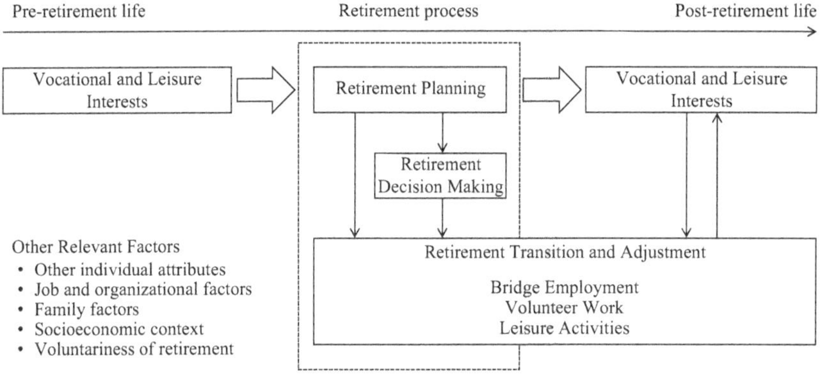

FIGURE 8.1 Theoretical model on the role of interests for understanding retirement.

TABLE 8.1 Propositions on the Role of Interests for Retirement

Interests as antecedents of retirement planning, decision making, and adjustment
1 Employees with higher vocational (leisure) interests will plan and decide to retire later (earlier).
2 Employees who experience (in)congruence between their vocational interests and their pre-retirement work environment will plan and decide to retire (earlier) later.
3 Retirees with relatively higher vocational interests will less well adjust to the retirement role, particularly when retirement was involuntary.
Interests as antecedents of post-retirement activities
4 In general, retirees will seek post-retirement employment, volunteer work, and/or leisure activities congruent to their interests. Voluntariness of retirement, financial status, and health are moderators of the relationship between interests and post-retirement activities.
5 Retirees' choice of specific post-retirement activities is a function of their experienced level of pre-retirement congruence between interests and environment.
Development and change of interests as a result of the retirement process
6 Vocational and leisure interests change and develop as a result of the retirement process.

career selection and entry (Fouad, 1999; Tracey & Hopkins, 2001). In this chapter, we propose interests to be likewise important antecedents for older adults' retirement choices and career exit decisions. Specifically, we describe how vocational and leisure interests might determine individuals' retirement planning, decision making, and adjustment as well as individuals' choice of post-retirement activities (i.e., bridge employment, volunteer work, and leisure activities).

Despite their stable qualities, interests continuously develop over the life span (Low et al., 2005). Not only do individuals become more certain of their interests with age (e.g., Csikszentmihalyi & Schneider, 2000), but interests also develop in response to certain life experiences and events (Lent, Brown, & Hackett, 1994; Leuty & Hansen, 2014). Therefore, we not only expect interests to manifest as important antecedents of retirement but also propose that vocational and leisure interests develop and change as a result of retirement. Specifically, the transition from employment to retirement depicts an important role transition (Ashforth, 2001), which provides new opportunities for self-development and occupational choices (Reis & Gold, 1993). Hence, retirement depicts an important life event that has the potential to initiate interest change as a part of further self-development.

When investigating the role of interests for understanding retirement, surely other potentially relevant factors and boundary conditions need to be considered. On that account, we discuss how individual attributes (i.e., health, wealth, age, and gender), job, organizational, and family factors, socioeconomic context, and voluntariness of retirement might interplay with interests in determining the retirement process.

Interests as Antecedents of the Retirement Process

Interests are individual preferences for certain activities, contexts in which activities occur, or outcomes of the preferred activities (Rounds, 1995). Accordingly, individuals differ from each other both in what they prefer (i.e., interest content, e.g., things vs. people; Prediger, 1982) and the contexts their preferences are situated in (e.g., work vs. leisure; Leuty et al., 2015). In the following, we argue how such individual differences in interest content and context may predict the individual retirement process.

Vocational choices are not made only once in life but individuals' careers keep developing across the entire life span (Super, 1980), ranging from individuals' career entry to their career exit. Recalling that interests represent rather stable individual preferences, vocational interests should play the same role in career choices at all ages (Costa, McCrae, & Holland, 1984). However, to date, empirical research mainly focused on the role of vocational interests for understanding the process of career planning, decision making, and adjustment of adolescents, college students, and young workers (Low & Rounds, 2006), whereas hardly any research examined interests in relation to the career exit and retirement process.

Interests as Antecedents of Retirement Planning, Decision Making, and Adjustment

In many cases, a worker's decision to retire is his or her individual motivated choice to behaviorally withdraw from work-related activities at a certain point in time (Adams et al., 2002; Topa et al., 2009). Scholars suggested that this voluntary retirement decision is influenced by several psychological factors, such as a person's career orientation (Dobson & Morrow, 1984), occupational commitment (Jones & McIntosh, 2010), retirement preferences (Barnes-Farrell, 2003), and the desire to pursue leisure activities (Shultz et al., 1998). Moreover, as Beehr (1986) pointed out, a person's retirement decision is likely to be based on a "combination of personal preferences and the environment's potential for matching these preferences" (p. 44). Accordingly, we propose personal interests to represent important antecedents of individual retirement planning and decision making.

Interests as antecedents of retirement planning and decision making.

Generally speaking, individuals are motivated to seek out activities and environments that best match their personal interests (Holland, 1996). Because voluntary retirement is commonly associated with a reduced commitment to work (Feldman, 1994) but increased time for leisure activities (Bidewell, Griffin, & Hesketh, 2006), we propose that individuals whose vocational interests are generally higher than their leisure interests (see Leuty et al., 2015) are more likely to decide to retire later as compared to "Leisurists" (ibid.). This expectation finds support in empirical studies that indicated a relationship between individual attitudes toward one's job and a person's retirement decision. For example, a study by Shultz and colleagues (1998) identified a person's dislike of his or her job as an antecedent of voluntary early retirement. Moreover, Adams and Beehr (1998) found those persons whose career is an important part of their self-identity to be less likely to retire. Schmidt and Lee (2008) also reported work centrality to negatively predict workers' retirement intentions. Meta-analytic findings further support the notion that the individual value of and involvement in work is related to a person's retirement decision and planning (Topa et al., 2009).

As for leisure interests, we expect "Leisurists" (Leuty et al., 2015) to be more likely to engage in retirement planning and to decide to retire, because "non-work interests can be a significant source of continuity for employees who do not experience continuity through their work. As a result, these individuals might be more likely to seek retirement instead of work, in order to achieve continuity in their lives (see Atchley, 1989)" (von Bonsdorff, Shultz, Leskinen, & Tansky, 2009, p. 84). Accordingly, leisure interests have been suggested to depict so-called "jump" factors that attract older workers toward (early) retirement (Nicolaisen et al., 2012). Likewise, Beehr (1986) proposed that employees who engage in leisure activities view retirement as more desirable because they deem it an attractive alternative to work. Again, empirical research supports this assumption. For example, the desire to pursue leisure interests or volunteer activities has been shown to predict early retirement (Shultz et al., 1998) and a high commitment to leisure activities is positively related to retirement intentions (Schmidt & Lee, 2008).

It is also conceivable that the fit (i.e., congruence) between interests and environmental factors in pre-retirement life plays a role in determining older workers' retirement planning and decision making (Feldman & Beehr, 2011). For employed adults, a high level of fit between a person's vocational interests and his or her work environment (i.e., high congruence) enhances the likelihood that this person stays in his or her job (Holland, 1996; Oleski & Subich, 1996; Nye, Su, Rounds, & Drasgow, 2017; Van Iddekinge, Roth, Putka, & Lanivich, 2011). Accordingly, we propose persons who experience a higher congruence between their vocational interests and their pre-retirement work environment to be more likely to stay in their job longer, that is, to retire later. On the other hand, individuals, whose work environment is incongruent with their vocational interests, will be more likely to engage in retirement planning and decision-making processes earlier. This proposition is in line with research that suggests a positive relationship between experienced incongruence and the perception of work stress on the one hand (Sutherland, Fogarty, & Pithers, 1995), and research that identified work stress as a predictor of retirement decisions on the other hand (Wang, Zhan, Liu, & Shultz, 2008). Moreover, job dissatisfaction, which is likely to be a result of incongruence (Holland, 1996), is related to retirement decisions (Wang & Shi, 2014).

Similarly, as for leisure interests, we argue that a missing pre-retirement fit between a person's leisure interests and his or her leisure environment might prompt the desire to retire in order to reach congruence. For example, an older worker with high leisure interests who feels that he or she does not have enough time to pursue his or her hobbies is likely to retire to have more leisure time (Shultz et al., 1998). However, older workers whose leisure interests are already met will not necessarily want to retire.

Interests as antecedents of retirement adjustment.

According to role theory (Ashforth, 2001), retirement depicts a role transition from work roles to retirement roles. This role transition influences individual retirement adjustment, depending on whether this transition matches a person's individual values, goals, and needs (Adams et al., 2002; Wang, 2007). Accordingly, as Barnes-Farrell (2003) stated, "the ability to follow one's preferences may have implications for a satisfying transition to the retirement role" (p. 160). As such, we argue that individual interests will influence the retirement transition and adjustment process. Specifically, we propose that retirees' paramount interest context affects their retirement adjustment: Retirees whose preferences are rather situated in the work context will have problems adjusting to the retirement role, because to them retirement means the loss of important work-role activities and, thus, of a major source of identity (e.g., Adams et al., 2002; Quick & Moen, 1998; Wang, 2007). This will particularly be true for those retirees whose retirement was involuntary, that is, for older workers who desired to keep their current employment but had to retire because of organizational policies or governmental regulations on compulsory retirement (e.g., pilots). At the same time, however, for those retirees whose interests are rather situated in leisure contexts, retirement involves the opportunity to meet and fulfill their preferences. Hence, retirees with high leisure interests will more easily adjust to retirement—irrespective of whether retirement was voluntary or not. This proposition finds empirical support in research indicating that interest-congruent persons typically show better psychological adjustment (Celeste, Walsh, & Raote, 1995; Walsh, Spokane, & Mitchell, 1976). Moreover, there is evidence showing that retirees who engage in activities of their own choice (i.e., activities that are congruent to their interests) remain in better health and are more satisfied with their lives (see Low & Rounds, 2006), with good health and satisfaction being indicators of good retirement adjustment (Wang et al., 2011).

Interests as Antecedents of Post-retirement Activities

The transition from work to retirement involves significant changes in how persons spend their time (Kranz-Kent & Stewart, 2007). At the same time, retirement does not necessarily imply a definite career exit, but can also involve the potential for changes and renewals in persons' careers (Fasbender et al., 2015; Wang et al., 2013; Wang & Shultz, 2010). Hence, from a life-span perspective on career development (Super, 1980), retirement provides an opportunity for further self-development and new occupational choices (Reis & Gold, 1993). This conceptualization of retirement as a career development stage highlights the important role of using persons' individual values, goals, and needs to explain their post-retirement activities (see Wang & Shi, 2014). Accordingly, interests have been suggested to play a role with regard to vocational and leisure activities of older people (Warren, Winer, & Dailey, 1981). Hence, we propose that interests will affect how people spend their post-retirement time. In particular, we suggest that retirees will seek post-retirement employment, volunteer work, or leisure activities accordant to their vocational and leisure interests. We base this proposition on the congruency assumption of Holland's (1997) theory of vocational choice, according to which individuals seek environments and activities that match their interests. This proposition is also congruent with Atchley's (1989) continuity theory of aging, according to which older workers seek continuity in their post-retirement lives by engaging in activities they highly value (see also Kim & Feldman, 2000).

Moreover, we suggest that retirees' choices of specific post-retirement activities are a function of their experienced pre-retirement vocational fit or misfit (i.e., level of pre-retirement congruence between interests and work environment). This proposition is, among others, based on findings from Griffin and Hesketh (2008) that showed peoples' evaluations of their pre-retirement work to be related to post-retirement activities. In particular, following notions on the relationship between job congruity and leisure activities put forward by Melamed and Meir (1981), we propose that retirees whose vocational interests were met in their pre-retirement life will choose post-retirement activities that match the type of activities they did at work. Retirees who worked in incongruent occupations, however, will seek post-retirement activities that might compensate for this lack of congruence.

Interests as antecedents of bridge employment.

As Atchley's (1989) continuity theory of aging suggests, bridge employment provides an opportunity for continuity for those retirees who place a high importance on their career. Hence, similar to the way that an individual's interests might predict his or her decision to retire, we propose retirees with more vocation-oriented interests (i.e., those who have interests that are more closely tied to vocational activities) to be more likely to engage in bridge employment. This proposition has not been directly tested by any empirical studies yet. However, researchers have found that constructs related to vocational interests can predict bridge employment. For example, workers' career attachment (Gobeski & Beehr, 2009) and retirees' motivational orientations (Zhan, Wang, & Shi, 2015) have been shown to predict bridge employment. Also, Fasbender and colleagues (2015) showed that the more an individual experiences meaningful work in his or her job, the higher the likelihood that he or she will engage in post-retirement employment. In addition, we propose the relationship between vocational interests and bridge employment to be even stronger for those who involuntarily retired, as those retirees might view bridge employment as a way to fulfill their need for work and to enhance the congruence between their personal interests and their environment.

We also expect individuals' fit between interests and environment to be related to the decision to take bridge employment. As Sutherland et al. (1995) showed, incongruence (i.e., misfit) is related to higher perceived work stress. Pre-retirement work stress, in turn, is negatively related to the likelihood to engage in bridge employment (Wang et al., 2008). Hence, incongruence between vocational interests and pre-retirement work environment might be negatively related to retirees' bridge employment. At the same time, contrarily, retirees' post-retirement misfit between their interests and the characteristics of their retirement environment might actually lead to the decision to engage in bridge employment in order to reach congruence (Wang & Shultz, 2010).

Comparable to vocational choices in young adulthood, when deciding to take bridge employment, the choice of a specific bridge employment is likely to be in accordance with one's vocational interests in terms of content. Indeed, Beehr and Bennett (2015) identified bridge employment as "the opportunity to explore personal interests" (p. 4) and stated that "older workers may be more motivated, for instance, to take bridge work that is consistent with their values and interests" (p. 5). Accordingly, for example, retirees with high Realistic vocational interests will be more likely to choose bridge employment in realistic work environments where they can use machines, tools, and materials, whereas retirees with high Social vocational interests will rather choose bridge employment that allows them to work with others (see Holland, 1996).

Individual differences in vocational interests may not only explain why some retirees engage in bridge employment while others do not, but also provide an explanation for why some retirees choose bridge employment similar to their pre-retirement employment (i.e., career bridge employment; Gobeski & Beehr, 2009; Wang et al., 2008), while others choose bridge employment in a field different from their previous job (i.e., noncareer bridge employment). Given that vocational interests direct occupational choices (Holland, 1996), for those retirees whose interests already were met in their pre-retirement life, choosing bridge employment similar to their main employment seems likely. However, for those retirees whose vocational interests were not met in their previous work life, bridge employment represents an opportunity to fulfill their vocational preferences and needs by choosing post-retirement employment in a different field according to their actual interests.

Interests as antecedents of post-retirement volunteer work.

Like bridge employment, engagement in volunteer work provides an opportunity for continuity in post-retirement life (Smith, 2004). Hence, we suggest the way interests antecede engagement in volunteer work to resemble the proposed way interests predict bridge employment. While bridge employment refers to paid work in post-retirement life, volunteer work is "unpaid work provided to parties to whom the worker owes no contractual, familial, or friendship obligations" (Wilson & Musick, 1997, p. 694). Accordingly, the main difference between bridge employment and post-retirement volunteer work is whether retirees get paid for their work or not. Hence, financial status might moderate the relationship between interests and choice of post-retirement activities (see Fasbender et al., 2015).

In addition, specific RIASEC interests—and particularly Social interests—will predict retirees' engagement in volunteer work. Clary and Snyder (1999) suggested several motivations to volunteer, including the desire to express one's social values and altruistic concerns for others. Accordingly, extant research suggests that volunteers indeed differ from nonvolunteers in their social motivational orientations (Zhan et al., 2015). For example, Erlinghagen and Hank (2005) showed older volunteers to have a higher desire to contribute something useful. Likewise, attitudes about helping people in need are related to the likelihood to volunteer (Toppe, Kirsch, & Michel, 2002) as are individuals' social and generative meaning of work (Fasbender et al., 2015). In addition, researchers reported a positive relationship between Social interests and community involvement in college students (Hansen & Scullard, 2002). Hence, we propose retirees with high Social interests (i.e., "Socials," Leuty et al., 2015) to be more likely to choose volunteer work in post-retirement life, because volunteer work often involves social interactions. Moreover, Kerby and Ragan (2002) identified high Enterprising interests to be related to leisure activities such as tutoring and volunteer work. Thus, we also propose retirees with high Enterprising interests to be more prone to engage in volunteer work in post-retirement life. In addition, it is also conceivable that the other four RIASEC interests might, at least to some extent, be related to volunteer work, as long as the volunteer work has the potential to meet a person's interests. For example, a retiree with high Artistic interests might volunteer for work that lets him or her do artistic work.

Interests as antecedents of post-retirement leisure activities.

Following the general assumptions of Holland's (1997) theory of vocational choice, we expect retirees to seek leisure activities that are likely to meet their interests. In particular, in line with our proposition that retirees who prefer work over leisure will be more likely to engage in bridge employment, we also propose retirees who prefer leisure over work to be more likely to use their post-retirement time to engage in leisure activities. Further, we expect interests to also predict retirees' choice of specific post-retirement leisure activities. First, based on extant research that used Holland's RIASEC system to classify interests in leisure activities of both working adults (e.g., Holmberg, Rosen, & Holland, 1991; Melamed & Meir, 1981) and retired adults (Kerby & Ragan, 2002), we propose that retirees seek leisure activities that match their interest content. For example, persons high in Social interests will prefer leisure activities that allow them to be in social contact, such as going out or taking care of their grandchildren. Persons high in Realistic interests, in contrast, will prefer leisure activities in which they can work with their hands (e.g., building furniture; Kerby & Ragan, 2002). That is, as also proposed in relation to bridge employment and volunteer work, we expect retirees to choose specific leisure activities congruent with their RIASEC interests. This, however, does not mean that retirees will necessarily engage in leisure activities that match their previous job (e.g., a former carpenter not necessarily engages in manual leisure activities). Rather, we expect retirees to use the autonomy that comes along with retirement to also explore new activities and make new experiences.

Again, we also expect individuals' fit between interests and environment to play a role. Specifically, particularly for those retirees who experienced incongruence between their occupational circumstances and their vocational interests in pre-retirement life, choosing new leisure activities in a content domain different from their previous job is likely. Moreover, vocational and leisure interests do not necessarily resemble each other. For example, people with a social job might, despite a high Social vocational interest, prefer "things" in their leisure time (see Sonnentag, 2001). Accordingly, retirees might want to choose post-retirement leisure activities that meet other needs and interests than have been fulfilled by their job. This idea is supported by research on incongruent vocational choices of working adults that shows that leisure activities can be compensatory when work activities are inconsistent with one's vocational interests (Melamed, Meir, & Samson, 1995).

Finally, we expect retirees to engage in leisure activities rather than in bridge employment or volunteer work if their interests are unlikely to be met by available bridge employment or volunteer work. For example, it is conceivable that retirees with high Artistic interests (i.e., "Artists," Leuty et al., 2015) will use their post-retirement time for creative activities such as painting or singing in a choir, particularly when they have not had the opportunity to follow those leisure interests in their pre-retirement life.

Development and Change of Interests as a Result of the Retirement Process

Although interests are quite stable across the life course (Low et al., 2005), they still can develop as a result of a person's individual experiences (Lent et al., 1994; Low & Rounds, 2006). Specifically, in their model of interest development, Lent and colleagues (1994) suggest that the initial process of interest formation during childhood and adolescence might repeat itself at any phase of the life span in response to compelling life experiences such as job layoff or the birth of a child. We argue that retirement, as a process involving fundamental changes in both work and non-work life, represents such a compelling life experience. Further, retirement depicts an important role transition (e.g., Wang, 2007) and new role demands are likely to trigger changes in interests (Low & Rounds, 2006, p. 256). Thus, we propose that vocational and leisure interests change and develop as a result of the retirement process.

In particular, retirement depicts one of the major life course transitions (Super, 1980) and is characterized by ongoing changes in peoples' circumstances and activities. Hence, it is reasonable to expect that retirement has a general impact on the individual (see Wang et al., 2011). Given that post-retirement life is filled with plenty of new opportunities, we argue that—to a certain extent—the post-retirement phase resembles the phase of career choice and entry in early adult life. Relating to young adults, Super (1957) stated that participation in leisure activities facilitates the development of vocational interests, because the engagement in new activities provides opportunities to develop an individual identity (see also Hendel & Harrold, 2004; Leuty et al., 2015). Likewise, Low and Rounds (2006) point out that the freedom people have in choosing contexts, such as work and leisure activities, affects the development of interests. When young adults enter the workforce, new activities and related "experiences serve to deepen the characteristics that lead people to those experiences in the first place, resulting in an elaboration ... of the interest dispositions being shaped by experience" (p. 254).

In a similar way, because retirement involves freedom and opportunity to choose and pursue new activities, we propose that by developing new daily activity structures and attaining new experiences, retirees might encounter interests they were not aware of while they were still employed. In particular, previous research suggests that retirement creates a large void in daily activity structure by freeing time from work, which requires retirees to develop new daily routines to restructure their life (Wang et al., 2011; Wang & Shi, 2014). Hence, we expect that retirement will provide opportunities for individuals to discover new interests or reprioritize their existing interests (see Nicolaisen et al., 2012). For example, a newly retired former bookkeeper (i.e., a conventional occupation; Holland, 1996) might join a friend in an arts class and only there find out about her Artistic interests. Or a former kindergarten teacher (i.e., a social occupation) might help his neighbor to build a pool and, thereby, encounter his Realistic interests. Moreover, because of the fact that retirement involves withdrawal from work-related activities but an increased orientation toward leisure activities (Krantz-Kent & Stewart, 2007), the relative order of vocational versus leisure interests or the mean level of vocational interests might change after retirement in a way that those persons who are already retired "might be expected to have lowered vocational interests in general" (Costa et al., 1984, p. 393).

Eventually, similar to factors that determine the development of interests in adolescence and young adulthood (see Lent et al., 1994; Low & Rounds, 2006), factors such as role models (e.g., the already retired friend who attends arts classes) and social influences such as stereotypic assumptions of retirees' activities (e.g., the typical retiree does gardening or knitting) will be influential in determining the activities retirees engage in and, ultimately, the further development of retirees' interests.

Other Relevant Factors to Understand the Role of Interests in Retirement

Though we propose interests to be an important potential antecedent of the retirement process, other relevant factors related to retirement planning, retirement decision making, retirement adjustment, and post-retirement activities need to be taken into account. More precisely, although interests will influence older workers' intentions to retire or retirees' intentions to pursue specific post-retirement activities, personal or contextual constraints might impede persons' opportunities to select activities. For example, a musician can no longer play his instrument if suffering from rheumatism and a person engaged in bridge employment may have to cut back his or her working hours if he or she has to take care of an ill spouse (see Kim & Feldman, 2000). Thus, based on Szinovacz's (2013) multilevel perspective of retirement and the potential impact factors on the retirement process proposed by Wang and Shultz (2010), we expect individual attributes besides interests, job and organizational factors, family factors, and the socioeconomic context to manifest as important boundary conditions or common causes for understanding the role of interests in retirement.

Retirement research consistently identified individual attributes such as health and financial status to have a strong influence on retirement decisions: workers with insufficient income and good health are less likely to retire (Barnes-Farrell, 2003). Likewise, health and wealth are important determinants of retirees' post-retirement activities. Poor health is negatively related to bridge employment (Topa et al., 2009), volunteer work (Choi, 2003), and retirees' engagement in leisure activities (Holmes & Dorfman, 2000). Further, Kim and DeVaney (2005) found indebted retirees to be more likely to engage in bridge employment. Thus, we expect health and wealth to be important boundary conditions of interests' influence on the retirement process, which limit the likelihood for interests to translate into actual career or leisure activities.

In addition, demographic variables like gender and age will interplay with interests in predicting the retirement process. As for gender, ample research shows its relevance for both interests and retirement. Specifically, men show higher Realistic and Investigative interests, and women show stronger Social, Artistic, and Conventional interests (Su, Rounds, & Armstrong, 2009). At the same time, men are more likely to take bridge employment (Davis, 2003; Wang et al., 2008), and women are more likely to plan for post-retirement volunteer work (Moen, Plassmann, & Sweet, 2001) and leisure activities (Petkoska & Earl, 2009). Following our previous propositions on interests as antecedents of post-retirement activities, we suggest that gender differences in interests could at least partly explain reported gender differences in post-retirement activities. In other words, we expect interests to serve as the potential underlying mechanisms (i.e., mediators) that link gender differences to post-retirement activities.

Furthermore, age surely plays an important role in predicting retirement decisions and post-retirement activities (Beehr & Bennett, 2015; Wang & Shi, 2014): The older the worker, the more likely it is that he or she will retire. At the same time, the younger a retiree is, the more likely it is that he or she will engage in bridge employment (e.g., Davis, 2003). As for interests, unfortunately, only few studies on the development of interests included participants older than 25 (Leuty & Hansen, 2014) and to the best of our knowledge no study examined development and change of interests as an outcome of retirement. However, the studies that included older participants indeed suggest slight changes in interests with age. In particular, Costa et al. (1984) found persons over age 55 to show slightly lower Realistic, Artistic, and Enterprising interests, whereas Thompson, Donnay, Morris, and Schaubhut (2004) reported a slight increase in Artistic and Social interests with age. Leuty and Hansen (2014) found a positive correlation between age and Enterprising as well as Conventional interests. Based on these—although inconclusive— findings, it is conceivable that age may play a role in explaining the afore-proposed relationships between interests and retirement.

Several job and organizational factors, such as pre-retirement job characteristics and flexible job options, may also play important roles in explaining the relationship between interests and retirement. For instance, as for Realistic jobs that involve a high amount of physical work (e.g., carpenter), despite potential continued high Realistic interests, due to decreasing health and physical strength, some "Realistic" bridge employment or leisure activities may not be possible anymore. Further, family factors like having a working spouse and dependent children at home are related to retirement (Kim & Feldman, 2000) and might influence interests' ability to predict retirement.

Finally, features of the social, physical, and cultural environment (see Lent et al., 1994) and societal factors (see Beehr & Bennett, 2015) also need to be considered. For example, stereotypical social expectations (e.g., gender socializing), typical role demands (e.g., "the typical retiree"), national and cultural norms (e.g., low versus high participation countries with regard to volunteer work of older people; Erlinghagen & Hank, 2005) as well as historic and political influences (e.g., governmentally restricted occupational choices as happened in the former German Democratic Republic or mandatory retirement ages) might impact the role that interests play in the retirement process.

Future Research Directions

For decades, vocational interests have been used in career counseling to match individuals with educational and work environments (Low et al., 2005). As our theoretical model on the role of interests for understanding retirement implies, interests may be likewise useful "for understanding and serving the needs of individuals at the end of their careers" (Warren et al., 1981, p. 104), and in particular for understanding the individual retirement process. However, as no studies so far have systematically considered interests as potential antecedents or outcomes of the retirement process, clearly research is needed to empirically examine and evaluate the current theoretical model. Therefore, we propose several research directions to help guide future empirical examinations on the role of interests in retirement.

Examining Interests as Antecedents of Retirement

We advocate future research to examine interests as antecedents of retirement. In order to approximate causal inferences as well as to capture the dynamic nature of retirement as a temporal process over multiple phases, longitudinal research designs seem adequate to test the current theoretical model (Shultz & Wang, 2011). Thereby, as discussed in this chapter, future studies might assess both leisure and vocational interests in pre-retirement life as predictors of retirement planning, retirement decision making, retirement adjustment, and choice of a wide range of post-retirement activities (i.e., career as well as noncareer bridge employment, volunteer work, and several leisure activities). In addition, peoples' congruence between interests and work and leisure environments in both pre- and post-retirement life should be taken into account.

Also, as elaborated earlier, other well-known antecedents of interests and retirement, including individual attributes such as age, gender, and health, job, organizational, and family factors as well as societal factors, should be incorporated when studying the relationship between interests and retirement. Moreover, because retirement is not always a result of personal choice, the utility of interests as antecedents of retirement planning and decision making may depend on the extent to which retirement is voluntary (Shultz & Wang, 2011). Likewise, voluntariness of retirement might be considered an important boundary condition of the relationship between interests and retirement adjustment and choice of post-retirement activities.

Examining Development and Change of Interests across the Entire Life Span

Although it is reasonable to expect certain continuity in interests (e.g., workers high in Realistic interests are unlikely to lose all interest in manual activities after they retire), it is conceivable that interest hierarchies (i.e., the importance of single interests) may change intra-individually over the life span. However, because most research on development and change of interests did not include participants over the age of 25 (Leuty & Hansen, 2014), we have little knowledge on possible age differences in interests for older aged workers and retirees. Hence, empirical studies are needed that shed light on if and how interests change across the entire life span. As previously discussed, Lent and colleagues' social cognitive theory of career development (1994) provides a theoretical framework for studying the development and change of interests. Accordingly, future research may pay particular attention to how compelling life experiences and role transitions, such as the transition from work to retirement, shape individual preferences, both in terms of vocational and leisure interests.

Finally, as discussed earlier, persons' past interests (e.g., retirees' pre-retirement leisure interests) and congruence experiences (e.g., retirees' perceived congruence between vocational interests and actual employment features in pre-retirement life) may have implications for the development and change of interests (e.g., for the change of interests as a result of retirement). Therefore, similar to the afore-proposed way to capture retirement as a temporal process, the development and change of interests across the life span is optimally examined using longitudinal studies.

Methodological Issues

Research on retirement as well as on the development of interests often suffers from several methodological problems. First, few studies have considered temporal issues in retirement processes and interest development. Instead, the majority of research constitutes cross-sectional studies that, for example, looked at the relationship between age and interests at one point in time. The resulting correlational findings are not suitable to draw causal inferences or to make statements on development and change (Wang et al., 2011). Hence, as advocated earlier, longitudinal research is needed.

Second, however, longitudinal research alone might not be sufficient to gain profound insight into retirement processes and interest development. In particular, the relevant factors may include not only intra-individual aging processes, but also generational experiences, birth cohort effects, and periodical influences (see Leuty & Hansen, 2014). For instance, both the retirement process and the development of individual interests have been linked to societal factors such as gender socializing and historical influences (see Leuty & Hansen, 2014; Shultz & Wang, 2011). Accordingly, cohort effects might play a role (e.g., Thompson et al., 2004). Similarly, it is plausible that different generations show different interest patterns that, in turn, might explain generational differences in retirement decisions. Likewise, potential changes in interests might be due to retirement, age, or cohort differences (Costa et al., 1984). Hence, it is crucial for future research to isolate the effects of age, generation, and cohort, for instance by using time-lag cohort designs.

Third, as for retirement, it seems crucial to understand retirement as a psychological process incorporating several phases (Shultz & Wang, 2011). Hence, instead of merely comparing retirees with non-retirees, individual retirement trajectories should be studied. The same applies for the examination of interests in retirement. More precisely, following the idea of retirement as a dynamic process, interest trajectories contingent upon retirement trajectories might be studied, showing how interests potentially develop in response to different retirement phases. Moreover, as for interests, future studies on the role of interests in retirement should independently measure leisure and vocational interests in order to disentangle their effects.

Summary and Conclusions

With the increasing number of workers of retirement age due to demographic changes, scholarly attention on retirement as an important career stage has grown. Following a temporal view on retirement, in this chapter, we presented a theoretical model on the potential role of interests for understanding retirement and derived a number of testable propositions. Specifically, we introduced vocational and leisure interests as antecedents of retirement planning, retirement decision making, and retirement adjustment as well as of post-retirement activities in terms of bridge employment, volunteer work, and leisure activities. Further, we discussed interests as potential outcomes of the retirement process shedding light on how interests may change and develop as a result of the retirement process. Finally, we discussed other potentially relevant factors to understand the role of interests in retirement, including other individual attributes besides interests, job, organizational, and family factors, retirees' socioeconomic context, and voluntariness of retirement. We ended the chapter providing suggestions for research to empirically examine and evaluate the here-proposed theoretical model on the role of interests in retirement.

References

Adams, G. A., & Beehr, T. A. (1998). Turnover and retirement: A comparison of their similarities and differences. *Personnel Psychology, 51*, 643–665. doi:10.1111/j.1744-6570.1998.tb00255.x

Adams, G. A., Prescher, J., Beehr, T. A., & Lepisto, L. (2002). Applying work-role attachment theory to retirement decision-making. *International Journal of Aging and Human Development, 54*, 125–137. doi:10.2190/JRUQ-XQ2N-UP0A-M432

Adams, G. A., & Rau, B. L. (2011). Putting off tomorrow to do what you want today: Planning for retirement. *American Psychologist, 66*, 180–92. doi:10.1037/a0022131

Armstrong, P. I., & Rounds, J. (2008). Linking leisure interests to the RIASEC world of work map. *Journal of Career Development, 35*, 5–22. doi:10.1177/0894845308317933

Ashforth, B. (2001). *Role transitions in organizational life: An identity based perspective.* Mahwah, NJ: Erlbaum.

Atchley, R. (1989). A continuity theory of normal aging. *The Gerontologist, 29*, 183–190. doi:10.1093/geront/29.2.183

Barnes-Farrell, J. L. (2003). Beyond health and wealth: Attitudinal and other influences on retirement decision-making. In G. A. Adams & T. A. Beehr (Eds.), *Retirement: Reasons, processes, and results* (pp. 159–187). New York: Springer.

Beehr, T. A. (1986). The process of retirement: A review and recommendations for future investigation. *Personnel Psychology, 39*, 31–55. doi:10.1111/j.1744-6570.1986.tb00573.x

Beehr, T. A., & Bennett, M. M. (2015). Working after retirement: Features of bridge employment and research directions. *Work, Aging and Retirement, 1*, 112–128.

Bidewell, J., Griffin, B., & Hesketh, B. (2006). Time of retirement: Including a delay discounting perspective in retirement models. *Journal of Vocational Behavior, 68*, 368–387. doi:10.1016/j.jvb.2005.06.002

Celeste, B. L., Walsh, W. B., & Raote, R. G. (1995). Congruence and psychological adjustment for practicing male ministers. *Career Development Quarterly, 43*, 374–384. doi:10.1002/j.2161-0045.1995.tb00442.x

Choi, L. H. (2003). Factors affecting volunteerism among older adults. *The Journal of Applied Gerontology, 22*, 179–196. doi:10.1177/0733464803251814

Clary, E. G., & Snyder, M. (1999). The motivations to volunteer: Theoretical and practical considerations. *Current Directions in Psychological Science, 8*, 156–159. doi:10.1111/1467-8721.00037

Costa, P. T., Jr., McCrae, R. R., & Holland, J. L. (1984). Personality and vocational interests in an adult sample. *Journal of Applied Psychology, 69*, 390–400.

Csikszentmihalyi, M., & Schneider, B. (2000). *Becoming adult: How teenagers prepare for the world of work*. New York: Basic Books.

Davis, M. (2003). Factors related to bridge employment participation among private sector early retirees. *Journal of Vocational Behavior, 63*, 55–71. doi:10.1016/S0001-8791(02)00016-7

Dendinger, V. M., Adams, G. A., & Jacobsen, J. D. (2005). Reasons for working and their relationship to retirement attitudes, job satisfaction and occupational self-efficacy of bridge employees. *International Journal of Aging and Human Development, 61*, 21–35. doi:10.2190/K8KU-46LH-DTW5-44TU

Dobson, C., & Morrow, P. C. (1984). Effects of career orientation on retirement attitudes and retirement planning. *Journal of Vocational Behavior, 24*, 73–83. doi:10.1016/0001-8791(84)90067-8

Dohm, A. (2000). Gauging the labor force effects of retiring baby-boomers. *Monthly Labor Review, 123*(7), 17–25. doi:10.2307/41845213

Erlinghagen, K., & Hank, M. (2005). *Participation of older Europeans in volunteer work*. Mannheim, Germany: University of Mannheim, MEA discussion papers. Retrieved from http://mea.mpisoc.mpg.de/uploads/user_mea_discussionpapers/0v0ohjjzj0wt6j7e_dp71-05.pdf

Fasbender, U., Wang, M., Voltmer, J.-B., & Deller, J. (2015). The meaning of work for post-retirement employment decisions. *Work, Aging, and Retirement, 2*, 12–23. doi:0.1093/workar/wav015

Feldman, D. C. (1994). The decision to retire early: A review and conceptualization. *Academy of Management Review, 19*, 285–311. doi:10.5465/AMR.1994.9410210751

Feldman, D. C., & Beehr, T. A. (2011). A three-phase model of retirement decision making. *American Psychologist, 66*, 192–203. doi:10.1037/a0022153

Fouad, N. A. (1999). Validity evidence for interest inventories. In M. L. Savickas & R. L. Spokane (Eds.), *Vocational interests: Meaning, measurement, and counseling use* (pp. 193–209). Palo Alto, CA: Davies-Black.

Gaudron, J.-P., & Vautier, S. (2007). Analyzing individual differences in vocational, leisure, and family interests: A multitrait-multimethod approach. *Journal of Vocational Behavior, 70*, 561–573. doi:10.1016/j.jvb.2007.01.004

Gobeski, K. T., & Beehr, T. A. (2009). How retirees work: Predictors of different types of bridge employment. *Journal of Organizational Behavior, 30*, 401–425. doi:10.1002/job.547

Griffin, B., & Hesketh, B. (2008). Post-retirement work: The individual determinants of paid and volunteer work. *Journal of Occupational and Organizational Psychology, 81*, 101–121. doi:10.1348/096317907X202518

Hansen, J.-I. C., Dik, B. J., & Zhou, S. (2008). An examination of the structure of leisure interests of college students, working-age adults, and retirees. *Journal of Counseling Psychology, 55*, 133–145. doi:10.1037/0022-0167.55.2.133

Hansen, J.-I. C., & Scullard, M. (2002). Psychometric evidence for the Leisure Interest Questionnaire and analyses of the structure of leisure interests. *Journal of Counseling Psychology, 49*, 331–341. doi:10.1037/0022-0167.49.3.331

Hendel, D. D., & Harrold, R. D. (2004). Undergraduate student leisure interests over three decades. *College Student Journal, 38*, 557–568.

Holland, J. L. (1959). A theory of vocational choice. *Journal of Counseling Psychology, 6*, 35–45. doi:10.1037/h0040767

Holland, J. L. (1996). Exploring careers with a typology: What we have learned and some new directions. *American Psychologist, 51*, 397–406. doi:10.1037/0003-066X.51.4.397

Holland, J. L. (1997). *Making vocational choices* (3rd ed.). Odessa, FL: Psychological Assessment Resources.

Holmberg, K., Rosen, D., & Holland, J. L. (1991). *The leisure activities finder*. Odessa, FL: Psychological Assessment Resources.

Holmes, J. S., & Dorfman, L. T. (2000). The effects of specific health conditions on activities in retirement. *Activities, Adaptation & Aging, 25*, 47–65. doi:10.1300/J016v25n01_04

Jones, D. A., & McIntosh, B. R. (2010). Organizational and occupational commitment in relation to bridge employment and retirement intentions. *Journal of Vocational Behavior, 77*, 290–303. doi:10.1016/j.jvb.2010.04.004

Kerby, D. S., & Ragan, K. M. (2002). Activity interests and Holland's RIASEC system in older adults. *International Journal of Aging and Human Development, 55*, 117–139. doi:10.2190/W0G9-NBYN-H6WC-LTDN

Kim, H., & DeVaney, S. A. (2005). The selection of partial or full retirement by older workers. *Journal of Family and Economic Issues, 26*, 371–394. doi:10.1007/s10834-005-5903-8

Kim, S., & Feldman, D. C. (2000). Working in retirement: The antecedents of bridge employment and its consequences for quality of life in retirement. *Academy of Management Journal, 43*, 1195–1210. doi:10.2307/1556345

Krantz-Kent, R., & Stewart, J. (2007). How do older Americans spend their time? *Monthly Labor Review*, 5, 8–26.

Lent, R. W., Brown, S. D., & Hackett, G. (1994). Toward a unifying social cognitive theory of career and academic interest, choice, and performance. *Journal of Vocational Behavior, 45*, 79–122. doi:10.1006/jvbe.1994.1027

Leuty, M. E., & Hansen, J.-I. C. (2014). Testing apart the relations between age, birth cohort, and vocational interests. *Journal of Counseling Psychology, 61*, 289–298. doi:10.1037/a0035341

Leuty, M. E., Hansen, J.-I. C., & Speaks, S. Z. (2015). Vocational and leisure interests: A profile-level approach to examining interests. *Journal of Career Assessment*. Advanced online publication. doi:10.1177/1069072715580321

Low, K. S. D., & Rounds, J. (2006). Vocational interests. In J. S. Thomas & D. L. Segal (Eds.), *Comprehensive handbook of personality and psychopathology* (Vol. 1, pp. 251–267). New York: Wiley.

Low, K. S. D., Yoon, M., Roberts, B. W., & Rounds, J. (2005). The stability of vocational interests from early adolescence to middle adulthood: A quantitative review of longitudinal studies. *Psychological Bulletin, 131*, 713–737. doi:10.1037/0033-2909.131.5.713

Melamed, S., & Meir, E. I. (1981). The relationship between interests-job incongruity and selection of avocational activity. *Journal of Vocational Behavior, 18*, 310–325. doi:10.1016/0001-8791(81)90018-X

Melamed, S., Meir, E. I., & Samson, A. (1995). The benefits of personality-leisure congruence: Evidence and implications. *Journal of Leisure Research, 27*, 25–40.

Moen, P., Plassmann, V., & Sweet, S. (2001). *The Cornell Midcareer Paths and Passages Study*. Ithaca, NY: Cornell University, Bronfenbrenner Life Course Center.

Nicolaisen, M., Thorsen, K., & Eriksen, S, H. (2012). Jump into the void? Factors related to a preferred retirement age: Gender, social interests, and leisure activities. *International Journal of Aging and Human Development, 75*, 239–271. doi:10.2190/AG.75.3.c

Nye, C. D., Su, R., Rounds, J., & Drasgow, F. (2017). Interest congruence and performance: Revisiting recent meta-analytic findings. *Journal of Vocational Behavior, 98*, 138–151. doi:10.1016/j.jvb.2016.11.002

OECD (Organization for Economic Cooperation and Development}. (2006). *Live longer, work longer.* Paris, France: OECD Publishing.

Oleski, D., & Subich, L. M. (1996). Congruence and career change in employed adults. *Journal of Vocational Behavior, 49*, 221–229. doi:10.1006/jvbe.1996.0041

Petkoska, J., & Earl, J. K. (2009). Understanding the influence of demographic and psychological variables on retirement planning. *Psychology and Aging, 24*, 245–251. doi:10.1037/a0014096

Prediger, D. J. (1982). Dimensions underlying Holland's hexagon: Missing link between interests and occupations? *Journal of Vocational Behavior, 48*, 59–67. doi:10.1016/0001-8791(82)90036-7

Quick, H. E., & Moen, P. (1998). Gender, employment, and retirement quality: A life course approach to the differential experiences of men and women. *Journal of Occupational Health Psychology, 1*, 44–64. doi:10.1037/1076-8998.3.1.44

Reis, M., & Gold, D. P. (1993). Retirement, personality, and life satisfaction: A review and two models. *The Journal of Applied Gerontology, 12*, 261–282. doi:10.1177/073346489301200209

Rounds, J. B. (1995). Vocational interests: Evaluation of structural hypotheses. In D. Lubinski & R. V. Dawis (Eds.), *Assessing individual differences in human behavior: New concepts, methods, and findings* (pp. 177–232). Palo Alto, CA: Consulting Psychologists Press.

Rounds, J., & Su, R. (2014). The nature and power of interests. *Current Directions in Psychological Science, 23*, 98–103. doi:10.1177/0963721414522812

Schmidt, J. A., & Lee, K. (2008). Voluntary retirement and organizational turnover intentions: The differential associations with work and non-work commitment constructs. *Journal of Business and Psychology, 22*, 297–309. doi: 10.1007/s10869-008-9068-y

Shultz, K. S., Morton, K. R., & Weckerle, J. R. (1998). The influence of push and pull factors on voluntary and involuntary early retirees' retirement decision and adjustment. *Journal of Vocational behavior, 53*, 45–57. doi:10.1006/jvbe.1997.1610

Shultz, K. S., & Wang, M. (2011). Psychological perspectives on the changing nature of retirement. *American Psychologist, 66*, 170–179. doi:10.1037/a0022411

Smith, D. B. (2004). Volunteering in retirement: Perceptions of midlife workers. *Nonprofit and Voluntary Sector Quarterly, 33*, 55–73. doi:10.1177/0899764003260591

Sonnentag, S. (2001). Work, recovery activities, and individual well-being: A diary study. *Journal of Occupational Health Psychology, 6*, 196–210. doi:10.1037//1076-8998.6.3.196

Su, R., Rounds, J., & Armstrong, P. I. (2009). Men and things, women and people: A meta-analysis of sex differences in interests. *Psychological Bulletin, 135*, 859–884. doi:10.1037/a0017364

Super, D. E. (1957). *The psychology of careers.* New York: Harper & Row.

Super, D. E. (1980). A life-span, life-space approach to career development. *Journal of Vocational Behavior, 16*, 282–289. doi:10.1016/0001-8791(80)90056-1

Sutherland, L., Fogarty, G., & Pithers, R. (1995). Congruence as a predictor of occupational stress. *Journal of Vocational Behavior, 46*, 292–309. doi:10.1006/jvbe.1995.1022

Szinovacz, M. E. (2013). A multilevel perspective for retirement research. In M. Wang (Ed.), *The Oxford handbook of retirement* (pp. 152–173). New York: Oxford University Press.

Thompson, R. C., Donnay, D. A. C., Morris, M. L., & Schaubhut, N. A. (2004). *Exploring age and gender difference in vocational interests*. Poster presented at the Annual Convention of the American Psychological Association, Honolulu, HI. Abstract retrieved from https://www.cpp.com/pdfs/Strong_Age_and_Gender.pdf

Tinsley, H. E. A., & Tinsley, D. J. (2015). Leisure. In P. J. Harting, M. L. Savickas, & W. B. Walsh (Eds.), *APA handbook of career intervention. Vol. 2: Applications* (pp. 209–222). Washington, DC: American Psychological Association. doi:10.1037/14439-016

Topa, G., Moriano, J. M., Depolo, M., Carlos-María Alcover, C.-M., & Morales, J. F. (2009). Antecedents and consequences of retirement planning and decision-making: A meta-analysis and model. *Journal of Vocational Behavior, 75*, 38–55. doi:10.1016/j.jvb.2009.03.002

Toppe, C. M., Kirsch, A. D., & Michel, J. (2002). *Giving and volunteering in the United States: Findings from a national survey*. Washington, DC: Independent Sector. Retrieved from http://www.cpanda.org/pdfs/gv/GV01Report.pdf

Tracey, T. J. G., & Hopkins, N. (2001). Correspondence of interests and abilities with occupational choice. *Journal of Counseling Psychology, 48*, 178–189. doi:10.1037/0022-0167.48.2.178

Van Iddekinge, C. H., Roth, P. L., Putka, D. J., & Lanivich, S. E. (2011). Are you interested? A meta-analysis of relations between vocational interests and employee performance and turnover. *Journal of Applied Psychology, 96*, 1167–1194. doi:10.1037/a0024343

Varca, P. E., & Shaffer, G. S. (1982). Holland's theory: Stability of avocational interests. *Journal of Vocational Behavior, 21*, 288–298. doi:10.1016/0001-8791(82)90037-9

von Bonsdorff, M. E., Shultz, K. S., Leskinen, E., & Tansky, J. (2009). The choice between retirement and bridge employment: A continuity theory and life course perspective. *International Journal of Aging and Human Development, 69*, 79–100. doi:10.2190/AG.69.2.a

Walsh, W. B., Spokane, A. R., & Mitchell, E. (1976). Consistent occupational preferences and academic adjustment. *Research in Higher Education, 4*, 123–129. doi:10.1007/BF00991379

Wang, M. (2007). Profiling retirees in the retirement transition and adjustment process: Examining the longitudinal change patterns of retirees' psychological well-being. *Journal of Applied Psychology, 92*, 455–474. doi:10.1037/0021-9010.92.2.455

Wang, M., Henkens, K., & van Solinge, H. (2011). Retirement adjustment: A review of theoretical and empirical advancements. *American Psychologist, 66*, 204–213. doi:10.1037/a0022414

Wang, M., Olson, D. A., & Shultz, K. S. (2013). *Mid and late career issues: An integrative perspective*. New York: Psychological Press.

Wang, M., & Shi, J. (2014). Psychological research on retirement. *Annual Review of Psychology, 65*, 209–233. doi:10.1146/annurev-psych-010213-115131

Wang, M., & Shultz, K. S. (2010). Employee retirement: A review and recommendations for future investigation. *Journal of Management, 36*, 172–206. doi:10.1177/0149206309347957

Wang, M., Zhan, Y., Liu, S., & Shultz, K. (2008). Antecedents of bridge employment: A longitudinal investigation. *Journal of Applied Psychology, 93*, 818–830. doi:10.1037/0021-9010.93.4.818

Warren, G. D., Winer, J. L., & Dailey, K. C. (1981). Extending Holland's theory to the later years. *Journal of Vocational Behavior, 18*, 104–114. doi:10.1016/0001-8791(81)90033-6

Wilson, J., & Musick, M. (1997). Who cares? Towards an integrated theory of volunteer work. *American Sociological Review, 62*, 694–713. doi:10.2307/2657355

Zhan, Y., Wang, M., & Shi, J. (2015). Retirees' motivational orientations and bridge employment: Testing the moderating role of gender. *Journal of Applied Psychology, 100*, 1319–1331.

9

NEW(ISH) DIRECTIONS FOR VOCATIONAL INTERESTS RESEARCH

Robert Hogan and Ryne A. Sherman

HOGAN ASSESSMENT SYSTEMS

Alfred North Whitehead once observed that all philosophy is an extended footnote to Plato. In the same way, we think that the modern study of vocational interests can be seen as an extended footnote to John Holland. Building on that metaphor, this chapter makes four points. First, Freud argued (correctly in our view) that the big problems in life concern choosing a mate and choosing a vocation, and that we never do either for rational reasons. Mainstream psychology spends vast amounts of time studying romantic relationships, and almost no time studying careers. However, a successful career usually potentiates a person's romantic prospects. Given the life-defining importance of vocational psychology, and the robust body of research supporting its major claims, we find it puzzling that (quoting Holland, 1976) "The interest literature still remains largely outside the mainstream of psychology" (p. 523). For example, few people at the annual meetings of the Society of Industrial/Organizational Psychology or Society for Personality and Social Psychology know John Holland's work. The first point of this essay, therefore, is to offer some suggestions for raising the profile of vocational psychology within academic psychology. Second, Holland regarded his RIASEC model as a contribution to personality psychology. We expand on this theme by analyzing the relationship between needs, values, interests, traits, and personality theory. That they are all related is seen in the following observation: "Personality... and such related constructs as values and interests—in some sense defines psychology for it is in the framing of the internal world of people that differentiates psychology from all others sciences. Personality conjures up thoughts about needs that people attempt to gratify (e.g., Maslow, 1954), the preferences people have for behaving in ambiguous or relatively unstructured situations (e.g., McCaulley, 1990), and the internal enduring interests and values of people that serve as guides or standards for their behavior (e.g., Holland, 1997)" (Schneider & Smith, 2004, p. 347). Third, vocational interest measures tell us about peoples' career aspirations, but to realize their aspirations, people must first be able to get a job. We describe a model of employability and argue that employability is an important part of vocational psychology. Finally, aspiring to and being employed in a particular vocation is no guarantee that a person will be successful in that vocation. In our judgment, the field of vocational psychology would be further enriched by focusing on the determinants of career success—in addition to the traditional focus on career fit. We offer some observations regarding generic determinants of career success. Attention to these issues should broaden the appeal of vocational psychology as a discipline.

Definitions

We begin by reviewing two conceptual/definitional issues. First, it is important to note that the terms *values, needs*, and *interests* are closely related—they are motivational terms that refer to the goals of peoples' actions. Although "values" are the most general and inclusive construct, Dawis (1980) argued that values are the same as beliefs (Allport, 1961), attitudes (Campbell, 1971), interests (Allport, 1961), and preferences (Katzell, 1964). The point is that psychologists use these terms interchangeably (and a bit carelessly). Values, needs, and interests differ primarily in their level of abstraction. Super (1973) defines needs as the most abstract, and suggests that values and interests are lower level constructs derived from needs. Values, says Super, are the generalized objectives that we seek in order to satisfy needs; interests are the specific activities through which people achieve their values and satisfy their needs. According to Super, then, interests are the least abstract/most concrete motivational terms. Dawis (1980) suggests that values, needs, and interests all reflect an "affective orientation" toward objects in the world, and like Super, he suggests the same hierarchical arrangement, with attitudes at the top, values and needs in the middle, and interests at the lowest and most concrete level. Thus, both Super and Dawis regard interests as the most concrete construct in the hierarchy of motivation terms.

Values, needs, and interests can be organized in terms of a hierarchy of abstraction, but the relations among them are poorly thought out. A person might *value* health, *need* exercise, and *be interested* in tennis; this seems to be a logical progression, but vocational interest researchers have shown little interest in making the connections. But to be very clear, the point we are trying to make is that *values are the real underlying subject matter of vocational psychology*. Values are the fundamental unit of individual differences *inside* the person.[1] They shape our understanding of the world and reflect our philosophy of life. Values drive us toward goals and careers. Understanding that values are at the core of individual differences opens a number of interesting research avenues, the most important of which concerns person-environment fit. Specifically, we like and are attracted to people, environments, and organizations that share our values. Likewise, we will become dissatisfied with and eventually leave people, environments, and organizations that do not share our values. Indeed, Schneider (1987) has always attributed his ASA model to his having read Holland. For the study of vocational interests then, values—not needs or interests—ought to be the starting point for vocational psychology.

Our second point about definitions involves an issue in the philosophy of science—namely, the explanation of social behavior. Harre and Secord (1973), Mischel (1968), and Peters (1958) all distinguish between "causes" and "reasons" as explanations for social behavior. Causes are biological processes inside people (hunger, fear, loneliness) that propel them into action. Causes are hard to study, and in any case they are more the province of physiology than psychology. In contrast, reasons refer to peoples' intentions, goals, and agendas; these constructs provide the focus and direction for peoples' actions, and they refer to psychological, not physiological processes. Peters (1958) points out that we normally use goals and intentions to explain everyday social behavior. Thus goals, intentions, and agendas are key concepts in the explanation of social behavior, *and* they are closely related to values, needs, and interests. Any competent theory of social action should begin with a clear view of what counts as an explanation, and vocational psychology explicitly deals with the reasons people do what they do. We will return to this point shortly when we discuss traits. For the moment let us note that values and interests are *not* traits; the terms refer to different psychological phenomena and serve very different linguistic functions.

We dwell on the point regarding the role of values and interests in the explanation of social behavior because, in the history of vocational psychology, researchers have paid little attention to a theory of interests. As a result, many writers regard the interest literature as conceptually barren, but we strongly disagree (cf. Hogan & Blake, 1996). According to Strong (1943), interests are "activities that are liked or disliked...remind me of tropisms. We go toward liked activities, go away from disliked activities" (p. 7). Note that Strong's statement contains an implicit assumption about the motivational properties of interests; he regards them as having "directional' properties: "Interest scores measure a complex of liked and disliked activities selected so as to differentiate members of an occupation form non-members. Such a complex is equivalent to a 'condition which supplies stimulation for a particular type of behavior,' i.e., toward or away from participation in the activities characteristic of a given occupation. Interest scores are consequently measures of drives" (p. 142). Once again, interests are motivational concepts that have a unique role to play in the explanation of social behavior, and they are the core of vocational psychology.

Personality and Vocational Psychology

Vocational psychologists have always acknowledged that personality variables (e.g., the Big Five traits) and career interests are related, and every major figure in the field has suggested that interests are manifestations of more basic personality characteristics. For example, Darley and Hagenah (1955) described the assessment of vocational interests as "a special case in personality theory" where "interests reflect…in the world of work, the value systems, the needs, and the motivations of individuals" (p. 191). Similarly, Layton (1958) described interests as "one aspect of what is broadly considered as the motivation of an individual…a part of the person's personality structure or organization" (pp. 3–4). Finally, Bordin (1943) defined interest inventory scores as measures of "self-concept" a point to which we will return shortly. John Holland states the point most directly: "If vocational interests are construed as an expression of personality then they represent the expression of personality in work, school subjects, hobbies, recreation activities, and references. In short, what we have called 'vocational interests' are simply another aspect of personality…If vocational interests are an expression of personality, then it follows that interest inventories are personality inventories" (1973, p. 7).

Given that vocational interests reflect personality and vice versa, the next question is, what is personality? In its most general form, personality theory concerns the nature of human nature. Nonetheless, following Mischel's (1968) situationist critique of the field, psychologists seemed to lose the plot. The subject today remains as vexed and confused as it is important. Many people think personality is personality and further specification is unnecessary. In contrast, we believe there are three distinct views of personality and it is important to be clear which one you sign up for. Stripped down to their essentials, the three views can be summarized quickly (and unfairly) as follows.

The first view comes from clinical psychology. Clinical psychology is rooted in the medical model wherein the goal is to identify and treat ailments (Alessandri, Heiden, & Dunbar-Welter, 1995). Thus, from a clinical perspective, the most important generalization we can make about people is that they are all somewhat neurotic (i.e., have ailments). It follows that the most important problem in life is to overcome one's neurosis, and that the goal of assessment is to identify the roots of one's neurosis. There are two problems with this perspective: (1) not everyone is neurotic, so the theories only concern a subset of the population, and (2) measures of psychopathology predict career failure not career success. If all you know about someone is that he/she is *not* neurotic, you don't know very much.

The second view is trait theory, as developed by Allport (1937), Cattell (1946), and Eysenck (1947). According to trait theory, the most important generalization we can make about people is that everyone has traits. It follows that the most important problem in life is to discover one's traits—perhaps as part of a more general process of self-discovery—and the goal of assessment is to measure traits. Trait theory defines traits both as: (1) observed consistencies in peoples' behavior, and as (2) hypothetical neuro-physiological structures that cause the observed consistencies, but which are postulated, not actually observed. So, for example, George Gordon, Lord Byron (1788–1824) was a compulsive lecher because he had a hypothetical (neuro-physiological) trait for lechery. Unless and until the underlying neuro-physiological traits are identified, trait theory is tautological—because trait theory uses trait terms both to predict and to explain behavior. In the terms of our earlier discussion, trait theorists use traits as both causes and reasons. Put differently, prediction is not explanation; we use trait terms to predict behavior, but we use motivational terms to explain behavior. In our view, people don't have traits, they have goals, intentions, and agendas, and it is these motivational terms that explain their behavior—which traits describe. Ultimately then, trait theory is intellectually incoherent—much as Mischel (1968) claimed.

The third view of personality is a combination of evolutionary psychology and sociological role theory (Mead, 1932) called socioanalytic theory (Hogan, 1982). According to this view, the most important generalization we can make about people is that they always live in groups and that every people-group has a status hierarchy. It follows that the most important problems in life concern gaining and retaining social acceptance and gaining and retaining status. In the modern world, careers are the vehicles for solving these two existential problems. Finally, in this theory, the goal of assessment is to predict individual differences in the ability to acquire social acceptance and status (i.e., individual differences in "getting along and getting ahead").

From the perspective of socioanalytic theory, personality and vocational psychology are linked in the following way (Hogan & Blake, 1996). People are all alike in that they need friends, power, and social influence—that is, people are motivated to get along and get ahead. People differ in terms of their identities (which concern career goals and strategies for getting along and getting ahead) and their reputations (which reflect their success at these activities). Peoples' Identities concern their hopes, dreams, and aspirations—largely the subject matter of vocational psychology. Peoples' reputations concern how others evaluate their efforts to get along and get ahead, and reputations are captured by trait words—largely the subject matter of personality psychology. Reputations (trait words) tell us what people typically do; identities (needs, values, and interests) tell us why they do it. Personality assessment is about reputation; vocational assessment is about identity. Personality assessment is about prediction, vocational assessment is about explanation.

Vocational assessment concerns identifying and clarifying peoples' goals—their identities. Personality assessment concerns how people typically behave, and are evaluated—their reputations—as they pursue their goals. People can usually describe their career goals—assuming they have some—pretty directly by means of reflection. But people tend not to understand how others see them; they need to rely on feedback from external observers to understand their reputations.

Personality and Vocational Assessment

The dynamics of assessing vocational interests and personality are quite similar. People respond to items on vocational preference or personality inventories in ways that are identical to how they behave during other ordinary social interaction. In our view, they do *not* respond with self-reports. Self-report theory assumes that people read an item, compare the item's content with a videotape stored in their memory, and then respond based on that comparison. But memories are not literal; memories are constructed based on the stories that we tell ourselves and others. In actuality, when people respond to items on inventories, they use their responses to tell other people how they, the respondent, would like to be regarded. In other words, when people respond to items on inventories, they provide self-presentations, not self-reports. There are important individual differences in how strategic, self-aware, and prudent these self-presentations tend to be; moreover, once again, what goes on in the context of responding to items on inventories is identical to what goes on in the context of responding to questions during any kind of interaction.

Vocational interest researchers have a more enlightened view of the meaning of test scores than personality researchers. Mainstream personality researchers (e.g., Cattell, Eysenck, Costa and McCrae) believe that the goal of personality assessment is to measure traits. This is problematic because, as noted above, people do not have traits, they have agendas. Observers ascribe traits to others as a way of making sense out of their behavior. Thus, there are no traits inside people to be assessed. An interesting transformation in the goals of assessment has taken place over the years: prediction has given way to measurement. Alfred Binet developed his original test to *predict* academic performance; Terman's version of Binet's test (the Stanford Binet) was intended to *measure* intelligence (Terman et al., 1916). The MMPI (Hathaway & McKinley, 1933) and the CPI (Gough, 1954) were designed to *predict* behavior; the NEO-PI is intended to *measure* traits. Thus the goals of assessment have migrated from predicting observable outcomes to measuring hypothetical entities. This critical difference has major implications for theory. In terms of validity, an instrument designed to *measure* something must be backed by a sensible theory for how the instrument measures the thing of interest. For example, (early) thermometers measured temperature on the basis of expansion of mercury in a tube. The validity of the thermometer is backed by known chemical and thermodynamic processes of mercury and heat. The assessment of psychological traits has no such corresponding theoretical basis (Borsboom, Mellenbergh, & van Heerden, 2004). One's level of extraversion does not directly cause one to strongly agree with the item "I like to go to parties." Some process must be involved, but we know very little about what makes respondents mark items the way that they do (though Funder's [1995] Realistic Accuracy Model might be a reasonable place to start). Prediction, on the other hand, does not require an underlying theory of the instrument. Instead, it only requires that the instrument predict some outcome of interest. Predicting outcomes is a practical and empirical activity; measuring hypothetical entities is a metaphysical pursuit. We believe that the goal of personality assessment is to predict outcomes and in this way, the goals of vocational interest and personality assessment come into alignment (see also Yarkoni & Westfall, 2017).

Vocational interest and personality assessment differ in a way that is worth noting. The difference has to do with the content of the items on the two types of assessment. Hofstee (1990) notes that personality items are typically "a hodgepodge of descriptions of overt and covert reactions, trait attributions, wishes and interests, biographical facts, attitudes and beliefs, descriptions of others' reactions to the subject, and more or less bizarre opinions (e.g., 'Somebody is trying to poison me')" (p. 79)—that is, personality items are an incoherent mess. In contrast, the content of interest items is much more focused: "(I)nterest items…involve preferences for behaviors (response and activity families), situations (the context in which the preferred behaviors occur, usually occupations or physical settings), and reinforcer systems (outcomes or reinforcers associated with the behavior in the situation)" (Rounds, 1995, p. 184).

Personality items lack thematic coherence, whereas interest items cluster meaningfully: they ask people about preferred activities, associated roles, and the types of people with whom they prefer to interact. In this way, interest measures get much closer to the actual content of peoples' self-concepts and allow people to project directly the image with which they would like to be credited. They also allow people to describe themselves in ways that are more consistent with what actually goes on in social interactions between near strangers. Question: "Tell me about yourself." Answer: "I like tennis" (as opposed to "Someone is trying to poison me"). People typically talk to others about themselves in terms of interests—interests are at the core of the ordinary language of social self-description and self-presentation. The conventional wisdom of applied psychology is that interests and values reflect affective responses to people and things. In contrast, we believe that interests reflect identities—when people tell us about their interests, they are telling us about how they hope we will regard them.

Validity

Most readers think the concept of validity has a straightforward definition, but they would be wrong: like many topics in the assessment business, there is little agreement on this subject. Trait theory (Cattell, Eysenck), for example, defines validity as the degree to which factor structures replicate across samples.

Cronbach and Meehl (1955) define validity as an inference researchers make about test scores given their relationships with a variety of other test scores and performance indices. And then Strong (1943) noted that there is "no better criterion (i.e., index of validity) for a vocational interests test than that of satisfaction enduring over a period of time" (p. 385); thus, for Strong, the validity of a sales interest scale is defined by the degree to which people with high scores on that scale are *satisfied* working in sales. Historically, vocational researchers have defined validity in terms of the degree to which, for example, incumbent sales personnel have higher scores on measures of sales interests. Finally, Dawis and Lofquist (1984) distinguish between validity as the degree to which people with certain scores are satisfied with certain working environments, and validity as the degree to which employers are satisfied with employees with certain scores. It follows that dissatisfied employees will leave their jobs and dissatisfied employers will ask them to leave.

At stake here is a fundamental distinction between the actor's and the observer's perspective on the actor's performance. This is the same as the distinction between identity (how people think about themselves) and reputation (how others think about them). Our point is that, in general, the study of identity (self-ratings) has yielded few useful results, whereas the study of reputation (observer ratings) has been quite productive. Using self-ratings of job satisfaction as a criterion is a case in point. A number of studies report no significant relationships between interests and job satisfaction (cf. Bartling & Hood, 1981; Dolliver, Irvin, & Bigley, 1972). Satisfaction matters to the employee; performance matters to the employer. A satisfied employee can still be incompetent. If the employer is satisfied, then there is hope for the employee; if the employer is unhappy with the employee, then the employee's satisfaction is largely irrelevant. Our point is, research in vocational psychology should prioritize the employers' (observers') reaction to an employee's (actor's) performance. Strong was wrong—employee satisfaction is not a good index of validity.

Regarding the links between assessed interests and the degree to which employers see employees as satisfactory, there is bad news and good news. The bad news is that there is little systematic research on the topic—and that is good news for vocational interest researchers. There is, however, a kind of fugitive literature (as John Holland called it). In the process of determining by brute empirical means what does and does not predict job performance, researchers (e.g., Barge & Hough, 1988) have found correlations between interest measures and performance that compare favorably with the validity of personality measures (see Nye, Su, Rounds, & Drasgow, 2012). Further, a recent cohort study in Germany (N = 3,023) found that vocational interests predict life outcomes (e.g., work outcomes, relationship outcomes, health outcomes), assessed 10 years later, over and above IQ and Big Five personality traits (Stoll et al., 2017). These results are interesting, but there is little analysis regarding why interests predict job performance.

Campbell (1987) compared a sample of U.S. Army generals with a sample of civilian executives using the Strong-Campbell Interest Inventory. As expected, the generals as a group received the highest scores on "military activities"; otherwise, however, the groups had rather similar scores. The similarity included very low scores for "artistic interests," which is curious because artistic interests would seem irrelevant to management activities. Borgen (1986) suggests (and we agree) that the blind empiricism that typifies vocational interest research ignores many intriguing questions—for example, why is it important to dislike art in order to be a successful executive? Unpacking this question should be quite revealing, because artistic interests are associated with creativity, entrepreneurship, and interest in innovation—characteristics that should be valuable in organizational leadership.

Employability and Vocational Interests

Employability concerns being able to gain and maintain a job in a formal organization, or to get a new one should that become necessary. In the United Sates, official unemployment has been high since the 2001 economic downturn, and no one knows how many people have stopped looking for work and are not counted among the unemployed. Whatever the numbers might be, employability is a topic with major social policy implications. We also believe the topic of employability belongs to vocational psychology, the problem has immense practical significance, and, best of all for vocational psychology, there has been almost no research done on the subject. Employability is a target of opportunity for vocational psychology researchers.

In the remainder of this section we offer some observations to orient readers toward this interesting but unexplored research topic. Much of the discussion concerns distinctions, the first of which is that job performance and career success are not the same; they only correlate about .30 (Carmeli, Shalom, & Weisberg, 2007; Van Scotter, Motowidlo, & Cross, 2000). This fact reflects an unpleasant reality of organizational life. Organizations often don't know who is doing a good job, but they always know whom they like. And people who are well liked in one administration may lose favor after a change in top leadership. This is compounded by the fact that performance appraisal systems—which directly control career success—are always imperfect. For example, Varma, DeNisi and Peters (1996), in a field study, found that performance appraisals are a function of how much supervisors like their employees and not the employees' objective performance.

A second distinction concerns the fact that what academic psychologists believe are the characteristics of a desirable employee is quite different from what employers want to see in a new hire. Academic psychologists argue that the best employees will have good academic credentials and high scores on measures of cognitive ability and conscientiousness (Baruch & Bozionelos, 2011; McArdle,

Waters, Briscoe, & Hall, 2007; Schmidt & Hunter, 1998). It is interesting to note that the same variables that predict academic performance (i.e., cognitive ability and conscientiousness) are those that psychologists believe predict career success. Although cognitive ability and conscientiousness are robust predictors of academic performance, academic performance is only modestly related to financial success (r = .21; Ng, Eby, Sorensen, & Feldman, 2005). Similarly, cognitive ability and conscientiousness nicely predict initial job performance, but the longer the employee's tenure, the more personality predicts performance. As for what employers want to see in a new hire, they don't care about educational attainment, and in some cases prefer candidates with lower GPAs (Chamorro-Premuzic & Furnham, 2010).

To answer the question of what employers look for in new hires, we must search what John Holland called the fugitive literature for an answer. We have identified three relevant papers. First, during the Reagan administration, the U.S. Department of Labor conducted a large-scale survey of what employers want and identified five broad competencies: (1) knowing how to find resources; (2) *interpersonal skills*; (3) being able to identify and use information; (4) being able to understand complex relationships; and (5) being able to work with technology. Items (1), (3), (4), and (5) seem to be a function of cognitive ability; item (2) is related to personality. Second, Hogan and Brinkmeyer (1994) conducted a detailed content analysis of newspaper want ads from all over the United States and found that the single most desired characteristic listed in the ads was *interpersonal skill*. Hogan, Lock, and Brinkmeyer (1997) then conducted a critical incidents study that revealed that the essence of interpersonal skill is "being rewarding to deal with," which largely involves being considerate and well-mannered. Third, in the only study we know that deals explicitly with employability, Van der Heijde and Van der Heijden (2006), proposed that employability is a syndrome with five measurable components: (a) competence at the job; (b) ambition; (c) personal flexibility (e.g., being willing to move for work); (d) ability to work in collaborative groups; and (e) having work-life balance. A sample of 314 employees in a Dutch manufacturing firm completed their inventory of employability, and they found that: (a) competence predicted salary level; (b) ambition predicted salary and promotions; (c) personal flexibility predicted salary and promotions; and (d) ability to work collaboratively was the best predictor of every criterion in their study, including promotions ($r = .32$) and salary ($r = .47$). It seems, therefore, that employers don't agree with I-O psychology's emphasis on cognitive ability and education as determinants of career success. The limited literature that exists suggests that employability is a function of interpersonal sensitivity, social skill, and being rewarding to deal with.

Hiring decisions allegedly concern how well applicants fit the competency requirement of a job, and evaluations of job performance allegedly depend on (duh) job performance, but these views are not supported empirically. Boudreau, Boswell, and Judge (2001) report that ratings for "employability" during the hiring process predict compensation levels after people are on the job. This suggests that hiring managers and subsequent managers who conduct performance appraisals are responding to similar employee characteristics. Thus, the biases in the selection process overlaps with biases in job performance evaluations; that is, supervisors reward the same attributes that are valued in the employment interview, even if the attributes don't enhance job performance. These conclusions are nicely supported by the Van der Heijde and Van der Heijden (2006) study: the essence of employability is socially desirable behavior during the hiring process and on the job. Historically, psychologists have regarded social desirability as a nuisance variable but we think it is valid and interpretable variance. Hogan and Shelton (1998) define socially desirable behavior as a particular kind of role performance that allows people to fit in and get along with others at work.

Hogan, Chamorro-Premuzic, and Kaiser (2013) reviewed the employability literature and concluded that the ability to gain and maintain employment depended on three competencies that they labeled Rewarding, Able, and Willing (RAW). Rewarding concerns interpersonal sensitivity and social skill; Able concerns quickly learning the job and showing good judgment; Willing concerns being dutiful and compliant. Employability is all about supervisors' ratings. In general, supervisors like employees who are pleasant to deal with, who learn quickly and show good judgment, and who are obedient and conforming (which explains the consistent correlations between Conscientiousness and job performance). This set of characteristics also explain why some high-IQ people are unemployable. Unemployable people: (1) are irritable and argumentative, (2) show bad judgment, and (3) are stubborn and nonconforming.

The foregoing considerations suggest that vocational psychology could go beyond person-job fit and study employability in the round. Psychologists study the fit between individuals and the demands of jobs, but employers are concerned with the fit between individuals and their organizations. Focusing vocational research on employability will encourage research that helps the unemployed as well as providing an empirical base for public policy decisions. For example, presently most vocational research assumes that there is a right job for everyone (i.e., that everyone is employable). Although this assumption might make us all feel good about ourselves (i.e., everyone is great in their own way!), it is simply false. Employability, like all individual differences variables, is normally distributed. A vocational psychology that is focused on employability could do several things. First, it could help low employable people become aware of what makes them unemployable (e.g., irritable and argumentative). Second, it could design behavioral change interventions to help the unemployable become more employable. Third, a vocational psychology that recognizes individual differences in employability would recommend more entrepreneurial careers for those who are low in employability, assuming these individuals have other prerequisite characteristics for entrepreneurship (e.g., ambition, creativity). Finally, a vocational psychology that focuses on employability could identify the base rate of employability and use this information to develop public policies to provide appropriate assistance for such individuals.

Career Success and Vocational Interests

Vocational psychology has traditionally studied the structure and the consequences of vocational interests. Our major claim in this chapter is that the true subject matter of vocational psychology is (or ought to be) careers, of which vocational interests form a crucial component and starting point. Knowing what career one would like to follow is, in the abstract, useful information, but in the absence of having a job, it is an empty exercise. We suggested in the preceding section that: (a) vocational psychology should attend to employability, and (b) employability is a wide open research area.

Employability concerns gaining and maintaining employment. In this section we briefly consider the next step in the evolution of careers—namely, career success. One index of success would be to be consistently employed, but that is the same as extended employability. What we are interested in here is high-level performance in any occupation. We think studying high-level performance in any occupation is an easy extension of the normal preoccupations of vocational psychology. It is also a topic on which there is not a great deal of informative research. We offer two thoughts as the beginning of an organizing framework for the study of career success. First, the one theme that characterizes the biographies of all highly successful people is they work longer and harder than less successful people—and John Holland would be an example. Holland called this the constant probability of success model: people who constantly turn out articles, paintings, poems, novels, inventions, or drawings are more likely to be successful in their fields than people who are less productive (Simonton, 2014).

Our second point concerns the psychological origins of the amazing level of productivity that characterizes high performers in any field. The answer, we believe, is individual differences in the desire to excel, to stand out, to be recognized as a superior performer—a syndrome that is captured by the term "ambition." Despite the importance of this syndrome as the driver of high-level performance, the concept has an odd history in academic psychology. At the start of psychology as a formal discipline, Charles Darwin, William James, and William McDougall all argued, based on their ideas about human evolutionary history, that people are inherently competitive and motivated by "rivalrous impulses." Rivalrous impulses are essentially the same as ambitious aspirations. What happened to this view that ambition is a core human motive? It just faded away.

Sigmund Freud powerfully stigmatized ambition by arguing that rivalrous impulses are manifestations of an unresolved Oedipal conflict and the unconscious desire to murder one's father. Carl Jung argued that the goal of life is individuation and ambition is "a regressive restoration of the persona." Ambitious people are stuck in an immature desire to have a successful career, as contrasted with fully coming to terms with the secrets of the collective unconscious. Alfred Adler characterized ambition as an unconscious and neurotic defense against feelings of unworthiness and inadequacy. Like Jung before him, Abraham Maslow thought that the goal of life is self-actualization and ambitious strivings are an immature distraction. Thus classic European depth psychology trivialized and stigmatized ambition (Jones, Sherman, & Hogan, 2017).

Today, the conventional wisdom of academic psychology is that ambition is a combination of extraversion and conscientiousness and ambition itself has totally disappeared. For example, the *American Psychological Association Dictionary* of psychological terms carries no entry for "ambition" (Jones et al., 2017). Extraversion concerns content-free social interaction. Extraverts are warm, sociable, impulsive, and talkative and do well in cold call sales. Conscientious people are diligent, dutiful, and conforming and they do well in accounting. The technical manual for the Hogan Personality Inventory (Hogan & Hogan, 2007) shows that persons with high scores for extraversion are described as sociable and energetic; persons with high scores for conscientiousness are described as not distractible and rule-abiding; persons with high scores for ambition are described as bold and assertive.

Career success and ambition have a place in the history of vocational psychology. The first author's long-lost copy of the 1964 technical manual for the Strong Vocational Interest Blanks (SVIB), contained, in the appendix, descriptive data for an empirically keyed ambition scale. Strong compared samples of high-achieving individuals (Nobel Prize winners) with lower achieving people, and selected the items that distinguished the two groups. The manual only contained normative data, but our point is, E. K. Strong thought the subject was important and was working on it at the end of his career.

Summary and Conclusions

Vocational psychology studies career choice—one of the most important problems in each individual's life. The discipline has a comprehensive taxonomy of career options, a well-developed measurement base, and a plethora of replicable findings to report. Nonetheless, it exists as an interesting subspecialty; it is not part of the mainstream of personality or Industrial/Organizational psychology. We suggest that the field could and should raise its profile by moving beyond the study of the structure and consequences of vocational interests by taking on two new (and underresearched) topics: (1) employability and (2) career success. The former is a problem with major public policy implications; the practical implications of career success research have yet to be demonstrated, but they are easy to imagine.

Note

1 As opposed to personality, which is the fundamental unit of individual differences that can be directly observed from the outside (i.e., behavior).

References

Alessandri, M., Heiden, L., & Dunbar-Welter, M. (1995). History and overview. In L. Heiden & M. Hersen (Eds.), *Introduction to clinical psychology* (pp. 3–19). New York: Plenum Press.

Allport, G. W. (1937). *Personality: A psychological interpretation*. New York: Holt, Rinehart & Winston.

Allport, G. W. (1961). *Pattern and growth in personality*. Oxford, UK: Holt, Reinhart & Winston.

Barge, B. N., & Hough, L. M. (1988). *Utility of temperament, biodata, and interest assessment for predicting job performance*. (ARI Research note 88-02). Alexandria, VA: U.S. Army Research Institute.

Bartling, H. C., & Hood, A. B. (1981). An 11-year follow-up of measured interests and vocational choice. *Journal of Counseling Psychology, 28,* 27–35.

Baruch, Y., & Bozionelos, N. (2011). Career issues. In S. Zedeck (Ed.), *Handbook of industrial and organizational psychology* (Vol. 2, pp. 67–113). Washington, DC: American Psychological Association.

Boudreau, J. W., Boswell, W. R., & Judge, T. A. (2001). Effects of personality one executive career success in the United States and Europe. *Journal of Vocational Behavior, 58*, 53–81.

Bordin, E. S. (1943). A theory of vocational interests as dynamic phenomena. *Educational and Psychological Measurement, 3,* 49–65.

Borgen, F.H. (1986). New approaches to the assessment of interests. In W. B. Walsh & S. H. Osipow (Eds.), *Advances in vocational psychology* (pp. 83–126). Hillsdale, NJ: Erlbaum.

Borsboom, D., Mellenbergh, G. J., & van Heerden, J. (2004). The concept of validity. *Psychological Review, 111*(4), 1061–1071.

Campbell, D. P. (1971). *Handbook for the Strong Vocational Interest Blank*. Stanford, CA: Stanford University Press.

Campbell, D. P. (1987). *Psychological test profiles of brigadier generals*. Paper presented at the annual meeting of Division 14 of the American Psychological Association, New York.

Carmeli, A., Shalom, R., & Weisberg, J. (2007). Considerations in organizational career advancement; What really matters. *Personnel Review, 36,* 190–205.

Cattell, R. B. (1946). *The description and measurement of personality*. Oxford, UK: World Book Company.

Chamorro-Premuzic, T., & Furnham, A. (2010). *The psychology of personnel selection*. Cambridge: Cambridge University Press.

Cronbach, L. J., & Meehl, P. E. (1955). Construct validity in psychological tests. *Psychological Bulletin, 52*(4), 281–302.

Darley, J. B., & Hagenah, T. (1955). *Vocational interest measurement*. Minneapolis: University of Minnesota Press.

Dawis, R. (1980). Measuring interests. *New Directions in Testing and Measurement, 7,* 77–91.

Dawis, R. V., & Lofquist, L. H. (1984). *A psychological theory of work adjustment: An individual-differences model and its applications.* Minneapolis: University of Minnesota Press.

Dolliver, R. H., Irvin, J. A., & Bigley, S.S. (1972). Twelve-year follow-up of the Strong Vocational Interest Blank. *Journal of Counseling Psychology, 19,* 212–217.

Eysenck, H. J. (1947). *Dimensions of personality.* London: Methuen.

Funder, D. C. (1995). On the accuracy of personality judgment: A realistic approach to person perception. *Psychological Review, 102,* 652–670.

Harre, H., & Secord, P. F. (1973). *The explanation of social behavior.* Totowa, NJ: Littlefield.

Hofstee, W. K. B. (1990). The use of everyday personality language for scientific purposes. *European Journal of Personality, 4*(2), 77–88.

Hogan, R. (1982). A socioanaltyic theory of personality. In M. M. Page (Ed.), *Nebraska symposium on motivation, 1982* (Vol. 29, pp. 55–89). Lincoln: University of Nebraska Press.

Hogan, R., & Blake, R. J. (1996). Vocational interests: Matching self-concept with the work environment. In K. R. Murphy (Ed.), *Individual differences and behavior in organizations* (pp. 89–144). San Francisco: Jossey-Bass.

Hogan, J., & Brinkmeyer, K. (2006). Bridging the gap between over and personality-based integrity tests. *Personnel Psychology, 50*(3), 587–599.

Hogan, R., Chamorro-Premuzic, T., & Kaiser, R. B. (2013). Employability and career success: Bridging the gap between theory and reality. *Industrial and Organizational Psychology, 6*(1), 3–16.

Hogan, R., & Hogan, J. (2007). *Hogan Personality Inventory Manual (*3rd ed.). Tulsa, OK: Hogan Assessment Systems.

Hogan, J., Lock, J., & Brinkmeyer, K. (1997). *A general taxonomy of interpersonal skills for work.* Tulsa, OK: Hogan Assessment Systems.

Hogan, R., & Shelton, D. (1998). A socioanalytic perspective on job performance. *Human Performance, 11,* 129–144.

Holland, J. W. (1973). *The psychology of vocational choices.* Englewood Cliffs, NJ: Prentice Hall.

Holland, J. W. (1997). *Making vocational choices.* Odessa, FL: PAR.

Jones, A. B., Sherman, R. A., & Hogan, R. (2017). Where is ambition in factor models of personality? *Personality and Individual Differences, 106*(1), 26–31.

Katzell, R.A. (1964). Personal values, job satisfaction, and job behavior. In H. Borow (Ed.), *Man in a* world of work (pp. 341–363). Boston: Houghton Mifflin.

Layton, W.L. (1958). *Counseling use of the Strong Vocational Interest Blank.* Minneapolis: University of Minnesota Press.

Maslow, A. (1954). *Motivation and personality.* New York: Harper.

McCaulley, M. H. (1990). The Myers-Briggs Type Indicator and leadership. In K. E. Clark & M. B. Clark (Eds.), *Measures of leadership.* Greensboro, NC: Center for Creative Leadership.

McArdle, S., Waters, L., Briscoe, J. P., & Hall, D. T. (2007). Employability during unemployment: Adaptability, career identity and hum and social capital. *Journal of Vocational Behavior, 71*(2), 247–264.

Mead, G. H. (1932). *Mind, self, and society.* Chicago: University of Chicago Press.

Michel, T. (1969). *Human action.* New York: Academic Press.

Mischel, W. (1968*). Personality and assessment.* Mahwah, NJ: Erlbaum.

Ng., T. W., Eby, T. T., Sorensen, K. L., & Feldman, D. C. (2005). Predictors of objective and subjective career success: A meta-analysis. *Personnel Psychology*, 58, 367–408.

Nye, C. D., Su, R., Rounds, J., & Drasgow, F. (2012). Vocational interests and performance: A quantitative summary of over 60 years of research. *Perspectives on Psychological Science, 7*, 384–403.

Peters, R. S. (1958). *The concept of motivation*. Oxford, UK: Humanities Press.

Rounds, J. B. (1995). Vocational interests: Evaluation of structural hypotheses. In D. Lubinski & R. V. Dawis (Eds.), *Assessing individual differences in human behavior: New concepts, methods, and findings* (pp. 177–232). Palo Alto, CA: Consulting Psychologists Press.

Schmidt, F. L., & Hunter, J. E. (1998). The validity and utility of selection methods in personnel psychology: Practical and theoretical implications of 85 years of research findings. *Psychological Bulletin, 124*(2), 262–274.

Schneider, B., & Smith, D. B. (2004). Personality and organizational culture. In B. Schneider & D. B. Smith (Eds.), *Personality and organizations*. Mahwah, NJ: Erlbaum.

Simonton, D. K. (Ed.) (2014) *The Wiley handbook of genius*. Oxford, UK: Wiley.

Stoll, G., Rieger, S., Lüdtke, O., Nagengast, B., Trautwein, U., & Roberts, B. W. (2017). Vocational interests assessed at the end of high school predict life outcomes assessed 10 years later over and above IQ and Big Five personality traits. *Journal of Personality and Social Psychology, 113*(1), 167–184.

Strong, E. K. Jr., (1943). *Vocational interests of men and women*. Stanford, CA: Stanford University Press.

Super, D. E. (1973). The Work Values Inventory. In D. G. Zytowski (Ed.), *Contemporary approaches to interest measurement* (pp. 189–2015). Minneapolis: University of Minnesota Press.

Terman, L., Lyman, G., Ordahl, G. Ordahl, L., Galbreath, N., & Talbert, W. (1916). *The Stanford revision of the Binet-Simon Scale for Measuring Intelligence*. Baltimore: Warwick & York.

Van Der Heijde, C. M., & Van Der Heijden, B. I. J. M. (2006). A competence-based and multidimensional operationalization and measure of employability. *Human Resource Management, 45*(3), 449–476.

Van Scotter, J. R., Motowidlo, S. J., & Cross, T. C. (2000). Effects of task performance and contextual performance on systemic rewards. *Journal of Applied Psychology, 85*, 5216–5535.

Varma, A., DeNisi, A. S., & Peters, L. H. (1996). Interpersonal affect and performance appraisal: A field study. *Personnel Psychology, 49*, 341–360.

Yarkoni, T., & Westfall, J. (2017). Choosing prediction over explanation in psychology: Lessons from machine learning. *Perspectives on Psychological Science, 12*(6), 1100–1122.

10

CONNECTING CONCEPTS

Effects of Diversity of Interests and Interests' Effects on Diversity

Ann Marie Ryan and Danielle D. King

MICHIGAN STATE UNIVERSITY

Diversity typically refers to differences and similarities among individuals in organizational contexts. While most often referencing demographic differences (race, ethnicity, gender, sexual orientation, religion, age, etc.), research on diversity in organizations has spanned a variety of individual attributes, including attitudes, knowledge, functions, skills and abilities. In this chapter, we consider the connection between interests and diversity.

We specifically focus on two ways the study of diversity and the study of interests intersect. First, we consider how "diversity of interests" in a work unit affects individual, group and organizational effectiveness. Workgroups that contain individuals with a variety of perspectives can produce more innovative solutions to problems (Bell, Villado, Lukasik, Belau & Briggs, 2011), although diversity can also decrease cohesion and increase conflict, negatively affecting team performance (Pelled, 1996; Thatcher & Patel, 2011). While researchers have addressed what conditions lead to more positive or negative effects of diversity, attention has not been specifically focused on diversity of vocational interests. We explore the questions: When there is greater heterogeneity or homogeneity in interests in a work unit, how, if at all, are relevant outcomes (e.g., attitudes, performance, withdrawal behaviors) affected? What moderates those effects? What can be done to foster positive outcomes when there is diversity in interests? While our primary focus on diversity of interests is at the work unit or interindividual level, we also briefly discuss how intraindividual diversity in interests (i.e., people who have more varied interest profiles) can affect these same outcomes.

Second, we consider how vocational interests themselves may influence the level of diversity in other characteristics in an organization. As a prime example, the lack of ethnic and gender diversity in certain occupational fields such as technology, physics, and elementary education has been widely noted (for a review of influences see Ceci, Williams, & Barnett, 2009; also, Iskander Gore, Furse, & Bergerson, 2013). Those seeking to diversify workforces in these fields often note the "pipeline problem" and the need to get underrepresented group members interested in these domains (Chen & Moons, 2015; Lubinski & Benbow, 1992). That is, vocational interests affect who is attracted to certain occupations (Le, Robbins, & Westrick, 2014) and given that there are demographic differences in some interests (Armstrong, Fouad, Rounds, & Hubert, 2010; Ryan, Tracey, & Rounds, 1996; Su, Rounds, & Armstrong, 2009), interests affect organizational demographic composition or diversity. While specific demographic differences in interest inventory responses are discussed in detail elsewhere in this volume, we consider how demographic correlates of interests may affect self-selection processes and thus influence the composition or diversity of an occupation, organization, or workgroup.

The first part of the chapter is devoted to a discussion of what little we know about the effects of the diversity of interests in workgroups, what research is needed, and practical implications. The second part focuses on how interests affect the demographic diversity of those in occupations and organizations, where that may be problematic, and the efficacy of efforts to change demographic composition.

Diversity of Interests

Diversity has most often been conceptualized and operationalized via a compositional approach, that is, the proportions of certain groups within a unit (Roberson, Ryan, & Ragins, 2017). However, Harrison and Klein (2007) proposed an influential typology of within-unit diversity that distinguishes between three forms of dispersion: separation, variety, and disparity. Separation refers to differences in values, beliefs, and attitudes, is associated with disagreement, and is most often operationalized as the average Euclidean distance of each member's attribute from all other members. Variety can be thought of as differences in the knowledge, networks, and experiences, reflects the amounts and types of information available to a group, and is often operationalized by a categorical variable such as Blau's index (1977). Disparity reflects differences in status or resources, is linked to power and influence, and is typically operationalized by coefficients of variation. How does this typology connect to interests? Typical thinking in discussions of diversity and interests resides around variety, and how differences in interests might lead to group members bringing something different to a task (van Knippenberg & Haslam, 2003). However, we should not neglect the fact that differences in interests may lead to differences in attitudes and beliefs or can be associated with status and resource differences. We draw on this related literature to speculate on how interest diversity in terms of variety, separation, and disparity might affect individual and organization

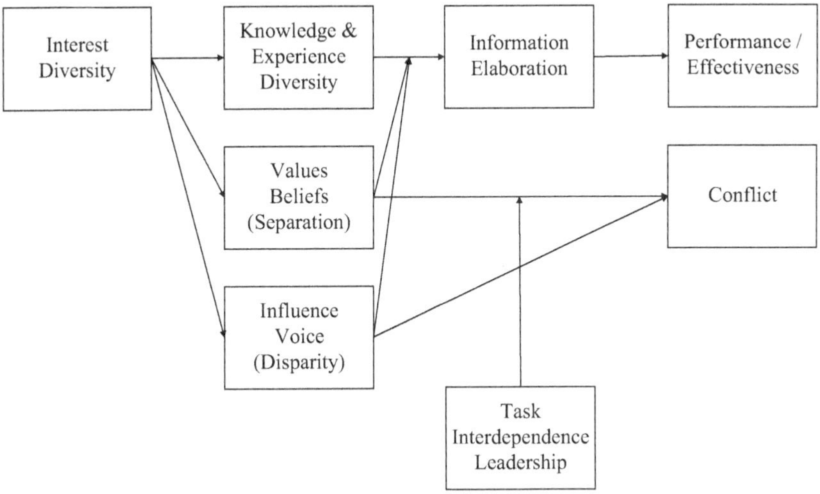

FIGURE 10.1 Relationship of Interest Diversity to Unit Level Outcomes.

outcomes in the sections that follow (see Figure 10.1 for an overview). Surprisingly, studies of interest diversity in organizational settings simply do not exist. There are a number of studies on potentially related variables—specifically on functional background (e.g., finance, sales) variety and educational background (i.e., major) variety, but not using measured interests. We draw on this related literature to infer likely effects of interest diversity.

Diversity in Interests as Variety

Work groups may be relatively homogeneous in interests (e.g., a team of accountants or microbiologists) or varied (e.g., a cross-functional task force). One might expect that variety in interests might be associated with differences in occupations, educational major, and/or specific knowledge, so research on diversity in these aspects is relevant to understanding potential effects of vocational interest variety. In a meta-analytic summary, Bell et al. (2011) found functional background variety to relate to group performance (ρ = .18) and in particular to creativity (ρ = .18); however, educational background variety related to creativity (ρ = .23) but not to team performance (ρ = .01). Thus, while knowledge variety can enhance decision-making (Huang, Hsieh, & He, 2014; Rietzschel, Nijstad, & Stroebe, 2007), this is not always the case. van Knippenberg and Schippers (2007), in their review of diversity research, concluded that the study of "main effects" of diversity on outcomes is not particularly useful, and that models should consider what moderators explain when positive effects occur. By extension then, we should not expect variety in interests to automatically lead to positive effects on creativity or performance.

In order to further research on how variety in interests affects functioning, one needs to consider whether that variety in interests leads to differences in experience and information, whether those differences are task relevant, and whether information sharing actually takes place. The Categorization-Elaboration Model (CEM; van Knippenberg, De Dreu, & Homan, 2004) holds that information elaboration is critical for experiencing the positive effects of diversity on group performance. Information elaboration refers to how information is exchanged and then expanded upon in a group where knowledge is initially distributed. The CEM suggests diversity can actually lead individuals to be less likely to share or to attend to information from others. Thus, while meta-analytic evidence hints that diversity in interests (as associated with functional and knowledge differences) should relate to greater effectiveness in problem-solving tasks, we need to understand under what conditions those differences lead to sharing of unique information versus discounting of others' views (i.e., what moderates the diversity-information elaboration link). Possible moderators include the role of the leader in encouraging and fostering sharing as well as task interdependence levels that require sharing. The next two sections indicate that the extent to which interest variety is coupled with separation or disparity might also be a moderator.

Diversity in Interests as Separation

Differences in interests can be associated with different beliefs about a work-related issue. For example, individuals may possess a desire to gather data to investigate a problem (Investigative interests) versus a belief that creative brainstorming is the best way to a solution (Artistic interests); a willingness to embark on a new approach (Enterprising interests) versus a desire to stick with the tried and true (Conventional interests). Thus, interests can be linked to separation between members of a group. When examining how interest separation affects work group functioning, one could assess the Euclidean distance of one individual's score on, say Investigative interests or data-people, from other group members.

How might separation in interests in a group affect outcomes? Research suggests that separation can be a source of conflict (Tsui, Ashford, St. Clair, & Xin, 1995); while task related conflict is often helpful in reaching a better solution, relationship conflict can have detrimental effects on group performance (O'Neill, McLarnon, Hoffart, Woodley, & Allen, 2015). As groups composed of members with homogeneous characteristics are likely to experience social cohesion and reduced interpersonal conflict (Pelled, 1996; Thatcher & Patel, 2011), interest similarity may produce such effects as well. Interest diversity that creates separation may have positive or negative effects depending on factors like task interdependence, conflict resolution processes, and how separation is managed by team leaders.

Diversity in Interests as Disparity

At first consideration, it may be hard to think of interests as associated with differences in status or resources. However, functions in organizations tend to contain people with different interests (HR, sales, manufacturing) and they can vary in status and power. One example would be the relative power and position of the sciences versus the humanities in most American universities (Hassan, 2010; Post, 2009). There may be many reasons for these power differences, but their link to interest diversity may have consequences for the effectiveness of a team/unit/organization. Groups with power differentials between members often do not have the best processes or perform the best (Berger, Fisek, Norman, & Zelditch, 1977; Berger, Rosenholtz, & Zelditch, 1980; Ragins, 1997). Also, Homan, van Knippenberg, van Kleef, and De Dreu (2007) note that "informationally diverse groups are often also diverse on other, more salient dimensions of diversity, such as gender, ethnicity, and age" (p. 79) and these are often linked to status and power. In terms of interests, any connections of interests to gender and ethnicity (reviewed in a subsequent section of this chapter) may prevent the positive effect of variety of information due to interest variety from emerging. For example, in a group with diverse interest profiles there can be unique information that individuals share, but there can also be categorization and stereotyping ("You are an artsy type so you will not attend to financial details") that is linked to power in the group.

Research Needs

Figure 10.1 outlines the proposed effects of interest diversity on group-level outcomes as discussed above. The lack of studies on interest diversity effects in organizational contexts indicates a clear need for more research. It is important, though, that researchers proceed mindful of key issues in diversity conceptualization and operationalization if the work is to produce meaningful contributions. First, researchers must specify whether the questions of focus relate to diversity in interests as a source of variety, separation, or disparity and ensure that the appropriate operationalization of diversity be used (Harrison & Klein, 2007). Measurement concerns also apply to how interests are considered: researchers have noted that the links between interests and performance at the individual level require attending to congruence, profiles, and patterns, not just to mean score levels (Nye, Su, Rounds, & Drasgow, 2012). Attention to potential differences in conceptualization and operationalization of "interests" is just as important as conceptualization and operationalization of "diversity in interests" in pursuing research on interest diversity.

Second, researchers need to heed van Knippenberg and Schippers's (2007) advice and focus on moderators rather than main effects of interest diversity and investigate *when* interest diversity has effects (i.e., what affects information elaboration, what affects social categorization based on interests). Third, researchers should measure proposed mediating mechanisms (e.g., information elaboration, voice) when possible in order to explicate *why* interest diversity may affect valued outcomes. One question to research is whether diversity in interests adds to prediction of outcomes above and beyond diversity in personality. Research on team personality composition shows the mean level of traits (e.g., conscientiousness, agreeableness) is positively associated with effectiveness (see Bell, 2007; LePine, Buckman, Crawford, & Methot, 2011 for reviews); however, that line of research does not suggest personality heterogeneity to be of benefit. It may be that homogeneity on high levels of some traits such as conscientiousness is critical, but heterogeneity on others (e.g., extraversion) can facilitate team performance in certain contexts (e.g., Kristof-Brown, Barrick, & Stevens, 2005). Whether the effects of interest diversity on performance are similar to those of personality diversity remains to be investigated.

Fourth, time may be an important consideration in understanding the effects of interest diversity. Specifically, Harrison, Price, and Bell (1998) found that the effects of deep-level diversity (differences in attitudes, beliefs, and values) become stronger the more frequently a group has interacted. This suggests that as groups interact more, any positive and any negative effects of interest diversity should magnify rather than decrease, as interests would be considered a deep rather than surface form of diversity.

Finally, levels of analysis should be given consideration in building theory on interest diversity. Work is needed that considers individual-level effects (e.g., how an individual's interest profile affects their performance), team-level effects (e.g., how and when the variety in interests in a team affect team performance), dyadic effects (e.g., how similarity in interests with one's supervisor might affect performance), broader context effects (e.g., how the type of organization might affect these outcomes), and the many potential cross-level effects (e.g., how being on a team with high interest variety might affect individual performance).

As a specific example of thinking at different levels noted earlier, "diversity of interests" can refer to the fact that some individuals have a more varied interest profile than others (also referred to as differentiation, Holland, Fritzsche, & Powell, 1994). How might this type of intraindividual diversity relate to workgroup functioning? While empirical research to address this question is lacking, we would expect that such individuals may be able to contribute more information and more social resources to a team. That is, their diversity of interests may allow them to take on multiple roles and functions in a work group. However, this would depend upon not just their interests but their abilities, as well as the relevance of those interests to the tasks at hand.

Practical Implications

There is ample advice out there on how to "manage diversity," which focuses on how to obtain the benefits of diverse perspectives while mitigating any negative effects (Stevens, Plaut, & Sanchez-Burks, 2008; van Knippenberg, Dawson, West, & Horman, 2011; Yang & Konrad, 2011). Beyond that advice, is there anything specific related to managing a diversity of interests?

First, we would advocate the importance of setting up processes within units to ensure that appropriate information exchange and elaboration is occurring. That is, individuals may tune out information from others that they find "uninteresting" and therefore miss out on the relevance of the information for task accomplishment. For example, an individual with strong conventional interests may be thinking through procedures and responsibilities while an individual with strong social interests may be focused on finding out more about who will be involved, and in doing so neither attends sufficiently to important information. Further, leadership can play an important role in facilitating information exchange and integration. Rico, Sanchez-Manzanares, Antino, and Lau (2012) demonstrated that the negative effects of educational specialization differences on group decision-making performance can be alleviated by cross-cutting roles and superordinate goals. Leaders can facilitate processes by which group members build on each other's ideas through discussion as well (Ellis, Mai, & Christian, 2013).

Second, when a diversity of interests is associated with separation on a particular issue (e.g., valuing feelings over rules), it is important to understand the separation and to ensure it does not devolve into a faultline in the group. Lau and Murnighan (1998) advanced a theory of faultlines, where attributes divide a group into smaller subgroups that individuals identify with more strongly. Faultlines can negatively impact group functioning (Thatcher & Patel, 2011) if their strength is not reduced. In the case of interests, individuals may form alliances with like-profiled others in the group. Chiu and Staples (2013) suggest one can reduce faultlines by having members that cut across subgroups (e.g., the scientist who also loves art). Faultline reduction can be facilitated by creating mechanisms for greater information elaboration and for individual disclosure of individuating information. Researchers have noted the value of perspective-taking (Hoever, van Knippenberg, van Ginkeyl, & Barkema, 2012) to ensure that members can appreciate others' views and why a particular focus might be appealing to someone with interests different from one's own.

Interests as an Influence on Unit Diversity

The second part of this chapter focuses on how interests affect demographic diversity in a unit. Despite advancements, the world of work remains somewhat demographically segregated (Blau, Brummund, & Liu, 2013). Given that individuals seek interest congruence by pursuing and remaining in environments that match their vocational interests (Dawis & Lofquist, 1978; Holland, 1959; Lent, Brown, & Hackett, 1994), investigating the relations between demographic characteristics and vocational interests provides insight into the processes that can limit unit diversity on demographic and other characteristics.

One of the most well-known findings in measurement of vocational interests is the gender difference in interests in people versus things (Su et al., 2009), as most males exhibit a greater preference for working with things, gadgets, and inorganic material; while females often prefer working with people and organic content. The subsequent differential representation in vocational options that match those interests also has been well-documented. For example, in the United States, more women work in service-type careers such as health care and teaching, whereas more men work in managerial or physically oriented jobs (Hegewisch & Matite, 2013). There are also significant gender gaps between male and female entries into the STEM fields, despite recent research suggesting that both genders are academically comparable in ability and achievement (Lindberg, Hyde, Peterson, & Linn, 2010). Indeed, in a meta-analysis Su and Rounds (2015) found that gender differences in interests of those in STEM fields ranged from d = .083 to 1.21 in engineering (favoring males) to d = -.40 in medical services (favoring females) and concluded that intervening to change interest levels may be key to attracting and retaining women in some STEM occupations. Research on gender development reveals that sex differences in interests are some of the earliest to emerge (Ruble, Martin, & Berenbaum, 2006) and Gottfredson (1981) asserts that, by 6 to 8 years of age, children begin to narrow their aspirations based on attitudes about gender-appropriate occupations. Weisgram, Bigler, and Liben (2010) showed that, when asked about interest in novel jobs, children, adolescents, and adults all were affected by the depicted sex of job holders, suggesting the effects of demographic composition on interests.

The link between ethnicity and interests has received support as well. Gottfredson (1978) demonstrated that a narrower range of occupations are considered among ethnic-racial minorities as compared to majority members. In addition, Tracey and Hopkins's (2001) research has shown that the specific occupations considered differ across ethnic groups. African Americans tend to have greater interest and subsequent representation in people-oriented social occupations as compared to others, Native Americans manifest the highest interest on the ideas pole of Holland's (1997) data-ideas dimension, Mexican Americans demonstrate more interests in careers characterized by the data pole, and Asian Americans tend to have higher interests and representation in investigative areas such as science and technology. Further, Tracey and Hopkins (2001) showed that ethnicity moderated the relationship between interests and occupational choice, as some groups place greater weight on interest fit in making career choices than others. Finally, research indicates that occupational segregation (in both actual jobs and as depicted in novel jobs) affects children's evaluations of job status and interest (Bigler, Averhart, & Liben, 2003).

These demographic differences in interests (which we will discuss in more detail later) can then lead to greater homogeneity and less demographic diversity in work units, although it is important to note that they are not the sole or even necessarily the primary contributor to occupational segregation and organizational demographic homogeneity. That is, sociocultural processes do fuel occupational segregation (Lee, Lawson, & McHale, 2015) and discrimination and perceptions of barriers affect the decision-making processes related to occupational choice (Chartrand & Rose, 1996; Hackett & Byars, 1996). Constrained opportunities—real or perceived—can limit individuals' feelings of accomplishment and drive for atypical career options, thus reducing the number of skilled job applicants for an occupation and contributing to the demographic gaps in representation (Hegewisch, Liepmann, Hayes, & Hartmann, 2010). Segregation has also been linked to differential status and power in the larger society, as masculine-typed occupations typically have higher salaries than feminine-typed occupations and are imbued with greater prestige (McCall, 2001; Lee et al., 2015). Thus, while we recognize that discrimination and other sociological and economic factors contribute to lessened occupational demographic diversity, we focus here specifically on how interests may contribute to the lack of demographic diversity through 1) attraction-selection-attrition (ASA) processes and 2) potential adverse impact of interest inventories as selection tools.

ASA and Diversity

Interests have been a major variable representing the "person" side in research applying the person-environment (PE) fit model (cf. Tinsley, 2000). This work is grounded in theories such as ASA theory (Schneider, 1987; Schneider, Smith, & Goldstein, 2000), which focuses on the interaction of personal attributes with environmental attributes in the prediction of perception of fit and subsequent attitudes and behaviors. How might each stage of the ASA process in terms of interests affect the diversity of an organization's membership?

First, as discussed earlier, demographic differences in interests may lead to proportionally more or less individuals self-selecting into and out of applying to certain occupations. Holland (1973, 1997) suggested that employees search for environments in which there is good fit between their own characteristics and the characteristics of their environment and where similar others (e.g. those with similar interests) can be found. The work of Schneider and colleagues (Schneider, 1987; Schneider et al., 2000) asserts that incumbents are those who were attracted to jobs and organizations that they believe will support their interests. There is empirical support for these ideas. Lent and colleagues (1994) conducted a meta-analysis examining interest's relationship with career choices and found that interests were significantly related to career choice (ρ = .60). Tracey and Hopkins (2001) also examined this relationship and determined that 27% of the variance in occupational choice was due to interests, and that interests were greater predictors of occupational choice than self-assessed ability. Thus, interests affect attraction and to the extent that interests display demographic differences, applicant pools will differ demographically for different occupations, affecting organizational diversity.

Second, selection processes may directly (through use of interest inventories) or indirectly (through use of educational credentials, biodata related to experiences and interests, fit assessments) screen out those lacking certain interests. For example, Ryan and Johnson (1942) presented one of the earliest examples of using interest inventory scores in the selection of sales and service employees. Van Iddekinge, Putka, and Campbell's (2011) validation efforts indicated that interests predicted a wide set of criteria including job knowledge and performance; Nye et al.'s (2012) meta-analysis also showed links from interest to outcomes. Thus, employers may find using interest inventories in selection a useful means of hiring employees that perform most effectively. However, as we will discuss in the next section, to the extent interests are linked to demographics, organizations may reduce diversity through selection on interests.

Third, attrition based on interests can affect organizational demographic diversity, as links between interests and continuance have been established (Van Iddekinge et al., 2011). One theoretical framework that presents a relationship between interests and employee retention is the social cognitive career theory (SCCT; Lent et al., 1994; Lent, Brown, & Hackett, 2000). This theory, drawn from the counseling psychology literature, focuses on the development of interests and their influence on intentions to pursue related activities over time. Empirically, Bolanovich (1948) found a correlation of .43 between interest scores and turnover in a sample of factory workers. Additional studies of U.S. forest service employee and police trainees and officers have also demonstrated significant correlations between interest inventory scores and turnover (Johnson & Hogan, 1981; Mayeske, 1964). Overall, individuals whose interest profiles are not congruent with characteristics of the environment will likely leave the environment (Schneider, 1987). Accordingly, interest profiles of those who stay in an environment come to represent the interest profile of the environment, thus fostering the expected outcome of the ASA process, homogeneity in interests. To the extent that interests relate to demographics, this also leads to demographic homogeneity.

In a straightforward relationship, those with interests that align less well with an occupation will tend to leave the occupation and those with aligned interests would stay. However, there is also a suggestion in the literature that the relationship of interests and attrition in segregated occupations is more complex. Interests that are seen as atypical for a group may relate to less perseverance and commitment to a career, such as when women drop out of sciences because they face or fear negative reactions for pursuing gender-atypical careers (Ceci et al., 2009; Heilman, Wallen, Fuchs, & Tampkins, 2004). That is, the interest-attrition relationship may be of a different form for those in a minority in an occupational setting.

Adverse Impact of Interest Inventories

One concern in selection processes in many countries is whether the use of certain procedures results in proportionally lower hiring rates for certain groups; that is, does the selection procedure have adverse impact? Interest inventories are seldom used in selection contexts, although recent evidence of their potential value in predicting performance may change that (Nye et al., 2012; Van Iddenkinge et al., 2011). Thus, it is important to consider whether interest inventories are likely to lead to adverse impact in hiring and, in particular, how the ways in which they are used might affect that.

As noted earlier, gender differences have been found to exist in interest inventory scores, with men showing greater scores on Realistic interests, and women scoring higher on artistic, conventional, and social scales (Fouad, 2002; Su et al., 2009). However, as Nye et al. (2012) note, using scale scores as direct predictors may not be the most effective way of selecting employees, and organizations may want to consider profiles as more meaningful. Armstrong et al. (2010) showed gender differences in the shape of profiles using Q correlations and Euclidean distance indices, so alternative methods of scoring interest inventories may still lead to adverse impact. Research is most definitely needed on this issue.

Further, since some interest inventories have separate norms for males and females, their use in selection settings can come under legal scrutiny in the United States. That is, the Civil Rights Act of 1991 prohibits the use of within-group norming in hiring contexts (Sackett & Wilk, 1994), which would disallow separate norming for males and females. While cautions and advice exist for using this information appropriately in career counseling contexts (e.g., Foud & Spreda, 1995), the ban on such use in selection contexts requires that organizations evaluate the interests of men and women on the same norms.

In general, there is inconsistent evidence of differences in interests across major ethnic and racial groups in the United States with some suggesting minimal differences (Fouad & Mohler, 2004), and others concluding that African Americans score higher on social, enterprising, and conventional interests than Whites (Tracey & Robbins, 2005). More recent meta-analytic work (Jones, Newman, Su, & Rounds, under review) suggests group differences in that Whites have greater realistic, investigative, and artistic interests, and African Americans have greater social interests. However, it is important to note that adverse impact is only in part determined by effect sizes of differences on an assessment tool, and is strongly affected by overall selection ratios (numbers hired out of numbers applying) as well as by applicant pool characteristics (Murphy, Osteen, & Myors, 1995). Thus, the effects of gender and ethnic group differences in interests on actual hiring rates and levels of adverse impact will likely vary across settings.

Further, one can look at how interests may indirectly relate to adverse impact through their correlations with cognitive ability, which exhibits large group differences (Cottrell, Newman, & Roisman, 2015). That is, in a meta-analysis, Jones et al. (under review) found cognitive ability correlates with investigative, artistic, and social interests, as well as to a small extent with enterprising interests. As Jones et al. demonstrated, considering mean group differences in interests as well as the correlation of cognitive ability with interests, one might have different expectations as to the level of expected adverse impact in different jobs. For example, in their study, they showed smaller Black-White differences on cognitive ability tests in investigative jobs because group differences in interests lead to greater portions of Whites applying as well as higher ability individuals applying (the A in ASA); however, Black-White subgroup differences were higher for social jobs because of greater attraction in terms of interests of African Americans as well as a greater range on cognitive ability in the applicant pool. The striking point made by Jones et al. is that indirect range restriction on interests affects observed adverse impact on cognitive ability predictors. Hence, interests affect demographic diversity in attraction directly, but also affect demographic differences in selection indirectly through their relation to cognitive ability test scores as well as to self-selection into hiring pools.

Research Needs

The research available on PE-fit and vocational interests is voluminous, so it may seem that we know all we need to know about interests, ASA, and diversity. However, there are some important unexplored questions. First, almost all of the work on ASA processes in organizations focuses on personality homogeneity, not interest homogeneity. Work on interest homogeneity has typically focused on the occupational level of analysis. Considering how interest homogeneity processes operate in occupations, but also in conjunction with potential effects in organizations and industries is important (i.e., a consideration of effects of multilevel ASA processes). For example, we might easily assume that there will be less diversity in interests among computer programmers (i.e., high in investigative and conventional interests) than across all jobs, and we can speculate a further extension to homogeneity in interest profiles when comparing computer programmers in a tech company to those in a retail or finance organization. Research on whether, how, and when interests affect homogeneity at levels other than the occupation may help us to understand potentially compounding effects on demographic diversity.

Another research area relates to faultlines in groups. In cases where interests and demographics are related, subgroups may emerge in groups where a "surface-level" characteristic (gender, ethnicity) may be strongly linked to a "deep-level" characteristic (interests). As we noted earlier, Harrison et al. (1998) found the effects of deep-level characteristics to become stronger over time and those of surface-level characteristics to lessen; in the case where surface and deep characteristics are linked, a stronger faultline may emerge that is harder to eradicate.

We see the research agenda on adverse impact and interest inventories as building on the work of Jones et al. (under review) regarding how interests can lead to indirect range restriction on other predictors, hence affecting pool demographic composition, as well as the work by Nye et al. (2012) suggesting greater direct use of interest inventories in selection. With regard to the latter, investigations are needed as to how to evaluate adverse impact when profiles and configural scoring are used as opposed to simply considering mean differences on interest scales. Further, how combinations of interest inventories with other selection assessments (DeCorte, Lievens, & Sackett, 2008; DeCorte, Sackett, & Lievens, 2010), as well as the order of assessments, might affect levels of adverse impact observed (DeCorte, Lievens, & Sackett, 2006; Finch, Edwards, & Wallace, 2009) will be important to investigate.

Practical Implications

As vocational interest fit has been shown to predict satisfaction with work (Dawis, 1991; Rounds & Tracey, 1990) and career stability (Holland, 1996), organizations composed of talented individuals pursuing environments that best match their interests will result in a satisfied and committed workforce (Robertson & Cooper, 2010). However, if greater homogeneity in interests does have negative effects on demographic diversity, organizations will need to consider how to counteract that influence while gaining the benefits of fit. Note that these effects on demographic diversity are not the result of a direct process of attracting, selection, or retaining only those of certain demographic groups, and are likely occurring *despite* strong efforts by organizations to recruit, select, and retain a diverse workforce. Organizational efforts to address ASA cycles based on legitimate job-fit criteria that happen to be demographically correlated can be resource-consuming and challenging to implement, but may be necessary. That is, for those interests where demographic differences do exist, there may be a need for targeted recruitment of women and minority group members to increase quality applicants in the initial pool (see Newman & Lyon, 2009, for analysis of how targeted recruiting can reduce adverse impact). Examples of this are currently happening in tech fields, where large employers of computer scientists make extra efforts to reach out to underrepresented individuals who have degrees in those fields through targeted recruitment and to retain such individuals through inclusion practices such as employee networks (e.g., Evans, 2012; Rice & Alfred, 2014).

Another practical implication would be the already popular notion of changing diversity of those in the field by changing interests (e.g., get girls interested in coding and engineering at an early age). While many of these interventions are relatively new efforts, their evaluation is important, particularly since—as we have already acknowledged—the reasons for lack of diversity in certain occupations may be multiple (e.g., discrimination and other barriers) and are not just based on interests. Interventions to develop interests may also need to be coupled with interventions to address other obstacles; for example, Woodcock, Hernandez, and Schultz (2015) demonstrated that a program for retaining underrepresented minorities in science was effective because of affecting students' responses to stereotype threats, not just enhancing their academic knowledge and interest in science.

While there may appear to be other practical implications easily drawn from this chapter, we would urge caution in plunging ahead to implement those related to employee selection. For example, one might conclude that there is a need to eliminate group differences on interest inventories by designing tools organizations can use in selection that do not show gender differences. While doing so might be quite feasible, it can occur at the cost of the construct validity of the measures and coverage of the content range of interests. As has been widely acknowledged by organizational psychologists, one does not wish to make tradeoffs between validity and diversity in selection contexts but may end up doing so (Ployhart & Holtz, 2008); considering ways to use interest inventories effectively in hiring processes while minimizing any potential adverse impact is important.

Summary and Conclusions

In this chapter, we have connected vocational interests and diversity in organizations in two distinct ways: through examining how diversity in interests affects team and organizational outcomes and through examining how interests affect the demographic diversity of workforces. In both cases, there is surprisingly limited research on which to draw conclusions, suggesting that making these connections is a worthwhile direction for enhancing our understanding of the importance of vocational interests in the workplace.

References

Armstrong, P. I., Fouad, N. A., Rounds, J., & Hubert L. (2010). Quantifying and interpreting group differences in interest profiles. *Journal of Career Assessment, 18,* 115–132.

Bell, S. T. (2007). Deep-level composition variables as predictors of team performance: A meta-analysis. *Journal of Applied Psychology, 92*(3), 595–615.

Bell, S. T., Villado, A. J., Lukasik, M. A., Belau, L., & Briggs, A. L. (2011). Getting specific about demographic diversity variables and team performance relationships: A meta-analysis. *Journal of Management, 37,* 709–743.

Berger, J. M., Fisek, H., Norman, R. Z., & Zelditch, M., Jr. (1977). *Status characteristics and social interaction*. New York: Elsevier.

Berger, J. M., Rosenholtz, S. J., & Zelditch, M. (1980). Status organizing processes. *Annual Review of Sociology, 6*, 479–508.

Bigler, R. S., Averhart, C. J., & Liben, L. S. (2003). Race and the workforce: Occupational status, aspirations, and stereotyping among African American children. *Developmental Psychology, 39*, 572–580.

Blau, F. D., Brummund, P., & Liu, A. Y. (2013). Trends in occupational segregation by gender 1970–2009: Adjusting for the impact of changes in the occupational coding system. *Demography, 50*(2), 471–492.

Blau, P. M. (1977). *Inequality and heterogeneity*. New York: Free Press.

Bolanovich, D. J. (1948). Interest tests reduce factory turnover. *Personnel Psychology, 1*, 81–92.

Ceci, S. J., Williams, W. M., & Barnett, S. M. (2009). Women's underrepresentation in science: Sociocultural and biological considerations. *Psychological Bulletin, 135*(2), 218. Retrieved from http://ezproxy.msu.edu/login?url=http://search.proquest.com/docview/203474291?accountid=12598

Chartrand, J. M., & Rose, M. L. (1996). Career interventions for at-risk populations: Incorporating social cognitive influences. *The Career Development Quarterly, 44*, 341–354.

Chen, J. M., & Moons, W. G. (2015). They won't listen to me: Anticipated power and women's disinterest in male-dominated domains. *Group Processes & Intergroup Relations, 18*(1), 116–128. doi:10.1177/1368430214550340

Chiu, Y., & Staples, D. S. (2013). Reducing faultlines in geographically dispersed teams: Self-disclosure and task elaboration. *Small Group Research, 44*, 498–531.

Cottrell, J. M., Newman, D. A., & Roisman, G. I. (2015). Explaining the Black–White gap in cognitive test scores: Toward a theory of adverse impact. *Journal of Applied Psychology*, doi:10.1037/apl0000020

Dawis, R. V. (1991). Vocational interests, values, and preferences. In M. D. Dunnette & L. M. Hough (Eds.), *Handbook of industrial and organizational psychology* (Vol. 2, pp. 831–871). Palo Alto, CA: Consulting Psychologists Press.

Dawis, R. V., & Lofquist, L. H. (1978). A note on the dynamics of work adjustment. *Journal of Vocational Behavior, 12*(1), 76–79.

DeCorte, W., Lievens, F., & Sackett, P. R. (2006). Predicting adverse impact and mean criterion performance in multistage selection. *Journal of Applied Psychology, 91*, 523–527.

DeCorte, W., Lievens, F., & Sackett, P. R. (2008). Validity and adverse impact potential of predictor composite formation. *International Journal of Selection and Assessment, 16*, 183–194.

DeCorte, W., Sackett, P., & Lievens, F. (2010). Selecting predictor subsets: Considering validity and adverse impact. *International Journal of Selection and Assessment, 18*, 260–270.

Ellis, A. P. J., Mai, K. M., & Christian, J. S. (2013). Examining the asymmetrical effects of goal faultlines in groups: A categorization-elaboration approach. *Journal of Applied Psychology, 98*(6), 948–961.

Evans, C. (2012). Recruitment initiatives aimed at increasing the gender diversity within ITEC employment. *Equality, Diversity and Inclusion: An International Journal, 31*(8), 741–752.

Finch, D. M., Edwards, B. D., & Wallace, J. C. (2009). Multistage selection strategies: Simulating the effects on adverse impact and expected performance for various predictor combinations, *Journal of Applied Psychology, 94*, 318–340.

Fouad, N. A. (2002). Cross-cultural differences in vocational interests: Between-group differences on the Strong Interest Inventory. *Journal of Counseling Psychology, 49,* 283–289.

Fouad, N. A., & Mohler, C. J. (2004). Cultural validity of Holland's theory and the Strong Interest Inventory for five racial/ethnic groups. *Journal of Career Assessment, 12,* 423–439.

Foud, N. A., & Spreda, S. L. (1995). Use of interest inventories with special populations: Women and minority groups. *Journal of Career Assessment, 3,* 453–468.

Gottfredson, L. S. (1978). An analytical description of employment according to race, sex, prestige, and Holland type of work. *Journal of Vocational Behavior, 13,* 210–221.

Gottfredson, L. S. (1981). Circumscription and compromise: A developmental theory of occupational aspirations. *Journal of Counseling Psychology, 28,* 545–579.

Hackett, G., & Byars, A. M. (1996). Social cognitive theory and the career development of African American women. *The Career Development Quarterly, 44,* 322–340.

Harrison, D. A., & Klein, K. J. (2007). What's the difference? Diversity constructs as separation, variety, or disparity in organizations. *Academy of Management Review,* 32, 1199–1228.

Harrison, D. A., Price, K. H., & Bell, M. P. (1998). Beyond relational demography: Time and the effects of surface- and deep-level diversity on work group cohesion. *Academy of Management Journal, 41,* 96–107.

Hassan, S. I. (2010). Humanities and the role of the university: To link university with market or with community. *Journal of Social Affairs, 27*(105), 9–32. Retrieved from http://ezproxy.msu.edu/login?url=http://search.proquest.com/docview/754047112?accountid=12598

Hegewisch, A., Liepmann, H., Hayes, J., & Hartmann, H. (2010). *Separate and not equal? Gender segregation in the labor market and the gender wage gap.* Institute for Women's Policy Research Briefing Paper IWPR C377. Retrieved from www.iwpr.org.

Hegewisch, A., & Matite, M. (2013). *The gender wage gap by occupation.* Institute for Women's Policy Research Fact Sheet IWPR C350a. Retrieved from www.iwpr.org.

Heilman, M. E., Wallen, A. S., Fuchs, D., & Tampkins, M. M. (2004). Penalties for success: Reactions to women who succeed at male gender-typed tasks. *Journal of Applied Psychology, 89,* 416–427.

Hoever, I. J., van Knippenberg, D., van Ginkeyl, W. P., & Barkema, H. G. (2012). Fostering team creativity: Perspective taking as key to unlocking diversity's potential. *Journal of Applied Psychology, 97,* 982–996.

Holland, J. L. (1959). A theory of vocational choice. *Journal of Counseling Psychology, 6,* 35–45.

Holland, J. L. (1973). Unfrocking college admissions. *PsycCRITIQUES, 18,* 327–328.

Holland, J. L. (1996). Exploring careers with a typology: What we have learned and some new directions. *American Psychologist, 51,* 397–406.

Holland, J. L. (1997). Making vocational choices: *A theory of vocational personalities and work environments.* Odessa, FL: Psychological Assessment Resources.

Holland, J. L., Fritzsche, B., & Powell, A. (1994). *The self-directed search: Technical manual.* Odessa, FL: Psychological Assessment Resources.

Homan, A. C., van Knippenberg, D., Van Kleef, G. A., & De Dreu, C. K. W. (2007). Bridging faultlines by valuing diversity: Diversity beliefs, information elaboration, and performance in diverse work groups. *Journal of Applied Psychology, 92,* 1189–1199.

Huang, X., Hsieh, J., J. P-A., & He, W. (2014). Expertise dissimilarity and creativity: The contingent roles of tacit and explicit knowledge sharing. *Journal of Applied Psychology, 99,* 816–830.

Iskander, E. T., Gore, P. A., Jr., Furse, C., & Bergerson, A. (2013). Gender differences in expressed interests in engineering-related fields ACT 30-year data analysis identified trends and suggested avenues to reverse trends. *Journal of Career Assessment, 21*(4), 599–613. doi:10.1177/1069072712475290

Johnson, J. A., & Hogan, R. (1981). Vocational interests, personality and effective police performance. *Personnel Psychology, 34,* 49–53.

Jones, K. S., Newman, D. A. Su, R. & Rounds, J. (under review). Vocational interests and adverse impact: A meta-analysis of black-white differences in vocational interests.

Kristof-Brown, A., Barrick, M. R., & Stevens, C. K. (2005). When opposites attract: A multi-sample demonstration of complementary person-team fit on extraversion. *Journal of Personality, 73*(4), 935–958.

Lau, D. C., & Murnighan, J. K. (1998). Demographic diversity and faultlines: The compositional dynamics of organizational groups. *Academy of Management Review, 23,* 325–340.

Le, H., Robbins, S. B., & Westrick, P. (2014). Predicting student enrollment and persistence in college STEM fields using an expanded P-E fit framework: A large-scale multilevel study. *Journal of Applied Psychology, 99*(5), 915–947. doi:10.1037/a0035998

Lee, B., Lawson, K. M., & McHale, S. M. (2015). Longitudinal associations between gender-typed skills and interests and their links to occupational outcomes. *Journal of Vocational Behavior, 88,* 121–130.

Lent, R. W., Brown, S. D., & Hackett, G. (1994). Toward a unifying social cognitive theory of career and academic interest, choice, and performance. *Journal of Vocational Behavior, 45,* 79–122.

Lent, R. W., Brown, S. D., & Hackett, G. (2000). Contextual supports and barriers to career choice: A social cognitive analysis. *Journal of Counseling Psychology, 47,* 36–49.

LePine, J. A., Buckman, B. R., Crawford, E. R., & Methot, J. R. (2011). A review of research on personality in teams: Accounting for pathways spanning levels of theory and analysis. *Human Resource Management Review, 21,* 311–330.

Lindberg, S. M., Hyde, J. S., Peterson, J. L., & Linn, M. C. (2010). *Psychological Bulletin, 136,* 1123–1135.

Lubinski, D., & Benbow, C. P. (1992). Gender differences in abilities and preferences among the gifted: Implications for the math-science pipeline. *Current Directions in Psychological Science, 1*(2), 61–66. Retrieved from http://ezproxy.msu.edu/login?url=http://search.proquest.com/docview/618301357?accountid=12598

Mayeske, G. W. (1964). Prediction of foster retention and advancement from the Kunder Preference Record. *USDA Personnel Research Series,* 1–13.

McCall, L. (2001). *Complex inequality: Gender, class, and race in the new economy.* New York: Routledge.

Murphy, K. R., Osteen, K., & Myors, B. (1995). Modeling the effects of banding in personnel selection. *Personnel Psychology, 48,* 61–84.

Newman, D. A., & Lyon, J. S. (2009). Recruitment efforts to reduce adverse impact: Targeted recruiting for personality, cognitive ability, and diversity. *Journal of Applied Psychology, 94,* 298–317.

Nye, C. D., Su, R., Rounds, J., & Drasgow, F. (2012). Vocational interests and performance: A quantitative summary of over 60 years of research. *Perspectives on Psychological Science, 7*(4), 384–403.

O'Neill, T. A., McLarnon, M. J. W., Hoffart, G. C., Woodley, H. J., & Allen, N. J. (2015). The structure and function of team conflict state profiles. *Journal of Management,* doi:10.1177/0149206315581662

Pelled, L. (1996). Demographic diversity, conflict, and work group outcomes: An intervening process theory. *Organization Science, 7,* 615–631.

Ployhart, R. E., & Holtz, B. C. (2008). The diversity-validity dilemma: Strategies for reducing racioethnic and sex subgroup differences and adverse impact in selection. *Personnel Psychology, 61*(1), 153–172.

Post, R. (2009). Debating disciplinarity. *Critical Inquiry, 35*(4), 748–770. Retrieved from http://ezproxy.msu.edu/login?url=http://search.proquest.com/docview/1320338759?accountid=12598

Ragins, B. R. (1997). Antecedents of diversified mentoring relationships. *Journal of Vocational Behavior, 51,* 90–109.

Rice, D., & Alfred, M. (2014). Personal and structural elements of support for African American female engineers. *Journal of STEM Education: Innovations and Research, 15*(2), 40–49.

Rico, R., Sanchez-Manzanares, M., Antino, M., & Lau, D. (2012). Bridging team faultlines by combining task role assignment and goal structure strategies. *Journal of Applied Psychology, 97,* 407–420.

Rietzschel, E. F., Nijstad, B. A., & Stroebe, W. (2007). Relative accessibility of domain knowledge and creativity: The effects of knowledge activation on the quantity and originality of generated ideas. *Journal of Experimental Social Psychology, 43,* 933–946.

Roberson, Q., Ryan, A. M., & Ragins, B. R. (2017). The evolution and future of diversity at work. *Journal of Applied Psychology, 102,* 483–499.

Robertson, I. T., & Cooper, C. L. (2010). Full engagement: The integration of employee engagement and psychological well-being. *Leadership & Organization Development Journal, 31*(4), 324–336.

Rounds, J. B., & Tracey, T. J. (1990). From trait-and-factor to person-environment fit counseling: Theory and process. In W. B. Walsh & S. H. Osipow (Eds.) *Career counseling: Contemporary topics in vocational psychology.* Hillsdale, NJ: Erlbaum.

Ruble, D. N., Martin, C. L., & Berenbaum, S. A. (2006). Gender development. In N. Eisenberg, W. Damon, & R. M. Lerner (Eds.). *Handbook of child psychology: Vol. 3, Social, emotional, and personality development* (pp. 858–932). Hoboken, NJ: Wiley.

Ryan, T. A., & Johnson, B. R. (1942). Interest scores in the selection of salesmen and servicemen: Occupational vs. ability-group scoring keys. *Journal of Applied Psychology, 26,* 543–562.

Ryan, J. M., Tracey, T. J., & Rounds, J. (1996). Generalizability of Holland's structure of vocational interests across ethnicity, gender, and socioeconomic status. *Journal of Counseling Psychology, 43,* 330–337.

Sackett, P. R., & Wilk, S. L. (1994). Within-group norming and other forms of score adjustment in preemployment testing. *American Psychologist, 49*(11), 929–954.

Schneider, B. (1987). The people make the place. *Personnel Psychology, 40,* 437–453.

Schneider, B., Smith, D. B., & Goldstein, H. W. (2000). Attraction-selection-attrition: Toward a person-environment psychology of organizations. In W. B. Walsh, K. H. Craik, & R. H. Price (Eds.), *Person-environment psychology: New directions and perspectives* (pp. 61–85). Mahwah, NJ: Erlbaum.

Stevens, F. G., Plaut, V. C., & Sanchez-Burks, J. (2008). Unlocking the benefits of diversity: All-inclusive multiculturalism and positive organizational change. *Journal of Applied Behavioral Science, 44*(1), 116–133. doi:10.1177/0021886308314460

Su, R. & Rounds, J. (2015). All STEM fields are not created equal: people and things interests explain gender disparities across STEM fields. *Frontiers in Psychology, 6*, 189.

Su, R., Rounds, J., & Armstrong, P. I. (2009). Men and things, women and people: A meta-analysis of sex differences in interests. *Psychological Bulletin, 135,* 859–884.

Thatcher, S. M. B., & Patel, P. C. (2011). Demographic faultlines: A meta-analysis of the literature. *Journal of Applied Psychology, 96,* 1119–1139.

Tinsley, H. E. (2000). The congruence myth: An analysis of the efficacy of the person-environment fit model. *Journal of Vocational Behavior, 56,* 147–179.

Tracey, T. J., & Hopkins, N. (2001). Correspondence of interests and abilities with occupational choice. *Journal of Counseling Psychology, 48,* 178–189.

Tracey, T. J., & Robbins, S. B. (2005). Stability of interests across ethnicity and gender: A longitudinal examination of grades 8 through 12. *Journal of Vocational Behavior, 67,* 335–364.

Tsui, A. S., Ashford, S. J., St. Clair, L., & Xin, K. R. (1995). Dealing with discrepant expectations: Response strategies and managerial effectiveness. *Academy of Management Journal, 38,* 1515–1543.

Van Iddekinge, C. H., Putka, D. J., & Campbell, J. P. (2011). Reconsidering vocational interests for personnel selection: The validity of an interest-based selection test in relation to job knowledge, job performance, and continuance intentions. *Journal of Applied Psychology, 96,* 13–33.

van Knippenberg, D., Dawson, J. F., West, M. A., & Homan, A. C. (2011). Diversity faultlines, shared objectives, and top management team performance. *Human Relations, 64*(3), 307–336.

van Knippenberg, D., De Dreu, C. K. W., & Homan, A. C. (2004). Work group diversity and group performance: An integrative model and research agenda. *Journal of Applied Psychology, 89*, 1008–1022.

van Knippenberg, D., & Haslam, S. A. (2003). Realizing the diversity divided: Exploring the subtle interplay between identity, ideology, and reality. In S. A. Haslam, D. van Knippenber, & J. Michael (Eds.), *Social identity at work: Developing theory for organizational practice* (pp. 61–77). New York: Psychology Press.

van Knippenberg, D., & Schippers, M. C. (2007). Workgroup diversity. In M. I. Posner & M. K. Rothbart (Eds.), *Annual review of psychology, 58*, 515–541. Palo Alto, CA: Annual Reviews.

Weisgram, E. S., Bigler, R. S., & Liben, J. S. (2010). Gender, values, and occupational interests among children, adolescents and adults. *Child Development, 81*, 778–796.

Woodcock, A., Hernandez, P. R., & Schultz, P. W. (2015). Diversifying science: Intervention programs moderate the effect of stereotype threat on motivation and career choice. *Social Psychological and Personality Science*, 1–9.

Yang, Y., & Konrad, A. M. (2011). Understanding diversity management practices: Implications of institutional theory and resource-based theory. *Group & Organization Management, 36*(1), 6–38.

11

VOCATIONAL INTERESTS IN A GLOBAL BUSINESS ENVIRONMENT

Jason L. Huang

MICHIGAN STATE UNIVERSITY

Shan Ran

MERCER UNIVERSITY

Mengqiao Liu

DEVELOPMENT DIMENSIONS INTERNATIONAL

Recent findings that vocational interests can predict individual job performance have underscored the potential instrumental role vocational interests can play in human capital management (Nye, Su, Rounds, & Drasgow, 2012; Van Iddekinge, Putka, & Campbell, 2011). However, it is unclear whether the science of vocational interests that is heavily rooted in research conducted in the United States may apply in different cultures. This is particularly important as businesses are faced with ever-increasing challenges to manage human capital across cultures and national boundaries (Kossek, Huang, Piszczek, Fleenor, & Ruderman, 2015). Thus, a critical review of cross-cultural research on vocational interests is in order.

The chapter serves two goals. First, we review the cross-cultural literature pertaining to vocational interests and its implications for global businesses, with a focus on how national and cultural contexts influence the structure of vocational interests and impact key correlates of interests. Second, we seek to identify directions for future research that can enhance current understanding of vocational interests' role in human capital management in a global economy.

Review of Cross-Cultural Vocational Interest Research

One of the focal questions in cross-cultural research is whether a phenomenon (e.g., the influence of vocational interests on job satisfaction) is universal, or is contingent on the culture in which it is enacted. In other words, one should examine, as posited by Graen, Hui, Wakabayashi, and Wang (1997), whether the phenomenon is etic (universal across all cultures) or emic (unique to a culture).

Traditional literature on vocational interests had assumed an etic approach, with the majority of the studies conducted in a single, typically Western, context. Emerging research endeavors have started to investigate some cultural contingencies concerning vocational interests. Addressing such complexity can lead to a more in-depth understanding of what is etic and what is emic, which can provide useful guidance for businesses managing human capital across national and cultural boundaries.

To provide an up-to-date review of vocational interest research with a particular focus on cross-cultural implications, we conducted a comprehensive literature search to identify relevant journal articles and book chapters. We organize our review into three sections: (a) the structure of vocational interests; (b) the relationships between interests and key individual difference variables (i.e., cognitive ability, personality, and self-efficacy); and (c) the influence of interests on occupational outcomes.

In each section, we first review the general findings in the literature, which are usually culture-blind and predominantly conducted in the Anglo cultural cluster. We then present research that focuses on the same relationships in different cultures.

Structure and Measurement

Since Holland (1959, 1966) proposed the influential RIASEC model (see the introduction to this volume for a description), the hexagon of vocational interests has been widely adopted in research and practice, especially for the occupational classifications in the United States (National Center for O★NET Development, 2015). Organized along six corners of a hexagon, people-things and data-ideas best describe the underlying two-dimensional structure (Donnay & Borgen, 1996; Prediger, 1982; Tay, Su, & Rounds, 2011). This circular structure predicts that the six pairs of adjacent interests (i.e., RI, IA, AS, SE, EC, and CR) show the strongest associations, followed by the six pairs of alternate interests (i.e., RA, IS, AE, SC, ER, and CI), and the three pairs of opposite interests (i.e., RS, IE, and AS) should show the weakest associations (Holland, 1973, 1985, 1997).

Cross-Cultural Differences in Structure

Gati (1979, 1984, 1991) challenged this circular structure and argued that vocational interests do not have different degrees of proximity. Instead, occupations are grouped based on their similarities in a hierarchically organized tree structure. This tree or hierarchical structure yields two major categories of "soft" and "hard" sciences. Under the "soft" science category, the AS pair represents service-related, social, and cultural interests, and the EC pair represents business-related interests. RI, under the "hard" science category, represent science-related interests. As a result, only three pairs of similar types (i.e., AS, EC, and RI) are expected to show stronger associations, whereas the twelve dissimilar pairs should be correlated to a weaker extent.

Although Holland's and Gati's models share some common predictions, Holland's model contains additional constraints: The magnitudes of correlations are expected to be weaker (a) between alternate interests than between adjacent interests and (b) between opposite interests than between alternate interests. A meta-analysis using 104 studies revealed favorable support for Holland's circular model (Tracey & Rounds, 1993). However, 77 out of 104 (74%) of the analyzed studies were from the United States, 19 studies (18%) were from Australia or New Zealand, and only 9 studies (9%) were from more culturally dissimilar countries (i.e., Guyana, Taiwan, and Mexico). Rounds and Tracey (1996) conducted another meta-analysis using 73 U.S. samples, 20 ethnic minority samples in the United States, and 76 studies from 18 non-U.S. countries. Results revealed that Holland's model failed to hold across countries, including countries culturally similar to the United States, such as Canada and Australia. In contrast, Gati's model was supported for the United States and non-U.S. datasets.

Despite the favorable evidence for Gati's hierarchical model, research following this meta-analysis has focused on Holland's model instead (for exceptions, see Einarsdóttir, Rounds, Ægisdóttir, & Gerstein, 2002 and Hedrih, 2008). These recent results regarding the fit of RIASEC have been mixed, including supportive evidence from Indian (Leong, Austin, Sekaran, & Komarraju, 1998) and Serbian samples (Hedrih, 2008), as well as unsupportive evidence from mainland China or Hong Kong (Goh, 2001; Tang, 2001, 2009; Yang, Stokes, & Hui, 2005), Japan (Long, Watanabe, & Tracey, 2006), the Philippines (Primavera et al. 2010), and Iceland (Einarsdóttir, Rounds, & Su, 2010). Likewise, Gati's model has also received favorable results from the Icelandic sample (Einarsdóttir et al., 2002) and unfavorable results from the Serbian sample (Hedrih, 2008). These findings suggest that prior knowledge regarding the fit of the two theoretical models may need to be qualified by the cultures in which the models are examined, and cultural differences might alter the structure of vocational interests.

Rounds and Tracey (1996) pointed out the necessity to specify the causes of these cross-cultural differences in interest structure and speculated that economic development and cultural values can moderate the correlations among interests. For instance, in individualistic cultures that value individual decisions (Hofstede, 1980, 2001), Artistic stood out as a unique type of interest rather than clustering with other interests as specified by the circular or hierarchical models. In addition, because interests are typically measured based on occupations, national differences in tasks, work roles, and work contexts within occupations may also explain some structural differences in vocational interests.

When taking into account the within-country variations, individuals' conformity to the national cultural values can explain the lack of fit to a theoretical structure. For instance, a cross-cultural study of college freshmen from Hong Kong and the United States indicated that only part of Holland's model fit well with students' responses (except A and S), and the fit was poor for students who endorsed traditional values (Farh, Leong, & Law, 1998). Therefore, cultural values are critical for explaining why these cross-cultural differences may have occurred.

Additional Dimensions of Vocational Interests

Besides Holland's circular model and Gati's hierarchical model, Tracey and Rounds (1996a, 1996b) expanded Holland's model to a three-dimensional, spherical structure by adding another prestige dimension. They suggested that prestige captures self-assessment of abilities and desired occupational culture, and it explained meaningful variance in vocational interests in a U.S. college student sample. Similar improvement in structural variance explained by prestige was also found in Japanese (Long et al., 2006), Serbian (Hedrih, 2008), and Icelandic (Einarsdóttir et al., 2010) samples. However, some structural dissimilarities between American and Japanese college students on this additional dimension imply distinctive views of prestige across cultures (Tracey, Watanabe, & Schneider, 1997). Specifically, Japanese workers often derive a perception of prestige from affiliations with specific organizations rather than certain occupations.

Sex-type of occupations is another dimension, which explains more variance in vocational interests than prestige (Einarsdóttir & Rounds, 2000). While not overlapping with prestige (Sodano & Tracey, 2008), sex-type is highly correlated with people-things in an Icelandic sample (Einarsdóttir et al., 2010), whereas the same relation tends to be weaker in the United States (Su, Rounds, & Armstrong, 2009). Thus, culture appears to influence various underlying dimensions of vocational interests.

Cross-Cultural Measurement

Meanwhile, measurement validation research also started to proliferate in other languages, such as in Dutch (Evers, 1995), French (Segal, 1995), Chinese (Fang, Bai, & Ling, 1996; Goh, 2001), Japanese (Tracey et al., 1997), Spanish (Glidden-Tracey & Greenwood, 1997), and Icelandic (Einarsdóttir et al., 2002). Most of the measures (i.e., Chinese, Japanese, Spanish, and Icelandic) were developed based on Holland's RIASEC model. As an exception, Einarsdóttir, Eyjólfsdóttir, and Rounds (2013) took an emic approach and used the occupational descriptions published in Iceland to develop an indigenous measurement of interests. Some studies also examined cross-cultural or cross-language structural invariance of the measurement on the basis of adopting back translation procedures for enhancing linguistic equivalence (Glidden-Tracey & Greenwood, 1997; Goh, 2001; Tracey et al., 1997). The methodology adopted by these authors provided an exemplar practice of the cross-cultural/language validation of the measurement. In addition to testing dimension-level invariance across cultures and languages, examining differential item functioning (DIF), or a lack of item-level invariance, can be informative about cultural differences in occupations. However, DIF and its potential contribution to the lack of dimension-level invariance can invalidate the cultural comparisons of interests (Church et al., 2011).

Individual Differences and Vocational Interests

Sex/Gender

Shortly after World War II, the United States began to shift from segregation to promoting equality of various social groups in the workplace (Katzell & Austin, 1992). However, the long-lasting stereotypes associated with sex/gender, race, and other socioeconomic factors continued to influence vocational interests held by individuals from different demographic backgrounds. In particular, sex has been considered as one of the most relevant demographic variables in relation to vocational interests, due to the sex-type dimension of occupations (Einarsdóttir & Rounds, 2000).

The developmental theory of occupational aspirations (Gottfredson, 1981) suggests that sex affects the extent to which an individual perceives a particular occupation to be compatible with and accessible to oneself, and this perception is a critical determinant for vocational interests. Su and colleagues (2009) meta-analyzed U.S. and Canadian studies published from 1964 to 2007, and their overall results revealed higher levels of Realistic (d = 0.84) and Investigative (d = 0.26) interests (or things), as well as lower levels of Artistic (d = -0.35), Social (d = -0.68), and Conventional (d = -0.33) interests (or people) among men compared to women. A more recent meta-analysis of gender differences of interests in specific STEM (Science, Technology, Engineering, and Mathematics) disciplines confirmed men's higher interests in things (i.e., engineering, ds = 0.83–1.21) and women's higher interest in people (i.e., social services, d = -0.33; medical service, d = -0.40; Su & Rounds, 2015). These two meta-analyses suggest that the unbalanced gender representations in the higher end of the distribution of each interest might have contributed to the sex disparities in actual occupational choices.

As society progresses, Betz, Heesacker, and Shuttleworth (1990) noted that women in the United States were increasingly aware of various career options. Supporting this increasing gender egalitarianism in the United States, a meta-analysis of studies from 1976 to 2004 revealed a decrease in sex differences in interests, including women's growing interests in Enterprising occupations and men's decreased interests in Realistic and Investigative occupations (Bubany & Hansen, 2011). Likewise, the meta-analysis conducted by Su et al. (2009) showed that the sex differences on the Artistic and Enterprising interests, as well as the data-ideas dimension, were smaller in younger cohorts (Su et al., 2009). On the contrary, Su and colleagues found that sex differences in STEM interests seem to persist over time. Research continues to support the substantial effect of sex on vocational interests in the United States across different racial/ethnic groups (Fouad, 2002; Leuty & Hansen, 2014; Rosenbloom, Ash, Dupont, & Coder, 2008). This sex effect is even noticeable within occupations. For example, male physician assistants were found to have considerably higher Realistic interests than their female counterparts (LaBarbera, 2005).

Cross-cultural Research on Interests and Sex/Gender

Researchers have observed decreasing, yet persistent sex differences in non-U.S. countries over the years as well. In a German college student sample obtained in 1990, men preferred majors related to things whereas women preferred majors related to people, resulting in limited representation of women in STEM disciplines (Pässler & Hell, 2012). College women in Switzerland, Austria, and Taiwan also showed lower interests in Realistic occupations and higher interests in Artistic and Social occupations (Proyer & Häusler, 2007; Tien, 2011). Paessler (2015) pointed out that sex differences in the variability of interests also partly contribute to the mean-level differences. Using two large samples of over 110,000 total respondents from Germany, Switzerland, and Austria, Paessler found large variations in Realistic and Enterprising interests for men, as well as Artistic and Conventional interests for women. In particular, there was a large ratio of men to women who score high on Realistic interests (5% tail ratio = 7:1) and things (5% tail ratio = 10:1). In contrast, women's representation in the top 5% of Artistic and Social interests was four times of men's representation. However, the increasing variability in younger adults' interests (i.e., R, A, and S) reflects the decreasing nature of sex differences in interests.

This movement toward decreasing sex disparities in different occupations in many countries implies that gender egalitarian values increase over time across different cultures, which may result in attenuated sex differences in interests in more recent studies. Therefore, we suggest that comparisons of sex differences in vocational interests should incorporate a temporal factor. Research has also indicated the complexity of the moderating role of gender egalitarianism on sex differences in interests, such that women and men may be more encouraged to embrace their preferred interests in egalitarian countries; therefore, sex differences in interests may be exacerbated in a different fashion as a society becomes more gender egalitarian (Ott-Holland, Huang, Ryan, Elizondo, & Wadlington, 2013). Based on a sample of approximately 400,000 workers obtained between 2001 and 2009, Ott-Holland et al. found that when gender egalitarianism (House, Hanges, Javidan, Dorfman, & Gupta, 2004) increases, there are lower sex differences in musical (ideas) and persuasive (people) interests, but higher sex differences in clerical (data) and scientific (things) interests, supporting the intricate role played by this cultural dimension.

Taken together, gender egalitarianism is a critical cultural moderator on the relationship between sex and vocational interests, and the direction of moderation can be complex. Beyond biological sex, researchers have also attended to how gender role orientation and sexual orientation are related to interests, suggesting some plausible positive effects of femininity-orientation (Betz et al., 1990; Pozzebon, Visser, & Bogaert, 2015) and male homosexuality (Ellis, Ratnasingam, & Wheeler, 2012) on female-typed occupations. As discussed above, the dynamic nature of gender egalitarian values in different societies needs to be considered when drawing inferences over time. Another unique challenge of studying sex differences is the violation of measurement invariance between men and women, which has been repeatedly found in studies across different countries (e.g., Proyer & Häusler, 2007; Tang, 2001)

Ability

Based on Holland's (1959, 1973, 1985) descriptions of vocational interests and theoretical propositions, vocational interests can be linked to cognitive abilities, both in terms of general intelligence (*g*) and specific cognitive abilities. Investigative interests were argued to be positively related to *g* (Holland, 1973, 1985, 1997). In addition, Holland (1959, 1973) posited that Realistic interests should be associated with mechanical abilities and (low) social skills, whereas Investigative interests should be related to numerical abilities and induction. In a qualitative review, Ackerman and Heggestad (1997) reported some general patterns regarding the interests-abilities associations: (a) Realistic interests were positively correlated with math, spatial, and mechanical abilities; (b) Investigative interests were positively correlated with math, spatial, mechanical, and verbal abilities; (c) Artistic interests were positively associated with verbal abilities; (d) Social interests negatively corresponded to mathematical and spatial abilities; (e) Enterprising interests were negatively correlated with cognitive abilities; and (f) Conventional interests were negatively related to cognitive abilities (except for perceptual speed and numerical abilities). Using O*NET' ratings, Anthoney and Armstrong (2010) found that the quantitative evidence generally supported these patterns with some exceptions. For instance, Realistic interests were negatively related to verbal abilities, and Investigative interests were negatively related to spatial orientation.

Ability may also be integrated as a dimension of interests. Armstrong, Day, McVay, and Rounds (2008) found that cognitive complexity required by the occupational activity was strongly associated with numerous ability components, such as oral and written comprehension, oral and written expression, and mathematical reasoning. They also argued for a correspondence between the complexity dimension and occupational prestige. Future work can continue examining the ability-interests link from this integrative approach.

Based on Holland's assumptions and Ackerman and Heggestad's review, Pässler, Beinicke, and Hell's (2015) meta-analysis (k = 29, N = 55,297) revealed meaningful relationships between vocational interests and both g and specific cognitive abilities (see Table 11.1). Investigative (ρ = .28), Realistic (ρ = .23), Social (ρ = -.19), and Enterprising (ρ = -.08) interests all shared significant correlations with g, whereas relationships between g and Artistic

TABLE 11.1 Summary of Relationships Between RIASEC and Abilities

	R	*I*	*A*	*S*	*E*	*C*
Meta–analytic correlations (Pässler et al., 2014)						
g	**.23**	**.28**	–.03	**–.19**	**–.08**	.01
Verbal ability	.05	**.21**	**.22**	**–.06**	–.08	–.05
Induction	**.13**	**.22**	.07	–.05	–.12	.06
Numerical ability	**.26**	**.25**	**–.18**	**–.21**	**–.08**	.08
Spatial ability	**.34**	**.27**	–.08	**–.22**	**–.13**	–.02
Perceptual speed	–.05	.08	.07	.03	–.06	.08
Mechanical knowledge	**.31**	**.17**	–.12	**–.28**	**–.14**	–.06
Australia (Carless, 1999)						
g		+				
Verbal ability		+				–
Numeric ability		+				
Austria (Proyer, 2006)						
Spatial ability	+	+				
Germany						
g (Mussel, 2013)		+			+	
g (Vock et al. 2013)	+	+	+	–	–	
Specific abilities (Pässler and Hell, 2012)						
Verbal ability	+	+	+	–	–	
Numerical ability	+	+	–	–		+
Spatial ability	+	+	–	–	–	

Note. For meta-analytic correlations, each number represents the estimated true score correlation (corrected for sampling error and unreliability in measurement) between the interests type and the ability. Numbers in boldface represent correlations with credibility intervals that exclude zero. For individual studies, + sign indicates a significant positive correlation; – sign indicates a significant negative correlation.

and Conventional interests were negligible. With regard to specific cognitive abilities, Realistic interests were significantly correlated with spatial abilities (ρ = .34), numerical abilities (ρ = .26), mechanical knowledge (ρ = .31), and induction (ρ = .13); Investigative interests were associated with verbal (ρ = .21), spatial abilities (ρ = .27), numerical abilities (ρ = .25), induction (ρ = .22), and mechanical knowledge (ρ = .17); Artistic interests were correlated with verbal abilities (ρ = .22) and numerical abilities (ρ = -.18); Social interests were related to mechanical knowledge (ρ = -.28), spatial abilities (ρ = -.22), and numerical abilities (ρ = -.21); Enterprising interests were associated with spatial abilities (ρ = -.13) and mechanical knowledge (ρ = -.14). Conventional interests did not share any meaningful correlations with specific cognitive abilities. In sum, the meta-analytical findings revealed small to medium relationships between vocational interests and cognitive abilities.

Cross-cultural Research on Interests and Abilities

We identified five studies that examined the interest-ability relationship in countries other than the United States (one in Australia, one in Austria, and three in Germany). An overview of the results is summarized in Table 11.1. Based on two samples in Australia, Carless (1999) identified weak to moderate positive relationships between Investigative interests and cognitive abilities (general abilities as well as verbal and numeric abilities), as well as negative relationships between Conventional interests and verbal abilities. Proyer (2006) studied the interest-ability relationship in a sample of 138 individuals from Austria. Results indicated that there was a positive relationship between spatial ability and both Realistic and Investigative interests.

Of the three studies conducted in Germany, Mussel (2013) examined the relationships between cognitive ability and vocational interests in a sample of 250 individuals. Results showed that both Intellectual-Scientific and Entrepreneurial interests were positively related to cognitive ability. However, with a relatively small sample size, the findings may have limited generalizability.

In contrast, the other two studies conducted in Germany were based on larger samples. Based on 1,990 students and alumni from universities, Pässler and Hell (2012) found that (a) both Realistic and Investigative interests were related to verbal, numerical, and spatial abilities, (b) Artistic interests were positively correlated with verbal and negatively correlated with numerical and spatial abilities, (c) Social interests were negatively related to verbal, numerical, and spatial abilities, (d) Enterprising interests were negatively related to verbal and spatial abilities, and (e) Conventional interests were positively associated with numerical abilities. Using another sample of students from Germany (N = 4,487), Vock, Köller, and Nagy (2013) demonstrated that high realistic, investigative, and artistic interests and low social and economic interests were significantly related to intelligence.

Personality

Although earlier research led to the conclusion that correlations between interests and personality traits were modest at best (Hansen, 1984), several meaningful relationships have since emerged in the literature. With regard to the Big Five personality traits (Digman, 1990), the most notable relationships identified by past meta-analyses (Barrick, Mount, & Gupta, 2003; Larson, Rottinghaus, & Borgen, 2002; see Table 11.2) and reviews (Ackerman &

TABLE 11.2 Summary of Relationships Between RIASEC and Personality Traits

	R	*I*	*A*	*S*	*E*	*C*
Meta–analytic correlations (Barrick et al., 2003; Larson et al., 2002)						
Extraversion	.03/.02	.02/.00	.09/.09	**.29**/.30	**.41**/.39	.06/.06
Conscientiousness	.05/.04	**.07**/.06	-.06/-.07	.07/.10	.08/.19	**.19**/.22
Agreeableness	.01/-.02	.01/.01	.02/-.02	.15/.16	-.06/-.10	-.01/.01
Openness to Experience	.06/.06	**.25**/.25	**.39**/.46	.12/.17	.05/.06	-.11/-.14
Neuroticism	-.08/-.12	**-.12**/-.13	.01/-.01	-.04/-.14	-.09/-.21	-.04/-.12
Netherlands & Belgium (van der Zee et al., 2003)						
Extraversion				+	+	
Conscientiousness			–			
Agreeableness						
Openness to Experience				+		
Neuroticism				+		
Germany (Henoch et al., 2015)						
Extraversion			+[a]	+		
Conscientiousness		+[a]	–[a]	+		
Openness to Experience		+	+	+		
Neuroticism	–[a]	–[a]	+	+[a]		
Australia (Carless, 1999)						
Extraversion				+	+	
Conscientiousness				+[a]	+	+[a]
Agreeableness						
Openness to Experience		+[a]	+	+[a]		+[a]
Neuroticism				–[a]		

Note. For meta-analytic correlations, each number represents the estimated true score correlation (corrected for sampling error and unreliability in measurement) between the interests type and the personality trait. Correlations left to the slash are from Barrick et al. (2003) and correlations right to the slash are from Larson et al. (2002). Numbers in boldface represent correlations with credibility intervals (available for Barrick et al., 2003, but not available for Larson et al. 2002) that exclude zero. For individual studies, + sign indicates a significant positive correlation; – sign indicates a significant negative correlation.; [a]Correlations were only significant one out of two subsamples in the study.

Heggestad, 1997; Ashton & Lee, 2007; Holland, 1997) are: (a) Investigative interests with openness to experience, (b) Artistic interests with openness to experience, (c) Social interests with extraversion, agreeableness, and openness to experience, (d) Enterprising interests with extraversion, and (e) Conventional interests with conscientiousness.

Researchers have argued that a further examination at lower order traits may increase the variance accounted for in vocational interests (e.g., Costa, McCrae, & Kay, 1995; Larson & Borgen, 2002; Staggs, Larson, & Borgen, 2003). For instance, Sullivan and Hansen (2004) found that several relationships between interests and higher order personality traits can be largely accounted for by the associations between interests and lower order personality traits: Warmth and assertiveness (facets of extraversion) accounted for the relationships extraversion shared with Social interests and Enterprising interests, respectively, while Aesthetics (a facet of openness to experience) accounted for the association between Artistic interests and openness to experience.

Using a neuro-biologically based approach, Hansen, Sullivan, and Luciana (2011) proposed a social neuroscientific model of the processes underlying vocational interests and examined the affective and motivational aspects of personality with vocational interests. Results showed that Social and Enterprising interests were positively associated with approach temperament (positive emotionality, extraversion, and behavioral activation scale), thus supporting the notion that interests might be driven by individual differences in the approach system.

Cross-cultural Research on Interests and Personality

Several studies have been conducted to examine the linkages between vocational interests and personality traits in countries other than the United States (see Table 11.2). van der Zee, Zaal, and Piekstra (2003) examined the relationships between vocational interests and personality in a sample of job applicants (n = 264) from the Netherlands and Belgium. The authors mapped the vocational interests they measured onto Holland's Social, Enterprising, Artistic interests and an additional factor of Managerial interests. Results suggested that (a) Social interests were positively related to agreeableness, neuroticism, and openness to experience, (b) Enterprising interests were positively related to extraversion, (c) Artistic interests were negatively related to conscientiousness, and (d) Managerial interests were negatively associated with neuroticism. The findings regarding Social and Enterprising interests were largely comparable with the interests-personality relationships identified from past reviews based on U.S. samples, whereas the relationships regarding Social/Managerial interests with neuroticism and Artistic with conscientiousness were inconsistent with the patterns from research in the United States.

In a large student sample (n = 1,463) from Germany, Henoch, Klusmann, Lüdtke, and Trautwein (2015) identified the following interest-personality associations that were unique from the meta-analytical findings summarized earlier: (a) Artistic interests were positively correlated with neuroticism, and (b) Social interests were positively associated with conscientiousness. Based on two working samples in Australia, Carless (1999) found similar vocational interest-personality associations based on research conducted in the United States, except for (a) a negative relationship between Social interests and neuroticism for males and (b) a positive relationship between Enterprising interests and conscientiousness for both females and males. In a Dutch sample (n = 656), Holtrop, Born, and de Vries (2015) largely replicated relationships between interests and personality traits that have been previously found in meta-analyses. The relations between neuroticism and RIASEC dimensions found in these non-U.S. studies are generally not supported in U.S. samples, which could be due to a substantive cross-cultural difference, or measurement nonequivalence, or both.

There has been limited cross-cultural research that directly focused on the substantive moderating effect of culture on the interest-personality association. Focusing on in-group collectivism, Ott-Holland et al. (2013) argued that individuals in collectivistic cultures might (a) focus more on group goals rather than personal goals, and (b) pursue vocations that meet family needs. Therefore, personality should have less impact on vocational interests in these cultures. Based on a sample of approximately 400,000 workers obtained between 2001 and 2009, Ott-Holland et al. (2013) confirmed that the relationships between occupational interests and personality traits were generally weaker in cultures with high in-group collectivism (based on the GLOBE ratings of in-group collectivism).

Self-efficacy

Introducing Bandura's (1977) theory of self-efficacy to vocational psychology, a substantial amount of research has been conducted to investigate the relationship between vocational interests and self-efficacy constructs, as well as how they relate to occupational and career outcomes.

Discussion on the causal linkages between vocational interests and self-efficacy has been largely informed by the social-cognitive career theory (SCCT; Lent, Brown, & Hackett, 1994, 2000), which suggests that vocational interests derive from the confluence of self-efficacy and outcome expectations. However, while some evidence from longitudinal and experimental studies supports the causal direction from self-efficacy to interests (e.g., Betz & Schifano, 2000; Campbell & Hackett, 1986; Luzzo, Hasper, Albert, Bibby, & Martinelli, 1999), other studies suggest a reverse directionality from interests to self-efficacy (Bonitz, Larson, & Armstrong, 2010; Nauta, Kahn, Angell, &

Cantarelli, 2002). One particular challenge on this topic is the substantial relationship between vocational interests and self-efficacy. Armstrong and Vogel (2009) offered evidence that indicates interests and self-efficacy should both serve as indicators for the RIASEC types, suggesting interests and self-efficacy are merely method factors. However, by reanalyzing earlier data from Armstrong and Vogel (2009), Lent, Sheu, and Brown (2010) reached a different conclusion that interests and self-efficacy are related yet distinct constructs.

Linking interests and career self-efficacy to vocational outcomes, researchers have studied and found that career self-efficacy can provide incremental validity in predicting occupational and educational outcomes above and beyond vocational interests (e.g., see Betz, Borgen, & Harmon, 2006; Rottinghaus, Larson, & Borgen, 2003; Tracey & Hopkins, 2001), suggesting that the two should be considered jointly for career assessment and counseling. As important factors in career planning activities, both self-efficacy and interests should be assessed, and interventions are needed if self-efficacy is too low to match a high level of interest (Bonitz et al., 2010; Nauta et al., 2002). Nauta and colleagues, in particular, discussed verbal persuasion, vicarious learning, and mastery experience as viable interventions for improving self-efficacy in career counseling, especially for encouraging women and minorities' participation in STEM disciplines.

Cross-cultural research on interests and self-efficacy

We identified only one study outside of the United States that focused on vocational interests and career self-efficacy. In a group of 301 Japanese university students, Adachi (2004) found positive associations between vocational interests and career self-efficacy, but the magnitudes of the relationships were generally smaller (*r*s ranging from .18 to .40) compared to those reported in meta-analyses ($\bar{r}$s ranging from .50 to .71; Rottinghaus et al., 2003; Sheu et al., 2010).

Vocational Outcomes

Satisfaction

Consistent with person-environment fit theory (Edwards, 1991), congruence (see Holland, 1959) between an individual's interests and his/her job environment contributes to job and career outcomes (e.g., De Fruyt, 2002; Rottinghaus, Hees, & Conrath, 2009; Wille, Tracey, Feys, & De Fruyt, 2014; Young, Tokar, & Subich, 1998). However, several meta-analyses have yielded positive yet nonsignificant relationships between overall interest congruence and job satisfaction (Assouline & Meir, 1987; Tranberg, Slane, & Ekeberg, 1993; Tsabari, Tziner, & Meir, 2005). Spokane, Meir, and Catalano (2000) speculated that congruence might be "a sufficient, though not a necessary, condition for job satisfaction" (p. 137).

Focusing on vocational interests as predictors of job satisfaction, Rottinghaus et al. (2009) combined and examined the predictive validity of Holland's six interest dimensions (measured by the Holland General Occupational Themes; GOTs) and basic interests (measured by the Basic Interest Scales; BISs) on satisfaction in 22 independent occupational samples (n = 9,647). Results suggested that Holland's six interest dimensions significantly distinguished the grouping between satisfied and dissatisfied workers.

In conclusion, the relationships between vocational interests and satisfaction and between interest congruence and satisfaction are generally weak or nonexistent with substantial variance across congruence indices, measures of interests, study settings, and research methodologies. Further advancement in research methodology and investigations of moderators (e.g., culture) are warranted to gain a better understanding of these relationships.

Cross-cultural Research on Interests and Satisfaction

In their meta-analysis, Tsabari et al. (2005) investigated the difference in mean correlations between interests congruence and satisfaction between the United States (k = 29) and Israel (k = 9). Results showed that the congruence-satisfaction linkage was stronger in Israel ($\bar{r}$ = 0.23, CI = 0.01 to 0.44) than in the United States ($\bar{r}$ = 0.13, CI = -0.02 to 0.27), although there was considerable heterogeneity in both cultures. The authors argued that the difference, albeit inconclusive, might be explained by the difference in the cultural dimension of in-group collectivism (d = .17, based on the GLOBE ratings of in-group collectivism) between the two cultures. Particularly, in cultures with relatively low in-group collectivism (e.g., the United States), individuals might be exposed to more employment opportunities, and other personal factors may influence job satisfaction than congruence alone. In comparison, job satisfaction might be more predictable in cultures where there is a moderate level of in-group collectivism, like Israel.

Job and Career Outcomes

Vocational interests have been theorized to influence job performance and turnover in two ways. First, a high level of congruence between one's interests and job characteristics will likely lead to satisfaction and commitment, which subsequently result in high performance and low turnover (Campbell, McCloy, Oppler, & Sager, 1993; Holland, 1973, 1997). Second, interests drive individuals to acquire and develop job-relevant knowledge and skills, which enable them to perform better on the job (e.g., Ackerman, 1996; Barrick et al., 2003; Lent et al., 1994; Sullivan & Hansen, 2004). Meta-analytic evidence has been supportive of the positive relationships between interests and job performance, training performance, organizational citizenship behavior, counterproductive work behavior, persistence, job level attained, tenure, and turnover (Hunter & Hunter, 1984; Nye et al., 2012; Van Iddekinge, Roth, Putka, & Lanivich, 2011). More criterion variance can be accounted for when using interests that are theoretically more relevant to the jobs (Van Iddekinge, Roth et al., 2011), or when congruence indices are used instead of interest scores alone (Nye et al., 2012). In a selection context, a concurrent validation project within the U.S. Army showed that specific RIASEC dimensions shared small to moderate correlations with job knowledge, interpersonal job knowledge, job performance, and continuance intentions above and beyond cognitive ability and personality traits (Van Iddekinge, Putka, & Campbell, 2011).

Vocational interests are related to career-related outcomes, such as educational choices, occupational choices, career indecision, career mobility, and income. Vocational interests can incrementally predict educational-occupational choices beyond cognitive abilities (Lubinski & Benbow, 2006). Individuals with high Realistic, Enterprising, and/or Conventional interests are more likely to be indecisive about their careers (Burns, Morris, Rousseau, & Taylor, 2013). With regard to career mobility, Enterprising interests were more likely to change jobs in general (internally and externally). Meanwhile, external job changes (across employers) were predicted by Investigative, Artistic, and (low) Conventional interests, whereas internal job changes (within an employer) were predicted by Realistic interests (Wille, De Fruyt, & Feys, 2010). Moreover, based on data from 665 occupations obtained from the U.S. Bureau of Labor Statistics and O*Net, Huang and Pearce (2013) showed that all six RIASEC dimensions were significantly correlated with annual income and the occupation level (with the relationships for I and C being negative). In addition, Investigative, Enterprising, and Realistic interests also emerged as the most important predictors for annual income based on relative weight analysis (LeBreton, Hargis, Griepentrog, Oswald, & Ployhart, 2007).

Cross-cultural Research on Interests and Job/Career Outcomes

Linking vocational interests congruence to job related outcomes, Meir, Esformes, and Friedland (1994) showed that vocational interests congruence was predictive of job stability and job performance (supervisor rated) a year later in an Israeli sample. When the findings were broken down based on gender and occupational field, however, significant relationships were only present for males in Business and Technology fields, and not for either males or females in the Organizational field. These findings suggested that there might be unique factors in the Organizational field (e.g., promotion opportunities impacting job stability) that contributed to job stability and performance other than vocational interests. In a sample of 272 German job apprentices in the food industry, Marcus and Wagner (2015) demonstrated that subjective congruence was predictive of only self-rated job performance, but not supervisory job performance ratings. In addition, objective congruence (where experts provided ratings on the work environment) was not related to either self- or supervisor-rated job performance.

In a sample of graduating college students in Belgium, de Fruyt and Mervielde (1999) conducted a longitudinal study linking vocational interests to employment status and employment nature. Results demonstrated that although Enterprising and Conventional interests were positively associated with employment status, they did not add incremental validity above and beyond personality traits. Meanwhile, the RIASEC types outperformed personality in predicting the nature of employment, suggesting that people are more likely to be attracted to and select jobs that match their interests.

In a cross-cultural study, Fan, Cheung, Leong, and Cheung (2012) used two university student samples in the United States (n = 369) and Hong Kong (n = 392) and found that Enterprising interests mediated the relationship between social potency and career exploration in the Hong Kong sample, whereas Artistic interests mediated the same relationship in the American sample, suggesting different processes in which personality affects career exploration across the two cultures. Particularly, the differential mediating mechanisms might be explained by the differences in environmental context. Given the substantial influence of the financial and commercial industries in Hong Kong, university students might be exposed to more opportunities than their American counterparts to develop interests that are business and entrepreneurial related. At the same time, there is a cultural tendency for Chinese parents to discourage career options that involve artistic interests, whereas American students might have more freedom to explore diverse career opportunities based on their creative nature.

Vocational interests have also been investigated as antecedents of educational and occupational choices in China, Germany, and Portugal. Based on a student sample collected in China, Song and Chon (2012) showed that vocational interests predicted person-job fit, which subsequently impacted choice goals (i.e., intention to work in the corresponding industry). In addition, the influence of vocational interests on choice goals was mediated by person-job fit. In a sample of 1,463 students from Germany, Henoch and colleagues (2015) found evidence that supports the predictive validity of vocational interests for major and career choices. In particular, students with higher Investigative and Realistic interests and lower Artistic and Social interests were more likely to choose STEM majors. While students enrolled in teacher education had higher Social and lower Realistic and Investigative interests, Social interests had the highest relative predictive validity compared to other interest dimensions in predicting one's decision to become a teacher candidate. In a sample of psychology students in Portugal, Ferreira, Rodrigues, and Costa Ferreira (2015) found that the RIASEC types were related to choices of going into organizational, educational, and clinical psychology fields.

Toward a Globalized Knowledge Base on Vocational Interests

Our review above suggests that, to a large degree, research on vocational interests has not stayed abreast of globalization. Instead, the review of extant research offered a glimpse of potential universal and cultural-specific phenomena related to vocational interests and highlighted the clear need for more research on vocational interests in non-U.S. countries. In this section, we offer three approaches researchers can consider in their efforts to explicate culture as a potential boundary factor that affects the measurement and utilization of vocational interests across the globe. Although not mutually exclusive, these approaches represent different likely scenarios that scholars may encounter to expand vocational interest research beyond the etic assumption.

In the first approach, researchers can continue to examine the cultural validity of vocational interest theories outside of the typical Anglo cultures. When generalizing the existing model of interests to non-Anglo cultures and conducting cross-cultural comparisons, measurement equivalence is necessary to ensure that the cross-cultural generalization and comparison is meaningful. Addressing this methodological challenge, Church et al. (2011) recommended that researchers examine differential item functioning (DIF) by conducting a multigroup confirmatory factor analysis (CFA) for every pair of cultures and test potential differences in DIF loading and intercepts at the item- and scale-levels. Besides generalizing Anglo-based theories to broader cultures, we call for a more proactive research strategy: In addition to testing cultural validity of existing theories, researchers can consider whether constructs stemming from a local culture can influence the development and consequences of vocational interest. This notion of testing the cultural specificity of indigenous constructs (Leong & Brown, 1995) will allow researchers to develop theories on vocational interests that are closely grounded in the local culture while acknowledging potentially universal aspects. For instance, Einarsdóttir et al. (2010) examined the structure of vocational interests in Iceland and identified two additional interest dimensions (finance/persuation and natural science). After removing the constraints of the RIASEC model, research may be able to reveal some qualitatively different components of vocational interests across cultures. Another illustration was provided by Leong, Huang, and Mak (2014) who demonstrated the cultural validity of the Protestant Work Ethic and the cultural specificity of Confucian values in predicting job satisfaction and organizational commitment in Singapore. As Confucianism has influenced the culture and ideology of several East Asia countries, one can conjecture the effects of Confucian values on vocational interests. For instance, Confucian emphasis on life-long learning and development may be positively associated with investigative interests. Furthermore, it is plausible that the Confucian value of harmony can attenuate the expected relationship between congruence and job satisfaction, as individuals espousing harmony values may attach greater significance to their coworkers and less so to the jobs they work on.

If the expected cultural validity is not supported in a particular study, we caution against the tendency to attribute the result to a particular dimension of the local culture. For instance, if a vocational interest study in South Korea yields a different finding than in the United States, one might be tempted to conclude that collectivism (high in South Korea and low in the United States) served as a moderator for the expected effect. However, the risk of such an attribution is, because two cultures can differ in a number of ways, one is unable to rule out alternative explanations (see van de Vijver & Leung, 2000). It should be recognized that the difference observed between two cultures, such as in the example above between South Korea and the United States, could have been caused by other cultural variables (such as power distance) instead. Because of this concern, researchers should, whenever possible, directly measure the underlying psychological mechanism that contributes to cultural difference (Okazaki & Sue, 1995).

In the second scenario, researchers can obtain data from multiple countries, and thus can utilize existing measures of cultural differences at the country level. Hofstede (1980) developed an early taxonomy of cultural dimensions, which were expanded later in Project GLOBE (House et al., 2004) in a 62-nation study. Specifically, GLOBE provides scores of cultures on nine dimensions, including performance orientation, future orientation, gender egalitarianism, assertiveness, institutional collectivism, in-group collectivism, power distance, humane orientation, and uncertainty avoidance (see Table 11.3). Although it is still advisable to collect data on the psychological mechanisms that lead to cross-cultural differences, imposing the existing scores at the country level can be advantageous when individual data collections are not feasible. Prior to the availability of GLOBE cultural scores, Rounds and Tracey (1996) identified cultural ratings for 13 countries from Hofstede (1980) and found that the individualism-collectivism dimension, but not the masculinity-femininity dimension, could explain differences in the fit of the RIASEC model among 13 countries. Similarly, when researchers utilize archival cross-cultural data, they assume the GLOBE cultural scores can provide meaningful analysis at the country/region level (e.g., Ott-Holland et al., 2013). It is also possible that researchers may utilize GLOBE scores in conjunction with their primary data collection to help rule out competing explanations.

An important, yet often overlooked issue in the assessment of vocational interest theories across cultures is appropriate sampling. Researchers often rely on convenient samples to represent cultures, making an inferential leap in such a representation. In cross-cultural research on vocational interests, sampling error can come into play in two focal areas. First, individuals selected in a particular sample may not reflect the population in a given culture. As Chao and Moon (2005) noted, each individual may possess distinct cultural identities that reflect the unique influences of culture on that person. If a particular sample differs from the overall population in terms of cultural beliefs, values, and

TABLE 11.3 GLOBE Cultural Dimensions (House et al., 1999, p. 25)

Cultural Dimension	*Definition*
Performance Orientation	The extent to which members are encouraged and rewarded to exhibit excellent performance and show improvement in an organization or society.
Future Orientation	The extent to which members are expected to plan for and invest in the future, as well as not seeking immediate gratification in organizations or societies.
Assertiveness	The extent to which members of organizations or societies are expected to be assertive, aggressive, and confrontational toward others.
Institutional Collectivism	The extent to which resources are distributed and actions are carried out in a collective manner based on institutional practices in organizations and societies.
In-group Collectivism	The extent to which individual members are encouraged to be proud of, loyal to, and cohesive in their organizations or families.
Power Distance	The extent to which power is expected to be shared unequally among members of an organization or society.
Humane Orientation	The extent to which members are encouraged and rewarded to be fair, caring, kind, friendly, altruistic, and generous to others in organizations or societies.
Uncertainty Avoidance	The extent to which members strive to avoid unpredictability of the future in an organization or society. Relevant practices include rituals and bureaucratic practices.

identities, one may be making a flawed inference from the sample to the population. Second, the sample in question may differ from the population in vocational interests. For instance, a convenient sample of undergraduate students from a private college may not represent the broader population of undergraduate students in the country. Taken together, ensuring the samples represent the populations of interest can allow researchers to draw valid inferences at the culture level of analysis.

In the third approach, researchers can track expatriate and sojourners during their adjustment process. Although much research has been conducted to understand how individuals experience changes and adjust to a new culture (e.g., Bhaskar-Shrinivas, Harrison, Shaffer, & Luk, 2005), little is known about potential changes in vocational interests during the adjustment process. Unique from other individual dispositions like personality, interests are highly contextualized and always directed toward an object (Rounds & Su, 2014). Therefore, opportunity to experience an activity in a certain cultural context can facilitate the development of interests. As sojourners and expatriates are under the confluence of two cultures—the home country culture that they are accustomed with, and the new host country's culture that they start to acculturate to—researchers can not only hypothesize the influence of a certain cultural variable, but also study the influence as it unfolds over time using methods such as growth modeling. For instance, applying growth modeling to study changes in extraversion in international students who newly arrived in the United States, Liu and Huang (2015) showed that increase of extraversion within the school context is associated with better cross-cultural adjustment. Using the same technique to investigate changes in vocational interest, researchers may identify changes in interests due to cross-cultural experience and model correlates of such changes. For example, one may examine whether sojourners from India, a country that highly emphasizes engineering education (Banerjee & Muley, 2008), would experience changes in vocational interests after prolonged experience in the United States; further, interindividual difference in changes in interests may predict vocational outcomes such as career satisfaction. Questions concerning cross-cultural changes should be adequately addressed before vocational interests can be used to select individuals for cross-cultural assignments.

Summary and Conclusions

In this chapter, we provided a review of cross-cultural vocational interest research, particularly focusing on the structure of vocational interests, the relationships between individual differences and vocational interests, and the associations between interests and vocational outcomes. We also discussed three likely approaches that researchers may utilize to examine culture as a boundary condition for vocational interests' development and effects. With in-depth cross-cultural research, vocational interests can become a valuable tool for organizations to assess, understand, and manage human capital across national and cultural boundaries.

References

Ackerman, P. L. (1996). A theory of adult intellectual development: Process, personality, interests, and knowledge. *Intelligence, 22*, 227–257.

Ackerman, P. L., & Heggestad, E. D. (1997). Intelligence, personality, and interests: Evidence for overlapping traits. *Psychological Bulletin, 121*, 219–245.

Adachi, T. (2004). Career self-efficacy, career outcome expectations and vocational interests among Japanese university students. *Psychological Reports, 95*, 89–100.

Anthoney, S. F., & Armstrong, P. I. (2010). Individuals and environments: Linking ability and skill ratings with interests. *Journal of Counseling Psychology, 57*, 36–51.

Armstrong, P. I., Day, S. X., McVay, J. P., & Rounds, J. (2008). Holland's RIASEC model as an integrative framework for individual differences. *Journal of Counseling Psychology, 55*, 1–18.

Armstrong, P. I., & Vogel, D. L. (2009). Interpreting the interest-efficacy association from a RIASEC perspective. *Journal of Counseling Psychology, 56*, 392–407.

Ashton, M. C., & Lee, K. (2007). Empirical, theoretical, and practical advantages of the HEXACO model of personality structure. *Personality and Social Psychology Review, 11*, 150–166.

Assouline, M., & Meir, E. I. (1987). Meta-analysis of the relationship between congruence and well-being measures. *Journal of Vocational Behavior, 31*, 319–332.

Bandura, A. (1977). Self-efficacy: Toward a unifying theory of behavioral change. *Psychological Review, 84*, 191–215.

Banerjee, R., & Muley, V. P. (2008). *Engineering education in India*. Mumbai, India: Indian Institute of Technology Bombay.

Barrick, M. R., Mount, M. K., & Gupta, R. (2003). Meta-analysis of the relationship between the five-factor model of personality and Holland's occupational types. *Personnel Psychology, 56*, 45–74.

Betz, N. E., Borgen, F. H., & Harmon, L. W. (2006). Vocational confidence and personality in the prediction of occupational group membership. *Journal of Career Assessment, 14*, 36–55.

Betz, N. E., Heesacker, R. S., & Shuttleworth, C. (1990). Moderators of the congruence and realism of major and occupational plans in college students: A replication and extension. *Journal of Counseling Psychology, 37*, 269–276.

Betz, N. E., & Schifano, R. S. (2000). Evaluation of an intervention to increase realistic self-efficacy and interests in college women. *Journal of Vocational Behavior, 56*, 35–52.

Bhaskar-Shrinivas, P., Harrison, D. A., Shaffer, M. A., & Luk, D. M. (2005). Input-based and time-based models of international adjustment: Meta-analytic evidence and theoretical extensions. *Academy of Management Journal, 48*, 257–281.

Bonitz, V. S., Larson, L. M., & Armstrong, P. I. (2010). Interests, self-efficacy, and choice goals: An experimental manipulation. *Journal of Vocational Behavior, 76*, 223–233.

Bubany, S. T., & Hansen, J.-I. C. (2011). Birth cohort change in the vocational interests of female and male college students. *Journal of Vocational Behavior, 78*, 59–67.

Burns, G. N., Morris, M. B., Rousseau, N., & Taylor, J. (2013). Personality, interests, and career indecision: A multidimensional perspective. *Journal of Applied Social Psychology, 43*, 2090–2099.

Campbell, J. P., McCloy, R. A., Oppler, S. H., & Sager, C. E. (1993). A theory of performance. In N. Schmitt & W. C. Borman (Eds.), *Personnel selection in organizations* (pp. 35–70). San Francisco: Jossey-Bass.

Campbell, N. K., & Hackett, G. (1986). The effects of mathematics task performance on math self-efficacy and task interest. *Journal of Vocational Behavior, 28*, 149–162.

Carless, S. A. (1999). Career assessment: Holland's vocational interests, personality characteristics, and abilities. *Journal of Career Assessment, 7*, 125–144.

Chao, G. T., & Moon, H. (2005). The cultural mosaic: A metatheory for understanding the complexity of culture. *Journal of Applied Psychology, 90*, 1128–1140.

Church, A. T., Alvarez, J. M., Mai, N. T., French, B. F., Katigbak, M. S., & Ortiz, F. A. (2011). Are cross-cultural comparisons of personality profiles meaningful? Differential item and facet functioning in the Revised NEO Personality Inventory. *Journal of Personality and Social Psychology, 101*, 1068–1089.

Costa, P. T., McCrae, R. R., & Kay, G. G. (1995). Persons, places, and personality: Career assessment using the Revised NEO Personality Inventory. *Journal of Career Assessment, 3*, 123–139.

De Fruyt, F. (2002). A person-centered approach to P-E fit questions using a multiple-trait model. *Journal of Vocational Behavior, 60*, 73–90.

De Fruyt, F., & Mervielde, I. (1999). RIASEC types and Big Five traits as predictors of employment status and nature of employment. *Personnel Psychology, 52*, 701–727.

Digman, J. M. (1990). Personality structure: Emergence of the five-factor model. *Annual Review of Psychology, 41*, 417–440.

Donnay, D. A. C., & Borgen, F. H. (1996). Validity, structure, and content of the 1994 Strong Interest Inventory. *Journal of Counseling Psychology, 43*, 275–291.

Edwards, J. R. (1991). Person-job fit: A conceptual integration, literature review, and methodological critique. In C. L. Cooper & I. T. Robertson (Eds.), *International review of industrial and organizational psychology* (Vol. 6, pp. 283–357). New York: Wiley.

Einarsdóttir, S., Eyjólfsdóttir, K. Ó., & Rounds, J. (2013). Development of indigenous basic interest scales: Re-structuring the Icelandic interest space. *Journal of Vocational Behavior, 82*, 105–115.

Einarsdóttir, S., & Rounds, J. (2000). Application of three dimensions of vocational interests to the Strong Interest Inventory. *Journal of Vocational Behavior, 56*, 363–379.

Einarsdóttir, S., Rounds, J., Ægisdóttir, S., & Gerstein, L. H. (2002). The structure of vocational interests in Iceland: Examining Holland's and Gati's RIASEC models. *European Journal of Psychological Assessment, 18*, 85–95.

Einarsdóttir, S., Rounds, J., & Su, R. (2010). Holland in Iceland revisited: An emic approach to evaluating U.S. vocational interest models. *Journal of Counseling Psychology, 57*, 361–367.

Ellis, L., Ratnasingam, M., & Wheeler, M. (2012). Gender, sexual orientation, and occupational interests: Evidence of their interrelatedness. *Personality and Individual Differences, 53*, 64–69.

Evers, A. (1995). The assessment of professional interests and work values. *Bollettino Di Psicologia Applicata, 215*, 3–10.

Fan, W., Cheung, F. M., Leong, F. T., & Cheung, S. F. (2012). Personality traits, vocational interests, and career exploration: A cross-cultural comparison between American and Hong Kong students. *Journal of Career Assessment, 20*, 105–119.

Fang, L., Bai, L., & Ling, W. (1996). Construction of the Chinese vocational interest inventory of Holland type. *Acta Psychoogica Sinica, 28*, 113–119.

Farh, J., Leong, F. T. L., & Law, K. S. (1998). Cross-cultural validity of Holland's model in Hong Kong. *Journal of Vocational Behavior, 52*, 425–440.

Ferreira, A. I., Rodrigues, R. I., & Costa Ferreira, P. (2015). Career interests of students in psychology specialties degrees: Psychometric evidence and correlations with the RIASEC dimensions. *International Journal for Educational and Vocational Guidance*. doi:10.1007/s10775-015-9289-3

Fouad, N. A. (2002). Cross-cultural differences in vocational interests: Between-groups differences on the strong interest inventory. *Journal of Counseling Psychology, 49*, 283–289.

Gati, I. (1979). A hierarchical model for the structure of vocational interests. *Journal of Vocational Behavior, 15*, 90–106.

Gati, I. (1984). On the perceived structure of occupations. *Journal of Vocational Behavior, 25*, 1–29.

Gati, I. (1991). The structure of vocational interests. *Psychological Bulletin, 109*, 309–324.

Glidden-Tracey, C., & Greenwood, A. K. (1997). A validation study of the Spanish self-directed search using back-translation procedures. *Journal of Career Assessment, 5*, 105–113.

Goh, D. S. (2001). Translation and validation of the Chinese form of the Strong Interest Inventory. *Applied Psychology: An International Review*, 50, 252–268.

Gottfredson, L. S. (1981). Circumscription and compromise: A developmental theory of occupational aspirations. *Journal of Counseling Psychology, 28*, 545–579.

Graen, G. B., Hui, C., Wakabayashi, M., & Wang, Z. (1997). Cross-cultural research alliances in organizational research: Cross-cultural partnership-making in action. In P. C. Earley, M. Erez, P. C. Earley, & M. Erez (Eds.), *New perspectives on international industrial/ organizational psychology* (pp. 160–189). San Francisco: The New Lexington Press/Jossey-Bass.

Hansen, J. C. (1984). The measurement of vocational interests: Issues and future directions. In S. D. Brown & R. W. Lent (Eds.), *Handbook of counseling psychology* (1st ed., pp. 99–136). New York: Wiley.

Hansen, J. I. C., Sullivan, B. A., & Luciana, M. (2011). A social neuroscientific model of vocational behavior. *Journal of Career Assessment, 19*, 216–227.

Hedrih, V. (2008). Structure of vocational interests in Serbia: Evaluation of the spherical model. *Journal of Vocational Behavior, 73*, 13–23.

Henoch, J. R., Klusmann, U., Lüdtke, O., & Trautwein, U. (2015). Who becomes a teacher? Challenging the "negative selection" hypothesis. *Learning and Instruction, 36*, 46–56.

Hofstede, G. (1980). *Culture's consequences: International differences in work-related values.* Newbury Park, CA: Sage.

Hofstede, G. H. (2001). *Culture's consequences: Comparing values, behaviors, institutions and organizations across nations* (2nd ed.). Thousand Oaks, CA: Sage.

Holland, J. L. (1959). A theory of vocational choice. *Journal of Counseling Psychology, 6*, 35–46.

Holland, J. L. (1966). *The psychology of vocational choice: A theory of personality types and model environments.* Oxford, UK: Blaisdell.

Holland, J. L. (1973). *Making vocational choices: A theory of careers.* Englewood Cliffs, NJ: Prentice-Hall.

Holland, J. L. (1985). *Making vocational choices: A theory of vocational personalities and work environments* (2nd ed.). Englewood Cliffs, NJ: Prentice-Hall.

Holland, J. L. (1997). *Making vocational choices: A theory of vocational personalities and work environments* (3rd ed.). Odessa, FL: Psychological Assessment Resources.

Holtrop, D., Born, M. P., & de Vries, R. E. (2015). Relating the Spherical representation of vocational interests to the HEXACO personality model. *Journal of Vocational Behavior, 89*, 10–20.

House, R. J., Hanges, P. J., Javidan, M., Dorfman, P. W., & Gupta, V. (2004). *Culture, leadership, and organizations: The GLOBE study of 62 societies.* Thousand Oaks, CA: Sage.

Huang, J. L., & Pearce, M. (2013). The other side of the coin: Vocational interests, interest differentiation and annual income at the occupation level of analysis. *Journal of Vocational Behavior, 83*, 315–326.

Hunter, J. E., & Hunter, R. F. (1984). Validity and utility of alternative predictors of job performance. *Psychological Bulletin, 96*, 72–98.

Katzell, R. A., & Austin, J. T. (1992). From then to now: The development of industrial-organizational psychology in the United States. *Journal of Applied Psychology, 77*, 803–835.

Kossek, E. E., Huang, J. L., Piszczek, M. M., Fleenor, J. W., & Ruderman, M. (2015). Rating expatriate leader effectiveness in multisource feedback systems:

Cultural distance and hierarchical effects. *Human Resource Management*. doi:10.1002/hrm.21763

LaBarbera, D. M. (2005). Physician assistant self-directed search Holland codes. *Journal of Career Assessment, 13*, 337–346.

Larson, L. M., & Borgen, F. H. (2002). Convergence of vocational interests and personality: Examples in an adolescent gifted sample. *Journal of Vocational Behavior, 60*, 91–112.

Larson, L. M., Rottinghaus, P. J., & Borgen, F. H. (2002). Meta-analyses of Big Six interests and Big Five personality factors. *Journal of Vocational Behavior, 61*, 217–239.

LeBreton, J. M., Hargis, M. B., Griepentrog, B., Oswald, F. L., & Ployhart, R. E. (2007). A multidimensional approach for evaluating variables in organizational research and practice. *Personnel Psychology, 60*, 475–498.

Lent, R. W., Brown, S. D., & Hackett, G. (1994). Toward a unifying social cognitive theory of career and academic interest, choice, and performance. *Journal of Vocational Behavior, 45*, 79–122.

Lent, R. W., Brown, S. D., & Hackett, G. (2000). Contextual supports and barriers to career choice: A social cognitive analysis. *Journal of Counseling Psychology, 47*, 36–49.

Lent, R. W., Sheu, H. B., & Brown, S. D. (2010). The self-efficacy-interest relationship and RIASEC type: Which is figure and which is ground? Comment on Armstrong and Vogel (2009). *Journal of Counseling Psychology*, 57, 219–225.

Leong, F. T. L., Austin, J. T., Sekaran, U., & Komarraju, M. (1998). An evaluation of the cross-cultural validity of Holland's theory: Career choices by workers in India. *Journal of Vocational Behavior, 52*, 441–455.

Leong, F. L., & Brown, M. T. (1995). Theoretical issues in cross-cultural career development: Cultural validity and cultural specificity. In W. B. Walsh, S. H. Osipow, W. B. Walsh, & S. H. Osipow (Eds.), *Handbook of vocational psychology: Theory, research, and practice* (pp. 143–180). Hillsdale, NJ: Erlbaum.

Leong, F. T. L., Huang, J. L., & Mak, S. (2014). Protestant work ethic, Confucian values, and work-related attitudes in Singapore. *Journal of Career Assessment, 22*, 304–316.

Leuty, M. E., & Hansen, J.-I. C. (2014). Teasing apart the relations between age, birth cohort, and vocational interests. *Journal of Counseling Psychology, 61*, 289–298.

Liu, M., & Huang, J. L. (2015). Cross-cultural adjustment to the United States: The role of extraversion change. *Frontiers in Psychology, 6*, 1–15.

Long, L., Watanabe, N., & Tracey, T. J. G. (2006). Structure of interests in Japan: Application of the Personal Globe Inventory Occupational Scale. *Measurement and Evaluation in Counseling and Development, 38*, 222–235.

Lubinski, D., & Benbow, C. P. (2006). Study of mathematically precocious youth after 35 years: Uncovering antecedents for the development of math-science expertise. *Perspectives on Psychological Science, 1*, 316–345.

Luzzo, D. A., Hasper, P., Albert, K. A., Bibby, M. A., & Martinelli Jr, E. A. (1999). Effects of self-efficacy-enhancing interventions on the math/science self-efficacy and career interests, goals, and actions of career undecided college students. *Journal of Counseling Psychology, 46*, 233–243.

Marcus, B., & Wagner, U. (2015). What do you want to be? Criterion-related validity of attained vocational aspirations versus inventoried person-vocation fit. *Journal of Business and Psychology, 30*, 51–62.

Meir, E. I., Esformes, Y., & Friedland, N. (1994). Congruence and differentiation as predictors of workers' occupational stability and job performance. *Journal of Career Assessment, 2*, 40–54.

Mussel, P. (2013). Intellect: A theoretical framework for personality traits related to intellectual achievements. *Journal of Personality and Social Psychology, 104*, 885–906.

National Center for O*NET Development. (2015). O*NET OnLine. Retrieved from https://www.onetonline.org/

Nauta, M. M., Kahn, J. H., Angell, J. W., & Cantarelli, E. A. (2002). Identifying the antecedent in the relation between career interests and self-efficacy: Is it one, the other, or both? *Journal of Counseling Psychology, 49*, 290–301.

Nye, C. D., Su, R., Rounds, J., & Drasgow, F. (2012). Vocational interests and performance a quantitative summary of over 60 years of research. *Perspectives on Psychological Science, 7*, 384–403.

Okazaki, S., & Sue, S. (1995). Methodological issues in assessment research with ethnic minorities. *Psychological Assessment, 7*, 367–375.

Ott-Holland, C. J., Huang, J. L., Ryan, A. M., Elizondo, F., & Wadlington, P. L. (2013). Culture and vocational interests: The moderating role of collectivism and gender egalitarianism. *Journal of Counseling Psychology, 60*, 569–581.

Paessler, K. (2015). Sex differences in variability in vocational interests: Evidence from two large samples. *European Journal of Personality, 29*, 568–578.

Pässler, K., Beinicke, A., & Hell, B. (2015). Interests and intelligence: A meta-analysis. *Intelligence, 50*, 30–51.

Pässler, K., & Hell, B. (2012). Do interests and cognitive abilities help explain college major choice equally well for women and men? *Journal of Career Assessment, 20*, 479–496.

Pozzebon, J. A., Visser, B. A., & Bogaert, A. F. (2015). Vocational interests, personality, and sociosexuality as indicators of a general masculinity/femininity factor. *Personality and Individual Differences, 86*, 291–296.

Prediger, D. J. (1982). Dimensions underlying Holland's hexagon: Missing link between interests and occupations? *Journal of Vocational Behavior, 21*, 259–287.

Primavera, M. T., Church, A. T., Katigbak, M. S., Bruna, L., White, J. R., & Peradilla, I. (2010). The structure of vocational interests in Filipino adolescents. *Journal of Vocational Behavior, 77*, 213–226.

Proyer, R. T. (2006). The relationship between vocational interests and intelligence: Do findings generalize across different assessment methods? *Psychology Science, 48*, 463–476.

Proyer, R. T., & Häusler, J. (2007). Gender differences in vocational interests and their stability across different assessment methods. *Swiss Journal of Psychology, 66*, 243–247.

Rosenbloom, J. L., Ash, R. A., Dupont, B., & Coder, L. (2008). Why are there so few women in information technology? Assessing the role of personality in career choices. *Journal of Economic Psychology, 29*, 543–554.

Rottinghaus, P. J., Hees, C. K., & Conrath, J. A. (2009). Enhancing job satisfaction perspectives: Combining Holland themes and basic interests. *Journal of Vocational Behavior, 75*, 139–151.

Rottinghaus, P. J., Larson, L. M., & Borgen, F. H. (2003). The relation of self-efficacy and interests: A meta-analysis of 60 samples. *Journal of Vocational Behavior, 62*, 221–236.

Rounds, J., & Su, R. (2014). The nature and power of interests. *Current Directions in Psychological Science, 23*, 98–103.

Rounds, J., & Tracey, T. J. G. (1996). Cross-cultural structural equivalence of RIASEC models and measures. *Journal of Counseling Psychology, 43*, 310–329.

Segal, Z. (1995). Etude des qualités métriques du «LIMEF»: inventaire d'intérêts professionnel multidimensionnel. *European Review of Applied Psychology, 45*, 127–134.

Sheu, H. B., Lent, R. W., Brown, S. D., Miller, M. J., Hennessy, K. D., & Duffy, R. D. (2010). Testing the choice model of social cognitive career theory across Holland themes: A meta-analytic path analysis. *Journal of Vocational Behavior, 76*, 252–264.

Sodano, S. M., & Tracey, T. J. G. (2008). Prestige in interest activity assessment. *Journal of Vocational Behavior, 73*, 310–317.

Song, Z., & Chon, K. (2012). General self-efficacy's effect on career choice goals via vocational interests and person-job fit: A mediation model. *International Journal of Hospitality Management, 31*, 798–808.

Spokane, A. R., Meir, E. I., & Catalano, M. (2000). Person-environment congruence and Holland's theory: A review and reconsideration. *Journal of Vocational Behavior, 57*, 137–187.

Staggs, G. D., Larson, L. M., & Borgen, F. H. (2003). Convergence of specific factors in vocational interests and personality. *Journal of Career Assessment, 11*, 243–261.

Su, R., & Rounds, J. (2015). All STEM fields are not created equal: People and things interests explain gender disparities across STEM fields. *Frontiers in Psychology, 6*, 189.

Su, R., Rounds, J., & Armstrong, P. I. (2009). Men and things, women and people: A meta-analysis of sex differences in interests. *Psychological Bulletin, 135*, 859–884.

Sullivan, B. A., & Hansen, J. I. C. (2004). Mapping associations between interests and personality: Toward a conceptual understanding of individual differences in vocational behavior. *Journal of Counseling Psychology, 51*, 287–298.

Tang, M. (2001). Investigation of the structure of vocational interests of Chinese college students. *Journal of Career Assessment, 9*, 365–379.

Tang, M. (2009). Examining the application of Holland's theory to vocational college students. *Journal of Career Assessment, 17*, 86–98.

Tay, L., Su, R., & Rounds, J. (2011). People-things and data-ideas: Bipolar dimensions? *Journal of Counseling Psychology, 58*, 424–440.

Tien, H. L. S. (2011). An exploration of adult career interests and work values in Taiwan. *Asia Pacific Education Review, 12*, 559–568.

Tracey, T. J. G., & Hopkins, N. (2001). Correspondence of interests and abilities with occupational choice. *Journal of Counseling Psychology, 48*, 178–189.

Tracey, T. J. G., & Rounds, J. (1993). Evaluating Holland's and Gati's vocational-interest models: A structural meta-analysis. *Psychological Bulletin, 113*, 229–246.

Tracey, T. J. G., & Rounds, J. (1996a). Contribution of the spherical representation of vocational interests. *Journal of Vocational Behavior, 48*, 85–95.

Tracey, T. J. G., & Rounds, J. (1996b). The spherical representation of vocational interests. *Journal of Vocational Behavior, 48*, 3–41.

Tracey, T. J. G., Watanabe, N., & Schneider, P. L. (1997). Structural invariance of vocational interests across Japanese and American cultures. *Journal of Counseling Psychology, 44*, 346–354.

Tranberg, M., Slane, S., & Ekeberg, S. E. (1993). The relation between interest congruence and satisfaction: A meta-analysis. *Journal of Vocational Behavior, 42*, 253–264.

Tsabari, O., Tziner, A., & Meir, E. I. (2005). Updated meta-analysis on the relationship between congruence and satisfaction. *Journal of Career Assessment, 13*, 216–232.

Van de Vijver, F. J., & Leung, K. (2000). Methodological issues in psychological research on culture. *Journal of Cross-Cultural Psychology, 31*, 33–51.

van der Zee, K. I., Zaal, J. N., & Piekstra, J. (2003). Validation of the Multicultural Personality Questionnaire in the context of personnel selection. *European Journal of Personality, 17,* S77–S100.

Van Iddekinge, C. H., Putka, D. J., & Campbell, J. P. (2011). Reconsidering vocational interests for personnel selection: The validity of an interest-based selection test in relation to job knowledge, job performance, and continuance intentions. *Journal of Applied Psychology, 96,* 13–33.

Van Iddekinge, C. H., Roth, P. L., Putka, D. J., & Lanivich, S. E. (2011). Are you interested? A meta-analysis of relations between vocational interests and employee performance and turnover. *Journal of Applied Psychology, 96,* 1167–1194.

Vock, M., Köller, O., & Nagy, G. (2013). Vocational interests of intellectually gifted and highly achieving young adults. *British Journal of Educational Psychology, 83,* 305–328.

Wille, B., De Fruyt, F., & Feys, M. (2010). Vocational interests and Big Five traits as predictors of job instability. *Journal of Vocational Behavior, 76,* 547–558.

Wille, B., Tracey, T. J., Feys, M., & De Fruyt, F. (2014). A longitudinal and multi-method examination of interest-occupation congruence within and across time. *Journal of Vocational Behavior, 84,* 59–73.

Yang, W., Stokes, G. S., & Hui, C. H. (2005). Cross-cultural validation of Holland's interest structure in Chinese population. *Journal of Vocational Behavior, 67,* 379–396.

Young, G., Tokar, D. M., & Subich, L. M. (1998). Congruence revisited: Do 11 indices differentially predict job satisfaction and is the relation moderated by person and situation variables? *Journal of Vocational Behavior, 52,* 208–223.

12

DEVELOPMENT OF VOCATIONAL INTERESTS IN ADULTHOOD

Bart Wille

GHENT UNIVERSITY

Filip De Fruyt

GHENT UNIVERSITY

Vocational interests are typically defined in work, organizational, and career psychology as *relatively stable* individual differences that influence behavior through preferences for certain work activities and work environments (e.g., Van Iddekinge, Roth, Putka, & Lanivich, 2011). This definition highlights that the assumption of within-person stability is central to the way vocational interests are traditionally conceptualized in the literature, and this perspective goes back to the early years of interest research. In essence, today's view on adult vocational interests is one in which individual differences in the stability of these constructs are conceived as a confounding factor. The question is, however, whether this view on vocational interests as stable entities is truly accurate given the lack of attention for adult interest development in the past (Low, Yoon, Roberts, & Rounds, 2005). Although the word *relatively* in the definition above implies that interests can change, the emphasis in the psychological literature has been on interest stability, resulting in relatively little theory and scarce empirical research on adult interest development. In this chapter, we review the extant literature on adult interest development and take this discussion one step further by framing it in the context of a transactional perspective on person-environment fit.

We begin by defining interest development in terms of five different indicators of stability or change. Based on this framework, we present some of the most important and recent empirical findings concerning interest development in adulthood, with particular attention on longitudinal research projects addressing this topic. Next, the social cognitive model of career interests (Lent, Brown, & Hackett, 1994) is reviewed as an existing theoretical framework that may help to understand the process of *how* individuals, young and old, may acquire and cultivate interests in specific vocational fields. In an attempt to take the discussion of adult interest development one step further, especially regarding *direction* of adult interest development, we elaborate on this topic from a transactional perspective on person-environment fit. Finally, at the backdrop of this chapter some considerations are presented concerning the relevance and practical implications of adult interest development in the twenty-first-century labor market.

Defining Interest Development

At the beginning of this chapter, it is relevant to point out that interest "development" should not be confused with interest "change." By *development*, we broadly mean *the process of how constructs, in particular vocational interests, evolve over time.* This concept of evolution covers both change and stability over time, as is indicated by the different indicators of development outlined below. Specifically, we distinguish between five different operationalizations of interest development that (i) either address the stability of interest dimensions separately or focus on entire interest profiles, (ii) provide information on interest development either at the group level or for individuals separately, and (iii) define development either in absolute or in relative terms.

1. *Rank-order stability.* Continuity and change in psychological constructs, and vocational interests in particular, are most commonly expressed in terms of correlations between scale scores between two time-points. This rank-order stability or change refers to individuals' relative standings within a group over time. The higher this test-retest correlation, the greater the likelihood that an individual will occupy the same position in the group ranking across time. This index is also referred to as relative stability or change.
2. *Profile stability.* Whereas rank-order stability addressed the development of one single interest domain, profile stability refers to change in the full profile of interest scale scores over time. Studies on the components of profiles and their stability have a long history in the psychological literature, possibly beginning with Cronbach and Gleser (1953) and, since that time, vocational and I/O psychologists have been studying the stability of profiles. In the personality literature, this index is also referred to as ipsative stability (Caspi & Roberts, 1999; De Fruyt et al., 2006) and "person-centered continuity" (Caspi & Roberts, 2001, p. 52) given that it addresses the stability of the configuration of personality traits within individuals. Concern for ipsative stability or change was inaugurated in personality psychology by Block (1971), who believed that it more adequately captured the integrated functioning of traits within the individual. Specifically, small changes in the relative balance of dispositions might lead to large changes in behavior, and the same might apply to vocational interests. This method enables

description of how much one person's profile is like another profile he or she produces at a later point in time. One means of assessing this aspect of development is to use intraindividual profile correlations that focus on the relative invariant ordering (i.e., shape) of an individual's scale scores at different times. When warranted, individual-level estimates of profile stability can also be aggregated to a higher-order or group-level estimate. In addition, there are also two indices available that take into account the absolute differences in profiles in addition to the relative-order differences generated by profile correlations. The profile difference index (Cronbach & Gleser, 1953) is the sum of squared differences of the individual's scores across the two time periods. This index can be used with any set of scale scores but is most appropriate for scales adhering to a simple structure. In contrast, the profile clarity index proposed by Tracey and Robbins (2005) uses the circumplex structure of the RIASEC scales. Interest clarity was defined as the vector length of RIASEC scores plotted in a two-dimensional interest space. Difference in profile clarity over time represents both absolute and relative stability of a profile across time.

3. *Structural stability.* One of the attractive features of vocational interest models, such as Holland's RIASEC model, is that the included interest dimensions are not supposed to be independent, but rather demonstrate a well-specified pattern of interrelations that describe their (dis)similarity. Using the Holland model as the most well-known example, the six RIASEC dimensions are theoretically expected to adhere to a specific interest structure. For instance, there is now evidence that RIASEC interests, as measured by the 2005 Strong Interest Inventory (Donnay, Morris, Schaubhut, & Thompson, 2005), can be structured according to a circular RIASEC ordering (Kantamneni, 2014). The issue of structural continuity addresses the degree to which this pattern of interrelations between interest dimensions (i.e., the covariance structure) remains stable across time. Structural models of vocational interests and, hence, change and stability interest structures, can be tested with a range of techniques (see also Darcy & Tracey, 2007; Gupta, Tracey, & Gore, 2008; Low & Rounds, 2007) providing information on relative as well as absolute development. Although structural validity (at one point in time) and structural stability (across time) may appear as abstract theoretical notions with little immediate practical relevance, they are of great importance for at least two good reasons. First, structural stability is the foundation of any research on continuity and change because it establishes whether the *same construct* is being measured at different time points (Little, 1997). Without structural continuity, comparing vocational interests or other constructs across time is, by definition, a pointless endeavor because of the risk of comparing apples and oranges. Second, the most promising practical implications that are derived from interest theory actually depend on this assumption of structural

validity of the RIASEC model. For example, in light of the new meta-analytic evidence regarding the criterion validity of vocational interest fit, it has also been suggested that organizations can assess applicants' interests and hire those individuals that will fit best with the job they are applying for (Nye, Su, Rounds, & Drasgow, 2012). Importantly, however, this and other examples of person-environment matching strongly depends on (the validity of) a predefined (e.g., hexagonal or circular) interest structure.

4. *Mean-level change.* Mean-level change refers to a group's increases or decreases on different interest dimensions over time. If groups of people demonstrate consistent mean-level changes over a certain age period, then it can be argued that interests undergo normative growth or decline that are consequences of maturational or historical processes shared by most of the members of a population (Low & Rounds, 2007). Note that in the absence of structural stability, changes in mean-level interest scores across time are difficult to interpret because the meaning of these constructs may have shifted over time. In other words, changes can only be unambiguously interpreted as a reflection of a developmental process when longitudinal measurement invariance or equivalence can be established (e.g., Allemand, Zimprich, & Hertzog, 2007; Little, 1997).
5. *Individual differences in change.* Whereas mean-level change focusses on gains or losses on interest dimensions averaged across the entire group, individual differences in change or "individual-level change" refers to the gains or losses (or lack thereof) in absolute levels of an interest dimension that an individual experiences over time (Nesselroade, 1991). The existence of individual differences in change has not received much (or any) attention in earlier reviews on interest development (e.g., Low & Rounds, 2007; Swanson, 1999). Nevertheless, it is exactly this type of change that we should be considering when talking about the interest development of individuals and how this may relate to individual career decisions. In the broader personality literature, this concept of individual differences in change has received considerably more attention, and is even regarded as a "cornerstone of lifespan-development theory," placed "front and center in the study of personality development" (Roberts & Mroczek, 2008, p. 33). These important individual-level changes may be masked in an analysis of mean-level continuity, because equal numbers of individuals may increase or decrease on a trait (or interest dimension), resulting in no change for the entire group (De Fruyt et al., 2006). The optimal way to track this type of interest change is to gather multiple (i.e., more than two) assessments over time and apply growth-modeling techniques to estimate individual differences in change over time. Additionally, it can be tested whether idiosyncratic life and/or career experiences are associated with these changes in vocational interests. Unlike recent advances in the personality literature on this topic (e.g., Hudson, Roberts, & Lodi-Smith, 2012; Le, Donnellan,

> & Conger, 2014), research on adult vocational interests has until now largely overlooked this possibility of individual differences in change. This is problematic from a theoretical (see further in this chapter) as well as from a practical point in view, since studies in the personality domain have pointed out that even relatively modest changes in traits may have significant consequences for individuals' lives. The same may be true for changes in interests and the effects on people's careers.

The overview above indicates that talking about interest development has a totally different meaning depending on the specific indicator that is used to map change or stability. Table 12.1 compares these five indices of interest development on three dimensions: (1) whether the index provides information on the development of interest dimensions separately or at the level of the entire interest profile, (2) whether the index represents an individual or a group-level statistic, and (3) whether the index informs about absolute or relative changes. The last column in Table 12.1 also lists some of the more frequently used analytical techniques to address each development index.

TABLE 12.1 Similarities and Differences Between Different Development Indicators

Indicator	*Interest dimensions or profiles?*	*Individual or group statistic?*	*Absolute or relative development?*	*Analytical technique*
1. Rank-order	dimensions	group	relative	Test-retest correlation
2. Profile	profile	individual, but can be aggregated to group-level	Relative and absolute	Intraindividual Q correlation (relative) / Profile difference index (absolute) / Profile clarity index (relative and absolute)
3. Structural	profile	group	Relative and absolute	Exploratory or confirmatory factor analysis / Correspondence Index
4. Mean-level	dimensions	group	absolute	Repeated measures analyses of variance / Growth curve modeling
5. Individual-level	dimensions	individual	absolute	Growth curve modeling

Findings on Interest Development

To date, most of the research findings concerning the development of vocational interests during adulthood come from early test developers interested in the relative stability of interest scores across time. Qualitative reviews of these longitudinal test-retest studies (e.g., Campbell, 1971; Swanson, 1999) converge on the conclusion that interests show remarkably high levels of relative stability. Hereby, stability typically increases with subjects' age at first testing, whereas stability is lower the longer the time interval between test and retest (Johansson & Campbell, 1971).

Complementing these earlier findings, Low et al. (2005) conducted a meta-analysis investigating rank-order and profile stability of vocational interests from early adolescence (age 12) to middle adulthood (age 40), summarizing the results of 66 longitudinal studies with test-retest intervals greater than or equal to one year. The first of their findings that deserves attention does not relate to vocational interest development itself, but rather to the literature search that preceded this meta-analysis. Specifically, these authors had to conclude that there is a striking lack of studies retesting vocational interests in adulthood. The vast majority of studies in this meta-analysis included participants in the adolescent (51.3%) or the college (40.5%) age groups. By contrast, only 7.8% of the studies examined interests after age 21. The general picture of interest development that emerged from synthesizing these studies was that rank-order and profile stabilities of vocational interests change very little during the greater part of adolescence. It was during the college years (i.e., ages 18–21.9) that interest stability increased dramatically from its previous estimates of about .55 to .67. After that, findings suggested interest stability plateaus for the remainder of the next two decades. The authors concluded that vocational interests were highly stable across all age categories, but that the stability estimates were insufficiently high to warrant the conclusion that no change occurred in adulthood.

A study by Wille, Tracey, Feys and De Fruyt (2014) considered various indicators of vocational interest development in a sample of Belgian college alumni that was followed across the first third of their professional careers. Participants (n = 167) completed a Holland RIASEC interest measure just before entering the labor market and then 15 years later when their careers had unfolded. For both assessment points (i.e., age 22 and age 37), the authors assessed the structural validity of Holland's circular RIASEC model using the Correspondence Index (CI; Hubert & Arabie, 1987), which provides a normalized descriptive index of the extent to which the hypothesized ordering of RIASEC types is met by a correlation matrix among RIASEC scales (Rounds, Tracey, & Hubert, 1992). The advantage of using the CI for this purpose is that the resulting estimate of this model-data fit can be compared to meta-analytically derived benchmarks (Rounds & Tracey, 1996) of CI = .70 for U.S. samples and measures and CI = .48 for international contexts. The results for the Belgian longitudinal sample demonstrated to be similar to the U.S. benchmark, with CI values of .69 and .72 for interest assessments at time 1 and time 2, respectively. When changes in structure were derived from differences in the CI at both time points (e.g., Low & Rounds, 2007), Wille and colleagues found that, as individuals grew older and became more advanced in their careers, interest scores tended to adhere more to Holland's circumplex structure, which is consistent with developmental trends observed in younger age categories (e.g., Tracey, Robbins, & Hofsess, 2005). For the study of adult interest development this is important because it indicates that it indeed makes sense to compare interest scores across different points in time; that we can be relatively sure that we are comparing the same constructs over time. From a more applied perspective, this evidence for increases in structural validity informs us that the necessary assumptions for widely used applications on interest congruence, are indeed met.

Wille and colleagues (2014) further reported rank-order stabilities and mean-level changes for the six RIASEC interest dimensions separately (see Table 12.2). There was a relatively high degree of rank-order stability in interest scores over the 15-year period, with an average test-retest correlation across interest dimensions of .51. However, at the same time there was quite some variation in rank-order consistency across interest types, with Enterprising interests in particular demonstrating the greatest potential for relative changes ($r = .37$). In addition, these authors also observed several mean-level changes in

TABLE 12.2 Test-Retest Correlations (r) and Mean-Level Changes (d) of RIASEC Dimensions (Interests and Occupations) and Big Five Personality Traits

	Interests		*Occupations (O*NET)*	
	Rank-order (r)	*Mean-level (d)*	*Rank-order (r)*	*Mean-level (d)*
Realistic	.76	-.14	.51	.00
Investigative	.51	-.28	.33	.00
Artistic	.50	-.24	.40	-.07
Social	.49	-.39	.53	.01
Enterprising	.37	.02	.31	.18
Conventional	.43	.14	.22	.01
Average	.51	-	.38	-
Neuroticism	.65	-.48	-	-
Extraversion	.69	-.09	-	-
Openness to Experience	.67	-.42	-	-
Agreeableness	.60	.21	-	-
Conscientiousness	.48	.54	-	-
Average	.62	-	-	-

interest scores over time that temper the claim of absolute stability of interests in adulthood. Albeit modest, significant mean-level decreases were observed in Realistic, Investigative, Artistic, and Social interests.

Low and colleagues (2005) also compared the results from their meta-analyses on interest stability with those reported by Roberts and DelVecchio (2000) on personality trait stability. Their conclusion was that vocational interests were markedly more stable than personality traits from ages 12 to 29. It was only until the second half of young adulthood (i.e., 30–40 years) that the rank-order stability estimates of both constructs converged at about .62. The longitudinal college alumni sample studied by Wille and colleagues (Wille & De Fruyt, 2014; Wille et al., 2014) extends these findings by offering a more direct and detailed comparison of change and stability estimates for vocational interest and personality trait data that were collected in the *same sample* and across the *same period of time*. The results of this analysis, summarized in Table 12.2, indicate that RIASEC interests were generally less stable compared to Big Five personality traits, with average test-retest correlations of .51 and .62, respectively. Two exceptions are noteworthy. First, of all six interest types, only Realistic interests were more stable compared to the average stability of Big Five personality traits. Second, of all Big Five traits, only Conscientiousness was less stable compared to the average stability of the interest types.

The evaluation of mean-level stability in adulthood is much more common for personality traits compared to vocational interests. This can be explained by the fact that there is no convincing theoretical rationale to explain mean–level changes in adult vocational interests, whereas normative changes in adult personality traits (e.g., increases in Agreeableness, Conscientiousness, and Emotional Stability; Roberts, Walton, & Viechtbauer, 2006) can easily be understood from a functional perspective in the sense that normative trait changes reflect a developmental process toward maturity (Hogan & Roberts, 2004). An unpublished study by Donnay, Thompson, Morris, and Schaubhut (2004) demonstrated significant but modest age differences in RIASEC interest scores. Unfortunately, the cross-sectional nature of these data did not enable to determine whether any of the observed age differences were actually due to interests *changing* over time. The longitudinal project by Wille and colleagues is particularly informative in this regard because a cohort of young professionals is tracked over a significant and meaningful period of time. Moreover, this same sample of college alumni also provided scores on Big Five personality traits at the beginning of their career and 15 years later, which allows a unique comparison of mean-level changes in interests and traits in the same sample and across the same time interval. For instance, prior research has converged on a relatively robust picture of personality–interest associations (e.g., between trait Openness and Investigative interests; Barrick, Mount, & Gupta, 2003; Larson, Rottinghaus, & Borgen, 2002), implying that, should there be normative changes in personality traits in the direction of greater maturity, then related vocational interests should probably also evolve in the same direction. As can be seen in Table 12.2, Wille and colleagues found some support for this hypothesis. For example, normative decreases in Openness to Experience were accompanied by decreases in Investigative and Artistic interests, and the increases in Conventional interests seems to be in line with the normative increase in Conscientiousness. One particular finding that contradicts this hypothesis is that despite people's mean-level increases in Agreeableness, their preferences for Social activities decreased.

An interesting question is also whether normative changes in interest scores might reflect changes in experienced work environments. The study by Wille and colleagues sheds some light on this by keeping track of occupational characteristics across the entire time period as well. For this purpose, participants' O*NET job titles and the accompanying RIASEC scores were registered at the very beginning of the career as well as 15 years later. The results shown in Table 12.2 indicate that, similarly as for interests, participants' RIASEC occupation scores simultaneously demonstrated both change and stability across the first third of their career. With an average rank-order stability of .38, the results suggested that occupational characteristics describing first jobs were moderately to strongly predictive for occupations as assessed 15 years later. This means for instance that those who started off in jobs with a strong Realistic component were significantly and substantially more likely to occupy a Realistic job 15 years later. Interestingly, only two of the six RIASEC occupation dimensions demonstrated significant mean-level changes over time: On average, occupations became slightly less Artistic (d = -.07) and slightly more Enterprising (d = .18) over time. This pattern of results suggests that there is no clear evidence for normative shifts in vocational interests that are also reflected in normative shifts in occupational characteristics over the same period of time.

However, one important shortcoming of the research presented above is that these findings say little or nothing about changes in vocational interests at the individual level. As a matter of fact, there is a glaring lack of research on individual changes in interests as adults progress in their careers, leaving a number of fundamental questions virtually unanswered. For instance, what happens to an individual's interest levels when he or she embarks on a new career? If there are any significant effects, how stable are these? Also, to what extent can someone learn to appreciate aspects of an occupation that do not fit with one's initial preferences? To answer these pertinent questions, longitudinal studies increasingly need to consider individual-level changes in vocational interests, comparable to recent trends in research on adult personality development. For example, Wille and De Fruyt (2014) demonstrated that people choosing Conventional occupations at the beginning of the career not only scored lower on Openness to Experience at the moment of their job choice, but they also decreased in Openness over time as they persisted in this occupation. In a similar way, research could start to consider the effects of occupational choices and experiences on individuals' personal patterns of interest development.

Theoretical Perspectives on Adult Interest Development

Existing theory on vocational interest development mainly attempts to explain how young children and adolescents gradually gain interest in academic or vocational fields, without much consideration of how these interests further develop once people have entered the workforce. This chapter discusses two theoretical perspectives that may shed light on the issue of adult interest development. First, we review the social cognitive model of interest development (Lent et al., 1994) as a theoretical framework that offers one explanation for *how* individuals gradually gain interest in certain fields of activity. Although the model is primarily intended to explain interest development up until late adolescence or early adulthood, at the same time it is assumed that this process repeats itself continuously over the lifespan, with the only difference that adult interest development requires more compelling experiences to provoke thorough change in basic interest patterns. Additionally, we aim to broaden theory of adult interest development by discussing this topic within the context of a transactional perspective on person-environment (P-E) fit. This second part deals with the *direction* of interest development rather than with underlying mechanisms, and departs from the assumption that personal and career-related development are fundamentally intertwined through a set of P-E fit dynamics.

The Social Cognitive Model of Interest Development

Figure 12.1 illustrates the sociocognitive determinants of career interests and the processes through which interests promote career-related activity involvement and skill acquisition. Central to this perspective is the idea that people form enduring interests in activities in which they view themselves to be efficacious and in which they anticipate positive outcomes (paths 1 and 2 in Figure 12.1). This does not necessarily mean that people need to be good at something right from the start in order to develop further interest, but at least there needs to be the belief that they can learn how to effectively master the activity in such a way that it brings them feelings of fulfillment. These self-efficacy beliefs and outcome expectations themselves are the result of a complex and enduring process of repeated exposure (both directly and vicariously), activity engagement, modeling, and feedback from important others (Lent et al., 1994). These different types of input to self-efficacy beliefs and outcome expectations illustrate that interest development is not restricted to childhood or adolescence. For instance, people may grow up in a commercial environment such as a family business and may gradually grow into the sales profession through observing their parents and even participating in this process at a young age. However, the model also allows people to come into contact with certain interest fields at a later age. People may learn through their interactions with peers that they are gifted negotiators and have good persuasion skills. Or people may find themselves in a

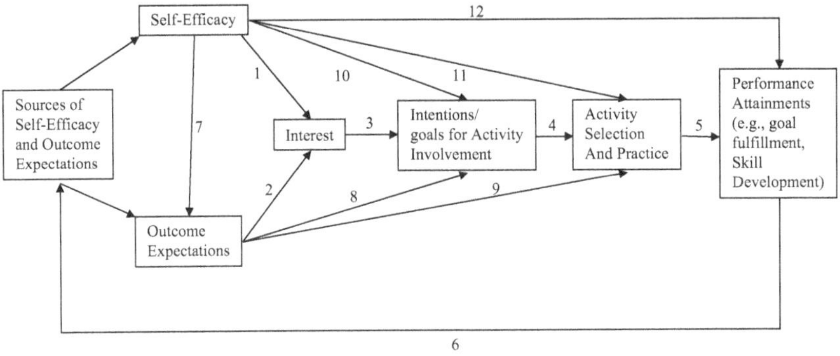

FIGURE 12.1 The social cognitive model of how basic career interests develop over time. Adapted from Lent, Brown, and Hackett, 1994.

new professional environment that suddenly challenges them to practice skills such as persuasion and negotiation; skills that they did not need so much in the past. When people embrace these talents and become aware of the benefits, both extrinsic and intrinsic, that they may bring them, this may lead them to develop an interest in professional activities such as sales and building a career in this direction.

The model further illustrates how these interests can lead to intentions or goals for further activity exposure (path 3), which increase the likelihood of subsequent task selection and practice (path 4). Activity involvement or practice, in turn, produces particular performance attainments (path 5) (e.g., successes and failures), resulting in the revision of self-efficacy and outcome expectancy estimates (path 6). This feedback loop from performance to self-efficacy and outcome expectations is important because it highlights the reciprocal nature of the associations between these constructs. Note that when the social cognitive model is presented as a developmental and causal model, self-efficacy and outcome expectations are used to predict interests, and interests are then used as a predictor of career-related behaviors. A number of empirical studies have supported the social cognitive model of placing self-efficacy before interests (Lent, Brown, & Hackett, 1994, 2000) but other studies by Tracey (2002) and Nauta, Kahn, Angell and Cantarelli (2002) suggest that the interest-efficacy links are reciprocal. In summary, there is discussion about the exact temporal ordering of these processes (see, for instance, Armstrong and Vogel, 2009) and this can only be resolved when additional longitudinal studies become available to further examine the interest-efficacy association from a developmental perspective.

The model further specifies that outcome expectation will also partly be determined by self-efficacy (path 7); this is because people presumably expect to achieve desirable outcomes in activities at which they view themselves to be efficacious (Bandura, 1986). Further, people's goals for activity development are formed partly indirectly, through their interest in these activities, and partly directly (path 8) because of the rewards (both extrinsic and intrinsic) that they anticipate. In a similar vein, outcome expectations may also contribute directly to activity choices (path 9).

With regard to the various types of outcome expectations, the model predicts that self-evaluative outcomes, such as anticipated self-satisfaction (Bandura, 1986), play a particularly influential role in interest development. Specifically, it is assumed that mastery of challenging tasks stimulates positive self-evaluation; the anticipation of additional mastery and self-satisfaction helps sustain task engagement, leading to skill development, and the growth of interest in activities that may have originally held little intrinsic allure (Lent et al., 1994). Like outcome expectations, self-efficacy perceptions are also assumed to have direct effects on activity goals and choices (paths 10 and 11). Finally, because of their role in helping persons to interpret, organize, and apply their skills, self-efficacy beliefs are also seen as contributing directly to one's performance accomplishments (path 12).

Although social cognitive theory especially narrows down on how children and adolescents form a sense of their efficacy in particular tasks and acquire certain expectations about the outcomes of their performance, it is relatively easy to translate this to an adult context. Over the course of their career, people's work environments expose them to a wide array of activities that can fall within and outside their current interest fields. They also observe or hear about others performing various occupational tasks. Further, they are differentially reinforced for pursuing certain activities, some of which they might not have considered pursuing themselves. The specific interactions between working adults and their occupational experiences, with potential implications for interest development, are discussed in greater detail following.

Interest Development from a Transactional Perspective on Person-Environment Fit

The social cognitive model of interest development illustrates the process of *how* interests can grow through individuals' experiences interacting with their environment. A different but equally important set of questions relate to the *direction* of adults' interest development. Assuming that there is room for individual differences in interest stability and change, how do adult workers select interest domains in which they want to specialize further? What are the triggers, internal and external, that may drive adults to deepen their current interests or to start exploring and developing alternative preference fields? In this section, we aim to shed some light on this complex issue by framing individual interest development in the broader context of

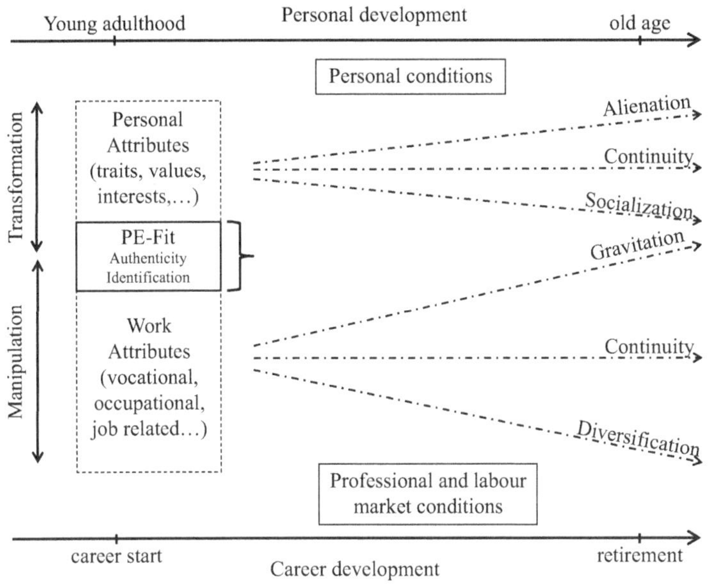

FIGURE 12.2 Transactional Model of Person-Environment Fit

a transactional perspective on P-E fit (see Figure 12.2). Specifically, we see interest development as one element of personal development over the life course, and we particularly hypothesize that personal development is in continuous transaction with career development through a series of fit dynamics. This transactional model of P-E fit combines elements from interest theory (Holland, 1985), gravitation theory (Schneider, Goldstein, & Smith, 1995; Wilk, Desmarais, & Sackett, 1995), socialization theory (Frese, 1982), work adjustment theory (Dawis & Lofquist, 1984), and frameworks of personality development at work (e.g., Roberts, 2006; Woods, Lievens, De Fruyt, & Wille, 2013).

Fit as an Individual Level Development Goal

Theory on development or growth often departs from the (implicit) assumption that this process should lead to some kind of an ideal end point. For instance, theory on personality trait development now more or less converges on the idea that people's personality evolves toward greater maturity (Roberts & Wood, 2006), and that this normative pattern of adult trait development is largely driven by social role investment (e.g., in work, marriage, or parental roles). In addition to these normative personality developmental changes, there is also room for individual differences in change and stability, and these are theorized to be the result of idiosyncratic experiences that people encounter in each of these roles (e.g., specific job characteristics, see Le et al., 2014; Roberts,

Caspi, & Moffitt, 2003). In our perspective, adult interest development is much more an individual-level process compared to adult personality trait development. This is because there is no such thing as a normative end result of interest development. Instead, we define the functionality of adult interest development solely at the individual level, and this is where the notion of P-E fit comes to the fore.

Person-environment fit or congruence can be broadly described as the degree of commensurability between an individual's personal attributes and his or her environment (Low & Rounds, 2007). Much of the work on P-E fit in Industrial/Organizational Psychology and Human Resources Management has been done from the perspective of Schneider's (1987) ASA-model, which suggests that people are *Attracted* to organizations with personal features similar to their own; that organizations will *Select* those people with personal features that resemble their own; and finally that people will be motivated to leave (*Attrition*) organizations that prove to be incompatible with their personal characteristics (see for instance Smith, 2008). The supposed result of this ASA-cycle is increased homogeneity or fit between people and their environments at the organizational level. Building on Roberts's (2006) Attraction-Selection-Transformation-Manipulation-Attrition (ASTMA) model to describe the reciprocal processes between personality traits and work in particular, our transactional model of P-E fit supplements the ASA-cycle with two additional mechanisms that refer to the dynamic qualities of personal and work-related attributes, respectively: Transformation and manipulation.

As illustrated in Figure 12.2, P-E fit in this view refers to a certain level of correspondence between personal attributes on one hand and environmental characteristics on the other. Personal attributes include traits, but also interests, values, goals, and so on. At the side of the environment, characteristics can be described and analyzed at varying levels of specificity including vocational, occupational, and job or task-related features. This degree of correspondence, represented by the intersection of personal and work-related attributes, has two defining characteristics in our view. First, P-E fit is essentially dynamic in nature, with the ability to increase as well as decrease over time. This is where our model is different from Schneider's (1987) ASA-cycle, which only predicts increases in fit over time. In our view, fit represents the outcome of the continuously evolving transaction between personal and career development. As people and their careers evolve over time, the degree of correspondence between personal and work-related attributes will either grow, shrink, or remain constant (see further). Most authors agree that P-E fit is indeed a dynamic process that unfolds over time (Tracey, 2007). For instance, French, Rodgers, and Cobb (1974) and Caplan (1987) describe P-E fit as an adjustment process where fit is the dynamic result of continuous attempts to alter person and environment characteristics. Along the same line, Holland (1997) described congruence as a *long-term* (p. 4) and *interactive* (p. 12) process, with mutual effects of interests and environments on each other. Nevertheless, remarkably little research has addressed the dynamics of congruence across time in adulthood. One notable exception is the 15-year longitudinal study by Wille et al. (2014) who failed to identify absolute (i.e., mean-level) increases in interest-occupation congruence across time. In this respect, more research is needed on the individual-level trajectories of P-E congruence, its antecedents, and its consequences.

The second elementary feature of P-E fit in the proposed transactional model is that congruence is considered to be inherently beneficial, for both the individual and the environment. For the individual, the assets of working in fitting environments are illustrated by higher levels of well-being and satisfaction (Assouline & Meir, 1987; Tsabari, Tziner, & Meir, 2005). Having fitting employees is also advantageous for the environment, given that they tend to perform better (Nye et al., 2012) and that they will demonstrate less deviant behavior (Iliescu, Ispas, Sulea, & Ilie, 2015). The basic idea is that people feel good in environments that—at least to a certain extent—are congruent with their personal attributes. Note that we do not make any assumption about the specific level of congruence that is optimal, nor do we hypothesize that more (congruence) is necessarily better. The transactional model of P-E fit does stipulate that congruence acts as an incentive, meaning that people are motivated to pursue and/or maintain a certain level of fit over time. This means that they will be attracted to environments with fitting features and that they will try to get themselves selected into these environments, much in line with Schneider's (1987) and Roberts's (2006) models. Further, our definition and representation of fit as the degree of overlap between personal and work-related attributes also illustrates that the evolution of fit over time results from two simultaneous and dynamic forces: Manipulation and transformation. Before explaining them in greater detail, it is already relevant to point out two fundamental features that characterize these basic forces. A first feature is that they can be either self-initiated or they can be driven by external conditions. Although I/O Psychology and Organizational Behavior typically focus on the personal factors that drive work-related behaviors and attitudes, developmental approaches cannot be blind to the impact that external conditions have on these behaviors and attitudes. In this regard, our interpretations of manipulation and transformation are also different from Roberts's (2006) approach where manipulation is exclusively self-initiated and transformation can only refer to changes in personal characteristics that make them more aligned with the work environment. As a second feature, these dynamic forces impacting fit can either enhance P-E fit or they can lead to decreasing fit. Although there is a lot of support from multiple areas of psychology that individuals do various things to increase fit with their environment over time, the same literature indicates that for various reasons, a substantial number of people also face a situation of misfit at least some of the time during their careers. Our developmental framework attempts to take this reality into account by hypothesizing on both the causes and consequences (for interest development) that follow from misfit. Finally, as can also be seen from Figure 12.2, it is assumed that there is generally a greater possibility for work-related characteristics to change over time compared to the rather limited room for maneuver for personal attributes.

The Interplay between Manipulation and Transformation

Manipulation in this model refers to possible changes in work-related characteristics made by individuals over time. It is a fundamental assumption in P-E fit theory that people actively shape their environment in order to make it more congruent with their personal characteristics. In Figure 12.2, this process of *gravitation* is illustrated by an upward shift in work-related attributes in the direction of the personal attributes, thus increasing the intersection of both sets of constructs (provided that personal attributes remain unchanged). In this regard, vocational interest development is an iterative process of increasing fit between the person and the environment as individuals choose activities and prune their social networks to conform with their identities, motives, goals, and values (Low & Rounds, 2007). In other words, people "pic their niches" (Scarr & McCartney, 1983)—aligning their environments with their interests such that the environmental press is in the direction of maintaining the direction of their interests. Evidence for this gravitational path comes from research showing that people who change jobs frequently switch to ones that are more congruent with their personalities (Oleski & Subich, 1996). Furthermore, Wille and colleagues (2014), tracking people's interests and occupations across the first third of their career, identified an increase in congruence from interests at time 1 with occupation at time 1 to interests at time 1 to occupation at time 2, thus indicating that individuals shifted jobs over time to better fit with their initial interests. This is consistent with the gravitational hypothesis, which states that people gradually and continually evolve toward better fitting environments (Wilk et al., 1995). It is unclear how exactly gravitational processes impact vocational interest development. Does gravitation lead to absolute increases in fitting interest levels? Does this have any consequences for the shape of the entire interest profile of people (e.g., Is there increased interest differentiation?). Future research is needed to shed light on these unresolved questions.

Still under the umbrella of manipulation, but in the opposite direction of gravitation, there may also be *diversification*: People may decide to or may be forced to change their work environment away from their personal characteristics. This process is illustrated in Figure 12.2 by a downward shift in work-related attributes moving away from the personal attributes, thus diminishing the amount of overlap between both sets of attributes. It is unrealistic to expect career moves to be solely inspired by a desire for increased P-E fit alone. Instead, it may be both personal considerations and labor market conditions that may encourage or force people to engage in diversification and there is research in the turnover literature (e.g., Hulin, Roznowski, & Hachiya, 1985), on job search behaviors (e.g., Saks & Ashforth, 2002), and on underemployment (e.g., McKee-Ryan & Harvey, 2011) to support this. Personal motives may either reflect deliberate choices, personal necessities, or a combination of both. To give a couple of examples, people may be motivated to switch to less fitting jobs because of financial reasons (i.e., higher compensation), better work/life conditions (e.g., choosing a job that is intrinsically less satisfying but that is closer to home), or health-related reasons (e.g., deciding to take a step back and/or to change direction after the experience of a burnout). In addition, diversification may also be driven by specific labor market conditions. For instance, young people searching for a first job may be forced to consider less fitting occupations because of a shortage of jobs in certain industries or interest fields. Regardless of the reasons why people get involved in work environments with attributes that diverge from their personal attributes, the case of diversification represents a crucial challenge in terms of personal attribute development. Applying this to interest development in particular, the question is whether involvement in less fitting occupations may also cause interests to change over time and, if yes, under which conditions? As can be derived from Figure 12.2, in the case of diversification, the only way in which people can restore their level of P-E fit is by gradually adjusting their personal attributes in such a way that these are more closely aligned with their new work-related attributes.

Before delving deeper into the possibility of change in personal attributes, it is worth pointing out that the transactional model of P-E fit also leaves the door open for stability or *continuity* in work-related attributes over time. Despite ongoing changes in the career landscape in the direction of greater mobility and flexibility (Arthur, Khapova, & Wilderom, 2005), a significant number of individuals still experience long periods of status quo. For example, Wille and De Fruyt (2014) observed that almost one third (32.3%) of the college alumni that were followed over time reported exactly the same job title in 2010 compared to 15 years earlier. When job titles were categorized based on the first letter of their O*NET RIASEC letter code, 45.4% demonstrated continuity in occupations held (i.e., retained the same primary RIASEC letter in their job code over time). Finally, acknowledging stability in work-related attributes, in addition to changes in these attributes, is also important to better understand several aspects of personal development. Specifically, this stability in environmental characteristics has been identified as one of the capital forces behind continuity in personal attributes (Roberts & Wood, 2006).

In addition to work environments developing over time, the transactional model also considers change and continuity in personal attributes as a mechanism steering P-E fit. This development of personal attributes, including vocational interests, is represented in the transactional perspective by a second dynamic force referred to as *transformation* (see Figure 12.2). In his framework on personality development and organizational behavior, Roberts (2006) uses the notion of transformation to exclusively refer to development in personality traits that happens in reaction to work-related characteristics. Our current conceptualization of transformation is broader than that in the sense that we also consider development in personal attributes that is not necessarily instigated by our work-related experiences. For instance, there is evidence that personality trait development in adulthood is also influenced by factors such as the experience of disease (Sutin, Zonderman, Ferrucci, & Terracciano, 2013), challenges that result from the parent role (Jokela, Kivimaki, Elovainio, & Keltikangas-Jarvinen, 2009; van Scheppingen et al., 2016), and changes in relationship status (e.g., finding a partner or breaking up; Specht, Egloff, & Schmukle, 2011). In sum, we find it relevant to also pay attention to development in personal attributes that may not directly originate from work experiences, but that may pose crucial challenges for people's career development anyway.

Socialization happens when individuals work on themselves, consciously or unconsciously, to better align their personal attributes with existing or new work-related attributes. Similar to the definition of socialization in the organizational literature (e.g., Bauer, Bodner, Erdogan, Truxillo, & Tucker, 2007), this personal development can either be self-initiated or not. Different than organizational socialization, however, is that the current conceptualization is not restricted to influences at the organizational level (e.g., to conform with an organization's culture), but also acknowledges occupational pressures (e.g., to conform with values, beliefs, and norms associated with a particular type of work). The goal of socialization is, hence, to gradually acquire (when it is self-initiated) or install (when it is initiated externally) the attributes that are regarded as appropriate and desirable in the respective setting (see also Schneider, 1987). In line with this, socialization is represented in our model by the downward path of personal attributes in the direction of the work-related attributes, thus enhancing the level of correspondence between both sets. Socialization may be happening for school leavers entering the world of work and embarking on a new career path. For instance, imagine a young adult choosing the profession of police officer. Holding the personal attributes that fit this profession is highly important for functioning as a police officer and being happy in this occupation. Police officers who do not hold the attributes (e.g., values; Bardi, Buchanan, Goodwin, Slabu, & Robinson, 2014) that fit the profession may find it hard to perform their duty under difficult conditions, such as arresting people who try to resist. Hence, although a certain level of fit will probably be ensured by processes of self-selection that affect the choice to become a police officer, there is also high potential for socialization as a way to improve fit over time. For instance, police recruits receive formal training and close mentoring by experienced officers, both of which are likely to be significant sources of socialization (Cable & Parsons, 2001; Chatman, 1991). Research on socialization effects has mainly focused on changes in personality traits in response to work-related experiences (e.g., Denissen, Ulferts, Luedtke, Muck, & Gerstorf, 2014; Hudson et al., 2012; Le et al., 2014; Wille & De Fruyt, 2014), and much of this work has relied on Roberts and colleagues' corresponsive principle (Caspi, Roberts, & Shiner, 2005; Roberts et al., 2003). Accordingly, life experiences accentuate those personal characteristics prospectively associated with those life experiences in the first place. There is existing support for the corresponsive principle when considering personality development in the workplace. For instance, earlier research has demonstrated that college alumni who score lower on Openness tend to prefer Conventional work environments at the start of their career, and these Conventional work characteristics in turn also predict changes in this trait over time (Wille & De Fruyt, 2014). Work experiences do not impinge themselves on people in a random fashion; rather, it appears that a work environment facilitates the development of traits that are functional in that specific work role. Interestingly, Holland (1997) suggested that similar processes should also exist for vocational interests when he talks about "secondary effects" in his theory of vocational personalities (p. 47). Accordingly, people do not only gravitate toward more fitting environments over time, but at the same time they are assumed to deepen the interests—and associated traits and motives—that got them selected into these environments in the first place. This combination of gravitation and socialization should result in vast increases in P-E fit over time, as is illustrated in Figure 12.2. As a scarce empirical illustration of such interest socialization processes, Meir and Navon (1992) found newly employed bank tellers to converge toward a Conventional interest profile after half a year of employment, with the tellers' level of congruence being highly associated with their performance evaluation.

It may be clear that much remains to be learned about interest socialization in adulthood. Particularly pertinent questions relate, for example, to the possibility of interest change as a reaction to drastic career switches, which can either be self-initiated or involuntary. Specifically, people switching jobs across interest fields may face the need to adjust to a new set of work-related attributes that appeal to personal attributes that may have remained underdeveloped until then. The advantages of considering the transactional approach to P-E fit in this context is that it provides researchers and counselors with a shared language to describe the mechanisms that are involved, and that it also allows specific predictions. Specifically, the case described above would be an example of potential *socialization* effects following *diversification*, and the hypothesis would be that the result of these two forces acting jointly would be stability in P-E fit across time. In the case that people do not succeed in adjusting to these changing work-related attributes—in Figure 12.2 this is indicated by continuity in personal attributes—this would mean a reduction in P-E fit over time.

Opposite to socialization, the model also allows personal attributes to move away from work-related attributes. The term *alienation* was chosen to highlight the process by which people lose touch with their current work environment as their interests develop over time. Applying this to interest development, alienation implies that people can lose interest in the type of work that they perform, and this diminished interest may or may not be accompanied by growing preferences for different kinds of work-related experiences, causing a shift in occupational preferences. Despite its obvious relevance from an applied perspective, this issue of alienation has not yet been systematically studied and to date very little is known about this phenomenon. Possible causes of alienation could be a lack of perceived challenge and variation, causing people to bore out (e.g., "*I have experienced everything there is to experience in this profession*"). In terms of outcomes, people may recognize an ongoing process of alienation by indicators such as a loss of intrinsic motivation in the work they perform and lower levels of engagement (e.g., being less motivated to "go the extra mile"). When it occurs, and people's interests cannot be rekindled anymore, the transactional model prescribes gravitation toward new work-related environments in order to make sure that personal and work attributes remain aligned and a desirable level of P-E fit is secured or restored.

Finally, it is important to note that the outlined developmental paths in this transactional model (i.e., continuity, alienation, socialization, gravitation, and diversification) are hypothesized to be discontinuous, as indicated by the dotted lines, meaning that people can switch between paths, depending on the specific challenges or "anchor points" that they encounter along their professional and personal development. The model is intended to give a broad overview of the different ways in which personal attributes, including vocational interests, can interact with aspects from our career development. In this regard, the transactional perspective complements rather than substitutes existing theoretical frameworks, such as the social cognitive model discussed earlier. Specifically, whenever the transactional model hypothesizes interest change, be it socialization or alienation, the underlying mechanisms described by the social cognitive model will come into play.

The Time Is Now: Challenges for Adult Interest Development in the Twenty-first Century

In this final section, the topic of adult interest development is discussed within the context of some prominent changes in the career landscape. We specifically highlight three recent evolutions that each present a set of challenges that relate directly to interest development: Increased flexibility, working at older age, and competitive workforces.

Increased Worker Flexibility

The theoretical perspectives covered in this chapter both describe interest development as the result of an interactive process between a person and his or her (work) environment. This emphasis on environmental influences could be one of the underlying reasons why interest change has received relatively little attention in the past: The traditional career was assumed to be largely linear and predictable, with little room for drastic changes in work-related attributes. This is in contrast with the idea of a boundaryless career (Arthur & Rousseau, 1996), which puts more emphasis on mobility and flexibility. For instance, whereas career success used to be mainly an issue of securing a specific career and succeeding in climbing the corporate ladder, being successful today involves being marketable or "employable," which includes demonstrating ability and flexibility to learn on the job, to adapt to professional structures, and to prepare for future challenges (De Fruyt, Wille, & John, 2015). More than in the past, people are expected to navigate their careers and to explore different directions, which—along the way—also exposes them to a variety of experiences from different interest fields. We hypothesize that twenty-first-century workers are challenged now to reappraise their career paths more frequently, which may stimulate the processes of interest development described above. The idea here is that increased flexibility and mobility may enable people to come upon interest fields that they had not considered earlier. Just as theory on personality development suggests that environmental stability is one of the important forces driving personality stability (e.g., Roberts & Wood, 2006), the same is true for interest development. It is only when people have the chance to explore—or, in certain cases, are pushed toward—new environments that they may start to develop new self-efficacy beliefs and growing interests. While prior research has typically considered interests as *predictors* of turnover (see for instance Van Iddekinge et al., 2011) and career mobility (e.g., Wille, De Fruyt, & Feys, 2010), more research is needed on the effects of job and career mobility on the development of interests over time.

Working at Older Age

Next to increased flexibility, the aging of the workforce is also a growing concern for organizations of the twenty-first century. For instance, studies on the projected retirement of older workers suggest that more than half of the organizations expect to experience a worker shortage as a result of Baby Boomers retiring (Mermin, Johnson, & Toder, 2008). If we want to motivate older workers to remain active in the labor market, at least two challenges need to be tackled that directly relate to interest development. First, we will need to prevent older workers from boring out or from alienating from work in other ways. Second, when older workers can no longer cope with the demanding (e.g., physical) requirements accompanying work in certain (e.g., Realistic) industries, they will need assistance in reorienting them toward different but more fitting work environments (i.e., diversification). Further, as the demographics of the workforce change, employers will be increasingly confronted with potential cohort and/or generational differences in personal attributes and vocational interests among their age-diverse staff. For instance, Twenge (2001) found more recent birth cohorts to be more assertive and describing themselves as having higher leadership abilities compared to the self-descriptions of earlier birth cohorts (Twenge, Campbell, & Gentile, 2012). Along the same line, Bubany and Hansen (2011) demonstrated an overall increase in Enterprising and Social interests among more recent birth cohorts. It should be noted, however, that the association between age, birth cohort, and vocational interests are still poorly understood and that more research on this topic is warranted before drawing firm conclusions (Leuty & Hansen, 2014). Nevertheless, the issue of people working at later ages, in collaboration with people from younger cohorts and generations, poses a second set of challenges with particular relevance to the topic of adult interest development.

Competitive Workforces Through Interventions

Finally, in order to meet the challenges that nations face of remaining competitive with other scientifically and technologically advanced countries, much emphasis is now placed on the production of more postsecondary and advanced degrees in the Science, Technology, Engineering, and Math (STEM) fields, as well as on promoting professional careers in these interest domains. Over the past decades, various strategies have been devised and implemented to address the challenges having to do with the quality, quantity, and diversity of the STEM educational pipeline. At the postsecondary level in particular, STEM intervention programs (SIPs) have emerged as a means to foster, support, and sustain the interest of students in STEM. Although research on the actual efficacy of these programs is still limited, there is some evidence that suggests that these interventions might indeed be successful, at least in middle-school adolescents (Turner & Lapan, 2005) and college students (Luzzo, Hasper, Albert, Bibby, & Martinelli, 1999). Moreover, the active ingredients of these interventions seem to be in line with theoretical perspectives on interest development, such as the social cognitive model outlined earlier. Specifically, a key element in increasing interests consists of increasing self-efficacy expectations, and these are relatively easily manipulated through intervention (e.g., Betz & Schifano, 2000). It remains to be examined, however, to which extent such interventions may help to affect the interests of more mature adults, whose interest profiles are more crystalized.

Practical Implications of Adult Development in Interests

Early investigations of interest development were mainly concerned with demonstrating continuity in interests over time, because this would facilitate the use and acceptance of interest inventories in applied settings such as counseling and selection. The evidence that emerged recently, demonstrating predictive validity of interest scales for various performance indicators, further supported the utility of interest assessment. So, when delving deeper into the issue of interest change, are we undermining this recent optimism concerning the role of interests in applied settings? After all, changes in, for instance, the rank-order of interest scores could be associated with relative changes in associated performance scores. In other words, should interests prove to be highly volatile, then single-shot interest assessments in the selection process would prove to be of little value for predicting future performance.

The extant knowledge on adult interest development offers no reasons to be pessimistic in this regard. Although a lot still remains to be learned in this field, it is safe to conclude from this literature that, just like other individual differences such as values, personality traits, and cognitive abilities, adult interests show sufficiently high levels of continuity to make predictive claims. This is backed-up by (a) longitudinal studies demonstrating moderate-to-high levels of stability in interests across different development indicators (see above), (b) studies demonstrating a substantial heritable component in interests (e.g., Kandler, Bleidorn, Riemann, Angleitner, & Spinath, 2011), and (c) studies integrating interests in a nomological network of relatively stable cognitive (e.g., Paessler, Beinicke, & Hell, 2015) and noncognitive (e.g., Mount, Barrick, Scullen, & Rounds, 2005) individual differences that are successfully used in assessment practice.

Summary and Conclusions

In the beginning of interest scholarship, there was mainly concern about the permanence of interests, because this would be a crucial factor in the acceptance and predictive validity of the newly developed interest measures. What we now know from the literature is that vocational interests are indeed relatively stable across adulthood, but that there is at the same time room for change. Unfortunately, this "dynamic quality" (Low et al., 2005, p. 727) of adult vocational interests has to date received little attention, and thus remains poorly understood. The current chapter attempted to integrate the available findings and theory relevant to adult interest development, and broadened the discussion of this topic by framing it in the context of a transactional perspective on person-environment fit. We should not be afraid of interest discontinuity; nor should we treat it as error. Instead, we need to put more effort in trying to better understand interest change at the individual level, its causes, and consequences. As was outlined above, it can be expected that recent changes in the career landscape, combined with expected transitions in labor force demographics, will further underline the need to pay more attention to adult interest development.

References

Allemand, M., Zimprich, D., & Hertzog, C. (2007). Cross-sectional age differences and longitudinal age changes of personality in middle adulthood and old age. *Journal of Personality, 75*(2), 323–358. doi:10.1111/j.1467-6494.2006.00441.x

Armstrong, P. I., & Vogel, D. L. (2009). Interpreting the interest-efficacy association from a RIASEC perspective. *Journal of Counseling Psychology, 56*(3), 392–407. doi:10.1037/a0016407

Arthur, M. B., Khapova, S. N., & Wilderom, C. P. M. (2005). Career success in a boundaryless career world. *Journal of Organizational Behavior, 26*(2), 177–202. doi:10.1002/job.290

Arthur, M. B., & Rousseau, D. M. (1996). Introduction: The boundaryless career as a new employment principle. In M. B. Arthur & D. M. Rousseau (Eds.), *The boundaryless career: A new employment principle for a new organizational era* (pp. 3–20). New York: Oxford University Press.

Assouline, M., & Meir, E. I. (1987). Meta-analysis of the relationship between congruence and well-being measures. *Journal of Vocational Behavior, 31*(3), 319–332.

Bandura, A. (1986). *Social foundations of thought and action: A social cognitive theory*. Englewood Cliffs, NJ: Prentice-Hall.

Bardi, A., Buchanan, K. E., Goodwin, R., Slabu, L., & Robinson, M. (2014). Value stability and change during self-chosen life transitions: Self-selection versus socialization effects. *Journal of Personality and Social Psychology, 106*(1), 131–147. doi:10.1037/a0034818

Barrick, M. R., Mount, M. K., & Gupta, R. (2003). Meta-analysis of the relationship between the five-factor model of personality and Holland's occupational types. *Personnel Psychology, 56*(1), 45–74. doi:10.1111/j.1744-6570.2003.tb00143.x

Bauer, T. N., Bodner, T., Erdogan, B., Truxillo, D. M., & Tucker, J. S. (2007). Newcomer adjustment during organizational socialization: A meta-analytic review of antecedents, outcomes, and methods. *Journal of Applied Psychology, 92*(3), 707–721. doi:10.1037/0021-9010.92.3.707

Betz, N. E., & Schifano, R. S. (2000). Evaluation of an intervention to increase realistic self-efficacy and interests in college women. *Journal of Vocational Behavior, 56*(1), 35–52. doi:10.1006/jvbe.1999.1690

Block, J. (1971). *Lives through time*. Berkeley, CA: Bancroft Books.

Bubany, S. T., & Hansen, J.-I. C. (2011). Birth cohort change in the vocational interests of female and male college students. *Journal of Vocational Behavior, 78*(1), 59–67. doi:10.1016/j.jvb.2010.08.002

Cable, D. M., & Parsons, C. K. (2001). Socialization tactics and person-organization fit. *Personnel Psychology, 54*(1), 1–23. doi:10.1111/j.1744-6570.2001.tb00083.x

Campbell, D. P. (1971). Handbook for the Strong Vocational Interest Blank. Stanford, CA: Stanford University Press.

Caplan, R. D. (1987). Person-environment fit theory and organizations: Commensurate dimensions, time perspectives, and mechanisms. *Journal of Vocational Behavior, 31*(3), 248–267. doi:10.1016/0001-8791(87)90042-x

Caspi, A., & Roberts, B. W. (1999). Personality and continuity and change across the life course. In L. A. Pervin & O. P. John (Eds.), *Handbook of personality: Theory and research* (pp. 300–326). New York: Guilford Press.

Caspi, A., & Roberts, B. W. (2001). Personality development across the life course: The argument for change and continuity. *Psychological Inquiry, 12*(2), 49–66.

Caspi, A., Roberts, B. W., & Shiner, R. L. (2005). Personality development: Stability and change. *Annual Review of Psychology, 56*, 453–484. doi:10.1146/annurev.psych.090902.141913

Chatman, J. A. (1991). Matching people and organizations: Selection and socialization in public accounting firms. *Administrative Science Quarterly, 36*(3), 459–484. doi:10.2307/2393204

Cronbach, L. J., & Gleser, G. C. (1953). Assessing similarity between profiles. *Psychological Bulletin, 50*, 456–473. doi:10.1037/h0057173

Darcy, M. U. A., & Tracey, T. J. G. (2007). Circumplex structure of Holland's RIASEC interests across gender and time. *Journal of Counseling Psychology, 54*(1), 17–31. doi:10.1037/022-0167.54.1.17

Dawis, R. V., & Lofquist, L. H. (1984). *A psychological theory of work adjustment*. Minneapolis: University of Minnesota Press.

De Fruyt, F., Bartels, M., Van Leeuwen, K. G., De Clercq, B., Decuyper, M., & Mervielde, I. (2006). Five types of personality continuity in childhood and adolescence. *Journal of Personality and Social Psychology, 91*(3), 538–552. doi:10.1037/0022-3514.91.3.538

De Fruyt, F., Wille, B., & John, O. P. (2015). Employability in the 21st century: Complex (interactive) problem solving and other essential skills. *Industrial and Organizational Psychology: Perspectives on Science and Practice, 8*, 276–281.

Denissen, J. J. A., Ulferts, H., Luedtke, O., Muck, P. M., & Gerstorf, D. (2014). Longitudinal transactions between personality and occupational roles: A large and heterogeneous study of job beginners, stayers, and changers. *Developmental Psychology, 50*(7), 1931–1942. doi:10.1037/a0036994

Donnay, D. A. C., Morris, M. L., Schaubhut, N. A., & Thompson, R. C. (2005). *Strong Interest Inventory Manual* (Revised Ed.). Palo Alto, CA: Consulting Psychologists Press.

Donnay, D. A. C., Thompson, R. C., Morris, M. A., & Schaubhut, N. (August, 2004). *Exploring age and gender differences in vocational interests*. Poster presented at the Annual Convention of the American Psychological Association. Honolulu, HI.

French, J. R. P., Rodgers, W., & Cobb, S. (1974). Adjustment as person-environment fit. In G. V. Coelho, D. A. Hamburg, & J. E. Adams (Eds.), *Coping and adaptation*. New York: Basic Books.

Frese, M. (1982). Occupational socialization and psychological development: An underemphasized research perspective in industrial psychology. *Journal of Occupational Psychology, 55*(3), 209–224.

Gupta, S., Tracey, T. J. G., & Gore, P. A., Jr. (2008). Structural examination of RIASEC scales in high school students: Variation across ethnicity and method. *Journal of Vocational Behavior, 72*(1), 1–13. doi:10.1016/j.jvb.2007.10.013

Hogan, R., & Roberts, B. W. (2004). A socioanalytic model of maturity. *Journal of Career Assessment, 12*(2), 207–217. doi:10.1177/1069072703255882

Holland, J. L. (1985). *Making vocational choices: A theory of vocational personalities and work environments* (2nd ed.). Odessa, FL: Psychological Assessment Resources.

Holland, J. L. (1997). *Making vocational choices: A theory of vocational personalities and work environments* (3rd ed.). Odessa, Fl: Psychological Assessment Resources.

Hubert, L., & Arabie, P. (1987). Evaluating order hypotheses within proximity matrices. *Psychological Bulletin, 102*(1), 172–178. doi:10.1037/0033-2909.102.1.172

Hudson, N. W., Roberts, B. W., & Lodi-Smith, J. (2012). Personality trait development and social investment in work. *Journal of Research in Personality, 46*(3), 334–344. doi:10.1016/j.jrp.2012.03.002

Hulin, C. L., Roznowski, M., & Hachiya, D. (1985). Alternative opportunities and withdrawal decisions: Empirical and theoretical discrepancies and an integration. *Psychological Bulletin, 97*(2), 233.

Iliescu, D., Ispas, D., Sulea, C., & Ilie, A. (2015). Vocational fit and counterproductive work behaviors: A self-regulation perspective. *Journal of Applied Psychology, 100*(1), 21–39. doi:10.1037/a0036652

Johansson, C. B., & Campbell, D. P. (1971). Stablity of Strong Vocational Interest Blank for men. *Journal of Applied Psychology, 55*(1), 34–36. doi:10.1037/h0030627

Jokela, M., Kivimaki, M., Elovainio, M., & Keltikangas-Jarvinen, L. (2009). Personality and having children: A two-way relationship. *Journal of Personality and Social Psychology, 96*(1), 218–230. doi:10.1037/a0014058

Kandler, C., Bleidorn, W., Riemann, R., Angleitner, A., & Spinath, F. M. (2011). The genetic links between the Big Five personality traits and general interest domains. *Personality and Social Psychology Bulletin, 37*, 1633–1643. doi:10.1177/0146167211414275

Kantamneni, N. (2014). Vocational interest structures for Asian Americans, Middle-Eastern Americans and Native Americans on the 2005 Strong Interest Inventory. *Journal of Vocational Behavior, 84*(2), 133–141. doi:10.1016/j.jvb.2013.11.003

Larson, L. M., Rottinghaus, P. J., & Borgen, F. H. (2002). Meta-analyses of big six interests and big five personality factors. *Journal of Vocational Behavior, 61*(2), 217–239. doi:10.1006/jvbe.2001.1854

Le, K., Donnellan, M. B., & Conger, R. (2014). Personality development at work: Workplace conditions, personality changes, and the corresponsive principle. *Journal of Personality, 82*(1), 44–56. doi:10.1111/jopy.12032

Lent, R. W., Brown, S. D., & Hackett, G. (1994). Toward a unifying social cognitive theory of career and academic interest, choice, and performance. *Journal of Vocational Behavior, 45*(1), 79–122.

Lent, R. W., Brown, S. D., & Hackett, G. (2000). Contextual supports and barriers to career choice: a social cognitive analysis. *Journal of Counseling Psychology, 47*(1), 36–49. doi:10.1037//0022-0167.47.1.36

Leuty, M. E., & Hansen, J.-I. C. (2014). Teasing apart the relations between age, birth cohort, and vocational interests. *Journal of Counseling Psychology, 61*(2), 289–298. doi:10.1037/a0035341

Little, T. D. (1997). Mean and covariance structures (MACS) analyses of cross-cultural data: Practical and theoretical issues. *Multivariate Behavioral Research, 32*, 53–76. doi:10.1207/s15327906mbr3201_3

Low, K. S. D., & Rounds, J. (2007). Interest change and continuity from early adolescence to middle adulthood. *International Journal for Educational and Vocational Guidance, 7*(1), 23–36.

Low, K. S. D., Yoon, M. J., Roberts, B. W., & Rounds, J. (2005). The stability of vocational interests from early adolescence to middle adulthood: A quantitative review of longitudinal studies. *Psychological Bulletin, 131*(5), 713–737.

Luzzo, D. A., Hasper, P., Albert, K. A., Bibby, M. A., & Martinelli, E. A. (1999). Effects of self-efficacy-enhancing interventions on the math/science self-efficacy and career interests, goals, and actions of career undecided college students. *Journal of Counseling Psychology, 46*(2), 233–243. doi:10.1037/0022-0167.46.2.233

McKee-Ryan, F. M., & Harvey, J. (2011). "I have a job, but...": A review of underemployment. *Journal of Management, 37*(4), 962–996.

Meir, E. I., & Navon, M. (1992). A longitudinal examination of congruence hypotheses. *Journal of Vocational Behavior, 41*(1), 35–47. doi:10.1016/0001-8791(92)90037-z

Mermin, G. B. T., Johnson, R. W., & Toder, E. J. (2008). *Will employers want aging boomers?* Washington, DC: Urban Institute Retrieved from http://www.in.gov/icw/files/aging_boomers.pdf.

Mount, M. K., Barrick, M. R., Scullen, S. M., & Rounds, J. (2005). Higher-order dimensions of the big five personality traits and the big six vocational interest types. *Personnel Psychology, 58*, 447–478.

Nauta, M. M., Kahn, J. H., Angell, J. W., & Cantarelli, E. A. (2002). Identifying the antecedent in the relation between career interests and self-efficacy: Is it one, the other, or both? *Journal of Counseling Psychology, 49*(3), 290–301. doi:10.1037//0022-0167.49.3.290

Nesselroade, J. R. (1991). The warp and woof of the developmental fabric. In R. Downs, L. Liben & D. S. Palermo (Eds.), *Visions of aesthetics, the environment, and development: The legacy of Joachim F. Wohwill* (pp. 213–240). Hillsdale, NJ: Erlbaum.

Nye, C. D., Su, R., Rounds, J., & Drasgow, F. (2012). Vocational interests and performance: A quantitative summary of over 60 years of research. *Perspectives on Psychological Science, 7*(4), 384–403. doi:10.1177/1745691612449021

Oleski, D., & Subich, L. M. (1996). Congruence and career change in employed adults. *Journal of Vocational Behavior, 49*(3), 221–229. doi:10.1006/jvbe.1996.0041

Paessler, K., Beinicke, A., & Hell, B. (2015). Interests and intelligence: A meta-analysis. *Intelligence, 50*, 30–51. doi:10.1016/j.intell.2015.02.001

Roberts, B. W. (2006). Personality development and organizational behavior. *Research in Organizational Behavior, 27*, 1–40. doi:10.1016/S0191-3085(06)27001-1

Roberts, B. W., Caspi, A., & Moffitt, T. E. (2003). Work experiences and personality development in young adulthood. *Journal of Personality and Social Psychology, 84*(3), 582–593. doi:10.1037/0022-3514.84.3.582

Roberts, B. W., & DelVecchio, W. F. (2000). The rank-order consistency of personality traits from childhood to old age: A quantitative review of longitudinal studies. *Psychological Bulletin, 126*(1), 3–25. doi:10.1037/0033-2909.126.1.3

Roberts, B. W., & Mroczek, D. (2008). Personality trait change in adulthood. *Current Directions in Psychological Science, 17*(1), 31–35. doi:10.1111/j.1467-8721.2008.00543.x

Roberts, B. W., Walton, K. E., & Viechtbauer, W. (2006). Patterns of mean-level change in personality traits across the life course: A meta-analysis of longitudinal studies. *Psychological Bulletin, 132*(1), 1–25. doi:10.1037/0033-2909.132.1.1

Roberts, B. W., & Wood, D. (2006). Personality development in the context of the neo-socioanalytic model of personality. In D. K. Mroczek & T. D. Little (Eds.), *Handbook of personality development* (pp. 11–39). Mahwah, NJ: Erlbaum.

Rounds, J., & Tracey, T. J. (1996). Cross-cultural structural equivalence of RIASEC models and measures. *Journal of Counseling Psychology, 43*(3), 310–329. doi:10.1037/0022-0167.43.3.310

Rounds, J., Tracey, T. J., & Hubert, L. (1992). Methods for evaluating vocational interest structural hypotheses. *Journal of Vocational Behavior, 40*(2), 239–259. doi:10.1016/0001-8791(92)90073-9

Saks, A. M., & Ashforth, B. E. (2002). Is job search related to employment quality? It all depends on the fit. *Journal of Applied Psychology, 87*, 646–654.

Scarr, S., & McCartney, K. (1983). How people make their own environments: A theory of genotype-environment effects. *Child Development, 54*(2), 424–435. doi:10.1111/j.1467-8624.1983.tb03884.x

Schneider, B. (1987). The people make the place. *Personnel Psychology, 40*(3), 437–453. doi:10.1111/j.1744-6570.1987.tb00609.x

Schneider, B., Goldstein, H. W., & Smith, D. B. (1995). The ASA framework: An update. *Personnel Psychology, 48*(4), 747–773. doi:10.1111/j.1744-6570.1995.tb01780.x

Smith, D. B. (Ed.) (2008). *The people make the place: dynamic linkages between individuals and organizations.* New York: Erlbaum.

Specht, J., Egloff, B., & Schmukle, S. C. (2011). Stability and change of personality across the life course: The impact of age and major life events on mean-level and rank-order stability of the big five. *Journal of Personality and Social Psychology, 101*(4), 862–882. doi:10.1037/a0024950

Sutin, A. R., Zonderman, A. B., Ferrucci, L., & Terracciano, A. (2013). Personality traits and chronic disease: Implications for adult personality development. *Journals of Gerontology Series B-Psychological Sciences and Social Sciences, 68*(6), 912–920. doi:10.1093/geronb/gbt036

Swanson, J. L. (1999). Stability and change in vocational interests. In M. L. Savickas & A. R. Spokane (Eds.), *Vocational interests: Meaning, measurement, and counseling use* (1st ed., pp. 135–161). Palo Alto, CA: Davies-Black.

Tracey, T. J. G. (2002). Development of interests and competency beliefs: A 1-year longitudinal study of fifth- to eighth-grade students using the ICA-R and structural equation modeling. *Journal of Counseling Psychology, 49*(2), 148–163. doi:10.1037//0022-0167.49.2.148

Tracey, T. J. G. (2007). Moderators of the interest congruence-occupational outcome relation. *International Journal for Educational and Vocational Guidance, 7*, 37–45. doi:10.1007/s10775-006-9111-3

Tracey, T. J. G., & Robbins, S. B. (2005). Stability of interests across ethnicity and gender: A longitudinal examination of grades 8 through 12. *Journal of Vocational Behavior, 67*, 335–364. doi:10.1016/j.jvb.2004.11.003

Tracey, T. J. G., Robbins, S. B., & Hofsess, C. D. (2005). Stability and change in interests: A longitudinal study of adolescents from grades 8 through 12. *Journal of Vocational Behavior, 66*(1), 1–25. doi:10.1016/j.jvb.2003.11.002

Tsabari, O., Tziner, A., & Meir, E. I. (2005). Updated meta-analysis on the relationship between congruence and satisfaction. *Journal of Career Assessment, 13*(2), 216–232. doi:10.1177/1069072704273165

Turner, S. L., & Lapan, R. T. (2005). Evaluation of an intervention to increase non-traditional career interests and career-related self-efficacy among middle-school adolescents. *Journal of Vocational Behavior, 66*(3), 516–531. doi:10.1016/j.jvb.2004.02.005

Twenge, J. M. (2001). Changes in women's assertiveness in response to status and roles: A cross-temporal meta-analysis, 1931–1993. *Journal of Personality and Social Psychology, 81*(1), 133–145. doi:10.1037//0022-3514.81.1.133

Twenge, J. M., Campbell, W. K., & Gentile, B. (2012). Generational increases in agentic self-evaluations among American college students, 1966–2009. *Self and Identity, 11*(4), 409–427. doi:10.1080/15298868.2011.576820

Van Iddekinge, C. H., Roth, P. L., Putka, D. J., & Lanivich, S. E. (2011). Are you interested? A meta-analysis of relations between vocational interests and employee performance and turnover. *Journal of Applied Psychology, 96*(6), 1167–1194. doi:10.1037/a0024343

van Scheppingen, M. A., Jackson, J. J., Specht, J., Hutteman, R., Denissen, J. J. A., & Bleidorn, W. (2016). Personality trait development during the transition to parenthood: A test of Social Investment Theory. *Social Psychological and Personality Science, 7*(5), 452–462. doi:10.1177/1948550616630032

Wilk, S. L., Desmarais, L. B., & Sackett, P. R. (1995). Gravitation to jobs commensurate with ability: Longitudinal and cross-sectional tests. *Journal of Applied Psychology, 80*(1), 79–85. doi:10.1037/0021-9010.80.1.79

Wille, B., & De Fruyt, F. (2014). Vocations as a source of identity: Reciprocal relations between Big Five personality traits and RIASEC characteristics over 15 Years. *Journal of Applied Psychology, 99*(2), 262–281. doi:10.1037/a0034917

Wille, B., De Fruyt, F., & Feys, M. (2010). Vocational interests and big five traits as predictors of job instability. *Journal of Vocational Behavior, 76*, 547–558. doi:10.1016/j.jvb.2010.01.007
Wille, B., Tracey, T. J. G., Feys, M., & De Fruyt, F. (2014). A longitudinal and multi-method examination of interest-occupation congruence within and across time. *Journal of Vocational Behavior, 84*(1), 59–73. doi:10.1016/j.jvb.2013.12.001
Woods, S. A., Lievens, F., De Fruyt, F., & Wille, B. (2013). Personality across working life: The longitudinal and reciprocal influences of personality on work. *Journal of Organizational Behavior, 34*, 7–25. doi:10.1002/job.1863

13

THE ROLE OF INTERESTS IN THE DEVELOPMENT OF EXPERTISE

A Multifactorial Perspective

David Z. Hambrick and Alexander P. Burgoyne

MICHIGAN STATE UNIVERSITY

Frederick L. Oswald

RICE UNIVERSITY

People with high levels of expertise in domains such as science, business, law, and music contribute to the prosperity of nations, the competitive advantage of organizations, and the well-being of families and communities. These individuals are often revered by society for their contributions—think of Marie Curie in science, The Beatles in popular music, Tiger Woods in sports, and Ruth Bader Ginsberg in the law. Scientific interest in expertise has a long history in psychology, dating to the earliest days of the field (Galton, 1869). Recent decades have witnessed an explosion of popular interest in research on expertise, as well, through books such as Malcolm Gladwell's (2008) *Outliers: The Story of Success* and Geoff Colvin's (2010) *Talent Is Overrated: What Really Separates World-Class Performers from Everybody Else.*

Not surprisingly, research has made it clear that an important determinant of both within-person and between-person variability in expertise is domain-specific experience: engagement in training and other types of activities within a given domain. Here, we consider the influence of interests on domain-specific experience. The chapter is organized into four major sections. In the first section, we provide a definition of expertise and discuss how expertise is measured in scientific research. In the second section, we briefly review evidence from recent research examining individual differences in expertise, including both domain-general and domain-specific factors. In the third section, we describe a multifactorial model of expertise (Ullén, Hambrick, & Mosing, 2016), and discuss predictions stemming from this model, particularly regarding the role of interests as a primary factor in learning and the development of expertise. In the final section, we offer several future directions for research on the role of interests in expertise over the lifespan.

What Is Expertise?

As a practical matter, people often identify or infer a person's expertise based on titles and credentials, as reflected by advanced degrees, certifications, and licenses. For example, we often assume that a person with an MD is an expert in medicine. And, given the strict laws around practicing medicine, we are generally willing to entrust the treatment of our physical ailments (and thus our lives) to such experts, with little vetting. However, as the old joke about what you call the person who finishes at the bottom of their medical school class (*doctor*) goes, being an MD only raises a patient's confidence that the doctor holds a minimum level of expertise. It certainly does not guarantee that the person is a *good* doctor.

As a scientific matter, expertise can be identified by measuring a person's performance on one or more tasks that capture the essential requirements of a domain (Ericsson & Smith, 1991). Performance can be measured directly (e.g., by having individuals perform laboratory tasks), or it can be measured more indirectly by means of estimation from various proxies for such tasks (e.g., ratings, rankings, grades, awards). For some domains, a single type of task may be sufficient to capture expertise. For example, playing good chess depends on choosing a series of good moves in actual chess games. Therefore, the researcher's obvious choice of a task to measure chess expertise is to give game positions to chess players and ask them to choose what they consider to be the best moves for White or for Black (de Groot, 1946/1978). The quality of each move can then be evaluated by comparing the participant's move using a chess analysis software program, given that current chess engines—such as Komodo, Stockfish, or Houdini—perform much better than even the best human players. One might also have expert chess players rate the moves. As another example, expertise in typing can be measured by giving participants a standardized passage of text to type that is of reasonable difficulty, and then measuring their speed and accuracy (highly skilled typists show both high speed and high accuracy, not one at the exclusion of the other).

For other domains, no single task can be argued to measure expertise, because there are specializations and even sub-specializations. For example, overall musical expertise comprises a wide range of activities, including sight-reading, improvising, composing, arranging, and so on. Similarly, lawyers perform a multitude of tasks, such as writing contracts and briefs, drumming up clients, negotiating settlements, and arguing cases before juries. In these domains, there are many classes of conceptually distinct situations that call on different types of specialized knowledge. Therefore, it is necessary to treat expertise as a multidimensional construct, or else to restrict the focus of research to a particular area of specialization (e.g., sight-reading in music). In some domains, it may even be misleading to use a single task to measure expertise, even if that task would seem to be the most obvious choice for doing so (Hambrick & Hoffman, 2016). For example, many stockbrokers may be no better at predicting the stock market than statistical algorithms (Andersson, 2004). Yet they may be measurably superior in a host of other critical domain-relevant activities, such as executing trades, interpreting economic data, and giving clients advice on how to diversify their investments.

As a final point, it is common in expertise research to classify people into distinct categories based on their level of performance in domain-relevant tasks, even though these categories are ultimately arbitrary labels. One common classification scheme is *beginner, novice, intermediate,* and *expert* (e.g., Chase & Simon, 1973); another is *initiate, apprentice, journeyman,* and *expert* (Hoffmann et al., 2013). These classification schemes can be useful for both research and applied purposes, but most, if not all, forms of expertise are *continuous* in nature (not discrete and univariate). Thus, cut-offs used to create categories representing different skill levels are necessarily arbitrary. That is, although skill level can certainly be distinguished as a practical matter, particularly at the extremes (e.g., beginner vs. expert), these groups do not represent discrete categories of individuals (like people who have brown, blue, or green eyes). Rather, levels of expertise refer to imperfect labels often applied to continuous measures of human performance. Thus, the goal of scientific research on expertise should not be to understand differences between groups of individuals such as "novices" and "experts," but rather to understand factors that contribute to individual differences in expertise across its full range.

Individual Differences in Expertise

Obviously, not everyone who enters a vocational or avocational domain will reach a high level of performance, even among people who have a strong desire to do so. For example, most people who take up a musical instrument will never become skilled enough to play in a local symphony, much less the Royal Concertgebouw Orchestra in Amsterdam, which is consistently ranked as the world's best symphony orchestra. Likewise, very few people who become an attorney will ever develop the legal expertise necessary to argue a case before the U.S. Supreme Court, and very few people who take up the game of golf will ever make it to a professional tour.

Success in these types of endeavors is, of course, influenced by opportunity. A child whose parents cannot afford to buy him a saxophone and pay for music lessons will probably not become the next Charlie Parker, just as the child whose parents cannot afford to buy her a proper set of golf clubs and pay for golf lessons will probably not become the next Michelle Wie. And legal expertise is surely not the only factor that determines whether a lawyer gets the chance to argue a case before the Supreme Court. Unfortunately, being in the "right place at the right time" and knowing the "right people" often matters for success. But, beyond differences in opportunity, what are the knowledge, skills, abilities, and other factors (KSAOs) that distinguish people who reach a high level of expertise in complex domains from those who fail to do so? To put it another way, among people with similar opportunity, who rises to the top in business, science, music, sports, and other domains?

Decades of research in industrial-organizational psychology have left no doubt that *general cognitive ability*—the psychological trait captured by IQ tests—is a statistically and practically significant predictor of job training success and subsequent performance (see Schmidt & Hunter, 2004). Especially in the expertise literature, some theorists have argued that this is true only early in training, and that general abilities drop out as a predictor of performance differences at high levels of skill. For example, in their book *Peak: Secrets from the New Science of Expertise,* Ericsson and Pool (2016) claimed that "While people with certain innate characteristics...may have an advantage when first learning a skill, that advantage gets smaller over time, and eventually the amount and quality of practice take on a much larger role in determining how skilled a person becomes" (p. 233).

This hypothesis has been called the *circumvention-of-limits hypothesis* (Hambrick & Meinz, 2011), because the idea is that the acquisition of domain-specific knowledge and skills enables the performer to circumvent (or bypass) performance limitations associated with general abilities (see, e.g., Ericsson & Charness, 1994). As appealing as it is, evidence for this hypothesis is weak. We recently reviewed the available evidence (Hambrick, Burgoyne, & Oswald, 2019), conducting systematic searches for articles in the literatures on expertise (in games, music, science, sports, surgery/medicine, and aviation) and on job performance. On balance, evidence from the expertise literature does not support the hypothesis. To be exact, only 3 of 15 studies were found to show evidence for a diminishing role of cognitive ability with increasing skill, either in terms of significantly different ability-performance correlations across skill groups or Ability × Skill interactions on performance. What might be regarded as the strongest evidence for the hypothesis comes from one of our own meta-analyses (Burgoyne et al., 2016). We found that the correlation between fluid intelligence (as measured by tests of reasoning ability) and chess expertise was significantly higher for less-skilled chess players than for more-skilled players. However, as we noted, this finding must be interpreted cautiously, because the measure of chess skill was highly confounded with age. In general, findings from the expertise literature relevant to the circumvention-of-limitations hypothesis are difficult to interpret because of methodological shortcomings, such as small samples and use of measures with poor or unknown psychometric properties (see Hambrick et al., 2019, for a discussion).

A more consistent picture emerged in the review of evidence from the job performance literature: Even after an extensive amount of job experience, general cognitive ability remains a statistically and practically significant predictor of job performance (see also Reeve & Bonaccio, 2011; Schmidt & Hunter, 2004). Some of the most compelling evidence for this conclusion comes from a re-analysis of data from the Joint-Service Job Performance Measurement/Enlistment (JPM) Standards Project, a large study initiated in 1980 by the U.S. Department of Defense to develop measures of military job performance (see Hambrick et al., 2019; see also Wigdor & Green, 1991).[1] The JPM data set includes 31 jobs and a total sample size of 10,088 military personnel; the measure of general cognitive ability was the Armed Forces Qualifying Test (AFQT) score from the Armed Services Vocational Aptitude Battery, and job performance was measured with hands-on job performance (HOJP) tests for the different jobs. As shown in Figure 13.1, the AFQT-HOJP correlation decreases from the first year to the second, stabilizes, and then, if anything, increases. The overall picture to emerge from this and other large-scale studies (e.g., Schmidt, Hunter, Outerbridge, & Goff, 1988; Farrell & McDaniel, 2001) is that general cognitive ability remains a significant predictor of job performance, even after extensive job experience and even if validity drops initially.

Of course, this is not to say that general cognitive ability (or any other general ability) is the only important factor in acquiring expertise. Even a very smart person must engage in some form of training to acquire expertise, as no one is *literally* born an expert (or even a novice). (We humans may not enter the world as blank slates, but we are certainly not innately endowed with the

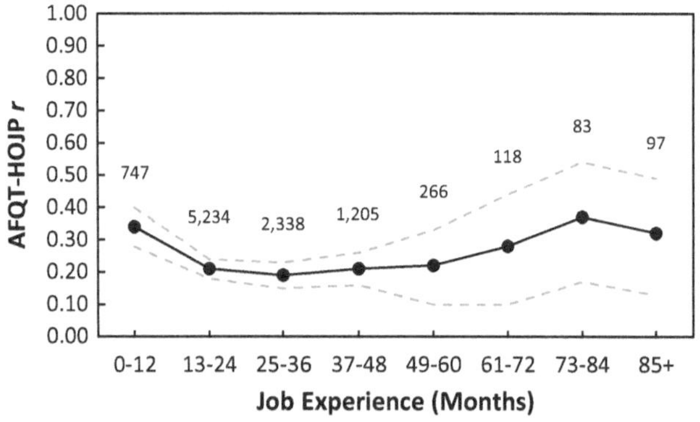

FIGURE 13.1 Correlations (with 95% confidence intervals) between AFQT scores and Hands-on Job Performance (HOJP) scores at 8 job experience intervals. Dashed lines are 95% confidence intervals; adjacent values are sample sizes. Data from Joint-Service Job Performance Measurement/Enlistment (JPM) Standards Project (N = 10,088). Adapted with permission of Oxford from Hambrick, Burgoyne, and Oswald (in press).

type of specialized knowledge that is necessary for success in domains such as science, business, music, and the law.) Ideally, training is adapted to fit to the level of the person's skill, beginning simple. Then, as basic skills are mastered, training builds in complexity. For example, a music student learns scales and arpeggios before attempting to sight-read complex pieces of music.

In technical terms, the training process contributes to *intra-individual variability* (change)—that is, improvement in performance over time. Even prodigies, who progress at an unusually rapid rate of domain-specific skill acquisition, must engage in extensive training to develop skill. For example, having learned the moves of chess at age 5, Magnus Carlsen started playing chess seriously at age 8 but did not become a grandmaster until age 13 (Gobet & Ereku, 2014), and then took another 6 years to reach number one in the Fédération Internationale des Échecs rankings. Notwithstanding reports from the North Korean government's state-run news media that the late Kim Jong-il shot a world-record demolishing 38-under par his first time playing golf (Longman, 2011), and bowled a perfect 300 on his first trip to Pyongyang Lanes despite drinking a pint of beer between each roll (Vasquez, 2012), there are no instant experts. Expertise is acquired gradually.

The more controversial question about expertise is not the need for training—everyone needs it to develop expertise—but the extent to which individual differences in training history can explain individual differences in expertise. Of particular interest has been the role of what Ericsson and colleagues (Ericsson, Krampe, & Tesch-Römer, 1993) termed *deliberate practice* in explaining individual differences in expertise. In a study made famous by Malcolm Gladwell in his bestselling book *Outliers: The Story of Success* (2008), these researchers asked violin students of varying levels of accomplishment to estimate the amount of time they had devoted to deliberate practice for each year since beginning their musical career. By young adulthood, the "best" group had accumulated an average of around 10,000 hours of deliberate practice. This was similar to the average for a group of professional musicians, and about 2,500 hours more than the average for the "good" group and 5,000 hours more than the average for the least accomplished group.

Applying their findings to several domains, Ericsson et al. concluded that "individual differences in ultimate performance can largely be accounted for by differential amounts of past and current levels of practice" (Ericsson et al., 1993, p. 392). To empirically test this claim, Macnamara, Hambrick, and Oswald (2014) conducted a meta-analysis of 88 relevant studies (157 effect sizes, with a cumulative sample size of $N > 11{,}000$) that quantitatively summarized correlations that were reported between activities interpretable as deliberate practice and performance. The results of the meta-analysis were summarized across five broad domains: games, music, sports, education, and professions. Across domains, deliberate practice accounted for an average of 14% of the variance in expertise. Furthermore, moderator analyses revealed that deliberate practice tended to be more predictive of expertise in some domains than in others.

For example, variance in expertise explained by deliberate practice was 24% for games, 23% for music, and 20% for sports, but only 5% for education and 1% for professions (for a correction to the original values, see Macnamara et al., 2018). Thus, regardless of domain, deliberate practice accounted for considerably less than half of the variance, and thus did not *largely account for* individual differences in expertise. In a meta-analysis on music, Platz, Kopiez, Lehmann, and Wolf (2014) similarly found that deliberate practice accounted for 37% of the variance in musical expertise, after accounting for measurement error.

Subsequently, Macnamara, Moreau, and Hambrick (2016) focused on the domain of sports, to assess the role of potential moderators of the relationship between deliberate practice and expertise. The study investigated whether this relationship might be moderated by whether the sport was a *closed-skill* sport (i.e., relatively predictable, such as running) versus an *open-skill* sport (i.e., less predictable, such as field hockey). The idea was that practice might be easier to design around closed-skill sports, meaning that practice would have a more standardized regimen, a more targeted effect, and thus have stronger correlations with performance. Conversely, open-skill sports might require skills that cannot be readily trained due to the complexity of the game requiring highly situation-contingent behaviors that are, relatively speaking, more difficult to practice and train for.

Moderation was not found for open- versus closed-skill sports, but was found for the skill level of the participants. Specifically, deliberate practice accounted for more variance in studies that sampled both elite and non-elite athletes (27%) than in studies that sampled only elite athletes (<1%). This finding could reflect a diminishing importance of training at high levels of skill. That is, among elite performers, it could be that abilities (talent) are the main distinguishing factor. To some degree, this finding could also reflect restriction of range among the elite athletes, although there was still a range of performance levels represented at the elite level (national- to international-level athletes).

Overall, evidence indicates that deliberate practice is an important piece of the expertise puzzle, just not as important as Ericsson and colleagues originally argued it is. That is, while deliberate practice appears to contribute substantially to individual differences in expertise, it leaves an even larger amount unexplained and potentially explainable by other factors. Ericsson and colleagues have further claimed that a minimum amount of deliberate practice (10 years, or 10,000 hours) is required to reach an elite level of performance. For example, writing in the *Harvard Business Review,* Ericsson, Prietula, and Cokely (2007) explained, "It will take you at least a decade to achieve expertise, and you will need to invest that time wisely, by engaging in 'deliberate' practice" (p. 116), adding: "Our research shows that even the most gifted performers need a minimum of ten years (or 10,000 hours) of intense training before they win international competitions" (p. 119).

This claim (the 10-year rule) may serve as a useful reminder to the layperson that expertise is acquired gradually, but as a testable proposition, it appears to be false. For example, as already mentioned, the Norwegian chess great Magnus Carlsen reached grandmaster status less than 6 years after he began playing chess seriously (and less than 9 years after learning the moves; Gobet & Ereku, 2014). And, in a study of chess players, Gobet and Campitelli (2007) found that the amount of deliberate practice that participants required to reach master status ranged from 3,016 to 23,608, and some players had not reached this level of skill despite more than 20,000 hours of deliberate practice. Ericsson (2006) allowed that "people are able to reach world-class levels in fewer than ten years in activities that lack a history of organized international competition" (p. 692), but as one of the world's oldest games, chess is clearly not such an activity. To be sure, there is *some* minimum amount of training that a person must engage in to become an elite performer, for reasons already discussed. However, that minimum does not appear to be 10 years (or 10,000 hours). Even in domains with a long history of organized international competition, it is considerably less for some performers.

In sum, key predictions stemming from Ericsson and colleagues' deliberate practice view are not well supported by empirical evidence. In the face of challenge, Ericsson has mounted a vigorous defense of his view. However, this defense has been undermined by repeated contradictions, inconsistences, and material errors in Ericsson's arguments (for further discussion, see Hambrick et al., 2014; Macnamara, Hambrick, & Moreau, 2016; Hambrick, Burgoyne, Macnamara, & Ullén, 2018). As a case in point, in an unpublished commentary, Ericsson (2014a; see also Ericsson, 2014b) criticized Macnamara et al. (2014) for deviating from his definition of deliberate practice, even though he has defined the term in conflicting ways, without acknowledging and explaining the shifts in the definition. For example, on the critical point of who designs deliberate practice, Ericsson has argued that a teacher ***must be involved:*** "In distinction from leisurely or normal job-related experience, Ericsson *et al.* defined *deliberate practice* as a very specific activity designed for an individual by a skilled teacher explicitly to improve performance" (Krampe & Ericsson, 1996, p. 333); that a teacher is ***typically involved:*** "When individuals engage in a practice activity (typically designed by their teachers), with full concentration on improving some aspect of their performance, we call that activity deliberate practice" (Ericsson, 2007, p. 14); and that a teacher ***need not be involved:*** "Ericsson et al. (1993) proposed the term deliberate practice to refer to those training activities that were designed solely for the purpose of improving individuals' performance by a teacher or the performers themselves" (Ericsson, 1998, p. 84).[2] Obviously, defining a theoretical term in conflicting ways is problematic, because it allows the theorist (and others) to flexibly select or reject evidence depending on whether it supports his theory.

Ericsson (2014a) also rejected studies that Macnamara and colleagues (2014) included in their meta-analysis for not meeting his criteria for deliberate practice that he previously used to explicitly argue for the importance of deliberate practice. Most perplexing, Ericsson even rejected some of his own studies, seeming to undermine the case he has made for the importance of deliberate practice. For example, he rejected his study of darts expertise (Duffy, Baluch, & Ericsson, 2004; see Ericsson's, 2014b, Table 2) because there is no record of a teacher/coach supervising all or most of practice, but in the article itself, based on the finding of skill group differences (i.e., amateur vs. professional) in measures labeled "deliberate practice" (see Duffy et al., Table 3, p. 240), he and his colleagues concluded: "This finding supports one of the main tenets of Ericsson et al.'s (1993) theory whereby expertise is acquired through a vast number of hours spent engaging in activities purely designed to improve performance, i.e., deliberate practice" (Duffy et al., p. 243). As another example, referring to another one of his own studies (Tuffiash, Roring, & Ericsson, 2007), Ericsson et al. (2009) noted that there are activities that meet the criteria for deliberate practice in the game of SCRABBLE: "Several researchers have reported a consistent association between the amount and quality of solitary activities meeting the criteria of deliberate practice and performance in different domains of expertise, such as...Scrabble (Tuffiash et al., 2007)" (p. 9). More recently, however, Moxley, Ericsson, and Tuffiash (2017) claimed that a person *cannot engage in deliberate practice in SCRABBLE:* "[T]he domain of SCRABBLE is a recently developed domain, and it lacks professional coaches and a large body of written knowledge about training. SCRABBLE players, therefore, must decide for themselves which types of training activities that they think are effective for improving their performance. Consequently, SCRABBLE players cannot engage in deliberate practice, but only purposeful practice and other types of practice" (p. 4). By all appearances, the "criteria of deliberate practice" have changed.

It is, of course, perfectly appropriate to revise a theory as evidence accumulates. This is a normal, and essential, part of the scientific process. However, it should go without saying that the revisions must be explicitly acknowledged and justified. A theorist must be willing to admit that his theory is wrong—or, at least, not quite right! Otherwise, a theory can be endlessly tweaked in response to challenge. Then, to use Ferguson and Heene's (2012) term, it becomes an *undead theory:* like the vampire or zombie that is deceased but behaves as if it is alive, a theory that is "ideologically popular but [has] little basis in fact" (p. 555) and "continues in use, having resisted attempts at falsification, ignored disconfirmatory data, negated failed replications...or having simply maintained itself in a fluid state with shifting implicit assumptions such that falsification is not possible" (p. 556).

The issues with deliberate practice theory aside, it is now relatively clear that deliberate practice (however operationally defined) is an important contributor to individual differences in expertise. That is, deliberate practice does not appear to be as important as Ericsson and colleagues originally argued, but it still accounts for a practically, statistically, and theoretically meaningful amount of the inter-individual variability in expertise—even if deliberate practice is confounded with aptitude. With that established, we now turn to the core of this chapter and examine interests as a key motivator for selecting a domain of expertise and then engaging in deliberate practice and other forms of domain-specific experience.

The Role of Interests in Expertise

Given evidence that training history contributes meaningfully to individual differences in expertise, it is important to ask what contributes to people's willingness to engage in training activities in the first place. Deciding to train is an important first step (e.g., deciding to enroll in college, or to pursue IT certification), but people vary greatly in how much they will then commit to the hard work that is required to reach a high level of expertise. For example, among children enrolled in piano lessons, some will practice diligently, whereas others will only practice before a lesson, if at all, before giving up.

Motivation is the fuel that drives sustained training, so before discussing interests as a form of motivation, we consider motivation more broadly. A high level of motivation is manifested in a willingness to engage in the activity (i.e., direction), to engage in that activity often (i.e., frequency), and to do so with a high level of focus (i.e., intensity). What are the factors that predispose a person to decide to spend thousands of hours training in some vocational or avocational domain, particularly when feedback may be ambiguous or discouraging to many, and particularly when success, however defined, is itself ambiguous or far from certain? For example, who among a classroom of high school students will be so taken with physics that they will go on to earn a PhD in the subject, and generate discoveries worthy of a Nobel Prize? Who among a group of music students will spend all of their free time in the practice room and earn a scholarship to Julliard? And who among a group of new attorneys at a large law firm will make partner? Interests reflect a form of motivation that presumably plays a key role in the formation of many types of expertise. In a free society, people often will invest a great amount of time and energy learning, practicing, and performing in a given domain, with domain-related interests forming, developing, and changing along the way. It is in this context that expertise in domains such as science, business, medicine, law, and any other profession is born.

As a psychological construct, interest can be thought of simply as a preference for engaging in some activity. Interests may be specific or general, although expertise eventually develops in specific domains, meaning that specific interests are usually the researchers' concern with regard to particular domains (e.g., music) and sub-domains (e.g., piano). Although specific interests are the primary focus of expertise research, general interests reflect preferences for engagement in broader classes of domains, and are therefore important to consider when considering how seeds of expertise get planted in the first place.

For example, it could be that a person who becomes highly skilled in oil painting could have also become highly skilled in metal sculpture under different circumstances, because both fall within the general domain of artistic interests.

Holland (1959, 1997) described general interest domains in his theory of vocational personalities and work environments. Specifically, as reviewed in the introductory chapter of this volume, he distinguished among six vocational interests: Realistic (R), Investigative (I), Artistic (A), Social (S), Enterprising (E), and Conventional (C). These interests may reflect different drives toward expertise. For example, the drive to hike El Capitan without a rope, as the rock climber Alex Honnold was first to do, seems to differ radically from the drive to become the Sage of Omaha, as Warren Buffet has been called for his financial investment strategies. From the RIASEC viewpoint, this makes good sense, because hiking is a Realistic task, and financial investment is Conventional (with some adjacent Enterprising interest).

RIASEC is as much a theory of environments (e.g., work, careers) as it is a theory of people, where over time, people tend to seek out activities congruent with their interests. The person-job fit literature in organizational psychology (e.g., Cable & Edwards, 2004; Kristof, 1996) capitalizes on this idea, addressing supplementary fit and complementary fit. With supplementary fit, the person and environment match on a similar profile of characteristics; for example, a job might require that a person have a high level of communication and teamwork skills, and employees that are hired possess this profile of requisite skills. Complementary fit, by contrast, represents the nature of transactional or reciprocal relationships between the person and the environment. For example, an organization might provide a good salary and benefits in exchange for an employee providing the aforementioned communication and teamwork skills (i.e., both parties are getting what they want through this exchange). Note that these two types of fit seem to mirror conditions that foster intrinsic and extrinsic motivation, respectively, and as noted earlier, motivation is the fuel for cultivating interests. Using the previous examples of fit, an environment that supports and rewards communication skills and teamwork allows employees with those skills to invest and refine them further. Or more generally speaking, once supplementary and complementary fit begin to be established in a person, and collectively in a team or organization, that can contribute to greater investment in interests over time. As interests strengthen, become refined, or otherwise change over time (Hoff, Briley, Wee, & Rounds, 2018), so might the domains of expertise in which one engages; or, if the domain is already fixed (e.g., one is already committed to a salesperson job and its sales objectives), then changing and refining one's interests might still occur in order to make task engagement and problem-solving more satisfying to oneself and effective for the organization. (For a theory of interests and interest refinement within a dynamic environment with cognitive and affective inputs, see the Four-Phase Model of Interest Development by Hidi and Renninger [this volume].)

The Multifactorial Gene-Environment Interaction Model of Expertise

Ullén et al's (2016) Multifactorial Gene-Environment Interaction Model (MGIM) provides a theoretical framework for thinking about the role of interests in the development of expertise. The model rests on three core assumptions. The first assumption is that expertise (i.e., domain-relevant performance) arises from the influences of domain-general traits (e.g., intelligence, personality) and the domain-specific characteristics (i.e., knowledge and skills) that arise from these traits. The second assumption is that these factors may have both direct and indirect influences on expertise. For example, domain-general traits may predict domain-specific characteristics, which in turn predict expertise. However, domain-general traits may also have direct effects on expertise. Finally, the model assumes that environmental and genetic influences operate throughout the model to produce individual differences in these factors. That is, consistent with a large body of evidence demonstrating that essentially all individual-difference characteristics are influenced by both genetic and environmental factors and their interplay (Plomin, DeFries, & Loehlin, 1977), the model makes no assumption that any individual-difference variable is purely environmental or purely genetic. Consistent with Turkheimer's (2000) *first law of behavioural genetics,* all individual-difference factors within the model are assumed to reflect both environmental and genetic influences.

As can be seen in Figure 13.2, training is one primary way that interests may operate to influence expertise. Specifically, people who have higher levels of interest tend to be more highly motivated and invest more of their time and effort in training on a consistent basis, eventually leading to greater expertise. There is empirical evidence to support these speculations. For example, in a study of 190 national spelling bee contestants, Duckworth, Kirby, Tsukayama, Berstein, and Ericsson (2011) found that *grit*—defined as perseverance and passion for long-term goals—predicted deliberate practice ($\beta = .30$, $p < .001$). In turn, deliberate practice predicted spelling performance ($\beta = .31$, $p < .001$). Thus, the type of people in the real world who decide to engage in deliberate practice was as important as deliberate practice itself. As another example, Miksza and Tan (2015) found that in a sample of 241 collegiate music students, grit was strongly and positively correlated with practice in terms of minutes per day ($r = .40$, $p < .001$). Although musical expertise was not measured in this study, Macnamara et al. (2014) estimated that the average correlation between deliberate practice and music expertise was .48, again suggesting that deliberate practice is an important mediator between individual differences (here, grit) and expert performance.

Another way to think about how interests influence performance through training is based on Vallerand et al.'s (2003) Dualistic Model of Passion. Within this model, *harmonious passion* (HP) refers to an internalization of an activity

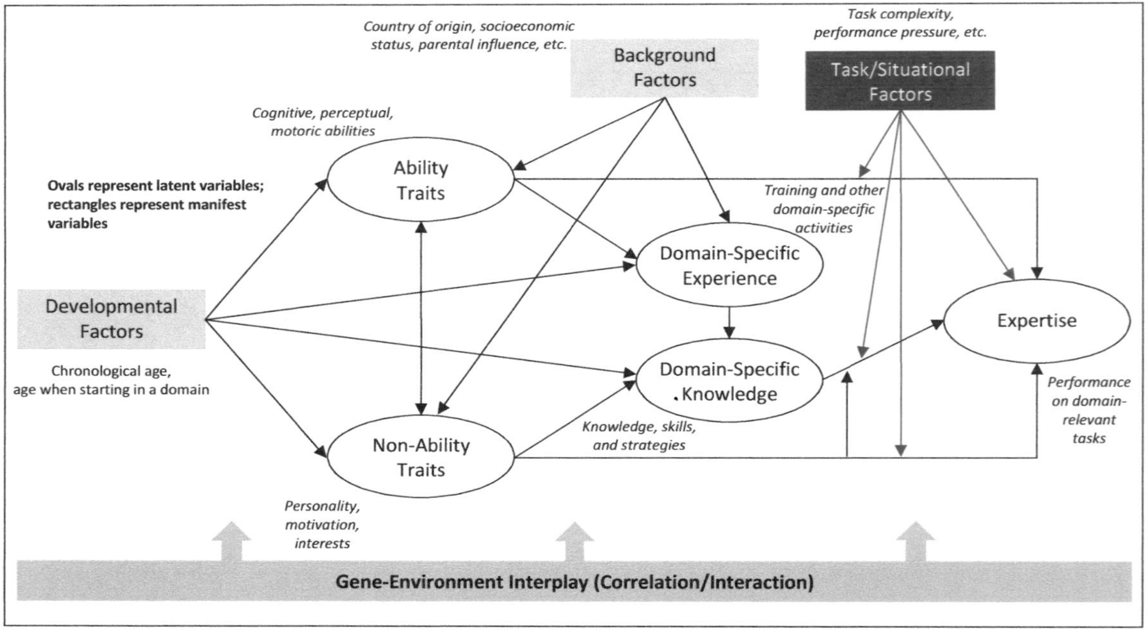

FIGURE 13.2 Instantiation of Multifactorial Gene-Environment Interaction Model (MGIM) of expertise (Ullén, Hambrick, & Mosing, 2016). Adapted with permission of Routledge from Hambrick, Campitelli, and Macnamara (2017).

into a person's identity, which motivates engagement in that activity and leads to positive affect. By contrast, *obsessive passion* (OP) refers to a controlled internalization of an activity into one's identity, such that one feels compelled to perform the activity despite conflicts with other aspects of one's life (Vallerand et al., 2003). HP and OP have been shown to jointly predict training time and perseverance under adverse conditions. In one study, Vallerand and colleagues examined the impact of HP and OP on cycling, despite unfavorable winter conditions found in Montréal. (During the winter, temperatures drop to an average of 8° F in Montreal, and slippery roads make cycling dangerous.) Only 30% of participants continued cycling through the winter, but those who persevered had higher levels of OP for cycling than those who did not. In another study, of water-polo and synchronized swimming athletes, Vallerand and colleagues (Vallerand et al., 2008) found that HP and OP correlated significantly with deliberate practice (*rs* of .30 and .32, *ps* $< .01$, respectively). Deliberate practice, which in this study referred to training activities performed independent of coaching or supervision, in turn correlated significantly with coach-evaluated performance ($r = .33$, $p < .01$).

Thus, across multiple empirical studies, a particular model of mediation is strongly supported: interest in a domain positively predicts engagement in training in that domain, which in turn positively predicts expertise. Note that interest and engagement themselves may be fuelled not only by the situational features, but by personality traits such as conscientiousness and grit. Furthermore, some research has discovered that conscientiousness and interest can compensate for one another across individuals (Trautwein et al., 2015). As a specific example of a compensatory relationship that may occur in the development of expertise, a person high in interest but low in conscientiousness may engage in more playful activities in the domain (forgoing "serious" practice). By contrast, a person high in conscientiousness but low in interest may engage in practice over the short term, but may ultimately experience burnout because they feel they should practice even though they lack interest in doing so. One can also reasonably speculate that compensation occurs *within* individuals over time as well. For example, sometimes playing the violin feels deeply interesting in certain moments of task engagement; yet in other moments, it can feel like sheer drudgery to practice. Anyone who is considered an expert has likely had both experiences in their pursuit of expertise.

Finally, it is possible that interests may also have effects on domain-relevant performance, independent of domain-specific knowledge. For example, a person with a high level of interest in a task may maintain greater task focus than a person with a lower level of interest, and consequently be less prone to mind-wandering (Unsworth & McMillan, 2013) and more likely to become immersed in the task and experience a "flow" state (Csikszentmihalyi, 1990).

Summary and Conclusions

We believe that adopting a multifactorial perspective involving a wide range of relevant personal characteristics and situational factors will push scientific understanding of the origins of expertise to new heights. This includes a better understanding of the role of interests as a key motivating factor for developing expertise. Traditionally, research on expertise has focused on what for all but a few people are hobbies, such as games, music, and sports. However, the insights gained through multifactorial research on expertise are equally applicable to the workplace, and efforts to bridge the gap between research in workplace performance and expertise will enhance understanding of both.

We already know that those who possess high levels of knowledge and interest in a given domain as children will likely continue into adult careers that fall within that same domain (Austin & Hanisch, 1990; Makel, Kell, Lubinski, Putallaz, & Benbow, 2016). A multifactorial perspective should incorporate interests, and also follow up on the personal, social, and situational factors that together can facilitate or limit interests and aspirations, and therefore subsequent development of expertise. Examples include feedback on one's task performance (e.g., timely, veridical, or normative feedback); family, peer, and teacher support (vs. discouragement or conflict); perceived and actual discrimination (e.g., by race, gender, or disability); and mental and physical health. Meta-analysis has investigated some of these factors within a larger developmental framework focused on academic achievement and success (Brown et al., 2018), and this framework could inspire a similar approach in the continued study of the development of expertise.

Teachers, mentors, and coaches have a whole host of intervention strategies to improve performance in others. They motivate and engage interests, and they attempt to tailor training to the specific needs of individuals, both of which can certainly be seen in the case of athletic training (e.g., Mann, Lamberts, & Lambert, 2014). An important goal for research on expertise is to conduct high-quality longitudinal research that can usefully inform the design and tailoring of these interventions that will improve a person's engagement with tasks and situations relevant to education, work, hobbies, and life, and thus ultimately accelerate the acquisition of knowledge, skill, and expertise. New technologies not only make more intensive data collection possible, to inform such research; these technologies may bring the interventions within reach of more people, including low-SES, underrepresented minorities, the disabled, and those living in rural settings, ultimately bringing expertise within the reach of more people than is currently the case. We may see more experts in our future as a function of technology and big data—so long as both are well-informed by psychological research and theories in areas such as interests, motivation, knowledge and ability, training and practice, and expertise.

Finally, it is critical to note that interests *shape* the process of developing expertise; they do not *dictate* that process. Cultivating interests, learning, and expertise throughout the lifespan surely benefits from both short-term interventions and longer-term nurturing environments (e.g., intensive mentoring, or college). However, those settings also allow for important-yet-unanticipated interests, learning experiences, and new insights into oneself to emerge (see the Happenstance Learning Theory of Krumboltz, 2009). In these beneficial settings, we agree with Louis Pasteur (1854) who famously said that luck favors the prepared mind. However, luck will also favor those who are more open to experience (von Stumm, 2018; Woo, Keith, Su, Saef, & Parrigon, 2017) and can identify and create expertise-building situations that present themselves.

Notes

1 We are grateful to Dr. Jane M. Arabian (Assistant Director, Accession Policy Office of the Under Secretary of Defense, The Pentagon, Washington, D.C.) for granting us permission to use the data, and to Dr. Rodney McCloy (Principal Scientist, Human Resources Research Organization, Louisville, KY) for sending us the data, with helpful notes.

2 What is Ericsson's current definition of deliberate practice? It depends on where you look. On his website, he defines deliberate practice as "activities designed, typically by a teacher, for the sole purpose of effectively improving specific aspects of an individual's performance" (see archived webpage here). However, in *Peak: Secrets from the New Science of Expertise,* he states that "deliberate practice requires a teacher who can provide practice activities designed to help a student improve his or her performance" (Ericsson & Pool, 2016, p. 98).

References

Andersson, P. (2004). *How well do financial experts perform? A review of empirical research on performance of analysts, day-traders, forecasters, fund managers, investors, and stockbrokers.* (EFI report 2004: 9). Stockholm, Sweden: Stockholm School of Economics.

Austin, J. T., & Hanisch, K. A. (1990). Occupational attainment as a function of abilities and interests: A longitudinal analysis using Project TALENT data. *Journal of Applied Psychology, 75,* 77–86.

Brown, S. D., Roche, M., Abrams, M., Lamp, K., Telander, K., Daskalova, P., Tatum, A., & Massingale, M. (2018). Relationships among supports and barriers and career and educational outcomes: A meta-analytic investigation. *Journal of Career Assessment, 26,* 395–412.

Burgoyne, A. P., Sala, G., Gobet, F., Macnamara, B. N., Campitelli, G., & Hambrick, D. Z. (2016). The relationship between cognitive ability and chess skill: A comprehensive meta-analysis. *Intelligence, 59,* 72–83.

Cable, D. M., & Edwards, J. R. (2004). Complementary and supplementary fit: A theoretical and empirical integration. *Journal of Applied Psychology, 89,* 822–834.

Chase, W. G., & Simon, H. A. (1973). Perception in chess. *Cognitive Psychology, 4,* 55–81.

Colvin, G. (2010). *Talent is overrated. What really separates world-class performers from everybody else.* New York: Penguin.

Csikszentmihalyi, M. (1990). *Flow.* New York: Harper and Row.

de Groot, A. D. (1946/1978). *Thought and choice in chess.* Berlin, Germany: De Gruyter Mouton.

Duckworth, A. L., Kirby, T. A., Tsukayama, E., Berstein, H., & Ericsson, K. A. (2011). Deliberate practice spells success: Why grittier competitors triumph at the National Spelling Bee. *Social Psychological and Personality Science, 2*, 174–181.

Duffy, L. J., Baluch, B., & Ericsson, K. A. (2004). Dart performance as a function of facets of practice amongst professional and amateur men and women players. *International Journal of Sport Psychology, 35*, 232–245.

Ericsson, K. A. (1998). The scientific study of expert levels of performance: General implications for optimal learning and creativity. *High Ability Studies, 9*, 75–100.

Ericsson, K. A. (2006). The influence of experience and deliberate practice on the development of superior expert performance. In K. A. Ericsson, N. Charness, P. J. Feltovich, & R. R. Hoffman (Eds.). *The Cambridge handbook of expertise and expert performance* (pp. 683–703). New York: Cambridge University Press.

Ericsson, K. A. (2007). Deliberate practice and the modifiability of body and mind: Toward a science of the structure and acquisition of expert and elite performance. *International Journal of Sport Psychology, 38*, 4–34.

Ericsson, K. A. (2014a). *Challenges for the estimation of an upper-bound on relations between accumulated deliberate practice and the associated performance of novices and experts: Comments on Macnemara (sic), Hambrick, and Oswald's (2014) published meta-analysis* (Unpublished manuscript.) Retrieved from https://psy.fsu.edu/faculty/ericsson/ericsson.hp.html

Ericsson, K. A. (2014b). *Supplemental online materials for "A challenge to estimates of an upper-bound on relations between accumulated deliberate practice and the associated performance in domains of expertise: Comments on Macnemara (sic), Hambrick, and Oswald's (2014) published meta-analysis."* (Unpublished manuscript.) Retrieved from https://psy.fsu.edu/faculty/ericsson/ericsson.hp.html

Ericsson, K. A., & Charness, N. (1994). Expert performance: Its structure and acquisition. *American Psychologist, 49*, 725–747.

Ericsson, K. A., & Pool, R. (2016). *Peak: Secrets from the new science of expertise.* New York: Houghton Mifflin Harcourt.

Ericsson, K. A., Krampe, R. Th., & Tesch-Römer, C. (1993). The role of deliberate practice in the acquisition of expert performance. *Psychological Review, 100*, 363–406.

Ericsson, K. A., Prietula, M. J., & Cokely. E. T. (2007). The making of an expert. *Harvard Business Review, 85*, 114–121.

Ericsson, K. A., Perez, R. S., Eccles, D. W., Lang, L., Baker, E. L., Bransford, J. D., Vanlehn, K. & Ward, P. (2009). The measurement and development of professional performance: An introduction to the topic and a background to the design and origin of this book. In K. A. Ericsson (Ed.), *Development of professional expertise: Toward measurement of expert performance and design of optimal learning environments* (pp. 1–26). Cambridge: Cambridge University Press.

Ericsson, K. A., & Smith, J. (1991). Prospects and limits of the empirical study of expertise: An introduction. In K. A. Ericsson & J. Smith (Eds.), *Toward a general theory of expertise: Prospects and limits* (pp. 1–38). New York: Cambridge University Press.

Farrell, J. N., & McDaniel, M. A. (2001). The stability of validity coefficients over time: Ackerman's (1988) model and the General Aptitude Test Battery. *Journal of Applied Psychology, 86*, 60–79.

Ferguson, C. J., & Heene, M. (2012). A vast graveyard of undead theories: Publication bias and psychological science's aversion to the null. *Perspectives on Psychological Science, 7*, 555–561.

Galton, F. (1869). *Hereditary genius: An inquiry into its laws and consequences.* London: Macmillan.

Gladwell, M. (2008). *Outliers: The story of success.* New York: Little, Brown and Company.

Gobet, F., & Campitelli, G. (2007). The role of domain-specific practice, handedness, and starting age in chess. *Developmental Psychology, 43,* 159–172.

Gobet, F., & Ereku, M. H. (2014). Checkmate to deliberate practice: the case of Magnus Carlsen. *Frontiers in Psychology, 5,* 878.

Hambrick, D. Z., Altmann, E. M., Oswald, F. L., Meinz, E. J., Gobet, F., & Campitelli, G. (2014). Accounting for expert performance: The devil is in the details. *Intelligence, 45,* 112–114.

Hambrick, D. Z., Burgoyne, A. P., Macnamara, B. N., & Ullén, F. (2018). Toward a multifactorial model of expertise: Beyond born versus made. *Annals of the New York Academy of Sciences, 1423,* 284–295.

Hambrick, D. Z., Burgoyne, A. P., & Oswald, F. L. (in press). Domain-general models of expertise: The role of cognitive ability. To appear in P. Ward, J. M. Schraagen, J. Gore, & E. Roth (Eds)., *Oxford handbook of expertise: Research and application.* Oxford, UK: Oxford University Press.

Hambrick, D. Z., & Hoffman, R. R. (2016). Expertise: A second look. *IEEE Intelligent Systems, 31,* 50–55.

Hambrick, D. Z., & Meinz, E. J. (2011). Limits on the predictive power of domain-specific experience and knowledge in skilled performance. *Current Directions in Psychological Science, 20,* 275–279.

Hoff, K. A., Briley, D. A., Wee, C. J., & Rounds, J. (2018). Normative changes in interests from adolescence to adulthood: A meta-analysis of longitudinal studies. *Psychological Bulletin, 144,* 426–451.

Hoffman, R. R., Ward, P., Feltovich, P. J., DiBello, L., Fiore, S. M., & Andrews, D. H. (2013). *Accelerated expertise: Training for high proficiency in a complex world.* New York: Psychology Press, Taylor & Francis Group.

Holland, J. L. (1959). A theory of vocational choice. *Journal of Counseling Psychology, 6,* 35–45.

Holland, J. L. (1997). *Making vocational choices: A theory of vocational personalities and work environments* (3rd ed.). Odessa, FL: Psychological Assessment Resources.

Krampe, R. T., & Ericsson, K. A. (1996). Maintaining excellence: Deliberate practice and elite performance in young and older pianists. *Journal of experimental Psychology: General, 125,* 331–359.

Kristof, A. L. (1996). Person-organization fit: An integrative review of its conceptualizations, measurement, and implications. *Personnel Psychology,* 49, 1–49.

Krumboltz, J. D. (2009). The happenstance learning theory. *Journal of Career Assessment, 17,* 135–154.

Longman, J. (2011, December 20). Remembering Kim Jong-il's ventures into the sporting world. Retrieved from https://www.nytimes.com/2011/12/21/sports/remembering-kim-jong-ils-ventures-into-the-sporting-world.html

Macnamara, B. N., Hambrick, D. Z., & Moreau, D. (2016). How important is deliberate practice? Reply to Ericsson (2016). *Perspectives on Psychological Science, 11,* 355–358.

Macnamara, B. N., Hambrick, D. Z., & Oswald, F. L. (2014). Deliberate practice and performance in music, games, sports, education, and professions: A meta-analysis. *Psychological Science, 25,* 1608–1618.

Macnamara, B. N., Moreau, D., & Hambrick, D. Z. (2016). The relationship between deliberate practice and performance in sports: A meta-analysis. *Perspectives on Psychological Science, 11,* 333–350.

Macnamara, B. N., Hambrick, D. Z., & Oswald, F. L. (2018). Corrigendum: Deliberate practice and performance in music, games, sports, education, and professions: A meta-analysis. *Psychological Science*, 29, 1202–1204.

Makel, M. C., Kell, H. J., Lubinski, D., Putallaz, M., & Benbow, C. P. (2016). When lightning strikes twice: Profoundly gifted, profoundly accomplished. *Psychological Science*, *27*, 1004–1018.

Mann, T. N., Lamberts, R. P., & Lambert, M. I. (2014). High responders and low responders: Factor associated with individual variation in response to standardized training. *Sports Medicine*, *44*, 1113–1124.

Moxley, J. H., Ericsson, K. A., & Tuffiash, M. (2017). Gender differences in SCRABBLE performance and associated engagement in purposeful practice activities. *Psychological Research*, 1–21.

Miksza, P., & Tan, L. (2015). Predicting collegiate wind players' practice efficiency, flow, and self-efficacy for self-regulation: An exploratory study of relationships between teachers' instruction and students' practicing. *Journal of Research in Music Education*, *63*, 162–179.

Pasteur, L. (1854). Lecture, University of Lille.

Platz, F., Kopiez, R., Lehmann, A. C., & Wolf, A. (2014). The influence of deliberate practice on musical achievement: A meta-analysis. *Frontiers in Psychology*, *5*, 646.

Plomin, R., DeFries, J. C., & Loehlin, J. C. (1977). Genotype-environment interaction and correlation in the analysis of human behavior. *Psychological Bulletin*, *84*, 309–322.

Reeve, C. L., & Bonaccio, S. (2011). On the myth and the reality of the temporal validity degradation of general mental ability test scores. *Intelligence*, *39*, 255–272.

Schmidt, F. L., & Hunter, J. (2004). General mental ability in the world of work: Occupational attainment and job performance. *Journal of Personality and Social Psychology*, *86*, 162–173.

Schmidt, F. L., Hunter, J. E., Outerbridge, A. N., & Goff, S. (1988). Joint relation of experience and ability with job performance: Test of three hypotheses. *Journal of Applied Psychology*, *73*, 46–57.

Trautwein, U., Lüdtke, O., Nagy, N., Lenski, A., Niggli, A., & Schnyder, I. (2015). Using individual interest and conscientiousness to predict academic effort: Additive, synergistic, or compensatory effects? *Journal of Personality and Social Psychology*, *109*, 142–162.

Tuffiash, M., Roring, R. W., & Ericsson, K. A. (2007). Expert performance in SCRABBLE: implications for the study of the structure and acquisition of complex skills. *Journal of Experimental Psychology: Applied*, *13*, 124–134.

Turkheimer, E. (2000). Three laws of behavior genetics and what they mean. *Current Directions in Psychological Science*, *9*, 160–164.

Ullén, F., Hambrick, D. Z., & Mosing, M. A. (2016). Rethinking expertise: A multifactorial gene–environment interaction model of expert performance. *Psychological Bulletin*, *142*, 427–446.

Unsworth, N., & McMillan, B. D. (2013). Mind wandering and reading comprehension: Examining the roles of working memory capacity, interest, motivation, and topic experience. *Journal of Experimental Psychology: Learning, Memory, and Cognition*, *39*, 832–842.

Vallerand, R. J., Blanchard, C., Mageau, G. A., Koestner, R., Ratelle, C., Léonard, M., Gagné, M., & Marsolais, J. (2003). Les passions de l'âme: On obsessive and harmonious passion. *Journal of Personality and Social Psychology*, *85*, 756–767.

Vallerand, R. J., Mageau, G. A., Elliot, A. J., Dumais, A., Demers, M. A., & Rousseau, F. (2008). Passion and performance attainment in sport. *Psychology of Sport and Exercise, 9*, 373–392.

Vasquez, R. (2012, March 25). *Kim Jong-il: The greatest sportsman ever.* Retrieved from http://www.dailyautocrat.com/kim-jong-il-the-greatest-sportsman-ever/

von Stumm, S. (2018). Better open than intellectual: The benefits of investment personality traits for learning. *Personality and Social Psychology Bulletin, 44*, 562–573.

Wigdor, A. K., & Green, B. F. (1991). *Performance assessment for the workplace. Volumes I & II.* Washington, DC: National Academy Press.

Woo, S., E., Keith, M. G., Su, R., Saef, R., & Parrigon, S., (2017). The curious dynamic between openness and interests in creativity. In G. J. Feist, R. Reiter-Palmon, & J. C. Kaufman (Eds.), *The Cambridge handbook of creativity and personality research* (pp. 44–63). New York: Cambridge University Press.

INDEX

Bold page numbers refer to tables; *italic* page numbers refer to figures and page numbers followed by "n" denote endnotes.